Restructuring Representation

The Merger Process and Trade Union Structural Development in Ten Countries

P.I.E.-Peter Lang

Bruxelles · Bern · Berlin · Frankfurt am Main · New York · Oxford · Wien

Jeremy WADDINGTON **(ed.)**

Restructuring Representation

The Merger Process and Trade Union Structural Development in Ten Countries

"Work & Society"
No.46

© P.I.E.-PETER LANG s.a.

PRESSES INTERUNIVERSITAIRES EUROPÉENNES

Brussels, 2005

1 avenue Maurice, 1050 Brussels, Belgium

info@peterlang.com; www.peterlang.net

ISSN 1376-0955

ISBN 90-5201-253-9

US ISBN 0-8204-6633-6

D/2005/5678/01

Printed in Germany

Bibliographic information published by "Die Deutsche Bibliothek"

"Die Deutsche Bibliothek" lists this publication in the "Deutsche Nationalbibliografie"; detailed bibliographic data is available in the Internet at <http://dnb.ddb.de>.

CIP available from the British Library, GB and the Library of Congress, USA.

Contents

Preface..9

CHAPTER 1. INTRODUCTION
Charting the Dimensions of the Merger Process.............................11
         Jeremy WADDINGTON

CHAPTER 2. AUSTRALIA
Top-down Strategic Restructuring...45
         Gerard GRIFFIN

CHAPTER 3. AUSTRIA
A Case of Limited Restructuring..67
         Sabine BLASCHKE

CHAPTER 4. DENMARK
The Survival of Small Trade Unions
in the Context of Centralised Bargaining..87
         Jesper DUE and Jørgen Steen MADSEN

CHAPTER 5. GERMANY
Towards a New Form of German Trade Unionism? 113
         Jeremy WADDINGTON and Jürgen HOFFMANN

CHAPTER 6. GREECE
From Divided "Quangos" to Fragmented "Social Partners".
Explaining the Absence of Mergers...139
         Christos A. IOANNOU

CHAPTER 7. NORWAY
Adapting Slowly...165
         Kristine NERGAARD

CHAPTER 8. PORTUGAL
Mergers within a Fragmented Union Structure, 1974-2000..........191
         Alan STOLEROFF

CHAPTER 9. SWEDEN
Mergers in a Class-segmented Trade Union System......................225
　　　　　Anders KJELLBERG

CHAPTER 10. UNITED KINGDOM
Merge, Merge and Merge Again..257
　　　　　Jeremy WADDINGTON

CHAPTER 11. UNITED STATES
Merging in a Hostile Environment...291
　　　　　Jeremy WADDINGTON

CHAPTER 12
Closer Working between Unions.
The Impact of the Bargaining Framework.....................................319
　　　　　Jesper DUE and Berndt KELLER

CHAPTER 13
Confederations and Mergers.
Convenience Rather Than True Love...337
　　　　　Christos A. IOANNOU and Anders KJELLBERG

CHAPTER 14
Are New Forms of Union Organisation Emerging?......................361
　　　　　Gerard GRIFFIN

CHAPTER 15. CONCLUSIONS
What Difference Has the Merger Process Made?.........................375
　　　　　Jeremy WADDINGTON

References...393

Notes on Contributors..413

Preface

Trade union movements throughout the industrialised world are in the midst of an extensive process of restructuring. Merger activity is a key aspect of this process of restructuring. Drawing on data from ten countries, this volume argues that much recent merger activity is a defensive reaction to adverse environmental circumstances. Although mergers have enabled a few unions to embark on programmes of renewal and modernisation, this volume shows that most mergers remain locked into the spiral of decline that promoted them and fail to address key aspects of union renewal.

The origins of this volume lay in a network established by the European Trade Union Institute (ETUI) and convened by Jeremy Waddington, the Project Co-ordinator of the ETUI. Members of the network identified four objectives for it to pursue. First, to trace the pattern of merger activity in ten countries. In several countries this necessitated the compilation of an original data series on the merger process. Second, to establish whether similar pressures were driving the merger process in the different countries. Third, to assess how merger partners were selected and to specify the procedures whereby mergers were brought about. Fourth, to examine the outcome of the merger processes in the ten countries by reference to the stated objectives of those engaged in the process and its contribution to the renewal or modernisation of trade unions. To these ends, members of the network resolved to prepare this volume, central to which is a combination of country-based or vertical chapters and thematic or horizontal chapters. Nationals of the different countries wrote most of the country-based chapters. These same people combined to write the thematic chapters. Both the vertical and the horizontal chapters were subject to scrutiny by the entire network. This collective approach to the volume facilitated the achievement of the aforementioned objectives, sharpened the analytical edge of the volume and, above all, made the process more enjoyable.

Although considerable efforts were made to ensure that each of the country-based chapters covered similar ground, it was inevitable that different emphases emerged, as there were marked variations between the different national merger processes. Motivated by an analytical approach that centres on the 'politics of bargaining', contributors assessed the merger process by reference to changes in three relationships: the bargaining position of unions relative to employers and the state; a

9

union's bargaining position relative to other unions; and factional bargaining within unions. While the impact on the merger process of changes to these relationships differed among the countries examined here, each relationship figures prominently in the analyses that follow. Different emphases within the country-based chapters are thus explained within the context of a unifying analytical framework.

A distinction that is central to this volume is that between amalgamations and acquisitions. In an amalgamation two or more unions combine to form a new union. In an acquisition one union absorbs another union and the identity of the acquired union is subsumed within that of the acquiring union. The term 'merger' is used as the collective noun to describe the process that comprises both amalgamations and acquisitions. The relative rates at which amalgamations and acquisitions occur within the merger process have a marked influence on its character and on its outcome.

Members of the network are grateful to Kathleen Llanwarne, Mette Bærentsen and Birgit Buggel-Asmus of the ETUI for their editorial assistance, and to Lilli Wilcox-Poulsen of the Documentation Centre at the ETUI for assistance with the compilation of the lists of abbreviations and the bibliography. The efforts of Catherine Closson of P.I.E.-Peter Lang were indispensable to ensuring the smooth and timely production of the volume. We would also like to thank the ETUI for its unstinting financial support for this initiative without which this volume would never have seen the light of day. The views expressed within the volume are those of the authors and do not necessarily accord with those of the ETUI.

CHAPTER 1. INTRODUCTION

Charting the Dimensions
of the Merger Process

Jeremy WADDINGTON

During the past two decades trade union movements have been dra-matically restructured. Long-standing principles of organisation, includ-ing industrial unionism, have been jettisoned in attempts to develop structures through which new agendas can be generated and delivered. Trade union mergers are central to this process of structural adaptation. As a consequence, membership is becoming more concentrated in fewer, larger unions; membership of the trade unions that remain is more heterogeneous; and relations between confederations and affiliated unions are subject to review. Each of these tendencies presents new challenges for trade union organisation and activity. In particular, exist-ing forms of membership representation are in need of overhaul to allow members from under-represented or minority groups to participate more fully in union affairs. Similarly, greater membership heterogeneity requires new means of articulation and co-ordination to ensure the coherence of union activities conducted at different levels or by different groups of members. This book examines these issues by reference to the merger processes underway in ten countries since 1950.

The principal challenges faced by trade unionists from these ten countries stem from changes to regulatory and to production regimes implemented by the state and employers in order to compete in an increasingly internationalised economy. Deregulation has tended to exclude trade unions from influence in the formulation of macro-economic and social policy and to restrict resources made available by the state to support trade union organisation and activity. Privatisation has also eliminated some of the traditional boundaries on which trade union organisation was founded, thereby generating new areas of com-petition for membership between unions. Furthermore, the greater 'distance' sought by social democratic parties from union movements has necessitated a reappraisal of the means whereby political influence is secured. In contrast, the introduction of social pacts has required trade unionists to engage in the formulation of macro-economic policy at a time when neo-liberal economic policies are in the ascendancy. For union movements within member states of the European Union (EU), the development of a new regulatory tier requires supra-national union organisation and activity. For unions operating within the framework of the North American Free Trade Agreement (NAFTA), international co-operation is also of a higher priority.

Employers have also restructured production regimes. Measures to enhance labour flexibility have undermined some of the traditional de-marcations between unions, and aspects of the human resource manage-ment (HRM) agenda are clearly directed to securing employee com-mitment to the enterprise at the expense of that towards unionism. Furthermore, for much of the twentieth century some employers have cited multi-unionism as an impediment to workplace re-organisation and have thus advocated union structural reform. Large-scale shifts of em-ployment away from manufacturing towards private sector services also exposed weaknesses in union organisation in all countries where the Ghent system is not in place.[1] Combined with persistently high levels of unemployment, the shift in the composition of the labour force resulted in widespread membership decline, which has restricted the resources available to unions. A further demand on resources has arisen from the decentralisation of bargaining, which has raised union operating costs as a larger number of bargaining arrangements have to be supported.

A challenge for unions has thus been to articulate organisation be-tween the international level and the locality, while material and politi-cal resources are diminishing. Advocates of union restructuring argue that economies of scale arising from the merger process will mitigate the effects of reduced resources and allow the delivery of improved support services to members. The increased size of post-merger unions is also envisaged as facilitating political engagement. Furthermore, mergers are viewed as the means whereby trade union structures can be 'simplified'; friction arising from inter-union competition for membership can be dissipated; and opportunities created for recruitment in areas of low density, notably private sector services. These claims for the benefits of

---

[1] In countries where the Ghent system operates trade unions undertake a role in the administration of unemployment benefits or insurance. Trade union membership in these countries (Belgium, Denmark, Finland and Sweden) thus tends to cover the en-tire economy as workers join unions to participate in unemployment insurance schemes as well as in union affairs. Shifts in the composition of the labour force, therefore, have not had as adverse effects on union membership in these countries as elsewhere (for details see Western, 1997).

the merger process are contested by those who question the extent of the efficiency savings and whether mergers have facilitated recruitment in unorganised areas (for example, Gill and Griffin 1981; Waddington and Hoffmann 2000). This volume thus focuses on an empirical question: are mergers defensive adjustments to adverse circumstances or a mainspring for the delivery of a new agenda appropriate to currently unorganised workers?

Positions are also contested within the academic community regarding the merger process. At one pole of the debate is the contention that there is no future for the development of a 'general theory of union mergers' (Chitayat, 1979: 9). From this perspective each merger should be treated as a unique case from which little can be generalised. Others identify 'merger types' that result from similar influences and exhibit similar merger outcomes (Hughes, 1967; Freeman and Brittain, 1977; Undy *et al.*, 1981). More wide-ranging explanations rely on industrialisation, institutionalisation or features drawn from both tendencies to provide a framework within which the merger process may be located and explained (Dunlop, 1948; Bernstein, 1960; Lester, 1958; Clegg, 1976). Debate between these competing positions is made more opaque by the use of different research methods; the relative 'explanatory weight' attached to internal and external influences on the merger process; and emphasis on different features of the merger process, such as its rate, character or impact on membership participation. Overall, as with the purpose of mergers, there is a need to critically assess these theoretical positions, with the objective of moving towards a comparative explanation of the merger process. Accordingly, the principal purposes of this book are threefold;

-   to outline and to explain the changing pattern of merger activity in ten countries since 1950;
-   to examine the extent to which merger policies are defensive adjustments to adverse circumstances or mainsprings for the generation and delivery of a new policy agenda;
-   to assess the competing explanations of merger activity in the context of data from ten countries and to move towards a comparative explanation of the merger process.

To introduce these themes this chapter comprises two sections. The first section reviews the literature on three key aspects of the merger process: reasons for merger, the 'choice' of specific merger partners and outcomes of the merger process. It identifies the terms of the debate on the merger process and a number of objectives of this volume that supplement the three key purposes. The second section presents evidence on merger intensity from the ten countries that are covered by this volume. It also defines the terms used throughout and briefly outlines the structure of the book.

Evidence on the Merger Process

It is generally accepted that merger activity constitutes a process along two inter-related dimensions (Chaison, 1986; Waddington, 1995). The first dimension concerns the impact of mergers on the process of trade union structural development. The completion of a specific merger may change inter-union relations, for example regarding competition for members, and thus create the circumstances for subsequent mergers. The chapters of this book demonstrate that this dimension of the merger process is country-specific, is influenced by elements of the regulatory regime of each country and rarely promotes convergence in union structure. This dimension of the merger process is introduced in the second section of this chapter by reference to the intensity of merger activity in ten countries.

The second dimension of the merger process concerns the process whereby a single merger may be completed. This dimension may commence with some form of closer working between unions before merger negotiations begin. Once the merger agreement is ratified, post-merger integration of governing structures and branch organisation may commence, with the result that this dimension of the merger process may take several years to complete. Ratification of the merger agreement is thus but one step in a process of integration. The literature on the second dimension of the merger process is reviewed below in three inter-related stages. The first presents the different reasons advanced to explain why unions merge. The second examines the factors that explain the choice of specific merger partners. In both of these stages consideration is also given to those factors which act as barriers to the completion of mergers. The third stage reviews the evidence on merger outcomes.

Reasons for Merger

More research has been conducted on this aspect of the merger process than on the subsequent stages. Existing explanations of merger activity tend to draw on external or internal influences, or a combination of both influences. The distinction between these influences in several instances is analytical rather than practical, as external influences may manifest themselves as internal issues. Membership decline, for example, may be treated as an external factor, yet is associated with the financial situation of a union, which is regarded as an internal influence. Four broad explanations of the merger process have been developed: the industrialisation thesis, the institutionalisation thesis, a political explanation, and an explanation based on the politics of bargaining.

Advocates of the industrialisation thesis argue that 'structural cycles', crises or periods of 'fundamental unrest' promote the 'really critical developments in the morphology of unions' (Bernstein, 1960; Dunlop, 1948). Integral to the industrialisation thesis is the position that particular forms of production are associated with 'fundamental structural periods in modern capitalism' (Dunlop, 1948: 191). These forms of production influence the development of trade union structure. The merger process is thus most pronounced when a shift from one form of production to another is underway and trade unions adjust to new prevailing circumstances. The industrialisation thesis predicts a cyclical pattern in the development of union structure and the intensity of union structural change is anticipated to be most pronounced during specific periods of economic long cycles (Bernstein, 1960; Dunlop, 1948). Recent analyses of the impact on union structure of industrialisation emphasise 'tertiarisation', the transfer of jobs from public to private suppliers and the outsourcing of support functions within manufacturing (Dølvik and Waddington, 2004). Qualified support for the industrialisation thesis is available from research which showed similarity in the timing of periods of intense merger activity in the Netherlands, Sweden and Britain (Visser and Waddington, 1996) and in Australia, Britain, Canada, New Zealand and the United States (Chaison, 1996). However, the assertion associated with some variants of the industrialisation thesis that periods of intense trade union structural change will promote convergence in union structure (Kerr, 1983) is neither supported by these studies nor by other comparative analyses (Campling and Michelson, 1997).

The timing of industrialisation influences the character of the merger process. Early industrialisation in the UK, for example, is associated with the predominant position initially achieved by craft unions. In contrast, relatively late industrialisation in Sweden and the Netherlands prevented craft unions from becoming as well entrenched and enabled industrial unions to establish stronger positions (Fulcher, 1991; Buiting, 1990). The timing of industrialisation thus influences the starting point of the trade union merger process in each country and the merger process enacted thereafter.

Different positions within the institutionalisation thesis emphasise either the 'acceptance' of unions by employers and the state (Lester, 1958) or the structure of collective bargaining (Clegg, 1976), as legitimising or consolidating trade union structure. The argument of the institutionalisation thesis is that union structure will be in flux before recognition and the establishment of bargaining structures. Only after employers and the state have recognised unions for bargaining purposes and bargaining structures have been established, is it anticipated that union structure will remain relatively stable. Among the influences identified by the advocates of the institutionalisation thesis are the 'liability of newness' (Stinchcombe, 1965) which, before the acceptance by employers and the state of trade unions, ensures considerable structural change as unions struggle to secure stable resources and legitimacy. After recognition and the establishment of bargaining structures, the impact of the liability of newness remains but in a different form, as established unions, often with the assistance of employers and the state, act to discourage the consolidation of newly formed unions that might challenge the position of established unions.

Variants of the institutionalisation thesis suggest rather different patterns of development of the merger process. The 'maturation' variant expects a period of marked trade union structural change involving intense merger activity before union recognition and political acceptance of unions, followed by a period in which union structure remains stable (Lester, 1958). Lester thus anticipated a phased pattern of development of the merger process. Clegg (1976: 9-11) argued that the structure of collective bargaining is the key influence on trade union structure. He entered two caveats, however, to suggest that trade union structure need not be stable once the initial structure of bargaining has been established. First, he argued that the dimensions of collective bargaining may change as a result of actions taken by employers and thus acknowledges that mergers are likely to occur as unions adjust to new bargaining circumstances. Second, mergers due to the 'pressures of internal union politics, or to boundary revisions inspired by doctrines of union organisation' may take place once initial bargaining structures are in place (1976: 10). The institutionalist explanation developed by Clegg thus anticipates merger activity after the initial structure of collective bargaining is established rather than the phased pattern of development of the merger process proposed by Lester. The data presented in this book cover the period after 1950. As unions were recognised by employers and the state before 1950 in all the countries examined here except Greece and Portugal, Lester would expect relatively low rates of merger activity throughout, but higher rates in Greece and Portugal as unions adjust to recognition. Clegg, however, would anticipate a continuing development of the merger process in all countries after 1950 as unions sought to adjust to changes in the dimensions of bargaining, internal union politics and principles of union organisation.

A third explanation of trade union structural development emphasises the effects of politics, the political organisation of labour movements and the impact of social and cultural cleavages on trade union structure. Borrowing from the 'freezing' hypothesis for party political systems (Lipset and Rokkan, 1967), it argues that 'the social cleavage structure at the time of consolidation is frozen' in trade union structure (Ebbinghaus, 1990). This results in the persistence of politico-religious cleavages (socialist, communist and Christian) and functional or status differentiation (industrial and craft unionism or manual and white-collar organisation) as features of trade union structure. While this explanation was initially developed to explain the diversity in trade union structure (Ebbinghaus and Visser, 1990), it also incorporated an analysis of changing union structures. In particular, 'contemporary trends towards secularisation and class decomposition' were shown to have lessened the salience of the original splits and thus enabled 'reunifying mergers', which were viewed as an 'adaptation strategy' to changed environ-mental circumstances (Ebbinghaus, 1990: 71). The range of factors identified as influencing these mergers was drawn from both the indus-trialisation and institutionalisation theses.

A fourth explanatory framework for the merger process was devel-oped with specific reference to the United Kingdom and emphasises the role of the 'politics of bargaining' (Waddington, 1995). Three features of the politics of bargaining influence merger activity: the bargaining position of unions relative to employers and the state; a union's bargain-ing position relative to competitor unions; and factional bargaining within unions (1995: 205). This explanation incorporates aspects of the industrialisation and institutionalisation theses. From the industrialisa-tion thesis it accepts that a union's bargaining position may change as forms of production are altered and levels of industrial conflict vary. From the institutionalisation thesis it acknowledges that changes in bargaining structure are influential. In particular, it argues that changes in the level at which bargaining takes place influence the development of trade union structure. For example, unions in the UK merged to meet the challenges arising from the establishment of national bargaining between 1910 and 1922. A further wave of mergers was associated with the decentralisation of bargaining after about 1970 (Waddington, 1995). The key question regarding this explanation is, does it constitute a satisfactory framework for the explanation of merger activity in coun-tries beyond the UK?

Within the terms of these aggregate explanations, a vast range of fac-tors has been identified as influencing the merger process. These factors do not influence all mergers, but, acting singly or in combination, are regarded as influencing the merger process at specific junctures. It is acknowledged that a web of inter-relationships exists between many of these influences, among which are included;

- the business cycle, specifically the impact of changing rates of unemployment and inflation on bargaining position (Waddington, 1988; Freeman and Brittain, 1977);
- company mergers and the rise of the multi-plant firm (Geroski and Knight, 1984; Galenson, 1952; Ulman, 1955);
- technological change, particularly when it impinges on craft unionism (Buchanan, 1981; Undy *et al.*, 1981);
- industrial restructuring, specifically its effect on established union jurisdictions and inter-union competition for membership (Campling and Michelson, 1997; Abrahamsson, 1993);
- absolute and relative changes in the membership size of individual unions (Buchanan, 1974; Chaison, 1981; Undy *et al.*, 1981);
- the level of union density (Voos, 1983; 1984);
- financial decline (Willman *et al.*, 1993; Waddington, 1995);
- employer recognition of the union for bargaining or representation, particularly for small unions (Morris 1986; Swabe and Price 1984);
- trade union leadership (Undy *et al.*, 1981);
- legislation that either limits the opportunities for trade union activity and organisation or specifies the procedures whereby mergers are brought about (Waddington, 1995; Chaison, 1996);
- the presence of membership size thresholds, such as those which allow union participation in unemployment insurance schemes in some Nordic countries (see Chapter 4).

Many of these influences have been identified in country-specific studies. An additional purpose of this volume is thus to establish whether these specific influences on the merger process are more geographically wide-ranging. Furthermore, it also attempts to establish the relationships between the aggregate explanations of the merger process and the specific influences on particular mergers.

Internal Processes of Negotiation and the Selection of a Merger Partner

Before selecting a specific organisation with which to merge, union representatives may enter into negotiations with a number of potential partners. Similarly, merger negotiations between unions may continue for a number of years, albeit with ebbs and flows in intensity, before a settlement acceptable to the parties is ratified. In both of these instances, the central issue is the identification and settlement of satisfactory terms to the merger agreement. Within these processes divergent priorities may be pursued both within and between different constituencies of the unions party to the merger proposal. Although members' interests tend to be associated with the protection of union identity or culture and officers with the terms and conditions of their post-merger employment (Chaison, 1986; Undy *et al.*, 1981), this distinction obscures the detail of the processes involved in selecting a merger partner. These processes necessarily involve discussion of issues that facilitate, and those that act as a barrier to, the conclusion of a merger agreement. The particular form of these issues and their impact depends on which unions are involved and the intended form of the post-merger union. In short, the greater the degree of intended post-merger integration, the more barriers that will have to be overcome (Chaison, 1996: 12-14). Measures that facilitate and impair the selection of specific merger partners are reviewed below with the purpose of identifying the terms that form the substance of merger agreements.

Union confederations or senior union officers in several of the countries examined in this volume (Australia, Denmark, Germany, Greece, Sweden and the UK) have formulated detailed plans for the systematic reform of trade union structure. Integral to these plans were recommenddations to unions to merge within a specific blueprint. Furthermore, in Austria, Norway, Portugal and the US, confederations tend to support union restructuring. With the exception of Australia (see Chapter 2) blueprints have not been realised and the merger policies enacted by individual unions have held sway, although confederal support has certainly encouraged initiatives taken by individual unions. In other words, the overwhelming majority of merger agreements are concluded between two or more unions acting independently, rather than as part of a pre-formulated blueprint. Merger agreements are also usually concluded between entire unions, rather than sections of unions. Such conditions ensure that the systematic restructuring of a trade union movement is extremely problematic because different sections of most large unions will have close links to a range of other unions. A single merger may enhance some of these links, but is unlikely to enhance them all. There are exceptions to this general formula. Recently in Denmark, for example, members of GF (Danish Union of Graphical Workers) voted to dissolve the union with the different sections electing to join no fewer than three other unions[2], thus ensuring the systematic restructuring of union organisation.

---

[2] Bookbinders, commercial artists, lithographers and typographers from the GF joined HK (Union of Commercial and Clerical Employees); cardboard product workers joined SiD (General Workers' Union); and the photographers joined DJ (National Union of Journalists) (see Jørgensen, 1999).

At the core of most merger agreements are terms concerning the authority of the post-merger union's executive and the employment of union officers and staff.[3] Central to the position of the executive is constitutional authority over a unified or centralised system of internal union finance and over the sanctioning of industrial action. The overwhelming majority of merger agreements stipulate these arrangements thereby ensuring centralisation of authority on these matters. Although arrangements that allow for the executives of the pre-merger unions to persist into the post-merger period are commonplace, they are usually accompanied by terms that stipulate the operation of a superior executive with authority over the entire post-merger union. Where agreements have allowed dual executives or have failed to assign authority on financial matters to a single body, the merger has often fallen apart. In order to secure support for a merger proposal, most merger agreements specify the continued employment of union officers and staff. Support for the merger from these groups before its ratification by members is usually too important to jeopardise, although post-merger rationalisation often involves recourse to some form of early retirement scheme through which staff numbers may be reduced.

The allowance of some degree of post-merger autonomy encourages the selection of a union as a merger partner. As a result of mergers there has been a proliferation of different forms of sectional representation intended to preserve some elements of pre-merger union identity. These may be accompanied by the retention of conferences, journals and newspapers. The degree of post-merger autonomy encouraged by these arrangements is often restricted to the collective bargaining function. Sectional representation raises questions concerning interest aggregation in post-merger unions. In particular, are horizontal linkages established between different post-merger sections and, if so, what form do they take and how do they influence union activity?

Mergers may also be facilitated where the senior union officers are nearing retirement, particularly if the proposed merger is to lead to the formation of a new union (Chitayat, 1979; Drucker, 1988). The argument here is that during the years following their election or appointment, senior officers are keen to implement the policies on which they were elected, whereas drawing to the end of their tenure different priori-

---

[3]   For the purposes of this chapter the terms 'executive' is used to refer to the senior body that is responsible for the day-to-day running of a union. This term is in common usage in Australia and Britain, but in Austria and Germany this body is usually termed the *Vorstand, Bundesvorstand* or *Hauptvorstand*; in Denmark, the *hovedbestyrelsen* or *forretningsudvalget*; in Norway, the *forbundsstyre*; in Portugal, the *quadro*; in Sweden, the *istyrelson*.

ties assume precedence. Similarly, guaranteeing the terms, conditions and pension provisions of union officers is key to ensuring that they are prepared to campaign for the merger. Union officers are also more likely to select a merger partner and to campaign for a merger with a union that offers superior terms and conditions. Evidence from the US suggests that union officers will 'seek mergers in pursuit of their self-interest', particularly if post-merger improvements are secured in the terms and conditions of employment among union officers and employees (Conant, 1993).

Political alliances among members and officers have a range of effects on the selection of a merger partner. A merger between unions may be supported if the political position of specific sections of members will be improved in the post-merger union. State employees of lower 'socio-economic status', for example, were more favourably disposed to merge their employee association with a union than were groups of a higher status, because they wanted 'the power to initiate strikes and join civil rights coalitions' (Cornfield, 1991: 334). Similarly, the majority position of engineers in the Association of Scientific, Technical and Managerial Staffs (ASTMS) was threatened by superior rates of member recruitment from other sectors of the economy. Engineers in ASTMS thus strongly supported a proposed merger with the Technical, Administrative and Supervisory Section (TASS), because engineers comprised a substantial majority within TASS and in the post-merger union the traditional political dominance of engineers was restored (Carter, 1991). Political differences may constitute a barrier to a merger agreement. The affiliation of a union to a particular political party or the different political persuasions of senior officers and members of the executive have inhibited merger initiatives. Similarly, long-standing rivalries between unions have often proved an insurmountable barrier to what appears to be a 'logical' merger and, in certain instances, have prompted alternative mergers.

The role of union confederations is also far from straightforward. Most union confederations tend to promote mergers and make mediation facilities available to assist the search for a satisfactory merger agreement. In addition, breakaway unions are usually refused affiliation by union confederations and recommended to merge with an affiliated union, thereby promoting mergers.[4] The chapters of this volume demonstrate, however, that in certain situations, representatives of confedera-

---

[4] Following Waddington a breakaway union is formed when 'a section of a union secedes to become an independent organisation without the sanction of the executive of the original union' (1995: 12)

tions advocate particular merger options in order to preserve political position. The boundaries of union confederations tend to act as barriers to mergers, irrespective of whether they are based on class and status, as in Denmark, Norway and Sweden; sector, as in Greece; or political affiliation, as in Portugal. Mergers thus tend to involve affiliates of the same confederation. Where single confederations have been established, affiliation acts as a boundary that tends to be permeable in one direction only. In other words, when a union affiliated to a confederation merges with a non-affiliated union, the post-merger union tends to retain confederal affiliation. There are very few instances of a union affiliated to a confederation merging with a non-affiliated union and the resultant post-merger union opting to remain outside the confederation.

Difficulties in reconciling constitutional or procedural differences also figure large in merger negotiations. In particular, failure to agree a membership contribution or fees structure for the new union, the range and level of friendly society benefits, the departmental structure of the proposed union and even the name of the new organisation are cited in most countries as having been at the core of lengthy discussions before agreements were settled. Similarly, disputes over the election or appointment of union officers have led to breakdown of merger proposals. Variations in the manner of collecting and distributing membership contributions are also problematic. This is certainly the case if one union allows local organisation to retain a proportion of the money collected from members and expects the remaining sum to be sent to head office, whereas the other union requires all money to be sent to head office which later remits a proportion of this sum back to local organisation. Irrespective of these, and other, peculiarities of specific mergers, it is apparent that a merger provides opportunities for constitutional change which otherwise might not have occurred. In part, the nature of the constitutional change depends on the intended outcome of the merger, differences over which may also be prominent in the selection of a merger partner. It is to these outcomes that we now turn.

Merger Outcomes

The range of benefits claimed to arise from the merger process is wide-ranging and encompasses micro- and macro-level issues. These are reviewed below with the object of introducing both claims and counter-claims concerning the benefits of increased post-merger union size and changes in the 'type' of union organisation. From the outset it should be acknowledged that the support of members for a merger is conditioned by their analysis of its costs and benefits (McClendon *et al.*, 1995). Immediately before a merger agreement is ratified, therefore, the terms of the merger may be contested within and between unions. There are often marked discrepancies between the claims made for the merger process and its outcome that, in part, are dependent on the structure of the trade union movement within which the merger process is underway. The extent of these discrepancies is examined in the country-based chapters of this volume. Irrespective of the structure of the national trade union movement within which restructuring is underway, mergers raise issues of union articulation and co-ordination. These issues are introduced in the context of merger outcomes because the merger process may transform both of them. Thus central to the merger process are means whereby union articulation and co-ordination can be maintained or restored.

The argument that fewer, yet larger, unions are able to provide a broader range of services and support to members more efficiently than smaller unions has had long-standing and widespread support within trade unions movements (ACTU, 1987; AFL-CIO, 1985; Rappe, 1992; TUC, 1966: 114-121). Underpinning this view is the expectation that economies of scale arise from involvement in the merger process. This expectation is often supplemented by a belief that small unions are unable to adequately service members, particularly where bargaining is decentralised. Advocates of mergers envisage that economies of scale may be achieved through the employment of fewer full-time trade union officers and union employees. Alternatively, some argue that services might be improved by retaining the same number of employees pre- and post-merger. The post-merger rationalisation of union offices is also viewed as a means of achieving savings and of releasing funds for other purposes through the sale of property. The amalgamation of training, legal, research and other support departments may be a further source of post-merger economies of scale, both through the reduction in staff and the requirement for office space.

Each of these positions is qualified. As it is very difficult politically for unions to declare redundancies as part of the merger process, many merger agreements guarantee the employment of union staff in the post-merger organisation, thereby limiting immediate post-merger economies of scale. Expensive early retirement or voluntary redundancy schemes introduced after the merger agreement is formally ratified may result in fewer union staff and, thus, longer-term economies of scale. Reductions in the number of staff, however, assume that post-merger economies of scale are more important than the provision of a wider range of services and support to members that the staff offered early retirement might provide. Furthermore, the extent of any economies of scale is dependent on which unions are involved in a merger. In short, economies of scale are more likely the greater the extent of overlap between the memberships of the pre-merger unions. If there is complete overlap, a single trade union officer may negotiate on behalf of the combined post-merger membership where two officers were involved before the merger. If there is no overlap between the memberships, it is necessary for the post-merger union to service two sets of negotiations, thereby requiring a similar staff complement. A further qualification of this point arises in the case of unions in Greece and Portugal, many of which employ no staff. Economies of scale may thus arise from the merger process, but only if the terms of the merger agreement and post-merger practice are directed to achieve such an outcome. Several recent prominent merger cases – for example, *Bondgenoten* in the Netherlands and UNISON in Britain – have encountered significant post-merger financial difficulties as the forecasts and assumptions on which the merger agreement was drawn up proved to be overly optimistic.

Advocates of restructuring by merger also argue that increased post-merger membership size may provide the platform for better-resourced recruitment campaigns, particularly into private sector services. Again, evidence on this proposition is equivocal. Large unions with decentralised systems of government and administration were more effective in winning certification elections in the US (Maranto and Fiorito, 1987), but large unions were also more likely to be decertified (Dworkin and Extejt, 1979). Membership growth factors were relatively marginal in a direct assessment of the benefits of mergers (Stratton-Devine, 1992). In Canada increased union size had no influence on organising (Gilson and Wagar, 1992). Pursuing the same tack, Willman (1989) argued that mergers in the UK have merely enabled some of the larger unions to maintain similar relative membership sizes or 'market shares', rather than act as a springboard for recruitment in unorganised sectors of the economy. The question raised by Brooks and Gamm (1976) thus remains pertinent; are mergers merely low-cost, low-risk alternatives to the costly, time-consuming and high-risk business of organising the unorganised?

Several union movements examined in this volume are committed to generating higher levels of membership participation in union affairs as part of a strategy to achieve higher rates of recruitment growth. The debate whether mergers curtail or enhance membership participation and democracy is thus associated with that concerning membership growth. Lower rates of membership participation were found within larger US unions, irrespective of their merger involvement (Barling *et al.*, 1992). The abandonment of the identity of pre-merger unions during the merger process, however, was linked to a diminution of membership participation (Williamson, 1995). Where high degrees of post-merger integration were achieved between union governing structures, membership participation declined due to the larger and more centralised committee structures, the creation of additional tiers of government and the increased time commitment required to run for union office (Chaison, 1986: 120). No evidence of any deleterious effects arising from amalgamations on the influence of members on union decision-making was reported in Australia (Peetz, 1998: 137), while in the UK the merger to form UNISON was not a significant factor in promoting members to leave the union (Waddington and Kerr, 1999). A systematic study of a specific Swedish merger showed that there were no differences in pre- and post-merger commitment to the union among members, although there was some decline in the rate of membership attendance at meetings of the post-merger union (Sverke and Sjöberg, 1997). As these authors acknowledge, however, one of the key criteria identified for this merger was the maintenance of levels of membership participation. This is unusual; most mergers are dominated by rather different agendas. The impact of the merger process on membership participation in different national circumstances thus remains to be seen.

Proponents of mergers also argue that increased bargaining strength and political influence result from engagement in the merger process. The consolidation of strike funds, an increased capacity to deploy experienced negotiators supported by professional lawyers, trainers and researchers, and different attitudes among employers towards a larger union leading to better results from bargaining are cited as benefits of merger involvement (Kochan and Wever, 1991; Chaison, 1997; Buchanan, 1981). Circumstances where such benefits might arise include:

- if a small union of insufficient size to sustain support departments or to afford full-time officers, merges with a larger union, access to a 'professional' negotiation service may be secured;
- in cases of long-term membership decline, merger may enable a union to retain staff originally employed when membership levels and income were higher;
- where a merger consolidates union organisation within bargaining units, whether at plant or industry level, there are fewer opportunities for employers to play groups of workers off against others and workers may act as a single unit.

Similar benefits may arise from other forms of closer working, such as federations or cartels of unions. The country-based chapters of this volume illustrate that these alternatives are consistently adopted in Denmark and Sweden for specific bargaining purposes in preference to mergers. The point here is that increased bargaining strength may result from mergers, but the effect is conditioned by the structure of bargaining, the structure of the trade union movement and the characteristics of the unions involved in any specific merger. A purpose of this volume is to establish how these conditioning factors impinge upon the merger process.

Increased political influence is a further possible outcome of the merger process (Waddington, 1995; Streeck and Visser, 1997). All other things remaining equal, representatives of larger unions are more likely to gain access to social, economic and political policy-making processes than their counterparts from smaller unions. As voting strength within many union confederations is determined by membership size, mergers may also improve voting positions within such institutions. The impact of shifts in the composition of the labour force on relative membership size has encouraged traditionally dominant unions to pursue mergers as a means to restore their influence. In several countries, for example, public sector unions are now larger than the traditionally dominant engineering unions, thereby encouraging mergers between engineering and other unions in manufacturing in order to regain their former position. The impact of the merger process on intra-confederal politics is thus wide-ranging. The different configuration of union confederations in the countries covered in this study is a further influence on the form of the merger process, as are variations in the political position of confederations within regulatory regimes.

Associated with the range of merger outcomes claimed for post-merger increases in union size are issues arising from increased membership heterogeneity and changes in 'type' of union organisation. Although increases in the membership heterogeneity of many large unions arise from changes in the composition of the labour force, mergers accentuate this trend. Furthermore, they do so in a single dramatic step, or a series of steps in the case of repeated merger involvement, rather than incrementally as occurs through recruitment. Mergers thus raise specific challenges for post-merger integration. In several of the countries examined in this study – Germany, Portugal, the UK and the US, for example – large unions are sustaining declines in membership simultaneously with increasing membership heterogeneity. Greater demands are thus placed on union organisation as a result of membership heterogeneity at a time of diminishing resources due to membership decline. Mergers also present opportunities for wide-ranging reforms of systems of union government. Such reforms may incorporate measures to ameliorate the effects of increasing membership heterogeneity. They may also facilitate the introduction of 'new' structures of representation, which are central to trade union 'modernisation', such as representative structures for women and young members. The effect of these reforms is not straightforward, however, as they may also increase operating costs and thus mitigate any post-merger economies of scale.

Increasing membership heterogeneity clearly impinges on trade union structure in different ways. The general tendency, however, is the abandonment of industrial, occupational or geographical restrictions to organisation. Where industrial unionism was the traditional basis to organisation, the merger process is resulting in multi-industry unions in a development similar to the establishment of multi-craft unions in the US during the early twentieth century (Glocker, 1915; Ulman, 1955). In Germany and the Netherlands, for example, the principle of industrial unionism is being jettisoned in favour of more conglomerate structures (Streeck and Visser, 1997). In countries where industrial unionism has been long abandoned the tendency is towards super- or mega-unions, which claim to recruit all workers irrespective of industry or occupation. The diverse membership of super-unions spreads organisational risk, in that losses from any one area of membership are unlikely to undermine the entire organisation. Furthermore, super-unions may perform many of the functions traditionally undertaken by confederations, thereby bringing into question the future role of union confederations.

These developments raise issues of union articulation and co-ordination. For our purposes, union articulation is defined in terms of the density of inter-linkages between vertical levels of a union. An articulated union is 'one in which strong relations of interdependence bind different vertical levels, such that the actions of the centre are frequently predicated on securing the consent of lower levels and the autonomous action of lower levels is bounded by the rules of delegation' (Crouch, 1993: 54-55). Once achieved, union articulation is not fixed or immutable, but requires the continuous reform of union activity and organisation if it is to be maintained. In several countries, for example, the decentralisation of bargaining is associated with the breakdown of union articulation, the isolation of workplace organisation and the failure to generate an agenda appropriate to current circumstances (Waddington, 2000). Union co-ordination refers to horizontal linkages within a union. Dense horizontal linkages facilitate cohesion between different groups of members and thus mitigate the adverse effects of increasing membership heterogeneity on interest aggregation.

Union mergers clearly illustrate the transitory nature of union articu-lation in that they disturb extant relationships and require the develop-ment of alternative networks. This is particularly the case where a merger results in the unification of local and regional, as well as na-tional, level organisations and activities. If union organisation is to be maintained or renewed in such circumstances, formal and informal networks need to be established which incorporate members from all pre-merger unions. As was illustrated above, internal union sections have proliferated to accommodate both the membership of acquired unions and the increasing heterogeneity of members that are recruited, but the horizontal linkages in many instances have not been sufficient to unify post-merger organisation. The conference of the post-merger union is often the only point at which the memberships of the different sections come into regular contact, thus leading some to suggest that unions are adopting the form of 'joint ventures' rather than serving as means of aggregating diverse interests (Willman and Cave, 1994). A further question asked by this book, therefore, is: does the merger process allow the development of articulated and co-ordinated post-merger union organisation and activity through which an agenda appropriate to current circumstances may be generated and delivered?

The Merger Process in Overview

This section introduces the countries that form the basis of this study, defines the terms that recur throughout, and reviews the data that are analysed in subsequent chapters. It thus establishes some of the parameters of the data and, in particular, introduces the different patterns of the merger process on the basis of broadly comparable data. Finally, this section briefly outlines the structure of the book.

The Ten Countries

Ten countries form the basis of this study: Australia, Austria, Denmark, Germany, Greece, Norway, Portugal, Sweden, UK and US. This range of countries provides examples of different regulatory regimes, union structures and confederal organisation. In particular, there are three examples of merger processes underway within Anglo-Saxon regulatory regimes (Australia, UK and US), three exemplars of the 'Nordic model' (Denmark, Norway and Sweden), two of trade union movements restructuring within Rhenish capitalism (Austria and Germany), and two cases that trace the development of trade union structure in the transition from totalitarian regimes (Greece and Portugal).

While industrial organisation has, at different times, been the objective of most of the trade union movements analysed here, only in Austria and Germany was something akin to industrial organisation achieved. In both of these cases and more markedly in the other countries under consideration, however, multi-industry or general unions and/or occupational unions have existed since 1950, which have restricted opportunities to establish industrial unions. There are also significant variations in the membership sizes of the unions within the selected countries. In Austria and Germany there is no 'tail' of small unions. In the other countries this 'tail' accounts for a small proportion of overall membership and a large proportion of total union numbers.

A further restriction to industrial unionism is the confederal structures of the ten countries. Unified confederations have existed in Austria, Germany[5] and the UK since 1950. In the US a single confederation has existed since 1955 when the American Federation of Labor (AFL) and the Congress of Industrial Organisations (CIO) merged to form the AFL-CIO. Multiple confederations exist elsewhere. In the Nordic countries occupation, education and political affiliation are the principal sources of demarcation, whereas in Greece it is sector and in Portugal it is political affiliation. As the country chapters illustrate, the impact of confederal boundaries on the form of the merger process is extensive. In the main, where there are multiple confederations, confederal boundaries act as a barrier to merger and thus restrict opportunities to adapt to changing labour markets.

Other countries could certainly have been included in the study. For example, extensive merger processes have occurred or are underway in Canada, Finland, Ireland, the Netherlands and New Zealand. While the inclusion of these and other countries would allow us to claim a more comprehensive coverage, our argument is that the selected countries enable us to identify the principal features of the trade union merger process within a broad range of institutional circumstances. They also allow us to trace the variation in the evolution of trade union structure and government.

Definitions

For the purposes of this book the following definitions are used for each of the chapters;

- A *merger* is the combination of two or more unions to form a single union. In the process, the independence of at least one of the unions is subsumed within another. Following Chaison (1982) there are two forms in which a merger may be brought about. In an *amalgamation* two or more unions combine to form a new union. Amalgamations usually, but not exclusively, involve unions of similar size and/or unions attempting to be seen as merging as

---

5   Chapter 5 on Germany considers only the merger process involving unions affiliated to the DGB (German Trade Union Confederation). In practice, the chapter, therefore, treats Germany as having a single trade union confederation. It is acknowledged, however, that the CGB (Christian Trade Union Confederation) also has a confederal role, albeit for only about 320,000 members, and that the DBB (Union of Civil Servants) is considered by many to be a confederation.

equal partners. In an *acquisition* one union acquires or absorbs another union and the identity of the acquired union is subsumed within that of the acquiring union. The acquiring union is usually larger than the absorbed union in an acquisition. The combination of local branches *within* an already established union is thus excluded from our definition. Also excluded from our definition is the affiliation of an independent local or an entire union to a national union. Such events are commonplace in the US. The exclusion of these affiliations thus understates the extent of trade union restructuring in the US.

- A *cartel* occurs where a number of unions, or parts of unions, unite, usually to engage in bargaining on a range of issues which may include wages. Such bargaining is usually undertaken at national level across an industry or sector. Cartels may be cross-confederal in Sweden and Denmark.

- A *confederation* is an umbrella organisation that seeks to represent the interests of affiliated unions and to adjudicate disputes between affiliated unions. As mentioned above, the countries examined here exhibit a range of confederal structures. The role of the confederation in bargaining and the peculiarities of the constitutional authority of the confederation are not taken into account in our definition, although these features certainly impinge on the merger process.

- A *federation* of unions comprises a group of trade unions that combine for specific purposes. As such, federations are similar to cartels, but they need not necessarily be directed towards bargaining, which is the principal function of a cartel. In a federation the independence of each trade union is not compromised. Federal arrangements between unions are often the forerunner of a formal merger. In Greece and Portugal federations are ever-present intermediary institutions between unions and confederations. Greek and Portuguese unions affiliate to federations, which pursue their interests within confederations. In consequence, unions in these two countries tend to be exclusive organisations, in terms of industry, occupation and/or geography, and operate with very low average membership sizes (see Table 1.1).

These definitions have been applied throughout this book. Where ambiguity occurs, for example in deciding whether a merger is an amalgamation or an acquisition, the decision has rested with the author(s) of each country chapter.

The Pattern of Merger Activity since 1950

The change in the number of trade unions since 1950 is shown in Figure 1.1. For most countries the trend is one of declining union numbers. This is particularly marked in the UK, although it is also present in Denmark, Sweden, Australia (among federally registered unions only) and the US. In Norway, Austria and Germany union numbers are relatively constant for much of the period after 1950. Only after 1990 are some declines recorded. A contrary trend is exhibited in Portugal. The number of trade unions increased sharply after democratisation until 1992 (from 316 in 1975 to 407 in 1992), before falling to 376 by 2000.

Figure 1.1: Number of Unions, 1950-2000

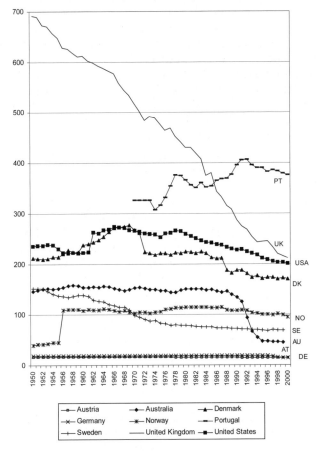

The country chapters illustrate that this decline in union numbers is not solely due to the merger process. Also contributing to the decline in union numbers is the dissolution of trade unions.[6] Table 1.1, however, shows that the decline in the number of unions has contributed to an increase in the average size of trade unions after 1950 in most of the selected countries. This increase is particularly marked in absolute terms in Denmark and Sweden where average union size in 2000 was about four times greater than in 1950. Larger average trade union sizes are attained in Austria and Germany where organisation most closely resembles industrial unionism due to post-war restructuring. Although average size increased in both of these countries, the rate of increase was lower than in Denmark and Sweden. The particularly low average union sizes recorded for Greece and Portugal result from the reliance on federations as the institutional means to unite exclusive unions organised on the basis of industry, occupation and/or locality. Average union size has also increased at a higher rate than membership in the countries shown in Table 1.1. This is particularly the case in Sweden where membership increased by 101.4 per cent between 1950 and 2000 while average union size increased by 350.0 per cent. Although periods of membership decline are recorded in several countries, it is only in Germany, between 1980 and 1985, and the UK, after 1980, that this was concurrent with a decline in average union size.

Comparative studies of membership concentration that use concentration ratios show increasing concentration to be associated with the decrease in the number of unions and the increase in average union size (Windmuller, 1981). Furthermore, using the same measure, country studies assign much of the rise in membership concentration to the impact of the merger process (Buchanan, 1981; Estey, 1966; Howells and Cathro, 1981). However, where measures of concentration are employed that include the entire population of unions, such as the Herfindahl Index, the rise in membership concentration since 1950 is less steep, particularly where there is a 'tail' comprising a large number of small unions, as in the UK (Waddington, 1993). In these circumstances, the continual renewal of the tail of small unions through the formation of new unions mitigates the impact on concentration arising from the merger process.

---

[6] In several of the countries under discussion the total number of unions was also influenced by the formation of unions and the establishment of breakaway unions. Of course, these events raised the number of unions. Where appropriate, these issues are examined in the country chapters.

Table 1.1: Trade Union Membership, Density and Average Size, 1950-2000

Year	Australia member-ship[1]	Australia density[1] %	Australia union average size	Austria member-ship	Austria density[3] %	Austria union average size	Denmark member-ship	Den-mark density[3] %	Den-mark union average size
1950	1,605,344	58	4,459	1,290,581	62.2	80,661	713,681	53.2	3,382
1955	1,801,862	59	4,844	1,398,446	63.8	87,403	839,666	58.3	3,924
1960	1,912,392	58	5,268	1,501,047	63.4	93,815	954,808	60.2	4,012
1965	2,116,200	55	6,336	1,542,813	63.0	96,453	1,049,454	61.1	3,975
1970	2,314,600	49	6,670	1,520,259	62.1	95,016	1,137,326	62.1	4,260
1975	2,813,800	56	8,711	1,587,500	58.5	99,219	1,314,183	70.0	5,947
1980	2,955,900	56	9,095	1,660,985	58.4	110,732	1,756,177	80.6	7,805
1985	3,154,200	57	9,766	1,671,381	58.2	111,425	1,990,058	83.3	9,343
1990	2,659,600	41	9,016	1,644,841	54.1	109,656	2,066,364	80.5	10,991
1995	2,251,800	33	15,858	1,583,356	47.1	113,097	2,162,759	85.5	12,648
2000	1,901,800	25	15,214[2]	1,442,393	35.8	103,028	2,161,616	82.1	12,715

Year	Germany member-ship[4]	Ger-many density %	Germany union average size	Greece member-ship[6]	Greece density[11] %	Greece union average size	Norway member-ship	Norway density %	Norway union average size
1950	6,600,400[5]	39.6	347,389				459,135		11,773[13]
1955	7,105,478	39.7	373,973				504,158	52.5[12]	11,204[13]
1960	7,562,776	37.5	398,041				622,388	52.3	5,763
1965	7,854,808	36.5	413,411				652,788	51.6	5,934
1970	8,012,607	36.2	421,716				683,205	50.4	6,633
1975	8,693,513	37.4	457,553				771,690	51.9	7,280
1980	9,364,800	38.3	492,884	667,000[7]	39.3	205	937,467	55.1	8,152
1985	9,179,790	36.0	483,147	761,000[8]	42.9	208	1,001,538	55.9	8,863
1990	9,408,380	34.9	522,688	766,000[9]	40.7	198	1,033,711	56.4	9,571
1995	11,085,557	32.4	615,864	656,000	31.8	183	1,061,140	55.4	10,611
2000	9,733,000	25.8	811,083	683,561[10]	30.4	189	1,117,604	53.2	11,764

Year	Portugal membership	Portugal density[14] %	Portugal union average size	Sweden membership	Sweden density %	Sweden union average size
1950				1,605,600	67.3	10,563
1955				1,758,900	69.2	12,839
1960				1,909,100	70.7	13,834
1965				2,103,300	65.4	17,528
1970				2,235,200	66.6	23,727
1975		52.0		2,766,700	73.0	33,334
1980		59.0		3,114,300	77.7	39,927
1985		44.0		3,349,800	80.8	44,664
1990	1,434,000		3,621	3,387,700	81.6	47,051
1995	800,000	36.0	2,051	3,390,200	85.0	49,133
2000				3,232,876	80.1	47,542

Year	UK membership (000s)	UK density %	UK union average size	US membership	US density %	US union average size[15]
1950	9,003,000	44.3	13,029	14,267,000	22.9	73,427
1955	9,460,000	44.5	14,599	16,802,000	25.8	92,131
1960	9,437,000	44.0	15,420	17.049,000	24.5	92,301
1965	9,715,000	43.0	16,692	17,299,000	23.2	100,147
1970	10,672,000	48.5	20,602	19,381,000	23.4	107,130
1975	11,561,000	52.0	24,237	19,611,000	20.9	125,625
1980	12,239,000	54.5	28,397	19,843,000	18.6	129,543
1985	10,282,000	49.0	27,058	16,996,000	18.0	136,552
1990	8,854,000	38.1	30,850	16,776,000	16.0	156,551
1995	7,275,000	32.1	29,816	16,360,000	14.9	158,622
2000	7,779,000	29.4	33,386	16,258,000	13.5	182,423

[1] Data for 1950-1985 are based on a now discontinued set of annual data collected by the Australian Bureau of Statistics directly from trade unions. Data for 1990-2000 are based on survey data collected by the Australian Bureau of Statistics.

[2] From 1997 onwards, the Australian Bureau of Statistics ceased to collect data on the number of trade unions. The average size figure for 2000 is based on estimates of the number of trade unions derived from data held by the office of the Industrial Registrar.

[3] Density data for Austria and Denmark are taken from Ebbinghaus and Visser (2000) and refer to union membership expressed as a proportion of the employed.

[4] Membership data include unions affiliated to the DGB, the DAG (Union of Salaried Employees) and the DBB (Union of Civil Servants). The membership of the GdP (Union of Police Officers) is included for all years, irrespective of whether it was affiliated to the DGB or not.

[5] Data are for 1951.

[6] Trade union membership data refer to members who voted at confederal congresses.

[7] Data are for 1983.

[8] Data are for 1986.

[9] Data are for 1989.

[10] Density calculated by reference to salary and wage earners in employment.

[11] Data are for 1998.

[12] Data refer to 1956, rather than 1955.

[13] The data on the number of trade unions in Norway before 1956 only cover LO-affiliated organisations whereas the membership data cover all unions. The apparent fall in the average size of trade unions between 1955 and 1960 is entirely due to this data shortfall. If the data on the number of unions was complete, it is assumed that the average size would fall beneath 5,500 for the period before 1960.

[14] Cerdeira (1997) provides density data for periods rather than specific years. To insert the data into this table, the following periods have been applied to specific years: 1974-78 is treated as 1975; 1979-1984 as 1980; 1985-90 as 1985; and 1991-95 as 1995.

[15] Union average size for the US was calculated by dividing the membership of the AFL-CIO by the number of national unions affiliated to the confederation. The membership data do not include the membership of unions that are affiliated to those unions that are affiliated to the AFL-CIO, but do include members that belong to locals that affiliate directly to the AFL-CIO. The number of unions data refer to the number of national unions affiliated to the AFL-CIO. Due to the direct affiliation of independent locals

Jeremy Waddington

and the exclusion of these organisations from the number of unions data, the union average size figures are likely to overstate the actual average size of AFL-CIO national union affiliates.

Sources: Australia, data taken from records maintained by the Australian Bureau of Statistics until 1985, thereafter from survey data collected by Australian Bureau of Statistics and data held by the Office of the Industrial Registrar.
Austria, data prepared by the author of Chapter 3.
Denmark, data prepared by the authors of Chapter 4, together with density data from Ebbinghaus and Visser (2000).
Germany, 1950-1995 data taken from Müller-Jentsch and Ittermann (2000), data for 2000 taken from Müller-Jentsch and Weitbrecht (2003).
Greece, data prepared by the author of Chapter 6 based on GSEE, ADEDY and Labour Force Survey evidence.
Norway, data from Stokke (1998) and Stokke *et al.* (2003).
Portugal, membership data taken from ILO (1997) and density data from Cerdeira (1997). These sources are spliced with data on the number of unions generated by the author of Chapter 8.
Sweden, data taken from series maintained by author of Chapter 9.
UK, membership data taken from various issues of *Labour Market Trends* or its predecessors.1950-1985 density data taken from Waddington (1992), 1990-2000 density data from Sneade (2001).
US, 1950-1980 data taken from Bureau of Labor Statistics, 1985-2000 data taken from Current Population Survey. The series on the membership of the AFL-CIO was assembled from various issues of the *Daily Labor Report* and the series on the number of national unions affiliated to the AFL-CIO was assembled by the author of Chapter 11. Details of its preparation are available there.

Figures 1.2, 1.4, 1.6, 1.7, 1.8, 1.9 and 1.10 show the trend in the intensity of merger activity in seven countries. Merger intensity may be represented as follows;

$$UA_t/TU_{t-1}$$

where:

UA is the number of unions absorbed in a year. This is calculated differently for an acquisition and an amalgamation. In an acquisition where a large union absorbs a small union the number involved is one. In an amalgamation the number is the total number of unions involved minus one. For example, if six unions amalgamate to form a new union, the number of unions absorbed is counted as five.
TU is the total number of trade unions. As data on the number of unions apply to December 31st of each year a t-1 denominator is used to express the total number of unions absorbed as a proportion of the population at the end of the previous year.

35

Merger intensity is thus a measure of the rate at which unions are absorbed in the merger process. As the number of unions and mergers in Austria and Germany is relatively small, a chart illustrating the entire merger process in these two countries is provided in Figures 1.3 and 1.5. The relatively few mergers in Greece and the absence of an appropriate data series preclude the visual presentation of the Greek merger process.

Figure 1.2: Merger Intensity Australia, 1950-2000

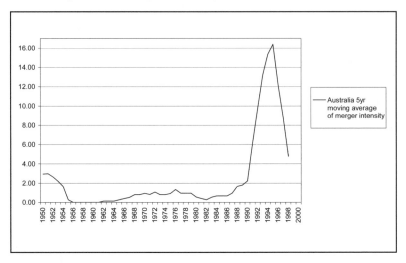

From the outset it is clear that there is no uniform pattern of merger intensity. In Australia and Sweden there is a single pronounced peak in merger intensity, whereas in Denmark, Portugal and the UK there is a peak followed by high levels of merger intensity relative to the period preceding the initial peak. Peaks of merger intensity suggest that influences that promote mergers were far stronger than the barriers to mergers for a limited period of time. This is particularly the case in Australia where the peak of merger intensity reaches almost 17, which is far greater than the height of the peaks recorded elsewhere. As the country chapters demonstrate, the nature of the influences that promote mergers during these peaks varies considerably. By contrast, the intensity of Norwegian merger activity is fairly stable throughout with no specific peak in merger intensity, suggesting a relatively constant process of trade union structural reform. A further pattern of merger intensity is illustrated in the US. Variations in merger intensity are evident throughout the period 1950-2000 with no single dominant peak. This suggests an uneven and irregular pressure for reform, but a pressure that has been present since 1950.

Figure 1.3: Austria: A Moderate Merger Process

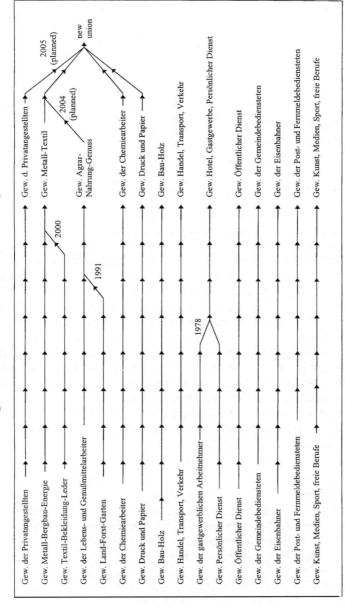

Notes: Gew.=Gewerkschaft Several unions changed their names since 1945, the chart contains only their present names or (where applicable) their names at the time of the merger. As merging unions had also changed their names before the merger, inclusion of the old as well as the current new names would have made the chart too complicated.

Figure 1.4: Merger Intensity Denmark, 1950-2000

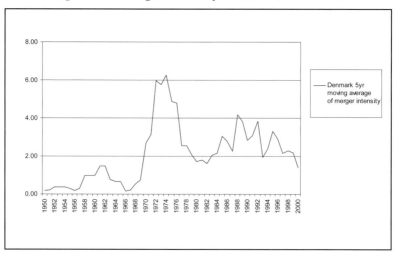

There is also consistency neither in the timing of the peaks in merger intensity nor in their relation to membership change. Peaks in merger intensity during the mid-1970s were features of the merger process in Denmark and Sweden, the late 1970s in the UK, early 1980s in Portugal and mid-1990s in Australia. The formation of ver.di (Unified Services Union) from five unions in 2001 effectively constitutes the peak of merger intensity in Germany. In Denmark, Sweden and the UK the initial peak in merger intensity occurred during a period of membership growth, whereas in Australia, Germany and Portugal it was concurrent with membership decline. Similarly, in the US there is no discernible difference in merger intensity between the period of union growth until about 1980 and the period of membership decline thereafter. The argument that mergers are the sole result of membership decline is thus immediately rejected.

High levels of merger intensity after 1950 immediately bring into question the view that merger activity should be marginal once employers and the state had recognised trade unionism (Lester, 1958). Only the consistent level of merger intensity in Norway and the sparse merger activity in Austria offer some support to this explanation. Institutional explanations of merger activity based on changes in the structure of collective bargaining are more strongly supported by the pattern of merger intensity. In several of the countries under discussion, for example, periods of intense merger activity coincide with the decentralisation of collective bargaining.

Figure 1.5: Charting the German Structural Transformation, 1950-2001

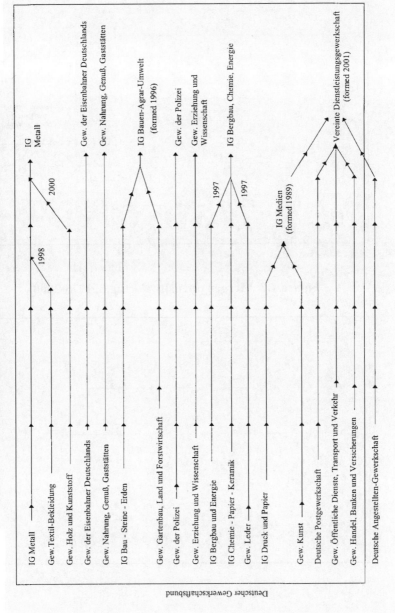

Figure 1.6: Merger Intensity Norway, 1950-2000

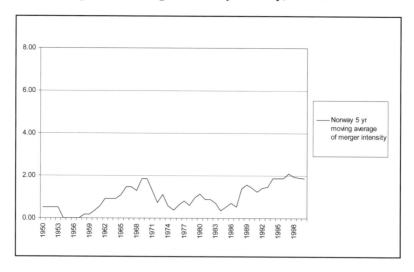

Figure 1.7: Merger Intensity Portugal, 1975-2000

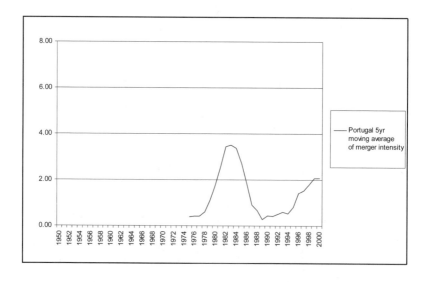

Figure 1.8: Merger Intensity Sweden, 1950-2000

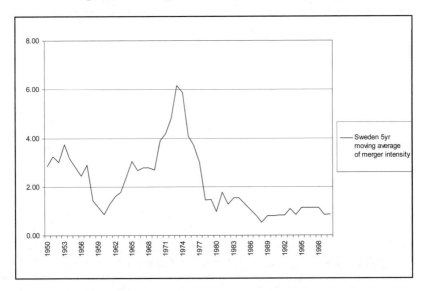

Figure 1.9: Merger Intensity UK, 1950-2000

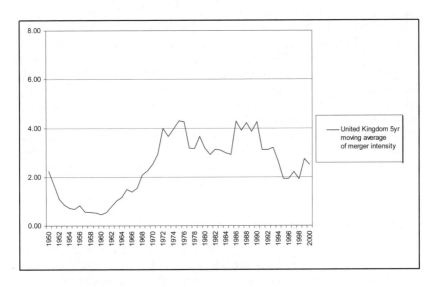

Figure 1.10: Merger Intensity US, 1950-2000

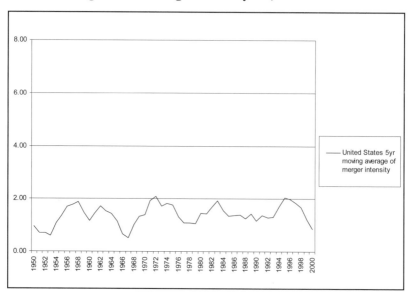

The industrialisation thesis is also supported insofar as there are peaks and troughs in the pattern of merger intensity, thus confirming the idea of cycles of trade union reform. Furthermore, merger activity in most countries is concentrated during the long downswing of the post-war boom. This is consistent with the industrialisation thesis, which suggests that trade union structural reform is a feature of these periods of 'crisis' or 'fundamental unrest' (Dunlop, 1948; Bernstein, 1960). By the same token the concentration of merger activity after about 1975 also lends some support to the explanation based on the politics of bargaining, as it is after about this date that the bargaining position of unions weakened relative to employers and the state. Subsequent chapters demonstrate the variation in the character of merger activity and wide differences in merger outcomes, which allow considerable elaboration of this initial overview.

The Structure of the Book

The book is divided into two parts. The first part comprises ten vertical chapters, which address the merger process in a single country. Wherever possible the authors have addressed similar issues in each of the country chapters, even if this is to report that a specific matter is not relevant to the merger process in that country. The second part comprises three horizontal chapters, each of which addresses a theme that is common to the merger process in several of the countries covered in the vertical chapters. The horizontal chapters elaborate whether mergers are primarily defensive, and examine the extent to which they offer opportunities for trade union 'modernisation'. Three themes are identified for such treatment: the interplay between collective bargaining and forms of closer working, the relationship between trade union confederations and the merger process, and the impact of the merger process on the emergence of new forms of union organisation. Authors who contributed a vertical chapter wrote the horizontal chapters, thereby developing the inter-linkages between the two sections of the book. Finally, a brief concluding chapter draws together the themes raised throughout and assesses the viability of the competing explanations of the merger process. To avoid loading the text with a mass of names, abbreviations and titles, each union is initially referred to by an abbreviation and the title provided in English. The full name of the union in the language of its country of origin is included in abbreviations sections, which are found at the end of each chapter.

List of Abbreviations

ASTMS   Association of Scientific, Technical and Managerial Staffs
CGB   Christlicher Gewerkschaftsbund Deutschlands (Christian Trade Union Confederation)
DBB   Deutscher Beamtenbund (Union of Civil Servants)
DGB   Deutscher Gewerkschaftsbund (German Trade Union Confederation)
DJ   Dansk Journalistforbund (National Union of Journalists)
EU   European Union
GdP   Gewerkschaft der Politzei (Union of Police Officers)
GF   Grafisk Forbund (Danish Union of Graphical Workers)
HK   Handels- og Kontorfunktionærernes Forbund (Union of Commercial and Clerical Employees in Denmark)
HRM   Human Resource Management
NAFTA   North American Free Trade Agreement
SiD   Specialarbejderforbundet i Danmark (General Workers' Union)
TASS   Technical, Administrative and Supervisory Section
ver.di Vereinte Dienstleistungsgewerkschaft (Unified Services Union)

Chapter 2. Australia

Top-down Strategic Restructuring

Gerard Griffin

Throughout the twentieth century trade unions played a key role in Australian industrial relations. Buttressed by the centralised conciliation and arbitration system, union membership remained relatively high and the movement's power and ability to improve their members' wages and conditions was quite strong. Perhaps inevitably, the structure of this successful union movement remained largely stable. Where change did occur it was slow and incremental, evolutionary rather than radical in nature. A union official of the 1920s transported to the 1980s would have felt at home in familiar organisational surroundings and would have had to make few adjustments. A move to the 1990s would, however, have left our official bewildered and lost in unfamiliar territory. In the intervening decade, the Australian trade union movement had undergone a massive restructuring, a restructuring that, arguably, has few parallels in other industrialised economies except in times of national crisis. This chapter details the contours of this restructuring, analyses the reasons for the massive change, and assesses its impact and influence to date. It commences with an historical overview of union structure until 1990.

Historical Overview

Although some nascent form of trade unionism and industrial relations existed prior to the 1850s (Quinlan, 1987), it was the discovery of gold in the early 1850s that created an economic environment suitable for the development of trade unionism. The rush to the gold fields, the dramatic growth of population and the general creation of wealth all contributed to a substantial demand for labour, especially skilled labour. In this environment trade unionism grew and flourished among skilled workers. In 1856, stone masons in Melbourne achieved a world first, in the form of the eight-hour day. Over the next three decades, buoyed by continuing economic growth, employees continued to improve gradually their working conditions. Unions for unskilled employees were formed and were as successful as their skilled counterparts. In the 1880s, white-collar public servants started to form unions.

The model for these early unions was the British horizontal or occupation-based union structure. This was not unexpected given that the vast majority of workers were British migrants who brought with them the culture and values of their homeland. Indeed, a number of the craft unions established in the 1850s, such as the Amalgamated Society of Engineers, were established as overseas branches of the 'parent' British union (Sheridan, 1975). In practice, this occupational structure dominated trade unionism until the 1980s.

The depression of the 1890s brought an abrupt halt to the march of trade unionism. Indeed, during the 1890s many of the advances in working conditions won over the previous three decades had to be surrendered. Between 1890 and 1894 a number of major strikes occurred, which practically destroyed the trade union movement. Subsequent and substantial exploitation by employers of workers, particularly unskilled and female workers, and some instances of child labour, led to major debates within the various colonies as to the most appropriate system of industrial relations. Commencing with New South Wales in 1892, the colonies gradually enacted legislation that granted the state a substantial interventionist role in the industrial relations system. This process culminated with the passing of the Conciliation and Arbitration Act 1904 that was to govern industrial relations in the new Commonwealth of Australia.

In many ways, a centralised system of arbitration necessitates the existence of a unionised workforce whose representatives can appear before its tribunals. The new commonwealth legislation provided for the registration of 'organisations of employees' and, among other things, granted these registered organisations exclusive jurisdiction over segments of the workforce. This legislation was mirrored in many of the former colonies, now states of the Commonwealth. Importantly, the then Commonwealth Court of Conciliation and Arbitration, now the Australian Industrial Relations Commission (AIRC), adopted the traditional occupational structure of unionism as the basis for its segmentation. Indeed, by giving legal force to exclusive occupational jurisdiction, the AIRC embedded this horizontal union structure for much of the twentieth century.

The role of the new AIRC was the major factor contributing to the re-birth of Australian trade unionism. As shown in Table 2.1, union density had dropped to around 6 per cent by 1901. Some ten years later density had increased to 28 per cent and reached over 50 per cent by

1921. Over the next 60 years, with the exception of the depression years of the 1930s, density remained above 50 per cent. In the decade following the 1904 legislation, the number of unions jumped significantly, reaching a peak of over 600. Many of these unions, however, disappeared in the post-World War I rationalisation and, by the early 1920s, the total number of trade unions had settled in the high three hundreds. Over the next six decades this total number of unions slowly decreased, but did not finally drop below 300 until 1989.

Throughout these decades, trade union structure was characterised by, first, a skewed distribution of union membership; second, multi-unionism at both the industry and enterprise level; and third, well-developed inter-union structures at the national and state level, but not at the enterprise level. Table 2.2 illustrates the number and membership size of trade unions as of June 1990.

Table 2.1: Membership of Trade Unions and the Number of Unions

	Number of Members (000s)	Total Members as Percentage of Employees	Number of Unions
1901	97.2	6.1	198
1911	364.7	27.9	573
1921	703.0	51.6	382
1931	740.8	45.0	361
1941	1,075.6	49.9	374
1951	1,690.2	60.0	359
1961	1,894.6	57.0	355
1971	2,436.6	52.0	303
1981	2,994.1	54.0	324
1986	3,186.2	55.0	326
1987	3,240.1	55.0	316
1988	3,290.5	53.0	308
1989	3,410.3	52.0	299
1990	3,422.2	52.0	295

Source: Australian Bureau of Statistics, Trade Union Statistics, Catalogue No. 6323.0

Clearly, a relatively large number of unions had a relatively small membership; indeed forty unions each had a membership of less than 100. A majority of unions, 170 out of the total of 295, had memberships lower than 2,000. These unions accounted for 57 per cent of all unions, but their combined membership was less than 3 per cent of total union membership. At the other end of the spectrum thirty-four unions, 11 per cent of all unions, each with a membership of more than 30,000, organised 73 per cent of all members. Not unexpectedly, few of the smaller unions operated outside the confines of more than one state. In 1990, only 134 unions (45 per cent) operated in two or more states; these unions organised 83 per cent of total membership.

Table 2.2: Number and Size Distribution of Australian Trade Unions, 1990

Number of members	Number of trade unions	Proportion of total members
Under 100	40	0.1
100 and under 250	34	0.2
250 and under 500	18	0.2
500 and under 1,000	44	0.9
1,000 and under 2,000	34	1.4
2,000 and under 5,000	41	3.9
5,000 and under 10,000	21	4.5
10,000 and under 20,000	18	7.8
20,000 and under 30,000	11	8.1
30,000 and under 40,000	11	11.0
40,000 and under 50,000	5	6.7
50,000 and under 80,000	6	11.9
80,000 and over	12	43.5

Source: Australian Bureau of Statistics, Trade Union Statistics, Catalogue No. 6323.0.

This large number of unions inevitably resulted in multi-unionism at the industry level. In 1981 the number of unions operating in fourteen industries was shown to range from six unions in the entertainment industry through to twenty-six unions in manufacturing to fifty-five unions in the transport industry (Plowman, 1981: 32). This multiplicity at the industry level need not necessarily translate into multi-unionism in the enterprise. It is not unusual for unions that organise similar workers to have negotiated demarcation lines, frequently along state boundaries. The first Australian Workplace Industrial Relations Survey (AWIRS) provided detailed data for 1989 on the number of unions in individual workplaces and showed that the average number of unions in enterprises with more than five employees was just under two. Not surprisingly, the larger the number of employees in the enterprise, the greater the number of unions. While only 5 per cent of workplaces with twenty or more employees had six or more unions, 43 per cent of workplaces with 500 or more employees were organised by six or more unions (Callus *et al.*, 1991: 118). Some large enterprises had to deal with a large number of unions. For most of the 1980s, for example, twenty-four unions had members within the State Electricity Commission of Victoria (Benson, 1991). Multi-unionism, and its attendant potential problems, was primarily an issue largely restricted to large enterprises.

With the exception of a limited number of industries, trade union structures at the workplace level have traditionally been relatively poorly developed. AWIRS found a low level of joint union organisation: only 11 per cent of managers at workplaces with more than one union reported the existence of a joint union committee. Even in manufacturing, such committees existed at only 18 per cent of workplaces. Of course, in small enterprises with relatively few unions, union and employee co-ordination can be organised relatively quickly and easily through forums less formal than joint committees. The survey highlighted the relative paucity of such committees, even in large enterprises: 'only 35 per cent of multi-union workplaces with 500 or more employers reported a joint union committee' (Callus *et al.*, 1991: 119).

The existence of one unified broadly based confederation (usually termed a peak council in Australia) stands in sharp contrast to this lack of structure at the workplace level. This unity, however, is a relatively recent development. When the Australian Council of Trade Unions (ACTU) was established in 1927 a 'rival' organisation was already in existence. The Australian Workers Union (AWU), by far the largest trade union, had, for some years prior to 1927, regarded itself as the logical organisational base for an all-Australian union confederation. In addition, as early as 1915 a peak council had been established covering associations of federal public sector employees. After the founding of the ACTU a number of peak councils, such as the Australian Council of Salaried and Professional Associations, were also established.

During the 1970s and 1980s, however, the ACTU absorbed most of these sectional union organisations. In 1967, the AWU chose to end its self-imposed exile and affiliated to the ACTU. In 1979, following a lengthy courtship, the Australian Council of Salaried and Professional Associations disbanded and most of its affiliates transferred to the ACTU (Griffin and Giuca, 1986). The small number of affiliates that decided not to join the ACTU at this time, subsequently did so during the 1980s. In 1981, the Council of Australian Government Employee Organisations, the federal peak council for the public sector, similarly disbanded and all its affiliates transferred their allegiance to the ACTU. In 1985, the Australian Public Service Federation, the confederation of the state-based public service associations, joined the ACTU. By 1990, 167 unions were affiliated to the ACTU and although this figure was not much more than half the total number of unions, these unions contained within their ranks over 90 per cent of all unionists. As a result of all of these mergers, the ACTU can legitimately claim to be the collective voice of organised labour and to speak with authority on its behalf.

Between the two extremes of enterprise and national union structures, lie two intermediate levels: industry federations and state-based

Trades and Labour Councils. Industry federations have played a significant role in a limited number of industries. The rationale for these
federations is to provide a forum for unions in the industry to both
resolve inter-union problems, such as demarcation disputes, and to
provide a mechanism for negotiations with employers at the industry
level. The Metal Trades Federation has been the most prominent federation, but similar organisations exist in industries such as mining and
building. Trades and Labour Councils, although pre-dating the formation of the ACTU, are now formally the state-based branches of the
peak council. Given that a majority of unions, as noted earlier, operate
in only one state, these councils undertake an important linking function
in trade union activities. Generally, most unions operating in each state,
with the exception of the very small unions, are affiliated to the appropriate Trade and Labour Council. Consequently, the level of influence
and degree of importance of these state-based councils has been significant, particularly when the Labor Party forms the state government.

Drawing together the pre-1990 changes, it would appear that a significant amount of structural change took place in the 1910-30 period.
These developments included a growth in the number of unions, a
number of mergers (discussed below), the development of workplace
joint committees and the triumph of occupational unionism, culminating
in the formation of the ACTU. Between 1930 and 1990, change was
slow and gradual, summarised in broad terms as comprising;

– more unionists and a reduced number of unions leading to a much
   larger average union membership size (see Table 1.1);

– the growth of white-collar employment and unionism;

– technologically-induced reductions in the blue-collar workforce
   and unions;

– the establishment of inter-union organisations such as workplace
   committees, industry groups and national union centres (Rimmer,
   1981).

These six decades of stability were, however, followed by a wave of
union mergers (see Figure 1.2).

Charting the Merger Process

Based on changes in the total number of unions between 1920 and
1990, it could readily be assumed that few mergers took place during
this period. This apparent stability hides some significant compositional
changes, particularly the disappearance of many blue-collar unions and a
growth in the number of white-collar unions. This trend was accentuated
in state jurisdictions. For the period 1961 to 1978, changes in the num-

ber of unions registered in the Queensland jurisdiction were analysed to find that '17 unions surrendered their registration and 12 unions were registered for the first time; these 17 unions had... usually fused with another organisation' (Gill and Griffin, 1981: 366). In New South Wales, while unable to offer exact data, it was speculated that a significant number of mergers had taken place (Rimmer, 1981). These state jurisdictions are the descendants of the colonial systems established during the 1890s and offer registration to trade unions operating solely within one state. Not unexpectedly, therefore, many such unions have relatively few members. In contrast, to achieve federal registration, unions must operate in two or more states.

Prior to presenting data on mergers between federally registered unions, the point should be made that there is a legal distinction between amalgamations and acquisitions. In cases where the membership of the smaller union is less than five per cent of that of the larger union, then only members of the smaller union have to vote on the merger proposal. In practice, no distinction exists and most mergers are completed after formal membership ballots. Indeed, in a number of mergers where one of the merging unions was significantly smaller than the other union, the politics of the merger frequently dictated the formation of a newly titled post-merger entity.

Between 1905 – when the federal system commenced operation – and 1986 a total of 313 organisations of employees were registered under the Conciliation and Arbitration Act within the federal jurisdiction. Some 164 of the organisations subsequently lost their registration (Griffin and Scarcebrook, 1989). At least 94 of these unions merged with other unions (Griffin and Scarcebrook, 1989), and the trends in this respect are illustrated in Table 2.3. While many of these mergers occurred in the early decades of this century, there has also been a consistent, if lower, number of mergers in recent decades. A substantial majority of defunct unions organised unskilled and semi-skilled employees with relatively few representing either skilled or white-collar workers. Most continuing unions that had been involved in mergers had absorbed either one or two unions only; three large unions, however, had been involved in a relatively large number of mergers.

Table 2.3: Merger Trends over Time

Time period	No. of mergers
1905-10	4
1911-20	28
1921-30	18
1931-40	3
1941-50	14
1951-60	2
1961-70	9
1971-80	9
1981-86	7
Total	94

Source: Griffin and Scarcebrook (1989: 260).

Over the next decade a relative tidal wave of union mergers oc-curred. Between 1987 and 1996, the last date for which official Austra-lian Bureau of Statistics (ABS) data was collected on unions, the total number of unions decreased from 316 to 132. *A priori*, it could be hypothesised that most of this reduction would have come from among the ranks of the large number of state-based unions with low member-ship.

Table 2.4: Number of Union Mergers, 1987-2000

Years	No. of Unions		No. of Mergers	
	Total	*Federal*	*Total*	*Federal*
1987	316	144	8	2
1988	308	146	8	6
1989	299	140	7	1
1990	295	134	4	4
1991	275	125	22	21
1992	227	94	44	18
1993	188	66	35	14
1994	157	54	27	8
1995	142	47	10	3
1996	132	47	7	0
1997[1]	N/A	46	N/A	1
1998	N/A	46	N/A	1
1999	N/A	45	N/A	0
2000	N/A	45	N/A	0

[1] After 1996, the Australian Bureau of Statistics ceased collecting data on trade unions.

Source: Australian Bureau of Statistics, Trade Union Statistics, Catalogue No. 6323.0; data from the Industrial Registrar's Office.

However, almost half of the total of 184 unions that disappeared comprised federally registered unions. In total, of the 172 mergers, 79 were between federally registered unions. The main concentration of mergers took place in the early 1990s, particularly between 1991 and 1994. During this period some 61 federal mergers occurred, an average of over fifteen each year (see Table 2.4).

These data can be contrasted with the data in Table 2.3, which show some 27 mergers between 1951 and 1986, an average of less than one merger per year.

In the post-1996 period only two mergers occurred between federally registered unions. A limited number of additional mergers may take place in the future. For example, in May 2000, two unions in the transport industry announced that they were entering merger discussions but no merger subsequently occurred. Equally, some mergers within state jurisdictions are likely to take place, but the principal merger wave has passed. In a very real sense, the ACTU thrust to restructure the Australian union movement (discussed below) has been largely achieved. Currently, trade unionism is dominated, both in terms of membership and power, by 20 large unions.

Reasons and Process

A wide range of factors influences the merger process. These factors are usually divided into external influences, such as the political, economic and legal environment, and internal factors such as leadership, finance and changing membership (see Chapter 1). Clearly, the role and relative importance of these factors can and will vary both over time and between different mergers. Nevertheless, the extent and the timing of the merger wave of the early 1990s indicate that some common factors were driving this massive change. There were three main driving forces. First, the decline in union membership, with its associated loss of income and power, which was coupled to a union desire to halt and then redress this decline. Second, the role of some union officials, particularly key decision-makers within the then all-powerful ACTU in pursuing a strategy to reverse membership decline. Third, the political environment that resulted in legislation which threatened the existence of a significant number of unions. This is not to argue that other influences, such as post-merger union structures to accommodate the various power groups in the new entity, or the move away from a centralised system of wage-fixation through arbitration towards an enterprise bargaining focused system, did not play a role in particular mergers. Rather, the argument is that, in the overall merger wave, these were the three key, inter-related driving forces.

Declining Membership

The starting point is trade union membership. Union membership appeared pretty healthy during the 1980s; continuing absolute membership growth, but a slight decline in density that, nevertheless, remained over 50 per cent (Table 2.1). The source of these data was the long-running annual census of union returns conducted by the Australian Bureau of Statistics (ABS). To complement these census data, in 1976, 1982, 1986 and then biennially to 1992, the ABS included questions on trade union membership in household surveys. These survey data (see Table 2.5) increasingly diverged from the census data, showing a lower density rate in 1976 of four percentage points, of nine points in 1986 and more than eleven points in 1990. In other words, rather than the small, if worrying, decline in density shown by the census data, the survey data were pointing to a crisis for the union movement. There is significant potential for error in both sets of data (Rawson 1992). By the late 1980s, however, the survey data were becoming widely accepted as the more accurate and reliable. Importantly, the union movement itself increasingly relied on the survey data. All of the ACTU policy and planning documents, for example, used these data. During the 1990s, the ABS ceased collecting the census data and now relies solely on the survey data.

These declining density figures created enormous discussion, debate and alarm within the union movement. Unusually, this debate spilled over into the print media as solutions were sought. A cogently argued booklet from the Building Workers Industrial Union was titled Can Unions Survive? Its conclusion was that the 'Australian model of trade unionism is dying. Our Anglo-Saxon, craft-based unionism has outlived its usefulness' (Berry and Kitchener, 1989). A book edited by senior officials of the New South Wales Trades and Labour Council asked 'What Should Unions Do?' (Crosby and Easson, 1992). The answer offered by the ACTU, its leadership and some senior leaders of key unions was simple: merge. The rationale was equally simple: economies of scale.

Table 2.5: Trade Union Membership

Year	No. of members (000s)	Overall Density (% Unionised)	Public Sector Density	Private Sector Density
1976	2513	51	N/A	N/A
1982	2568	49	73	39
1986	2594	46	71	36
1988	2536	42	68	32
1990	2660	41	67	31
1992	2509	40	67	29
1993	2377	38	64	28
1994	2283	35	62	26
1995	2252	33	56	25
1996	2194	31	55	24
1997	2110	30	55	23
1998	2037	28	53	21
1999	1878	26	50	20
2000	1902	25	48	19
2001	1903	25	48	19

Source: Australian Bureau of Statistics, Trade Union Members, Catalogue No. 6325.0; Employee Earnings, Benefits and Trade Union Membership, Catalogue No. 6310.

Declining membership, and associated financial problems, have long been identified in the literature as one of the main causes of union mergers (see, for example, Buchanan, 1974; Janus, 1978). The new, post-merger union is assumed to be better able to defend and/or service membership, and, importantly in this case, organise new members. This was the line of argument used by senior officials from both the ACTU and some affiliated unions. In addition, they argued that, because of structural problems, the existing union movement did not possess the resources to attack effectively declining density. Specifically, the large number of small unions (Table 2.2) did not possess, and could not find, either the finance or the personnel to engage in membership recruitment. On the other hand, such resources could be 'put to much better use through the economies of scale possible with larger, better resourced unions' (ACTU, 1987).

The role of the ACTU in leading this merger drive is analysed shortly. Some brief explanation is necessary of why some obvious alternative strategies, such as organising drives and enhancing the role of workplace union structures, were not regarded as viable alternative options. Because of the centralised arbitration system, the Australian industrial relations system had several distinct characteristics. Among other things, trade unions received recognition and membership coverage not through industrial action but through a legal, bureaucratic device. Wage increases and improved working conditions were won more by advocacy in courts than through bargaining with employers. These characteristics led some to claim that Australian unions were not true unions in the normal and usual sense of the word, because of their dependency on the state (Howard, 1977). While the level of state dependency can be argued (Gahan, 1996), there can be no doubt that the dominant, centralised arbitration system had a major impact on union structure and strategy. Accordingly, when seeking to respond to declining membership, the range of possible responses was limited by the historical restrictions imposed on trade unions. Put simply, the full range of strategic responses available to other union movements was not readily and immediately available to Australian unions.

One traditional remedy for declining membership is an organising drive, utilising a combination of experienced organisers and workplace-based officials. For many unions these combinations simply did not exist. For decades, membership had been delivered and guaranteed through the arbitration model. Technically, compulsory unionism *per se* was, and is, illegal. A number of substitute devices, for example, a preference clause in an award that legally guarantees preference on a whole range of issues to union members over non-members, produced de facto closed shops. Between 1969 and 1979 estimates of the number of unionists in closed shops varied between 63 per cent and 72 per cent (Peetz, 1998). A 1988 survey arrived at a figure of 57 per cent, while the AWIRS 1990 data suggest a figure of 54 per cent. Two points can be drawn from these data. First, the gradual demise of the centralised system contributed to reduced union density. Second, until the 1990s, a majority of union members were covered by closed shops; Australian unions did not have to fight to secure these members. Consequently, they had neither the organisational structure nor the mindset necessary to organise workers. The strategy of the then all-powerful ACTU, to merge prior to launching a major recruitment drive, appeared sensible and appropriate.

Role of the ACTU

The union movement had been aware for a number of decades of the need for structural change. Clause 3 of the original 1927 ACTU constitution set out the following goal;

The closer organisation of the workers by:
  a) The development of the trade union movement towards an industrial basis.
  b) Groupings of related unions for the purpose of co-ordination with the ACTU on matters of common interest.

c) Amalgamation of unions where practicable to establish one union in each industry or sector.

The ACTU, however, did not have the power or authority to enforce such goals. Consequently, as noted earlier, union structure remained largely unchanged for the next 60 years. During the 1980s a remarkable transformation took place in the role of the ACTU. In brief, it became the dominant union body within Australian trade unionism and, accordingly, was the strategic driver responding to and initiating change. Some brief discussion on this new role is necessary to understand the leadership offered by the ACTU in the merger process (for details, Griffin, 1994).

The background to this change was the election of a federal Labor Party government in 1983. A Labor government had been a rare event during the previous decades. Indeed, between 1949 and 1983 Labor held federal office only for the 1972-5 period. Labor Party officials had identified a poor industrial relations record – 1973/4 remain the peak years for strikes – as a key reason why the Labor government lost power in 1975. Accordingly, when elected in 1983, the incoming Labor government negotiated a social contract, known as the Accord, with trade unions (Carney, 1988). Among other things, the Accord provided for the reinforcement of the centralised system of industrial relations and the re-introduction of a centralised wage-fixing system that linked wages with movements in the Consumer Price Index. A key component of this centralised wage indexation system was that no additional wage claims should be made. Inevitably, some claims were advanced. Somewhat surprisingly, particularly to economists predicting the swift demise of the Accord, such claims were largely contained. Between September 1983 and December 1985, 96 per cent of all wage increases were achieved through the centralised system (NWC, 1986). Only in the building industry was there any increase outside wage indexation (Dabscheck, 1989: 96), while Griffin (1994) points to a dispute where, after the union had won a wage increase, the ACTU forced the union to give back the increase to the employer because of 'flow-on' implications. Outside of the wages arena, the ACTU, in its new role as police officer, rigorously enforced the provisions of the Accord. A number of 'challenges to the Accord' were noted, although 'the response of the ACTU leadership... to unions which challenged the Accord has been ruthless' (Kuhn, 1993: 37). The new-found authority of the ACTU was based on a range of factors, including economic and political forces, support from other actors in the industrial relations system, particularly the federal government and the Industrial Relations Commission, and leadership and inclusiveness within the union movement (Griffin, 1994). Our concern here, however, is with the impact of this authority on union mergers.

Despite the 1927 constitutional provision noted earlier, a formal ACTU policy on union amalgamations was not developed until 1981 and, indeed, was not detailed until 1987. At the 1987 ACTU Congress a document titled 'Future Strategies for the Trade Union Movement' was adopted. This document proposed the restructuring of the Australian trade union movement within broad industry categories. More specifically, it provided for the establishment of eighteen to twenty union groups and nominated each affiliate to a specific group. It was envisaged that these groups would be the catalyst for subsequent formal amalgamations. Between the 1987 and 1989 Congresses, little progress was made in implementing this policy. For example, of the nine mergers in the 1987-9 period, only three, at best, could possibly be attributed to ACTU policy. The 1989 Congress provided the major turning point. At the 1987 Congress there had been significant concern about declining membership. At the 1989 Congress there was alarm: density rates had declined from 49 per cent in 1982 to 46 per cent in 1986 and to 42 per cent in 1988. Furthermore, for the first time in decades, absolute membership also dropped by approximately 60,000 between 1986 and 1988 (Table 2.5). A new sense of urgency clearly existed within some unions. The task of reviving and restoring union membership 'dominated the four days of the Congress' (Davis, 1990: 100) and that concern over this 'significant erosion of membership permeated all of the major addresses to Congress' (Davis, 1990: 101). The ACTU President, for example, claimed that 'unions had failed to rationalise their often antiquated structures', while the ACTU Secretary argued that unions 'must amalgamate and rationalise their organisations' (Davis, 1990: 102). Of at least equal importance was a formal Congress resolution that supported union restructuring, which received strong cross-factional support. A senior official from the political left, in proposing the formal motion, argued that 'restructuring was essential because unions could not afford to persist with structures that squandered financial and human resources'. A leader of the right faction seconded the motion and noted that it was 'suicidal for unions to neglect the challenge of restructuring' (Davis, 1990: 102). Accordingly, building on the inclusiveness then evident within the ACTU and its Executive, the ACTU policy and strategy on mergers had the strong support of key, individual union leaders.

The subsequent lengthy debate did indicate, however, that some, particularly craft, unions did not support restructuring. The Federated Clerks Union (FCU) and the Electrical Trades Union (ETU), with horizontally organised memberships embracing several industries, moved an amendment to the recommendation of the Executive of the ACTU on union structure. Both unions 'stressed that they did not see industrial unionism as a panacea; they feared that the Executive's motion would lead to the imposition of reform from above' (Davis, 1990: 103). In short, they wished to remain independent. The ACTU Secretary's response was blunt: he argued that 'narrowly-based unions such as the FCU and ETU could not survive in their current form' and that 'they must face up to the challenge of reform' (Davis 1990: 103). In other words, despite their wishes they must merge. The Executive motion was carried with few dissenters.

Inevitably, a range of operational difficulties and continuing opposition by some unions meant that, post-1989, the merger path was far from smooth. Equally, political reality dictated that, in a number of industries, when mergers did occur, the preferred ACTU model of industrial unionism was not achieved. Throughout 1990, ACTU Executive meetings were dominated by restructuring issues. These meetings, comprising senior ACTU officials and the powerbrokers of the key affiliates, strongly supported this merger thrust. Accordingly, by the time of the 1991 Congress the merger process was well underway, despite the ETU persisting with its demand for autonomy (Davis 1992). By the time of the 1993 Congress, the process was underway at 'almost breathtaking pace' (Kelly, 1993: 1138) and both the ETU and the FCU had found merger partners. Based on a survey of unions, the restructuring policy of the ACTU was singled out as having the 'largest impact on the propensity of the respondent organisations to participate in a union merger' (Tomkins, 1999: 70). Clearly, the views and policies of the confederation, supported by leading officials of all political factions, had prevailed.

Politics and Legislation

Prior to 1972, the Conciliation and Arbitration Act did not specify any formal requirements or procedures to be followed by unions seeking to merge. In that year, however, the Liberal-Country Party government introduced legislation dealing with mergers. A section of this legislation specified that a merger could not proceed unless least half of the unions' members voted in a ballot on the merger. In 1983 the newly elected Labor government abolished this 50 per cent membership vote requirement. The replacement legislation specified that where a 'community of interest' exists between intending parties, as determined on very broad grounds by the Australian Industrial Relations Commission (AIRC), no formal minimum percentage of members need vote in a ballot. Where the Commission rules that no community of interest exists then the minimum voting requirement is 25 per cent.

Given that voting turnout at union elections in Australia tends to be less than 50 per cent, the easing of this legal voting requirement facilitated a significant number of mergers. Equally, some merger proposals that had failed under the old legislation were completed under the new provisions. For example, a proposed merger between the Australian Textile Workers' Union and the Australian Boot Trade Employees' Federation was not completed, despite a substantial majority of voting members supporting the merger, on the grounds that less than half the members participated in the ballot. Following the legislative change, a second, successful ballot was held; under the old requirements, this second attempt would also have failed.

Overall, the changes to the voting requirement fit into the facilitating change category. More relevant to the merger wave of the early 1990s was a form of prescriptive legislation passed in 1990. Section 193 of the then Industrial Relations Act 1988 allowed a senior member of the AIRC to review the registration of trade unions with less than a specified number of members. In such a review, the onus was on the union to convince the AIRC member that special circumstances warranted its continuing registration. The Act specified a minimum membership of 1,000 when it was enacted in 1988. Following extensive lobbying by the ACTU throughout 1990, an amendment to the Act increased this figure to 10,000 in December 1990. Unions were, however, given a three-year period of grace prior to the commencement of AIRC review. Clearly, this deadline was a major impetus to merge. A larger number of unions came within the scope of the amendment than came within the terms of the original provision. In June 1990, 136 unions each had less than 1,000 members while the number with less than 10,000 was 232 (ABS, 1990). Importantly, because many of the 136 unions were registered under state jurisdictions, few were affected by federal legislation. In contrast, most unions with membership sizes of between 1,000 and 10,000 were registered in the federal jurisdiction and were thus subject to the new provisions.

The peak employer body, now called the Australian Chamber of Commerce and Industry, complained to the International Labour Organisation (ILO) that this legislation contravened the ILO Convention on Freedom of Association. The ILO upheld this complaint in late 1992 and the Labor government responded to this decision, initially by suspending the review process in June 1993 and later that year omitting the process completely from the Industrial Relations Reform Act 1993. In practice, however, the disappearance of this review process was irrelevant: its impact had already been felt in the merger wave.

Some additional legislative changes also focused on the merger process. For example, the minimum membership requirement for new unions was raised from 1,000 to 10,000 in 1988 and in 1990 a new object was written into the Act, 'to encourage and facilitate the amalgamation of organisations'. These provisions were, however, relatively minor in the overall impact of legislative change on mergers.

Overall, legislative change, based on the close political relationship between a federal Labor government and the ACTU, and supplemented by a frequently close personal relationship between ministers and union officials, contributed significantly to the merger wave of the early 1990s. If the lure of halting a declining membership was the carrot offered by the ACTU, the threat of de-registration through legislative intervention was the stick. Together, they achieved the goal of restructuring the Australian union movement through mergers.

Outcomes

The outcomes of the merger process are assessed in term of the goals set out by the ACTU in promoting the merger process. Although changes to the external shape of Australian unionism were achieved through the merger process, there is little evidence to suggest that improvements in union organisation and servicing were achieved on the same scale.

Membership

The main rationale for mergers in Australia was to combat declining membership by, initially, halting the decline and, ultimately, increasing membership. On any measure employed, union mergers have failed utterly to achieve this desired outcome. If anything, the decline in membership accelerated in the immediate post-merger years. Between 1994 and 1999, absolute membership decreased by approximately 400,000 (from 2,283,000 to 1,878,000) while density dropped by approximately 2 percentage points each year (from 35 per cent to 26 per cent). In 2000 and 2001, absolute membership stabilised, while density continued to fall. In an historical sense, the total number of unionists is now back to the level of 1960, while density has returned to the level of 1910. These declines have been spread throughout the economy and are found among male and female workers, public sector and private sector workers, younger workers and older workers, workers from English-speaking and non-English speaking backgrounds and among workers in different states.

Inevitably, the merger process has been held responsible for some of these developments, both within and without the union movement. Criticisms usually centre around the 'small is better' argument, which states that smaller, more friendly and intimate unions, operating close to the workplace are more likely to recruit and retain members than are large, bureaucratic unions. The flavour of this argument is captured by Costa (1995), a union official, who termed the new unions the 'dinosaurs of the information age'. Based on a time-series analysis of aggregate membership statistics, the merger process was shown to have contributed to membership decline (Bodham, 1998). This claim, however, was effectively rebutted in analyses of panel data drawn from the two AWIRs studies (Wooden, 1999). Regardless of this debate, it is clear that prior to the 1990s, these small unions did not recruit, attract and retain membership; rather, they relied on the centralised arbitration model for their membership. What seems to have occurred is that the merger wave came too late to achieve what may potentially have been a major influence on membership density. In short, the forces that decimated union ranks, including industrial restructuring, massive shifts within the workforce towards casual, part-time and contract employees, changes in public policy, anti-union legislation, and more ideological employers (see Griffin and Svensen, 1996), were well in train prior to the 1990s and swamped the potential membership benefits of mergers. The failure of the union movement to achieve rapidly the maximum potential benefits of mergers did not, however, assist their cause.

Structure and Government

As argued earlier, a core theme driving mergers was the ACTU belief that a small number of large unions could take advantage of economies of scale to reverse declining membership. Some analyses have questioned the validity of this claim (Gill and Griffin, 1981; Costa and Duffy, 1991). 'Even if it is accepted that economies of scale are available in some union activities, it must be acknowledged that these economies may not be realised in practice where increased size is a result of amalgamation' (Davis, 1999: 11). Noting that the extent to which any economies are realised is an empirical question, Davis used multivariate analysis of financial data from a representative sample of federally registered unions to offer some support to the economies of scale argument. He concludes, however, that 'such an interpretation should be treated cautiously' (1999: 30).

Clearly, the extent to which post-merger unions integrate their operations is a key factor in determining the levels of economies of scale that are actually achieved. The clear evidence from Australia is that many of the merger partners did not, at least initially, fully integrate their operations. In many cases this was a deliberate strategy dictated by the pragmatic realisation that the various powerbrokers had to be accommodated within the post-merger union. In practice, a number of merged unions were the equivalent of conglomerate companies, with separate, and frequently different, administrative structures for 'sections' or 'divisions' of the union. Furthermore, these groups usually retained all of their existing staff. Joint National Secretaries and Joint National Presidents abounded. In a number of unions these administrative arrangements were put in place for an interim period only, usually three or five years. In many cases, however, these arrangements have continued in place. Frequently, this is necessitated by the very basis of the merger.

The initial 1987 ACTU 'Future Strategies' proposal recommended restructuring along industrial lines. Over time, however, and in the pursuit of mergers at all costs, a number of unlikely partners merged. Frequently, political affiliation or personal or other factors influenced the choice of merger partner. For example, two groups emerged in the metal industry, one linked to the left of labour politics, one to the right. In the public sector, while unions covering federal and state public servants merged, the two unions covering local government and municipal employees merged with the private sector union covering clerical workers. The titles of some unions reflect their rather unwieldy coverage. For example, it is difficult to find an integrating rationale, other than political orientation, for the Communications, Electrical, Electronic, Energy, Information, Postal, Plumbing and Allied Services Union. The Construction, Forestry, Mining and Energy Union also covers a significant range of employees. Notably, both unions include 'energy' in their remit, while the Australian Municipal, Administrative, Clerical and Services Union has, within its ambit, an Energy Branch. In fairness, it should be noted that a significant number of mergers adhered to the industrial model, notably the Finance Sector Union. Equally, there is no doubt that interim arrangements are being phased out slowly in a number of unions. It must also be conceded that, even where industrial unionism does not exist, the practical outcome of the merger wave is that, with a few notable exceptions, most industries are now covered by one key union only. Trade union structure after the merger wave is thus dominated by a relatively small number of twenty or so unions.

The governance of these unions is frequently very complex, with the degree of complexity related to factors such as the extent of 'membership fit' of the merger partners, historical power relationships and the structures agreed at the time of the merger. In brief, it has been easier to integrate pre-merger structures where some overlaps in membership were present. Conversely, little integration has occurred where the memberships had little in common. The historical distribution of power between the state and federal levels of the pre-merger unions has also influenced integration. Similar loci of power facilitated integration. Finally, some mergers were consummated on terms that militate strongly against full integration; in some cases these terms were formalised in the rules of the post-merger union.

Some years after the main merger wave ended, at least two groups of unions can be identified. The first group comprises those unions that have either fully integrated their operations or are on the way to doing so. These unions have, for example, one set of leaders and officials, common policies and common administrative systems and rewards, or are well on the way to achieving such integration. This group remains in the minority. The second group operates as conglomerate unions, with separate divisions or branches de facto running their own operations. Some common features, such as sharing offices, training facilities and specialised staff, may exist, although, in a number of large unions, even such minimal integration has not occurred. In a structural sense, the merger process has not been completed in a number of unions.

Links to the ACTU

All significant federally registered unions are affiliated to the ACTU. As with its affiliates, however, the current version of the ACTU is very different from the 1990 version. The demise of the Accord, the election of a conservative government at the federal level, and, particularly, the move away from a centralised system of wage fixation towards an enterprise bargaining system has dramatically reduced the power, influence and role of the ACTU. The emergence of the twenty key unions, with their larger memberships and resources, has seen these organisations win back their traditional roles from the ACTU. The confederation has, in the main, retreated to its pre-1980s role involving the co-ordination of the activities of affiliates, encouraging training and other activities, and making representations nationally and internationally. It is no longer the pivotal union body in Australian industrial relations.

Services to Members

Trade unions now offer a very wide range of services to their members. Broadly, these can be divided into two categories, industrial and non-industrial services. Focusing on the latter initially, there has been a veritable explosion in the number and range of such services in merged unions. The list is now incredibly long and ranges from legal services through financial services, shopping, medical, travel and telephone discounts, and computer rental and access to the internet. Unquestionably, merged unions, because of their ability to facilitate access to larger numbers of members/customers, have been able to deliver a much broader, and cheaper, range of non-industrial services. The issue, of course, is whether or not these are services that influence potential members to join or existing members to retain their membership, thus making the union a more effective organisation. The only Australian study of non-industrial services found a positive link between intention to use these services and levels of membership participation and satisfaction, but could not assess the impact on decisions to join or remain in a union (Griffin *et al.*, 1997).

Do the merged unions deliver a better range of industrial services to members? There are at least two aspects to any answer to this question: the actual range of services and the membership perception of the range and quality of these services. Clearly, post-merger unions deliver a broader range of services and, arguably, deliver them more effectively and efficiently. This is because the industrial relations system was transformed during the 1990s. Essentially, this system has moved from a centrally regulated, arbitration model, within which unions had a secure, legally guaranteed role and a related *modus operandi*, to a decentralised, enterprise bargaining system where unions have to fight for their existence while establishing new and differing methods of negotiation and interaction. On virtually all dimensions, increased demands are routinely made of trade unions. Crucially, membership fees have not increased to any great extent and remain clustered around 0.5 per cent of gross income. Accordingly, a case can be made that the broader range of services is being delivered more efficiently. How do members perceive these services? At the core of the 'small is beautiful' argument discussed earlier is the concept of quality of interaction between member and union. To date, only one study has examined in a systematic way membership perceptions of industrial services in merged unions. It found that two post-merger unions were perceived as providing better wages and benefits, and keeping members informed about union issues, but were not seen as performing well in terms of employment security or in giving members a say in running the union (Hanley, 1999).

Conclusion

During the first half of the 1990s the structure of Australian trade unionism changed dramatically. An unparalleled wave of mergers took place that dramatically decreased the number of trade unions. Currently, some twenty unions, a mix of multi-industry and industrial unions, organise around 80 per cent of all union members. Despite the success of this restructuring, the prime goal of halting the decline in union membership was not achieved. Indeed, membership density levels have continued to decline dramatically. On this basis, mergers and restructuring must be judged a failure. At the same time, with the shift to a decentralised enterprise bargaining system, it is highly unlikely that the union movement would have had any greater membership success if the mergers had not taken place. The union movement must now look to the future. It is aware of its lack of success and is attempting to respond by refocusing attention on the workplace and inculcating what it calls an organising culture into all of its officials and structures. Structurally, some additional, incremental changes are possible. The possibility of de-mergers exists. New legislation introduced by a conservative government, philosophically disposed to enterprise-based unionism, allows for any dissatisfied elements in a merged union to initiate de-merger moves. In the first five years of this legislation, one such de-merger has occurred, so the possibility of others cannot be dismissed. A more likely development is that a limited, additional number of mergers will take place. There are, for example, three unions remaining in education. It is also likely that some of the smaller state-based unions will be absorbed into the larger, federally registered unions over time. For the foreseeable future, however, trade union structure is likely to remain fairly stable. Certainly, a merger wave comparable to that of the 1990s will not occur.

List of Abbreviations

ABS	Australian Bureau of Statistics
ACTU	Australian Council of Trade Unions
AIRC	Australian Industrial Relations Commission
AWIRS	Australian Workplace Industrial Relations Survey
AWU	Australian Workers Union
ETU	Electrical Trades Union
FCU	Federated Clerks Union
ILO	International Labour Organisation

CHAPTER 3. AUSTRIA

A Case of Limited Restructuring

Sabine BLASCHKE

Since 1945 there have been only three mergers of Austrian trade unions, although a fourth large-scale amalgamation involving five unions is now planned (see Figure 1.3). This chapter examines these mergers and assesses their impact on trade union structure. From the outset, it should be noted that there is no state involvement in internal union affairs and unions conclude mergers according to rules laid down in their constitutions. The chapter comprises four sections. The first section locates trade unions within the Austrian system of industrial relations and identifies the specific mergers that have taken place. The second section examines the character of merger activity and the third section isolates the reasons that underpin such restructuring in Austria. The fourth section reviews the outcome of the merger process in terms of whether it has achieved the objectives intended by its advocates.

Trade Unions and Industrial Relations in Austria

This section reviews the key features of union structure in Austria within the context of social partnership and collective bargaining. It then identifies the three mergers that have taken place and the constituent parties to an intended fourth, large-scale merger that will have a long-term impact on the relationship between all Austrian unions.

Union Structure

After World War II the Austrian Trade Union movement was reconstituted by the foundation of the unified ÖGB (Austrian Trade Union Confederation). The ideologically divided trade union structure of the era before 1934, when unions were abolished, was replaced by an all-party confederation. On an informal level, however, the ÖGB was subdivided into ideological factions.

The ÖGB was founded before the sectoral unions were set up. Its structure was then constructed from the top down with the political aim of preventing inter-union rivalry. Though the unions' jurisdictions do not overlap, industrial unionism was not established in the strict sense of 'one establishment – one union'. In the private sector, blue-collar and white-collar workers were organised separately. In addition, one small union was established for both white-collar and blue-collar workers in the arts and the media. Sixteen unions were established to form the ÖGB: ten private sector blue-collar workers' unions,[1] one private sector white-collar workers' union, four public sector unions and one mixed union (Table 3.1). The separate organisation of blue-collar and white-collar workers prevented the formation of an autonomous white-collar union outside the ÖGB, but led to a recurrent conflict between the unions (Klenner and Pellar, 1999: 547).

Mergers of smaller blue-collar workers' unions resulted in a drop in the number of unions from 16 to 13: the GGA (Hotel and Restaurant Workers' Union) merged with the GPD (Personal Services Workers' Union) to form the HGPD (Hotel, Restaurant and Personal Services Workers' Union) in 1978; the GLFG (Agricultural and Forestry Workers' Union) merged with the GLG (Food and Tobacco Workers' Union) to form the ANG (Union of Food, Agriculture and Tobacco Workers) in 1991; and the TBL (Textile, Clothing and Leather Workers' Union) merged with the largest blue-collar workers' union, the MBE (Metal, Mining and Energy Workers' Union) to form the GMT (Metal and Textile Workers' Union) in 2000.

According to the ÖGB constitution, member unions are not independent associations, but sub-units of the ÖGB itself, which therefore exercises control over their finances, officials and negotiating function. This means that the unions collect dues from members in the name of the ÖGB, that formally their full-time officials are employees of the ÖGB and that only the ÖGB is authorised to conclude collective agreements. In practice, however, the member unions possess greater autonomy than laid down in the ÖGB constitution: the actual level of membership dues varies slightly between unions; in reality the individual unions exercise authority in respect to the full-time officials in their particular constituency and collective agreements are negotiated and signed by them on behalf of the ÖGB (Traxler, 2000: 119). Austrian trade unionism is thus exceptional in its centralisation and unity. A union affiliated to the Freedom Party was created outside the ÖGB in

---

[1]   The Printing and Paper Workers' Union is usually classified as a blue-collar workers' union although it also organises technical white-collar workers.

1998, but so far this union has remained very small, virtually without any influence, and has no right to conduct collective bargaining. In 2001, an independent teachers' union was founded, but this too will probably remain without influence.

Social Partnership

The Austrian social partnership regime (*Sozialpartnerschaft*) builds on the close co-operation between state authorities and the representative organisations of capital and labour. Capital is represented by the WKÖ (Economic Chamber of Austria) and the PKLWK (Standing Committee of the Presidents of the Chambers of Agriculture); the PKLWK plays only a minor role in the bargaining process and is restricted to agricultural issues. Labour is represented by the ÖGB and the BAK (Federal Chamber of Labour). While collective bargaining is exclusively the ÖGB's domain, the BAK operates mainly as a source of expertise both for the ÖGB and for government authorities in matters relating to employees' interests (Traxler, 2000: 23). Through the social partnership arrangements, labour and capital exert a strong influence on economic and social policy matters. The peak organisations are consulted on the drafting of policy regulations and also perform regulatory functions. Furthermore, there are close ties between the representative interest associations, the state and the political parties.

In principle, by adapting to various challenges the Austrian model remained fairly stable until the end of the 1990s. After about 1990 political changes, in the form of deregulation, privatisation of public enterprises, increasing international competition, as well as increasing unemployment, weakened social partnership and made capital more independent of labour's support (Traxler, 1998: 259). In the 1990s social partnership lost influence outside the core fields of labour law, labour market policies, and industrial relations (Kittel and Tálos, 1999: 129-30). Since the election of the conservative-populist government in 2000, social partnership has lost influence outside collective bargaining much more rapidly. As capital is able to exert influence via its close ties with the government, it is labour that is adversely affected by the dismantling of social partnership. In practice, labour's opportunities to influence policy-making have been reduced markedly. In addition, measures taken or planned by the conservative-populist government are aimed at weakening the union movement.[2]

---

[2] For example, the reform of the management of the social insurance system (cf. http://www.eiro.eurofound.eu.int/2001/08/inbrief/AT0108225N.html).

Collective Bargaining

In Austria the conclusion of collective agreements is confined to the private sector. Collective bargaining is highly inclusive due to compulsory membership in the WKÖ. Although the ÖGB has the exclusive right to conclude collective agreements, wage bargaining has been delegated to the affiliates, while the ÖGB negotiates only general non-wage issues involving the entire labour force.

Until the early 1950s there were central pay agreements. Since then bargaining on pay and other terms and conditions of employment has taken place on the sectoral level. There are separate collective agreements for white-collar and blue-collar employees. In the public sector employment conditions are regulated by law, but in practice they are determined by bargaining rounds between state authorities and public employees' unions. For a long period, co-ordination across sectors was performed by the *Paritätische Kommission* (Parity Commission, consisting of the social partners) and was aimed at influencing the timing of bargaining, but not the agenda or outcome. Since the early 1980s, co-ordination has been performed by pattern bargaining with the metal industry[3] as the pacesetter. From the early 1990s the MBE and the GPA (Union of Salaried Private Sector Employees) have conducted joint negotiations for blue- and white-collar employees in the metal industry.[4] This, in turn, sets the pattern for the GPA's 'global' agreement for white-collar workers in most of the rest of manufacturing (Traxler, 1998: 257; 2000: 145-46). Starting in the first half of the 1990s, joint negotiations for white-collar and blue-collar employees spread to an increasing number of sectors. Now, in most sectors, all unions in charge of various groups of employees conduct joint negotiations with the employers.

Flexibility in collective bargaining has been increased, following the path of organised decentralisation (Traxler, 1998: 256). Efforts to enlarge flexibility in collective bargaining have concentrated on issues of working time, a development that started in the mid-1980s. Legislation still sets the frame within which collective agreements may authorise agreements at the enterprise level to introduce more flexible working time schedules. Flexibility in wage bargaining has been very limited, with the exception of an option clause in some sectors. Since the end of the 1990s several collective agreements in industry[5] have authorised

---

3   Only large enterprises, the artisan sector bargains separately.

4   See previous note.

5   Only collective agreements for large enterprises in industry.

works councils to negotiate more flexible increases for those who earn more than the collectively agreed standard rates. When the flexibility option is chosen, wage increases in sum have to be higher than without its application.[6]

Union Restructuring

Total union membership has declined since the mid-1980s and union density started to decrease from the early 1970s (Ebbinghaus and Visser, 2000). The growth of service employment, together with other changes in the composition of the work force, explain this downturn in union density to a large extent (Blaschke, 1999: 68-69). Structural changes in employment not only affected union size, but also union composition. The number of agricultural workers and blue-collar workers in industry among union members declined, while the number of white-collar workers, blue-collar workers in services and public employees grew steadily in the 1970s and early 1980s (Table 3.1). After 1985 the majority of unions experienced a membership decline, whereby the share of blue-collar workers' unions in industry shrank further. As the GPA organises white-collar employees across the entire private sector, it became the largest union in 1973.

The structural shift from blue-collar to white-collar employment has had a particular impact in the private sector where these groups are organised by different trade unions. Given this demarcation, structural change becomes a kind of zero-sum game between the unions. The 'losers' in structural change are the blue-collar workers' unions in industry and the 'winner' is the GPA. This is happening not only on account of the expansion of the services sector in the narrow sense, but also because within the secondary sector the proportion of blue-collar to white-collar workers is decreasing. In consequence, there is conflict between the GPA and the blue-collar unions in manufacturing over the non-realisation of industrial unionism (Klenner and Pellar, 1999: 883-4; Peissl, 1994: 215-221).

---

[6] In 1993 an opening clause on wage flexibility was agreed for the metal industry. It allowed agreements concluded within plants to trade increases for wages above the standard rates against measures to promote employment. Only a small group of enterprises included this clause in the plant agreements (Auer and Welte, 1994). The union considered the clause to be a failure, primarily because it was not utilised as intended, that is, to promote employment. In consequence, the opening clause was not taken up again in the subsequent collective agreements.

Table 3.1: Union Membership and Density

	1950	1960	1970	1980	1990	1995	2001
	Total Membership[1]						
Blue-Collar Unions (Private Sector)							
Construction and Wood Workers' Union	172,757	192,257	192,022	197,575	185,065	184,257	158,065
Chemical Workers' Union	55,060	66,014	69,919	64,824	56,998	46,525	35,177
Printing and Paper Workers' Union[2]	22,441	25,102	25,334	24,280	23,362	19,585	19,817
Agricultural and Forestry Workers' Union[3]	66,502	67,644	39,074	20,679	18,387	50,576	39,736
Food and Tobacco Workers' Union[3]	50,047	58,755	50,578	46,079	39,517		
Metal, Mining and Energy Workers' Union[4]	202,649	274,753	283,006	273,841	239,839	219,462	216,799
Textile, Clothing and Leather Workers' Union[4]	109,227	104,724	69,146	60,224	38,094	25,215	
Commerce, Transport and Traffic Workers' Union	24,656	25,108	27,233	35,330	37,855	37,541	35,177
Hotel and Restaurant Workers' Union[5]	19,493	13,796	17,122	43,378	53,656	52,280	50,131
Personal Services Workers' Union[4]	31,934	23,097	21,314				
White-Collar Union (Private Sector)							
Union of Salaried Private Sector Employees	138,193	224,950	263,565	338,290	337,564	326,372	284,633

	1950	1960	1970	1980	1990	1995	2001
Public Sector Unions							
Union of Public Employees	105,993	116,918	129,414	193,716	230,570	231,968	229,079
Union of Municipal Workers	112,086	117,787	136,340	158,647	172,792	179,621	172,456
Railway Workers' Union	117,875	124,492	120,127	117,464	114,721	110,933	96,730
Union of Postal and Telegraph Workers	40,488	49,183	60,625	70,074	80,145	82,552	71,137
Mixed Union[6]:							
Union for Arts, Media, Sports and Freelancers	21,180	16,467	15,440	16,584	16,276	16,289	12,090
ÖGB Total	*1,290,581*	*1,501,047*	*1,520,259*	*1,660,985*	*1,644,841*	*1,583,176*	*1,421,027*
Share of ÖGB Membership							
Blue-Collar Unions in Industry and Agriculture (Private Sector)	52.6	52.6	48.0	41.4	36.6	34.5	33.0
Blue-Collar Unions in Services (Private Sector)	5.9	4.1	4.3	4.7	5.6	5.7	6.0
White-Collar Union (Private Sector)	10.7	15.0	17.3	20.4	20.5	20.6	20.0
Public Sector Unions	29.2	27.2	29.4	32.5	36.4	38.2	40.1
Net Density							
ÖGB Total	*54.8[7]*	*56.6[8]*	*62.6*	*56.6*	*46.9*	*40.7*	*35.1*

[1] Union members including retired, unemployed and self-employed, by end of December

[2] In 2001 the Printing and Paper Workers' Union was joined by the journalists (who left the Union for Arts, Media, Sports and Freelancers) and changed its name to Union of Journalists, Printing and Paper Workers.

[3] Merger of the Agricultural and Forestry Workers' Union and the Food and Tobacco Workers' Union in 1991 to form the Union of Food, Agriculture and Tobacco Workers.

[4] Merger of the Metal, Mining and Energy Workers' Union and the Textile, Clothing and Leather Workers' Union in 2000 to form the Metal and Textile Workers' Union.

[5] Merger of the Personal Service Workers' Union and the Hotel and Restaurants Workers' Union in 1978 to form the Hotel, Restaurant and Personal Services Workers' Union.

[6] White- and blue-collar workers, private and public sector.

[7] 1951.

[8] 1961.

Sources: ÖGB, Ebbinghaus and Visser 2000, own calculations.

In reaction to the structural shifts in employment and other changes in its environment, the 1991 ÖGB Congress decided to initiate a process of structural reform and established a commission. The programme of reform recommended by this commission comprised substantive reforms of policy and aims, reforms of ways of working, and structural reforms (Tomasek, 1999: 140-41). Following the proposal of the reform commission, the 1995 ÖGB Congress decided to 'orient refocusing co-operation among affiliates and advancing concentration of resources towards the basic grouping categories of industry, services and the public sector', the so-called 'three pillars'.

Following the decision of the 1995 ÖGB Congress, several unions concluded co-operation contracts: the HGPD, the HTV (Commerce, Transport and Traffic Workers' Union) and the GdE (Railway Workers' Union) in 1998; the GBH (Construction and Wood Workers' Union), the GdC (Chemical Workers' Union), and the ANG in 1998; the TBL and the MBE in 1998; the GPA, the DuP (Printing and Paper Workers' Union), the KMSfB (Union for Arts, Media, Sports and Freelancers), and the GPF (Union of Postal and Telegraph Workers) in 1999 (several months before, the DuP and the GPF had already concluded a co-operation contract); and the ANG, the GÖD (Union of Public Employees) and the GPA for the agricultural sector in 1999. Co-operation contracts aim, albeit to different degrees, to encourage co-operation in various fields, including collective bargaining, co-ordination of politics and campaigns, and the joint use of resources, such as offices and services to members. The unions involved in a co-operation contract remain independent and usually there is no formal intention to merge. Only the TBL and the MBE concluded their co-operation contract in 1998 in order to prepare their merger in 2000.

It is striking that the most obvious combination of partners, between blue-collar and white-collar unions within the same sector, is not prevalent among existing co-operation contracts, although co-operation in bargaining exists in several sectors. Differences in labour law for blue-collar and white-collar employees have been identified as a main obstacle for closer co-operation between the GPA and the various blue-collar workers' unions. Even more important, however, it seems that the GPA has tried to avoid any development that entails it being broken up and its members in industry distributed to blue-collar unions. Breaking up the GPA is what the decision of the 1995 ÖGB Congress would mean, if it was taken seriously. The GPA, however, will not accept such a solution. Thus, mergers between *parts* of the GPA and blue-collar unions are unlikely and the development does not point in the direction of a transformation towards a 'three-pillar' model, in the sense of 'three pillars – three unions'.

Blue-collar unions with shrinking membership size have resorted to mergers as a solution. So far, only blue-collar unions have been involved in mergers. As the number of blue-collar workers in manufacturing continues to decline, it is clear that this will not be a feasible strategy in the long run. At the beginning of 2001, the ÖGB President relaunched the debate on restructuring by suggesting that the thirteen unions should be transformed into eight industrial unions without differentiation by employee status. Just as in the pursuit of the 'three-pillar' model, this proposal would imply breaking up the GPA, which the GPA will not be willing to accept. Furthermore, the GMT and the ANG were already considered a merger that was not in line with the demarcation of union domains proposed in the President's plan. After the presentation of the President's plan, a commission was instructed to develop several alternative models of reorganisation. While the commission was working, ANG and GMT continued their preparations for a merger and in the autumn 2001 GPA and GMT announced that they intended to merge, probably in the year 2005. Because of earlier merger plans involving GMT and ANG, the ANG will also be a partner in this merger. In addition, two other small blue-collar unions, the DJP (Union of Journalists, Printing and Paper Workers, the former DuP) and the GdC, joined the merger project. In spring 2002 the five unions signed a memorandum of association. In autumn 2001 it was decided that GMT and ANG will merge in 2004, before the large-scale merger takes place (see Figure 1.3). Only four unions, therefore, will be involved in the large-scale merger, but until the merger of GMT and ANG is carried out, the ANG is a full partner in the process of the large-scale merger. As a consequence of this development, the plan of the President and the work of the commission became obsolete. The planned large-scale merger will finally realise industrial unionism, uniting organisation for blue-collar and white-collar workers for large parts of the secondary sector. This will be possible because, in contrast to previous plans to bring about industrial unionism, which entailed a splitting up of the GPA, the GPA will remain undivided.

In reaction to the planned large-scale merger, almost all of the other unions – the GBH, the HTV, the HGPD, the KMSfB, the GdG (Union of Municipal Workers), the GdE and the GPF – formed an alliance called 'infra'. The GÖD will remain on its own. Co-operation between GÖD and the GdG would seem more logical, but is rather unlikely for party-political reasons: the President of the GÖD belongs to the Christian Unionists faction of the ÖGB (*Fraktion Christlicher Gewerkschafter*) while the President of the GdG is a member of the Faction of Social Democratic Unionists (*Fraktion Sozialdemokratischer GewerkschafterInnen*), as are the Presidents of the other unions.

The Character of Merger Activity[7]

In each of the three mergers carried out so far, the ÖGB played a supportive role. In the case of the amalgamation of the GPD and GGA, the ÖGB had advocated such a merger for many years and the ÖGB's wish played an essential part in bringing it about. One main reason for the generally positive attitude of the ÖGB towards these mergers was the small size of one or both of the unions involved. The smaller the size of a union, the less likely it is that the costs of running can be covered by membership contributions. A deficit may be covered by the ÖGB for some years, but if a union permanently has not enough financial means to maintain its infrastructure, then cuts, such as closing offices, will be necessary. That, in turn, will lead to a decline in union membership and a weakening of the union movement. Union mergers are seen as a means to avoid such a development.

The ÖGB favoured mergers as a means to prevent a weakening of the union movement and to make it more powerful. The ÖGB profited financially from mergers, because they allowed it to stop payments to the economically weak unions. A strengthening of the union movement was also expected to result from mergers, not only because mergers lead to more efficient use of resources and thus to more capacities for recruiting members and supporting them (and, in consequence, keeping them), but also because in the negotiations on the sectoral level a union with more members is perceived to be in a stronger position *vis-à-vis* the employers.

While in the case of the GPD and the GGA the ÖGB played an active role to achieve the merger, for the other two mergers the ÖGB took on the role of an agent with only an indirect influence. In both cases, the smaller of the unions involved (the GLFG and the TBL) had been looking for a partner because of financial difficulties resulting from membership decline. In the case of the TBL, the ÖGB tried to support it in its search. In the case of the GLFG the ÖGB exerted an indirect influence via statements in support of mergers involving smaller unions.

In the case of the planned large-scale merger, the role of the ÖGB was different. GPA and GMT announced their intention to merge completely unexpectedly. Their plan probably was not approved by each of the other unions, but after the announcement that the ÖGB could do nothing against the merger, the ÖGB gave its consent. At a time when

---

[7]   The main sources of information for this section and the following sections were interviews conducted with union representatives and union congress proceedings.

the involvement of the GdC was not yet fixed, the ÖGB even recommended that the GdC should join the large-scale merger.

When looking for a partner, both TBL and GLFG conducted talks about the possibility of a merger with several unions. In each case, one union finally crystallised as the one with which a merger seemed most feasible. The decisive criterion for becoming the final merger partner was the extent of overlapping in sectors and/or affinity between the sectors where both potential merger partners were active. In the case of the GLG the decisive criterion was that the membership share of sectors where both unions were active was larger than that of other unions under consideration as merger partners. In the case of the TBL incompatible regional distribution of offices[8] in combination with sinking membership of the potential partner, which might have necessitated a further merger within several years, hindered the more plausible merger with the GdC, which organises more similar sectors to the TBL than those organised by the MBE. In addition, dissonance between union officials seems to have constituted another obstacle to merging (Karlhofer, 1999: 29). In both merger cases (TBL and GLFG), the larger union took the initiative to start talks about a merger.

With the exception of the planned large-scale merger, every merger was preceded by periods of thorough internal discussions. In the course of these, most of the opponents were convinced to support the planned merger. Finally the mergers were concluded by delegates at union congresses. The merger of the TBL and MBE was preceded by a period of co-operation, specified in a contract, which had been concluded to prepare for the merger. In the case of the planned merger between GMT and ANG, co-operation started without a formal co-operation contract.

The merger which resulted in the formation of the HGPD was an amalgamation in the strict sense, as both unions dissolved themselves and founded a new union where the seats in the various bodies and the two peak positions were divided between the two parts which had been the predecessor unions. From a formal point of view the other two mergers were acquisitions: the smaller unions (GLFG and TBL) dissolved and were incorporated into the larger unions (GLG and MBE).[9] In both cases the number of seats in the governing bodies of the acquir-

---

[8] In one of the federal states the GdC has no office. The TBL would thus have had to retain its offices in this federal state, but this was not possible without a partner. Therefore, after a merger with the GdC, the TBL would have needed another partner for running the offices in this state. Such a procedure would have been too complicated.

[9] The planned merger between ANG and GMT will also formally be an acquisition.

ing union were enlarged by a certain proportion and, although not wearing a label, it was clear that they were intended to be filled by officials coming from the acquired union. After a while the number of seats in union bodies will be reduced again.

It has to be stressed that, in both acquisitions, the character of the merger was that of an amalgamation. The acquisitions were always termed 'amalgamations' and never 'acquisitions' or 'absorption'. The identity of the absorbed union was not lost, but was incorporated into the acquiring union. This was expressed most clearly in the fact that the acquiring union changed its name to include the domain of the absorbed union. Pragmatic reasons were decisive for performing acquisitions instead of amalgamations.

Reasons for Merger

In Austria the main reason for union mergers has been pressure on finances. In the cases of the TBL and the GLFG, financial means were not sufficient because of a decline in membership. This decline was mainly caused by a shrinking membership base due to economic change (Table 3.2). The same applies to the smaller partners of the planned large-scale merger, GdC, DJP and ANG. In the case of the GGA and the GPD neither union had ever been large enough, but the GGA had more difficulties.

Insufficient size of membership leads to difficulties in maintaining infrastructure. In the long run, the consequence would be to close offices and thus reduce the support for members, which would accentuate membership decline. A merger is expected to be a solution to this problem. The resulting amalgamation of the infrastructure leads to a more efficient use of resources, and this should make it possible to keep or even to extend the level of support for members. In general, pressure on union resources can be assumed to have been aggravated by rapid changes in the economy and labour market since the 1980s.

Enforced international competition led to business restructuring involving company mergers, company sell-offs and company restructuring. In consequence, the unions had to extend their advisory activities for members and works councils. Furthermore, the proportion of workers employed at small enterprises grew, which has made it more time consuming for union officials to attend to the needs of individual enterprises. The increased possibilities of including flexible working time schedules in plant agreements, which, to a large extent, are a result of increased international competition, also contributed to the growing demand for union advice. However, the influence of the decentralisation of bargaining on the working time of union officers and, via pressure on union resources, on the merger process can be assumed to be relatively weak.

Table 3.2: Pre-merger Membership Trends
of Unions Involved in Mergers

	MERGER 1978	
	Hotel and Restaurant Workers' Union	Personal Service Workers' Union
1960	13,796	23,097
1965	15,473	22,598
1970	17,122	21,314
1975	20,007	21,882
1976	19,668	22,070
1977	21,484	22,107

	MERGER 1991	
	Agricultural and Forestry Workers' Union	Food, Beverage and Tobacco Workers' Union
1970	39,074	50,578
1980	20,679	46,079
1985	19,730	42,881
1987	18,805	42,404
1989	18,549	40,113
1990	18,387	39,517

	MERGER 2000	
	Metal, Mining and Energy Workers' Union	Textile, Clothing and Leather Workers' Union
1980	273,841	60,224
1990	239,839	38,094
1995	219,462	25,215
1997	206,241	20,236
1998	205,898	18,439
1999	204,674	16,887

Source: ÖGB.

A second reason for merger is the objective of making labour more powerful *vis-à-vis* capital. On the one hand, it is expected that this will be achieved by the larger size of the union. It is assumed that a large union with many members and many full-time officials is likely to be more successful in reaching its aims than a small union. On the other hand, co-ordination works better within a union than between unions. The objective of becoming more powerful seems to be relevant for all unions involved in mergers, as well as those involved in co-operation contracts. There have been rapid changes in the organisation of business. Increasingly, enterprises are merging and splitting up again, some are active across various national boundaries and directly or indirectly across various industries by outsourcing and subcontracting. By merging, unions try to establish a counterweight to these developments in enterprise structures. Industrial restructuring and business restructuring are among the consequences of enforced international competition. Together with high unemployment, enforced international competition has weakened the position of unions *vis-à-vis* employers. The factors weakening the position of unions seem to exert some influence on the merger process, because the weakened position makes unions search for possibilities to recover their position, and merging is seen as a strategy whereby this might be achieved.

Another kind of reason seems to have been relevant for the MBE's decision to merge with the TBL: maintaining influence within the confederation. Though the large MBE was far from being put under financial pressure by membership decline, its powerful position within the confederation was being adversely affected by its shrinking share of total membership (Table 3.1).

Among the factors identified as possible influences on the merger process in the literature (see Chapter 1), structural and technological changes in the economy – the employment shift from manufacturing towards services, and, within industrial sectors, the shift from blue-collar work towards white-collar work – which resulted in membership and financial decline can be identified as main causes for union mergers in the case of the TBL and the GLFG. In the case of the GGA and GPD the precarious financial situation which led to the merger was caused by insufficient union size. A few other factors exerted some influence on the merger process, but were of minor importance: industrial restructuring, enterprise restructuring, enforced international competition in general, and rising unemployment. These factors exerted their influence either via challenging the position of unions and making them choose merger as a counterstrategy, or via enforcing the pressure on resources because of an increase in demand for union advice. Apart from increasing demands for union advice which contributed to the pressure on union resources, developments in collective bargaining had no effect on mergers.

To date, mergers have been driven by the defensive motivation[10] of small unions with a deteriorating financial position. This applies to the mergers already completed, as well as to the intended merger of GMT and ANG. With the exception of the merger between GGA and GPD, the partner union of the small union was a larger union. The larger unions pursued the mergers as a means of consolidating their position within the union movement. Though the larger unions had their motives, the mergers would not have happened, had there not been smaller unions in financial difficulties seeking a partner.

The planned large-scale merger of five unions differs from previous mergers in several respects, one of which is the mix in motives. The two large and strong unions GPA and GMT want to merge with each other for two main reasons. First, the merger is a response to the attacks on the union movement by the conservative-populist government. Second, the merger will strengthen the position of both unions within the ÖGB and will enable them to resist proposals for reform that are deemed against their interests. The latter applies especially to the GPA as the merger will bring to an end reform plans which entail splitting up the GPA. Furthermore, like previous mergers, GPA and GMT see the merger as a means to strengthen the union movement *vis-à-vis* the employers. Finally, the GMT welcomes the merger because it will abolish the separate organisation of blue-collar and white-collar workers in its domain. As with the other mergers, the motives of the smaller partners in this planned large-scale merger are primarily defensive; they need to merge because of increasing financial pressure. In addition they see the merger as a means to strengthen the union movement. Compared to previous mergers, the consolidating motives of the two large unions have in sum a stronger weight in the planned large-scale merger.

Merger Outcomes[11]

The outcomes of the Austrian merger process are briefly reviewed in terms of resources, constitutions, membership heterogeneity and multi-industry unionism. It is clear that the merger process will result in further shifts away from industrial unionism.

---

[10] According to Undy *et al.* (1981: 214-5) motives and strategies of merging unions can be categorised as defensive, consolidating, or aggressive.

[11] To date the outcomes of the recent merger between the MBE and the TBL are only partly visible.

Resources

As intended, mergers led to a more efficient use of resources; offices and administrations were amalgamated and staffing levels were reduced. The more efficient use of resources also allowed improved recruitment and support of members. This effect was pronounced in the case of the HGPD where a significant rise in post-merger membership was achieved (Table 3.1), although this resulted in only slight increases in density.[12] The ANG improved support for members, but the decline in membership, which both pre-merger unions had experienced, continued because of shrinking employment in the union's domain. The former members of the TBL enjoyed improved services after the merger of TBL and MBE.

After the mergers, the number of union administrative staff usually declined, but the numbers engaged in recruitment and support of members remained relatively constant. The HGPD even employed more personnel for recruiting and supporting members. Declines in staff were usually achieved by natural wastage. In a few cases, however, union employees had to change to the ÖGB or to change their position within the union because of the restructuring of personnel.

Structural and Formal Aspects

During the first years after a merger the seats in various union governing bodies and the leading positions were usually divided up between the pre-merger parts of the new union. Many unions are divided into sections by groups of industrial sectors. In the case of the HGPD and the ANG the demarcation of these sections (*Sektionen* in the HGPD, *Fachgruppen* in the ANG) were identical to the domains of the pre-merger unions. The GMT has no sections, but operated with less-formal sectoral or industrial working groups (*Branchenarbeitskreise*). Representation *vis-à-vis* employers at the sectoral level and in collective bargaining is usually performed by members of sections or sectoral working groups. Thus, it is guaranteed that these tasks are performed by unionists who are acquainted with the sectoral conditions.

Dealing with Heterogeneity

Usually the cultures of the two partners in a merger differ to some extent. Combined training courses with no sectoral subject specificity, such as general labour law or speaking skills, for officials, activists and members of the pre-merger unions have proved a successful means of

---

[12] Figures on density are not available.

becoming acquainted with each other. In the case of HGPD, it took several years before the different union cultures of the GGA and GPD grew together. The final step could be taken only after the retirement of key persons. In the case of the ANG, the different culture of the former GLFG was incorporated, with the result that the culture of the GLFG and that of the GLG coexist without problems. The pre-merger GLFG became a section within the post-merger ANG. Stemming from their difference in size, the culture of TBL and MBE differed in one key aspect. In the small TBL, works councils had more opportunities to participate in union policy-making than in the large MBE. In the post-merger union this feature of TBL practice was abandoned because the size of the union made it impracticable. This change was accompanied by many talks to convince those who were affected by it and is said now not to be problematic.

Labour law for agricultural and forestry workers differs from general labour law. In forming the ANG, this variation was handled by leaving these affairs within the section that previously was the GLFG. There were no additional substantial differences between members of merging unions. Some problems occurred for the HGPD after the merger, because strong tendencies towards craft unionism had existed in the GGA and, to a much lesser extent, in certain parts of the GPD. The transformation of their union into a services union was not approved by members adhering to craft unionism.

From Industrial Unionism to Multi-industry Unionism

Because of the separate organisation of white-collar workers in the private sector, industrial unionism in the sense of 'one establishment – one union' was established in the public sector only. Strictly speaking, the public sector unions are not industrial unions, but enterprise unions. They organise all employees of a certain employer. With the privatisation of public services this demarcation becomes increasingly blurred and makes less sense. The GPA organises white-collar workers across all sectors and therefore is a multi-industry union. The unions of blue-collar workers in the private sector are usually seen as industrial unions, but from the outset some of them organised workers across more than one industry and are thus more multi-industry unions than industrial unions. As a result of the mergers, industrial unions vanished and more multi-industry unions emerged. The planned large-scale merger will continue this process.

Conclusions

Austria's union movement possesses a high degree of centralisation and unity. After World War II there were sixteen affiliates to the only confederation, the ÖGB. Starting in the late 1970s three union mergers took place and the number of affiliates was reduced to thirteen. The main driving force for merger activity was the precarious financial situation of, at least, one of the unions involved. In two of the three mergers, financial difficulties were the result of declining membership due to shrinking employment in the jurisdictions of the unions.

Given these circumstances, the more efficient use of resources was the main objective pursued by merger activity. Its achievement should allow post-merger unions to keep, or even extend, the level of activities in recruiting and supporting members. Another objective pursued by merger activity was a strengthening of the union movement. The mergers among the affiliates of the ÖGB met the intended objectives. Resources were used more efficiently, and thus a larger share of resources was devoted to recruiting and supporting members. Further, in the view of union officials, the larger size made the unions more powerful. Due to the developments in the Austrian economy, the blue-collar unions in manufacturing will experience further membership decline and, therefore, pressure on resources. In consequence, merging of unions has to continue. For around the year 2005 another merger involving five unions is planned.

In Austria, as in other countries, union restructuring via mergers follows a sectoral logic to only a limited extent. A more 'logical' restructuring along sector boundaries, as the abandoned plan of the ÖGB President in 2001 intended, is precluded by a number of factors: first, the fact that union structures have grown over the years and cannot be changed easily; second, the attachment of officials, activists and members to existing union structures and traditions; third, party-political differences; and fourth, other internal power struggles.

The planned large-scale merger will change the role and function of the ÖGB fundamentally. The new union will comprise around 40 per cent of total union membership. It will need less support from the confederation and, therefore, is likely to reduce its payments to the ÖGB. In addition, the distribution of power between the confederation and this affiliate probably will shift to the disadvantage of the confederation. This development is thus similar to the situation in Germany where three unions organise between 75 per cent and 80 per cent of the total membership and the position of the DGB is becoming more precarious (see Chapter 5).

List of Abbreviations

ANG   Gewerkschaft Agrar-Nahrung-Genuß (Food, Drink and Agricultural Workers' Union)

BAK   Bundesarbeitskammer (Federal Chamber of Labour)

DJP   Gewerkschaft Druck, Journalismus, Papier (Printing, Journalism and Paper Workers' Union)

DuP   Gewerkschaft Druck und Papier (Printing and Paper Workers' Union)

GBH   Gewerkschaft Bau-Holz (Building and Wood workers' Union)

GdC   Gewerkschaft der Chemiearbeiter (Chemical Industry Workers' Union)

GdE   Gewerkschaft der Eisenbahner(Railway Workers' Union)

GdG   Gewerkschaft der Gemeindebediensteten (Local Government Employees' Union)

GGA   Gewerkschaft der gastgewerblichen Arbeitnehmer (Hotelworkers' Union)

GLFG   Gewerkschaft Land-Forst-Garten (Agriculture, Forestry and Horticultural Workers' Union)

GLG   Gewerkschaft der Lebens- und Genußmittelarbeiter (Food and Tobacco Workers' Union)

GMT   Gewerkschaft Metall-Textil (Metal and Textile Workers' Union)

GÖD   Gewerkschaft Öffentlicher Dienst (Civil Service Union)

GPA   Gewerkschaft der Privatangestellten (Union of Salaried Private Sector Employees)

GPD   Gewerkschaft Persönlicher Dienst (Personal Service Workers' Union)

GPF   Gewerkschaft der Post- und Fernmeldebediensteten (Post Office and Telecommunication Workers' Union)

HGPD   Gewerkschaft Hotel, Gastgewerbe, Persönlicher Dienst Hotel and Personal Services Workers' Union)

HTV   Gewerkschaft Handel, Transport, Verkehr (Trade and Transport Workers Union)

KMSfB   Gewerkschaft Kunst, Medien, Sport, freie Berufe (Arts, Media, Sports and Entertainment Workers' Union)

MBE   Gewerkschaft Metall-Bergbau-Energie (Metal, Mining and Energy Workers' Union)

ÖGB Österreichischer Gewerkschaftsbund (Austrian Trade Union Confederation)

TBL Gewerkschaft Textil-Bekleidung-Leder (Textiles, Clothing, Leather Workers' Union)

WKÖ Wirtschaftskammer Österreich (Austrian Chamber of Commerce)

The Survival of Small Trade Unions in the Context of Centralised Bargaining

Jesper DUE and Jørgen Steen MADSEN

Historically, Danish trade union structure was highly differentiated and characterised by a large number of small trade unions. Much of this structure has been sustained. Its weaknesses have been overcome through a strongly centralised bargaining system in which negotiations have taken place either directly through, or with a strong involvement of, union confederations, or through bargaining cartels. The significant changes that took place after 1950 were associated with the structure of collective bargaining. When major changes were implemented to the bargaining structure, subsequent reforms were introduced to union structure, in order to maintain effective representation of members' interests.

The development of Danish unionism has thus been consistent with explanations that emphasise the connection between the establishment of a collective bargaining system and the internal and external structures of trade unions (Clegg, 1976). The degree of centralisation of a bargaining structure, which is often dictated by employers as a condition for concluding collective agreements, forces trade unions to adapt their decision-making processes so that they function effectively at the decisive bargaining levels. If the union structure does not hinder effective decision-making, then the bargaining system will legitimate the existing union structure. Changes to the bargaining structure may put union structure under pressure, especially should the structure become an obstacle to adaptation to new forms of bargaining (Clegg, 1976; Due et al., 1993; 1994).

Although the establishment and development of the collective bargaining system has had a significant influence upon the structure of trade unions, other factors have also been influential. Technological and industrial developments have encouraged mergers through the erosion of occupations and industries. These developments influenced union mergers at an early stage by promoting, for example, the disappearance of specialised craft unions during the first half of the twentieth century and, during the past decade, amalgamations. The state has also played an important role, mediated through the close relationship between unemployment insurance funds and trade unions in Denmark. Several waves of union mergers have been generated by the state introducing legislation to raise the membership threshold required by unions to gain official recognition of unemployment insurance funds (see Figure 1.4).

Danish Trade Union Structure

Trade unions in Denmark are grouped around four confederations: LO (Danish Confederation of Trade Unions), FTF (Confederation of Salaried Employees and Civil Servants in Denmark), AC (Danish Confederation of Professional Associations) and LH (Confederation of Managerial and Executive Staff in Denmark). There are clear membership overlaps between LO and FTF and between FTF and AC. These lead to disputes and to the existence of some competition, but the general borderlines are fixed, thus limiting destructive competition in the confederations' relations with employers. This demarcation was facilitated by the continuous growth in membership between 1900 and 1990. The affiliation of LO to the SD (Social Democratic Party) has been the main dividing line between LO and FTF.

The LO was set up in 1898 under the name of the DSF (Federation of Trade Unions in Denmark). By 1899 the new organisation was engaged in a decisive battle with the also recently established association of employers, DA (Danish Employers Association). At the time, this was the largest industrial dispute in Europe (Crouch, 1993) and it ended with the first basic agreement, the so-called September Compromise, which constitutes the foundation of the collective bargaining system in Denmark (Due *et al.*, 2000; Strøby Jensen *et al.*, 2001). Today LO has nearly 1.5 million members, about 1.2 million of whom are employed, organised into 22 affiliated trade unions. LO is not empowered to conduct collective bargaining, but has been able to exert influence in cases where the bargaining process has been referred to the Public Conciliator.

Though LO has its roots in the manual working class, it also began, relatively early, to organise salaried employees in the private sector, such as office workers. In addition, LO organised public employees, mainly blue-collar workers, but some white-collar workers were also included.[1] In recent decades the growth of white-collar workers gene-

---

[1]   It should be mentioned that employees in the public sector are covered by the Legal Relationship (Employers and Salaried Employees) Act (*Funktionærloven*) and must

rally, and, in particular, in the public sector, has meant that exclusively white-collar unions have grown faster than LO-affiliated unions. This is a development that led to the formation of two new confederations, FTF in 1952, which mainly organises white-collar workers with a medium-level education, and AC in 1972, which organises workers educated to university degree level, referred to as "academic staff".

FTF has 104 affiliated unions with 350,000 active members. FTF, which represents salaried employees and public/civil servants, was formed as an alternative to LO. FTF adopted a neutral stance in terms of party politics, thus dissociating itself from LO's links with SD.[2] Nearly 75 per cent of the members of FTF are public sector employees. The unions affiliated to FTF play a vital role in public sector bargaining. FTF is not empowered to conclude collective agreements, but like LO, plays a major role in tackling political issues, at both the national and the international level.

AC has 22 affiliated unions with 150,000 members. It was set up in 1972 as an aggregation of professional unions. About 40 per cent of its members work in the private sector. As a union for 'professionals', AC also organises the self-employed. It promotes its members' interests at the highest political levels and is represented on numerous public bodies. Unlike LO and FTF, AC is directly empowered to conclude collective agreements, although solely for members in the public sector.

At the behest of the employers, a clause of the September Compromise stipulated that supervisory staff should not be members of the same unions as other workers. This clause led to the formation of LH, which has now almost developed into a unitary organisation for medium-level managers, with a principal focus on the private sector. It has nearly 80,000 active members and comprises only three organisations, two small unions alongside LH itself. LH has a special bargaining role in relation to the employer confederation DA, and, similarly to the other confederations, is represented on a number of public councils and boards.

---

as such generally be defined as white-collar workers. The division into blue-collar workers and white-collar worker in relation to public employees is thus mainly based in the nature of the work functions and the background for exercising these functions (manual work versus non-manual work, unskilled and low-educated versus medium-level educated/higher educated).

[2] During the mid-1990s the formal links, through mutual representation, between the LO and the SD were cut, thus reducing the distance. The main obstacle to a merger between LO and FTF appeared to be removed (Due and Madsen, 1996: 527-31). But at the practical level the ties between LO and SD were still strong. LO's cutting of the financial support to SD in 2003 may lead to new discussions about mergers but it could be years before any real moves are made in this direction.

Table 4.1: Membership of the Confederations, 1950-2000

	LO Members	LO % of total	FTF members	FTF % of total	AC members	AC % of total	FR/LH Members	FR /LH % of total	Others members	Others % of total	Total members
1950	656,406	92							54,641	8	677,721
1955	687,464	82	88,465	11			20,831	2	43,006	5	838,666
1960	775,457	81	112,221	12			23,789	3	42,341	4	954,808
1970	895,995	79	156,101	14			30,285	3	54,945	5	1,137,326
1975	953,318	73	210,190	16	44,047	3	21,178	2	85,450	6	1,314,183
1980	1,249,562	71	277,374	16	69,692	4	23,986	1	135,563	8	1,756,177
1990	1,422,969	69	324,585	16	102,497	5	70,529	3	145,684	7	2,066,364
2000	1,458,742	67	350,255	16	150,060	7	79,778	4	122,778	6	2,161,616

Sources: Statistical Yearbook and the annual reports of the confederations. The figures for LO, unlike those of the other confederations, include passive members (pensioners and persons on early retirement pay) and conscripts. LO's share is thus slightly over-stated. The figures for AC are exclusive of self-employed persons, that is, they include only employees.

Through the establishment of the four confederations and their division of the labour market, trade unions have managed to maintain a high density rate in Denmark.[3] The rate of organisation has been steadily increasing since 1950. The total membership has tripled from nearly 700,000 in 1950 to 2.2 million members in 2000 (see Table 4.1). Although there was a marked increase in the size of the labour force during this period, union density also increased from about 55 per cent in 1950 to about 90 per cent in 2000.[4]

---

[3] The four confederations belong to what could be called the established trade union movement in Denmark, i.e. confederations that have obtained, through their affiliates, direct or indirect rights to negotiate and conclude collective agreements. These confederations are recognised by public and private sector employer associations and are embedded in the political system. From the start of the trade unionism about 1900, there have been attempts to create alternatives to the established movement. The only persistent alternative is the Christian Trade Union, which was established at the same time as LO, but which has never developed into more than a marginal organisation. As at 1st January 2000, the Christian Trade Union had nearly 60,000 members. But the number of members in the associated Christian unemployment insurance fund is nearly twice as high.

[4] Ebbinghaus' figures are at the same level as DA's calculation of the union density. According to DA, the union density was 88 per cent in 1999 (DA, 2000: 172). According to LO's analysis, this is an exaggeration. A more accurate number of the unionised wage earners in relation to the total number of employed and unemployed wage-earners is 82.5 per cent. (Madsen, 2000: 38-41). The difference is the calculation of the size of the denominator, i.e. the labour force.

Bargaining Structure

The regulation of pay and working conditions in Denmark takes place primarily through sector-based centralised negotiations at the national level. This system was established at the start of the last century and has functioned on the same basic principles since 1930. Decentralisation has characterised recent decades, however, initially in the private sector during the 1980s, and latterly in the public sector, with the introduction of a local wage system in the late 1990s. In spite of an increase in local bargaining, centrally established frameworks at sector level remain predominant.

Private sector agreements concluded between the member organisations of LO and DA are trend-setting. In principle, DA covers the entire private sector, but there is a clear division between it and two other principal organisations of employers, the SALA (Danish Confederation of Employers' Associations in Agriculture) and the FA (Danish Employers' Association for the Financial Sector). DA thus covers industry, building and construction, transport and services, but not forestry, agriculture or the financial sector.

The establishment of centralised negotiations at confederal level has its roots in the September Compromise of 1899. Most of the important elements in the centralisation process were in place by the mid-1930s. Centralisation did not mean that LO dominated its affiliates. The agreements concluded by affiliated unions preserved their authority and competence. But on the important general demands, negotiations took place jointly, with power placed in the hands of the negotiation body of LO, which comprised representatives of the major unions and the leadership of LO. Only special demands were negotiated by affiliated unions and even these negotiations were often conducted with the assistance of LO.

Employers advocated this centralised structure. The structure of Danish industry was then, and continues to be, characterised by a large number of small enterprises. Employers, therefore, saw centralised collective bargaining as a pre-condition to safeguarding their interests in relation to the trade unions. From the outset, DA was thus assigned strongly centralised decision-making powers. The leadership of LO could not obtain similar powers. The national trade unions stuck to their right to negotiate collective agreements. But, due to centralisation, which was strengthened by legislation on the conciliation service in the 1930s – empowering the public conciliator to submit draft settlements and linking the voting of the members in the many trade unions together – LO affiliates only formally kept their sovereignty. In reality, their negotiations were inter-linked.

The centralisation of bargaining enabled many small unions to exist during the entire period of the LO. The establishment of the collective bargaining system around 1900, and its maintenance until the 1960s, allowed them to represent their members' interests under the auspices of the LO. This meant that there was no incentive to merge. The unions that disappeared through this period were those whose occupational recruitment bases were undermined by technological development.

In the public sector a similar centralised bargaining system was established around the predominant group of civil servants, those working for the state. Negotiations did not take place with the individual unions, many of which were small. The unions were aggregated, under pressure from the state employer, in four large bargaining cartels. Each cartel negotiated specific relations, whilst the more general questions were jointly negotiated by the cartel TFU (Danish Central Federation of Public and Civil Servants). From the 1960s, but especially through the 1970s and 1980s, changes in employment conditions meant that there were ever fewer public civil servants and more employees' contracts were settled by collective agreements. The bargaining system therefore needed to be changed. The employees on group contracts were included in the four confederations and the name of their joint bargaining was changed from TFU to CFU (Danish Central Federation of State Employees). However, it was not only at the cartel level that the organisational structure had to be adjusted to the new reality; the unions merged either through amalgamation or acquisition.

A similar development occurred, albeit it at a later time, in the counties and municipalities where the employers also wanted a greater degree of centralisation. In the first instance, the negotiations for the civil servants in the municipalities were centralised into the collective bargaining cartel KTU (Committee of Public Servants in the Municipal Sector). KTU consisted of sixty unions. Later on, as employees on collective agreement contracts were included in the joint negotiations, the name of KTU was changed to KTO (Association of Local Government Employees' Organisations).

Thus, in the public sector, the establishment of bargaining cartels enabled a large number of very small unions to survive within the context of centralised bargaining. There were no incentives to merge as the most important task, the bargaining of members' terms and conditions, was handled through the cartels. The formation of cartels was thus a solution to a problem, both for the employers and for unions in the public sector. It was only when the inclusion of employees on contracts settled through collective agreements necessitated a change in the organisational structure that any changes took place. It was within the "academic" field, however, where the most profound development occurred.

Here the changes in union structure took place partly as a consequence of the changes in the bargaining system and partly due to the development of a new profession-based union ideology.

Traditional Union Structure

Late industrialisation and the persistence of strong guild traditions in Denmark led to the establishment of trade unions based on craft or occupational lines. The unionisation process, both initially, and in its subsequent development, was influenced by two conflicting ideologies. First, a craft- or occupation-based approach characterised both crafts-people and professionals, resulting in the establishment of exclusive unions. A second ideology was based on solidarity as a prerequisite for the protection of shared interests, which has as its objective the establishment of industrial unions. Craft ideology was more influential during the formative period of trade unionism, and strong unions for skilled workers became the norm. Industrial unions were rare and unskilled workers, who were excluded from such unions by skilled workers, formed their own general unions. Later, unskilled women also set up their own union (Due *et al.*, 1993; 1994).

The establishment of trade unions in the different sectors took place along two rather separate tracks. The first was the establishment of trade unions in the private sector. Most of these unions were established during the latter part of the nineteenth century. The second track comprises the unionisation of the public sector, which started at the turn of the century. This differentiation resulted in unions with different roots and structures and this historical background is still visible in the union structures of today. However, there have been significant adaptations and the development of some overlaps, as some unions organise members in both the private and the public sector.

It has always been the official view of LO that industrial unions should be set up. Within the LO there have been many debates about the structure of the trade union movement, most of which agreed a target of establishing industrial unions. But in spite of intense efforts, the traditional structure has been too strong to overcome. Only during the last decade are large, sector-based unions with federal systems of internal government emerging, primarily as a result of structural reform on the employer side.

In the public sector, union structure followed departmental lines. In the traditional civil service the structure was, at the same time, hierarchically divided into two or three unions for blue-collar workers, white-collar workers and, in some cases, "academic staff" in each department. These unions were characterised by a public servant ideology, which was often strongly related to a specific government service and gave employees a special sense of loyalty. With specific government service as the starting point, but combined with hierarchical and occupational divisions, this resulted in a large number of small unions, typically with only a handful of members. Particularly in the public sector, there were in addition some profession-based unions: for instance, for nurses, teachers, doctors and engineers. A shared professional ideology was decisive in the establishment of these unions.

Development of Union Mergers

The main lines in this structural development are examined below. For reasons of clarity, we divide the Danish merger process by confederation. By way of introduction we must emphasise that there are no legally binding rules on how union mergers should or must take place. It is, therefore, solely up to the individual unions to decide on amalgamations or acquisitions in accordance with their constitutions or other regulations. This usually implies both a majority of votes on the highest level, the congress, and a majority of votes in a ballot among the members. This is both a time-consuming and complicated procedure which, to a large extent, has been a barrier to mergers, because a ballot in a decision-making process often proves a conservative factor.

Almost all of the reduction of 48 unions affiliated to LO between 1950 and 2000 took place after 1960. This reduction was achieved primarily by the acquisition of very small unions by larger unions. The largest total number of unions was 277 in 1969. Since then 108 unions have disappeared in the merger process to result in 169 unions by 2000, a reduction of 39 per cent. FTF also peaked in 1969 with 173 affiliated unions, a number that was reduced to 104 by 2000, a fall of 40 per cent.

The third confederation, AC, was not established until 1972 and, in relation to the initial number of affiliated unions, there has been little change. But, as we shall see, this gives a completely distorted picture of the impact the establishment of AC had on the process of union mergers in Denmark. AC is best described as a gigantic acquisition process. More than 50 small unions in the Joint Council of Public Servants in the State Sector (usually referred to as the Joint Council) were acquired by 20 profession-based unions for "academic staff". In practice, one should compare the 22 unions affiliated to AC today with the 73 unions for "academic staff" in the Joint Council and the AS (Co-operation Committee of Academics) together in 1970. AS was a forerunner to AC, formed by the profession-based unions for academic staff. This means that more than two-thirds of the AC unions have disappeared. But since

94

the Joint Council was affiliated to FTF these acquisitions are visible only as a diminishing number of FTF unions between 1970 and 1980.

Table 4.2: Number of Unions Affiliated to each Confederation, 1950-2000

	LO	CO I[1]	FTF[2]	AC[3]	FR/LH[4]	Others	Total
1950	70	24	(101)		(4)	12	211
1960	68	16	125	(15)	8	6	238
1970	56	14	167	17	7	6	267
1980	40	6	133	19	8	19	225
1990	30	16	100	21	5	16	188
2000	22	8	104	22	3	10	169

[1] CO I is a bargaining cartel in the state sector with some member unions in LO and, during specific periods, some in FTF, but in addition, a large number outside of the confederations. Only these independent unions are included here in order to give a correct picture of the total number of unions.

[2] FTF was established in 1952, but we have included an estimated number of member unions in 1950 as virtually all member unions existed prior to the formation of FTF.

[3] AC was set up in 1972 and here too we have indicated the number of member unions for the immediately preceding years.

[4] LH was first included in the Statistical Yearbook from 1953. We have included an estimated number of member unions in 1950 as virtually all member unions existed prior to the formation of LH.

Sources: Statistical Yearbook and annual reports of the main and central organisations.

The period from 1950 to 2000 was characterised by a significant fall in the number of unions, but the fall did not take place until the 1970s. Before then, there was an increase in the total number of unions. This reflects the large number of union formations that took place during the 1960s and, to some extent, the 1970s. With the growth in the number of white-collar workers and the introduction of new technologies, new unions were formed in the private sector. Similarly, the extension of the welfare state led to a number of new unions.

Table 4.3 shows that most mergers took place during the 1970s. But the merger process gained momentum during the second half of the 1960s and continued into the 1980s. This is the period when the major-ity of acquisitions took place in LO, which meant that most of the small unions, initially those with under 1,000 members, latterly under 5,000, disappeared as a result of changed requirements in unemployment insurance legislation. Until the late 1970s, the centralised collective bargaining system solved many problems for the small unions. The first signs of crisis were not seen until after the legislative intervention in the collective bargaining process in 1979. The employers changed their strategy and there was pressure for decentralisation. However, it was a

decade before this decentralisation actually became reality and created a
need for structural change.

**Table 4.3: Number of Unions Disappearing
in Amalgamations and Acquisitions, 1950-2000**

	LO	FTF	AC	FR/LH	Others	**Total**
1950-59	6	9	0	0	0	15
1960-69	6	12	0	0	0	18
1970-79	21	43	42	0	0	106
1980-89	16	44	1	2	1	64
1990-99	12	23	2	2	4	43
Total	61	130	45	4	5	245

Source: Statistical Yearbook and the annual reports of the main and central organisations.[5]

Within FTF and AC, the merger process accelerated with the shift
from employment as public servants to employment on the basis of
collective agreement and the new Public Servants' Act, 1969. It was
followed up by the integration of agreement-covered employees in the
bargaining system of the public servants during the second half of the
1980s. In other words, it was the collective bargaining system that was
the engine of structural development. The change to the unemployment
insurance legislation, which explained the acquisition of small unions
within LO, did not have the same effect on the FTF and AC. In contrast
to LO unions, FTF and AC were legally allowed to establish one cross-
sectoral unemployment insurance fund each, with the consequence that
there was no incentive for small unions in FTF and AC to consider
mergers.

---

[5] It is not possible to compare directly the statistics concerning the number of trade
unions (Table 4.2) with the actual number of unions disappearing in mergers (Table 4.3). This is because many new unions were formed during the period until the
mid-1970s. There was a continuous flow of unions affiliating or seceding from the
confederations and some unions remained independent from the confederations during some periods and are thus excluded from official statistics. It is not possible on
the basis of available evidence (the official index of organisations in Statistical Yearbook, which is not exhaustive, and the annual surveys of the confederations and
cartels) to keep complete track of all the acquisitions and amalgamations which have
taken place; nor is it possible to make a precise registration of the cases where mergers fail and the unions regain their independence. The data are thus, to a degree, dis-
cretionary, but nevertheless are the most accurate achieved to date.

Union Mergers in LO

Table 4.4 illustrates the development in the number of unions, membership and the size of the unions affiliated to LO from 1950 to 2000. From 1950 to 1960, the number of affiliated unions fell by only two and, as Table 4.3 shows, only six acquisitions and no amalgamations took place during the period 1950-59.

Table 4.4: Development of LO Structure, 1950-2000

	Number of unions	Number of branches	Membership	Average size of union	Members per branch
1950	70	3,541	656,377	9,377	185
1960	68	3,568	776,457	11,418	218
1970	56	2,120	895,995	16,000	429
1980	40	1,453	1,249,562	31,239	790
1990	30	1,309	1,422,969	47,432	1,087
2000	22	988	1,458,742	66,306	1,476

Sources: Annual reports of DSF/LO, Statistical Yearbook.

The average size of unions increased six-fold, although the number of members more than doubled during the same period. In order to understand how the unions in LO are composed, it is necessary to examine their size. It is the relationship between a few very large unions and a significant number of small unions that is conspicuous when we look at LO as a confederation during the period 1950 to 1970.

Table 4.5: The Size of LO-affiliated Unions, 1950-2000

	1950 number	1950 %	1960 number	1960 %	1970 number	1970 %	1980 number	1980 %	1990 number	1990 %	2000 number	2000 %
Under 1,000	23	33	23	34	14	25	3	8	0	0	0	0
Under 5,000	46	66	42	62	34	61	16	40	3	10	2	9
5,000-25,000	19	27	22	32	16	29	16	40	17	57	9	41
25,000-75,000	4	6	1	1	3	5	3	8	5	17	6	27
Over 75,000	1	1	3	5	3	5	5	13	5	17	5	23
Total	70		68		56		40		30		22	
CR$_5$[1]		62		64		67		72		70		76

[1] The concentration ratio at five (CR$_5$) expresses the membership of the largest five unions of the population as a proportion of the total membership.

Sources: Annual reports of DSF/LO, Statistical Yearbook.

LO can be characterised as a confederation with a dichotomised structure. On the one hand, 30 per cent of the trade unions had less than

1,000 members in both 1950 and 1960. This share fell to 25 per cent in 1970. Unions with less than 5,000 members accounted for 66 per cent in 1950 and just over 60 per cent in 1960 and 1970. In other words, small unions comprised the majority of the unions in LO. LO also comprised a few relatively large unions. The five largest unions organised more than 60 per cent of all members in LO by 1950, and this share increased to 66 per cent by 1970 and 76 per cent by 2000.

To a significant extent, questions concerning changes in union struc-ture have been handled by the large unions affiliated to LO. Disagree-ment between the large unions has often meant that changes towards the establishment of industrial unions have been difficult to carry through, even though LO has supported industrial unionism, in principle, for over a hundred years. This especially applies to the battle between the large general workers' union SiD (General Workers' Union in Denmark) and the largest craft-based union Metal (National Union of Metalworkers). Throughout the history of the LO, these two unions have dominated the bargaining system and political processes, and they have always dis-agreed about structural change. Metal, with its strong foundation in the iron and metal industry, has favoured large industrial unions, whilst SiD, as a general union that covers a wide range of sectors, has been against such a development, as it implies that its members would be scattered across a number of industrial unions.

SiD and Metal are today the second and fourth largest unions within LO, with 315,000 and 140,000 members respectively. The largest union, with almost 375,000 members, is HK (Union of Commercial and Cleri-cal Employees in Denmark), which, as the name implies, is a general union for large groups of commercial and clerical employees in both the public and the private sector. The third largest union is FOA (Danish Trade Union of Public Employees), with almost 200,000 members.

The most important change in the period 1970 to 2000 was that the share of small unions gradually fell and by 2000 had been reduced to almost zero. Between 1950 and 2000, forty-six small unions were reduced to two. Small unions with less than 5,000 members merged. As a consequence, there has been an increase in unions of intermediate size between 5,000 and 25,000 members. By 1990, this was clearly the most numerous group. During this period the development of the collective bargaining system gained momentum and, in combination with a trend toward professionalisation in unions, it became difficult for small unions to cope with the development. These reasons also explain the decline in the number of medium-sized unions up to 2000. In 1990, unions with up to 25,000 members still accounted for 66 per cent of unions in LO. By 2000, unions with more than 25,000 members constituted half of the unions. This is a development that is expected to continue as part of an overall reduction in the total number of affiliated unions.

Amalgamations during the Past Fifty Years

Between 1950 and 1970 there were no amalgamations. Since 1970 eight amalgamations have taken place. Two amalgamations in the 1970s involved fairly equal unions in terms of size, although each of the pre-merger unions had less than 20,000 members.

1. The Union of Workers in the Clothing Industry and the Union of Textile Workers formed DBFT (Union of Clothing Industry and Textile Workers) in 1979. DBTF did not survive as an independent union until the turn of the century. The number of members in DBTF almost halved before it joined the industry group of SiD in 1998.

2. The Union of Joiners and the Union of Carpenters formed ST (Union of Joiners and Carpenters). ST was involved in a second amalgamation during the 1990s.

The amalgamation during the 1980s involved four unions in the food and beverage industry: the Union of Bakery, Confectionery and Mill Workers, the Union of Confectionery Hands and Chocolate Workers, the Union of Tobacco Workers and the Union of Danish Slaughterhouse Workers. This amalgamation differed from those of the 1970s in that the largest union in terms of members, the Slaughterhouse Workers with nearly 22,000 members, joined the three smaller organisations, which organised between 2,000 and 8,000 members, to form NNF (National Union of Food and Beverage Workers). NNF is unlikely to continue for many years ahead. The food and beverages industry does not constitute a sufficient basis for an independent union. NNF will probably join the industry group of SiD.

As Table 4.6 indicates, amalgamations in the 1990s were different again. Superficially, the predominance of amalgamations over acquisitions during the 1990s could be viewed as a radically new development. These amalgamations, however, have not provided any long-term solutions to structural problems. Only three of the newly amalgamated unions survived until 2003 and two of these have started further merger negotiations. The other two amalgamations dissolved before 1st January 2000.

Table 4.6: Union Mergers in LO, 1950-2000

	Number of unions	Total number of members	Average union size	Size range	Unions formed by amalgamation
1950-1959					
Acquisitions	6	3,173	529	113-1,580	
1960-1969					
Acquisitions	6	951	159	54-349	
1970-1979					
Acquisitions	19	27,359	1,440	16-9,975	
Amalgamations	4	72,812	18,203	16,057-20,596	2
1980-1989					
Acquisitions	13	21,716	1,670	162-3,380	
Amalgamations	4	35,123	8,781	2,455-21,902	1
1990-1999[1]					
Acquisitions	4(5)	38,201 (43,792)	9,550 (8,758)	3,008-17,229	
Amalgamations	13(19)	329,821	18,323	220-119,408	5
Total 1950-1999					
Acquisitions	48(49)	91,400 (96,991)	1,904 (1,979)	16-17,229	
Amalgamations	21(27)	437,756	16,837	220-119,408	8

[1] We have included in brackets FTF unions and independent unions outside LO, which were part of the mergers.

Source: LO Reports and Statistical Yearbook. The figure in the first column indicates the number of unions which have been either acquired or involved in an amalgamation. The total number of members refers to the final membership of the acquired or amalgamating unions.

The principal surviving amalgamation is FOA, which organises the county/municipal sector, and was formed through the amalgamation of DKA (National Union of Municipal Employees) and HAF (National Union of Cleaners and Domestic Workers) with about 120,000 and 75,000 members respectively. At the time, these were the third and sixth largest LO affiliates. It was a forward-looking amalgamation of two large unions with members in caring occupations.

In contrast, the formation of TKF (Union of Danish Telecommunication Workers) through the amalgamation of the LO-affiliated union *Dansk Teleforbund* and five small FTF unions within *Dansk Telesamvirke* (Association of Danish Teleworkers) involved a combined membership of less than 15,000 members. In 2003, however, TKF decided to join Metal. Similarly, the formation of TIB (Union of Joiners, Carpenters and Wood Industry Workers) with 70,000 members was not strong enough to survive. Compared with TKF, TIB was a relatively strong new union, but it was from the outset obvious that it would not last long. TIB will probably not be able to maintain its long-term independence and in 2003 started a new merger process planning an amalgamation with SiD. A part of this process is another strong union KAD (National Union of Women Workers) with more than 80,000 members.

During the 1990s, there were two other amalgamations, which failed to establish a form that could survive even in the short run. They broke apart before 1st January 2000 and all or part of the members joined either SiD or HK. The amalgamation in 1990 of four small unions (between 5,000 and 9,000 members) to form RBF (Union of Restaurant and Brewery Workers) failed when the brewery section left the amalgamation and joined SiD. GF (Print Union) was formed on 1st January 1994 by an amalgamation of four small unions, which each organised between 1,804 and 8,473 members. After a few years, the union ran into a dispute with HK concerning the operation of new technologies. GF was defeated in this dispute, and on 1st January 2000 GF was dissolved and its members joined a number of other unions, including HK and, in the case of workers in cardboard, SiD.

A total number of 27 unions have been involved in amalgamations during the period from 1970 to 2000. Thirteen LO-affiliated unions have disappeared, together with five unions affiliated to FTF. A total number of 438,000 union members have been affected by amalgamations, more than 193,000 (44 per cent) of whom were involved in the formation of FOA. This single amalgamation exaggerates the extent of amalgamations. It is relatively weak unions that have amalgamated. Typically, the outcome has not been very radical or far-reaching.

Acquisitions over the Past Fifty Years

After 1950, larger unions acquired a total of 48 unions. The acquired unions organised a total of 91,400 members, with an average membership of 1,904. The membership size of the acquired unions varied from 16 to 17,229 members. During the first four decades from 1950 to 1990, 44 small unions were acquired. The main reason underlying these acquisitions was changes in the unemployment insurance legislation. A change introduced during the late 1960s stipulated that, in order to obtain state recognition, and thus public support for an unemployment insurance fund, a minimum membership of 1,000 was required. This threshold was subsequently raised to 5,000 by legislation enacted in 1979, albeit operative only from 1985.

The pattern of acquisition of small unions changed in the 1990s. Only four LO-affiliated unions, with an average size of 9,500 members, were acquired. Relatively large unions were acquired, including DBTF (Union of Clothing and Textiles Workers), with over 17,000 members, and MF (Union of Bricklayers), with more than 13,000 members. The latter became part of the building and construction group within SiD. Two factors contributed to this development. The first was professionalisation, which occurred from the end of the 1970s. The secretariats of the unions became much larger with academically trained consultants and a range of support departments. This was deemed necessary to safeguard the interests of the members. The second factor was the decentralisation of the collective bargaining system. To illustrate, about 85 per cent of all employees coming within the sphere of DA/LO are now covered by collective agreements, integral to which are flexible systems where wages are negotiated at the individual enterprises. The handling of a decentralised bargaining system places a heavy burden on unions, many of which find it increasingly difficult to meet expectations.

Union Mergers in FTF, AC and LH

From 1952, the starting point of FTF, until the end of the 1960s, FTF grew rapidly as many new affiliates joined. Table 4.7 shows that throughout its history FTF has been characterised by large numbers of small affiliated unions. The vast majority of FTF unions organised less than 1,000 members in 1960 and, although their share declined, they still accounted for nearly two thirds of affiliates in 2000. Although the average size of FTF unions increased fourfold between 1960 and 2000, their average size decreased relative to that of LO-affiliated unions. The larger LO-affiliated unions were, and are, significantly larger than their FTF counterparts. In 1960, the two largest FTF unions were DSR (Union of Danish Nurses) and DLF (Union of Danish Teachers), with 30,000 and 19,000 members respectively. In LO, SiD and Metal organised 240,000 and 88,000 members. By 2000, DSR and DLF had switched places and had 52,000 and 60,000 members respectively, whereas HK had 374,000 members and SiD 315,000 members. In 1960, CR_5 of FTF was 55 per cent. This grew to 61 per cent in 2000. In LO, the CR_5 was 64 per cent in 1960 and 76 per cent in 2000.

FTF is also characterised by the presence of public sector cartels. In 1960 both the Joint Council, comprising 50 mainly small unions, and CO II (State Public Servants Trade Union – Central Organisation II) comprising 32 mainly small unions in the civil services, still formed part of FTF. After 1970, only CO II remained.

Table 4.7: Structural Development of FTF, 1950-2000

	Number of unions	Total membership	Average size of FTF unions	Average size of LO unions
1950	(101)	(80,000)	(792)	9,377
1960	125	112,221	898	11,418
1970	167	156,101	935	16,000
1980	133	277,374	2,086	31,239
1990	100	324,609	3,246	47,432
2000	104	350,255	3,371	66,306

Sources: Reports of FTF, Statistical Yearbook. FTF was not formally established until in 1952. The figures for 1950 are thus an estimate, which indicates the member organisations existing before the formation of FTF.

Acquisitions and Amalgamations in FTF

Although the total number of union mergers is large, they do not involve many members, especially the acquisitions. The merger process in FTF has primarily involved the acquisition of small unions, but this process has not, measured by numbers of members involved, been comprehensive. As Table 4.8 shows, some of the acquired unions had a membership of less than ten. Amalgamations have been larger, but one specific amalgamation skews the results. This was the amalgamation of three unions in the finance sector to form FF (Financial Services Union) in 1992. The post-merger FF organised more than 50,000 members and thus accounted for half of the members involved in amalgamations over the past fifty years. This merger also resulted from changes in the collective bargaining system. A change in the structure of the finance industry, involving the merging of banks and savings banks, removed the basis for independent unions and collective agreements in these two areas. The remaining seventeen amalgamations resulted in post-merger unions with an average size of 3,607 members.

If we examine the timing of this merger process, it is conspicuous that almost nothing happened up to 1970. Only minor adjustments took place and, as can be seen from Table 4.7, the number of affiliated unions increased until the late 1960s. A significant wave of mergers took place during the 1970s. Of the 43 mergers occurring during this period, 24 took place in 1970. That was the year following the introduction of the Public Servants' Act, which was an attempt to adapt the state bargaining system for public servants to a new era in which the recruitment of employees covered by collective agreements had become more common. It was the professional unions for occupations, such as doctors, lawyers, engineers and economists, which assumed the task of organising these "academic staff". This meant that many small unions for academic staff in the Joint Council were squeezed. A merger between the Joint Council and the other unions, which had formed the AS, was thus placed on the agenda.

Table 4.8: Union Mergers in FTF, 1950-2000

	Number of unions	Total number of members	Average union size	Size range	Unions formed by amalgamation
1950-1959					
Acquisitions	9	1,819	202	9-491	
1960-1969					
Acquisitions	11	3,319	302	14-1,346	
Amalgamations	2	2,989		1,404-1,585	1
1970-1979					
Acquisitions	28	4,262	152	5-879	
Amalgamations	19	9,139	485	10-2,456	4
1980-1989					
Acquisitions	19	1,232	65	9-184	
Amalgamations	33	25,836	783	10-ca.4,000	8
1990-1999					
Acquisitions	12	5,448	454	6-3,110	
Amalgamations	16[1]	73,863	4,942	220-35,576	5
Total 1950-1999					
Acquisitions	79	16,080	204	5-3,110	
Amalgamations	70[2]	111,881	1,598	10-35,576	18

[1] Only 5 were members of FTF. They all left FTF. The new union became member of LO.

[2] Only 69 FTF-unions.

Sources: Reports of FTF, Statistical Yearbook, CO II reports.

The new confederation, AC, did not become a reality until 1972, but the unions of the Joint Council had started the adaptation process during the preceding years. It was in connection with this process that no fewer than twenty-three unions of the Joint Council were acquired on 1st January 1970. For our purposes, they are counted as acquisitions taking place in FTF of which the Joint Council was still a member. With the formation of AC, academic staff had in reality left FTF and, therefore, we have recorded the next wave of acquisitions in which the remaining unions of the Joint Council were acquired as part of the AC merger process.

After this merger wave, during which one of the FTF cartels disappeared and was resurrected in the form of a new confederation, amalgamation activity again assumed modest dimensions. During the 1980s the merger process resumed, but was concentrated into a single year,

1988. That was the year when CO II reduced its member unions from 48 to 26. Twenty-two unions disappeared through amalgamation or acquisition.[6] The background to this process was the attempts by the confederation to adapt to a new bargaining system not only for public servants but also for agreement-covered employees. This did not change the fact that the shift in the bargaining system weakened CO II. Thus CO II remained primarily a cartel of public servants.

An opposite development affected the other large cartel with members in the traditional civil services CO I (State Public Servants Trade Union – Central Organisation I), which from the beginning was closely tied to LO. CO I succeeded, through amalgamation with larger groups of agreement-covered employees, in forming a new strong cartel, StK (Association of Danish State Employees Organisations). StK was recognised as an official cartel by the LO.

In summary, the merger process in FTF has produced modest results: FTF still has more than 100 affiliated unions, about 20 per cent of which have less than 100 members, and almost 66 per cent of which have less than 1,000 members. In spite of the amalgamation to form FF, during the 1990s there has not been a significant change in the average size of the member unions, which increased only marginally to nearly 3,500 members.

Acquisitions and Amalgamations in AC

The structure of AC remained unchanged during the entire period from its establishment on 1st January 1972 to date. Only during the formation of AC was there a wide-ranging merger process, when more than fifty unions of academic public servants dissolved when their members joined craft- or profession-based unions. The most noteworthy feature since the establishment period is the amalgamation in the 1990s of two unions of engineers, which were already the two largest affiliates of AC.

The number of members increased threefold over the thirty years of AC's existence. Concurrently, the average size of the member unions also increased significantly. Before the establishment of AC, unions of academic staff were significantly smaller than FTF unions. After the small unions of the Joint Council had merged with the professional

---

[6]   To illustrate the nature of these mergers: unions were formed for public servants in the Ministry of Labour and the Ministry of Ecclesiastical Affairs which involved, respectively, 5 unions (with a total of 436 members) and 3 unions (with a total of 615 members). A union was also formed from 5 unions of public servants in the national defence. From the outset this union had nearly 3,000 members.

unions, the average size of the affiliates of AC increased six-fold and AC unions became larger than the FTF affiliates. It is also noteworthy that the largest unions of FTF have considerably more members than the largest AC unions. With DLF, DSR, FF and BUPL (Danish Federation of Early Childhood and Youth Education), FTF has four unions with more than 40,000 members. In AC, only IDA (Union of Danish Engineers), is at a similar level, with just under 40,000 members, while DJØF (Danish Association of Lawyers and Economists) and DM (Danish Association of Masters and PhDs) have around 20,000 members.

Table 4.9: Development in the Structure of AC, 1950-2000

	Number of unions	Total membership	Average size of AC unions	Average size of LO unions	Average size of FTF unions
1970	(73)	(40,000)	(548)	16,000	935
1980	19	67,615	3,559	31,239	2,086
1990	21	102,597	4,886	47,432	3,246
2000	22	150,060	7,146	66,306	3,371

Sources: Reports of AC, Statistical Yearbook. AC was not formally established until 1972. The figures from 1970 indicate the number of organisations which existed in 1970 and which together joined AC, i.e. the organisations which were then members of the Joint Council and AS.

The main trend in the merger process in AC is illustrated in Table 4.10. Not all the union mergers between 1970 and 1979 can be attributed to the acquisition of the small unions from the Joint Council. The most important exception was the amalgamation of *Juristforbundet* (Association of Lawyers) and *Økonomforbundet* (Association of Economists) to form DJØF. At the time, the new union had nearly 5,000 members. This amalgamation was of decisive importance for AC. It united two main academic groups in the public sector and removed many of the problems arising from the new professionally-based structure that followed educational lines, which meant that employees at the same workplace were split between several unions.

The issue of large numbers of small unions is also addressed by allowing AC to negotiate on behalf of member unions. Prior to each round of negotiations, a negotiation agreement is concluded among the member unions. In practice, AC then negotiates the so-called general demands, while concurrent negotiations take place on specific demands at the level of the affiliated unions. The implementation of the finalised agreements also involves the affiliated unions.

Table 4.10: Union Mergers in AC, 1970-2000

	Number of unions	Total number of members	Average union size	Size range	Unions formed by amalgamation
1970-1979					
Acquisitions	61	7,479	123	5-879	
Amalgamations	6	6,961	1,160	90-ca.2,500	2
1980-1989					
Amalgamations	2	1,006[1]		165-307	1
1990-1999					
Acquisitions	1	50	50	50	
Amalgamations	2	35,978		16,208-18,754	1
Total 1950-1999					
Acquisitions	62	7,529	121	5-879	
Amalgamations	10	43,945	4,395	90-18,754	4

[1] Includes membership of FTF unions that were engaged in the amalgamation.

Sources: Reports of AC, reports of FTF, Statistical Yearbook.

In the private sector, AC has no bargaining rights. The norm is individual agreements concluded at enterprise level. It has thus been an important goal for AC unions to break down employers' opposition. The largest academic group in the private sector is the engineers. Two large unions for engineers amalgamated in the 1990s to form IDA, in an attempt to strengthen their position and to have collective bargaining introduced.

A total of five unions have affiliated to AC, explaining the rise from 19 to 22 affiliates over the past decades. Special mention should be made of the affiliation of *Civiløkonomforeningen* (Union of Bachelors of Economics) in 1984, *Bibliotekarforbundet* (Union of Danish Librarians) in 1992, and *Erhvervssprogligt Forbund* (Danish Association of Business Language Graduates) in 1994. Together, these recent affiliates had more than 20,000 members in 2000, which corresponded to 14 per cent of the total membership of AC.

Confederation of Managerial and Executive Staff

The fourth confederation, which primarily organises intermediate-level managers in the private sector, underwent a major organisational change during the 1990s. The September Compromise in 1899 between LO and DA established that work managers, including supervisors and foremen, could not be organised in the same unions as other employees. This is why various unions were formed for intermediate-level managers. These later federated in the FR (Joint Representation of Work

Supervisors and Organisations of Technical Employees). In 1950 there were eight unions in this loose federation.

Some mergers took place, which reduced the number of member unions in FR to five by the end of the 1980s. But it was still a divided organisation. The largest union, FAD (Association of Supervisors in Denmark), with about 40,000 members, had remained apart from FR for more than ten years and did not rejoin it until January 1987. This can be seen as the starting point of a process that transformed FR into a confederation and created a unitary organisation for supervisors and managers in the private sector. The decisive step was taken on 1st January 1992 when the two largest member unions, FAD and *Foreningen af Værkstedsfunktionærer* (Association of Employees in Workshops) amalgamated to form LH (Organisation for Managerial and Executive Staff in Denmark). At the outset, LH had just over 63,000 members. FR was thus reduced to a total number of three affiliates including, in addition to LH, *Maskinmestrenes Forening* (Association of Master Engineers) and *Dansk Formands Forening* (Association of Foremen in Denmark). These two other unions had a combined membership of 7,000, so LH had a completely dominant position. It has not been possible to take the decisive step to merge these three unions, but FR has been dissolved and common interests handled by LH, which thus represents managers within the polity.

Conclusion

Five inter-linked factors have had a decisive influence on the development of trade union structure in Denmark and on the role of the merger process in this development.

First, technological development and associated shifts in the structure of the labour market were very dramatic during the second half of the twentieth century. Recently the most characteristic change has been strong growth in the services sector, not least in the public sector. These changes have exerted considerable pressure on traditional structures based on occupation in the private sector and a multitude of divisions in the public sector. Although changes have been implemented and new confederations formed, the basic structure of Danish trade unionism has nevertheless proved surprisingly resistant. The most important institutions that have ensured the survival of existing unions are the cartels, which have been able to undertake negotiations.

The second important influence on the structure of the trade union movement is the political development and legislative change. Legislative initiatives taken in the light of technological and structural developments have directly and indirectly promoted structural change. More generally, the continued development of the welfare state has led to shifts in union structure and, specifically, changes in unemployment insurance legislation accelerated the merger process. No other single factor has had a more far-reaching influence. This influence applies mainly to the development of the structure of LO. This influence was not as strong within FTF and AC because these confederations established cross-sectoral unemployment insurance funds as an exception within the legislation, which stipulates that unemployment insurance funds follow occupational lines.

A third factor arises from the professional ideologies and attitudes that are held by union members. During the establishment of Danish trade unionism at the turn of the twentieth century and immediately after World War II, proposals in favour of industrial unions were tabled in response to a perceived strengthening of a common sense of solidarity. But craft- and professional-based attitudes have continued to hold sway and have acted as a barrier against mergers, which are seen as a threat to professional identities.

A further effective barrier against more fundamental structural change is the fourth influential factor: the conservative tendency of complex social organisations and institutions. At one level, this tendency is intimately connected with the third factor. Established attitudes and values make it difficult to change, and labour market specialisation and segmentation consolidate professional-based ideologies rather than solidaristic ideologies. This conservative tendency is thus an expression of an institutionalisation of power and resources. Established administrative and political apparatuses create their own inertia, merely as a result of the fact that structural changes will threaten the positions of a number of persons and groups.

The fifth decisive influence is the collective bargaining system. As long as this bargaining system has functioned, the pressure for changes has been too weak to overcome internal resistance to change. The case of Denmark also shows that change in the collective bargaining system will also influence union structure. This was evident in the public sector in connection with the shift in the relationship between recruitment as public servants and agreement-covered employees. The same trend was apparent in the private sector towards the end of 1980s when the member organisations of DA changed their strategy and decentralised bargaining to enterprise level, albeit within a structure of framework agreements. This organised decentralisation constituted the start of a radical change of the structure of the employers' side. These changes also influenced debate within the LO and led to a fresh round of structural change.

Typical of Danish trade union structural development, the most important step was not an amalgamation, but expansion of the close co-operation that had been established between, amongst others, Metal and SiD in the bargaining cartel within the iron industry, CO-Metal (Central Organisation of Metal Workers in Denmark). Since the 1940s CO-Metal comprised all the blue-collar unions within the iron industry. With the unifying of all industry employers during 1993 in the form of DI (Confederation of Danish Industries), it was necessary to expand CO-Metal so that it correspondingly covered the entire industrial sector. This happened with the reform of CO-Metal to CO-industri (Central Organisation of Industrial Employees in Denmark). CO-industri covers both blue- and white-collar workers, with the exception of academic staff. Thus, the trade union movement within industry, the key bargaining sector, matched the extensive merging and acquisition process towards large sectoral organisations that had taken place amongst the employers. Yet the question remains whether, in the long run, cartel co-operation will be sufficient. The employers are establishing sector-side organisations that form a strong and coherent opposition to the weaker cartels, which still consist of independent trade unions. In the long run, therefore, the trade union movement can be weakened by the fact that it has not been able to break through the barriers that prevent mergers.

List of Abbreviations

AC	Akademikernes Centralorganisation (Danish Confederation of Professional Associations)
AS	Akademikernes Samarbejdsudvalg (Co-operation Committee of Academics)
BUPL	Forbundet for pædagoger og klubfolk (Danish Federation of Early Childhood and Youth Education)
CFU	Centralorganisationernes Fællesudvalg (Danish Central Federation of State Employees)
CO I	Statstjenestemændenes Centralorganisation I (State Public Servants Trade Union Central Organisation I)
CO II	Statstjenestemændenes Centralorganisation II (State Public Servants Trade Union Central Organisation II)
CO-industri	Centralorganisationen af industriansatte (Central Organisation of Industrial Employees)
CO-Metal	Centralorganisationen af Metalarbejdere (Central Organisation of Metal Workers)
DA	Dansk Arbejdsgiverforening (Danish Employers' Confederation)

DBTF	Dansk Beklædnings- og Textilarbjderforbund (Union of Clothing Industry and Textile Workers)
DJØF	Danmarks Jurist- og Økonomforbund (Danish Lawyers' and Economists' Association)
DKA	Dansk Kommunalarbejderforbund (National Union of Municipal Workers)
DLF	Danmarks Lærerforening (Danish Teachers' Union)
DM	Dansk Magisterforening (Danish Association of Masters and PhDs)
DSF	De samvirkende Fagforbund (Federation of Danish Trade Unions)
DSR	Dansk Sygeplejeråd (Danish Nurses' Organisation)
FA	Finanssektorens Arbejdsgiverforening (Danish Employers' Association for the Financial Sector)
FAD	Foreningen af Arbejdsledere i Danmark (Association of Supervisors in Denmark)
FF	Finansforbundet (Financial Services' Union)
FOA	Forbundet af Offentligt Ansatte (Danish Trade Union of Public Employees)
FR	Fællesrepræsentation for danske Arbejdsledere og Tekniske Funktionærforeninger (Joint Representation of Organisations of Work Supervisors and Technical Employees)
FTF	Funktionærernes og Tjenestemændenes Fællesråd (Confederation of Salaried Employees and Civil Servants in Denmark)
GF	Grafisk Forbund (Graphic Union)
HAF	Husligt Arbejderforbund (National Union of Cleaners and Domestic Workers)
HK	Handels- og Kontorfunktionærernes Forbund (Union of Commercial and Clerical Employees in Denmark)
Joint Council	Danske Statsembedsmænds Samråd (Joint Council of Public Servants in the State Sector)
IDA	Ingeniørforbundet i Danmark (Union of Danish Engineers)
KAD	Kvindeligt Arbejderforbund i Danmark (National Union of Women Workers)
KTO	Kommunale Tjenestemænd og Overenskomstansatt (Association of Local Government Employees' Organisations)
KTU	Kommunale Tjenestemænds Udvalg (Committee of Public Servants in the Municipal Sector)

LH	Ledernes Hovedorganisation (Confederation of Managerial and Executive Staff in Denmark)
LO	Landsorganisationen i Danmark (Danish Confederation of Trade Unions)
Metal	Dansk Metalarbejderforbund (National Union of Metal-workers)
MF	Murerforbundet (Union of Bricklayers)
NNF	Nærings- og Nydelsesmiddelarbejder forbundet (National Union of Food and Beverage Workers)
RBF	Restaurations- og Bryggeriforbundet (Union of Restaurant and Brewery Workers)
SALA	Sammenslutningen af Landbrugets Arbejdsgiverforeninger (Danish Confederation of Employers' Associations in Agriculture)
SD	Socialdemokratiet (Social Democratic Party)
SiD	Specialarbejderforbundet i Danmark (General Workers' Union in Denmark)
ST	Snedker- og Tørmrerforbundet (Union of Joiners and Carpenters)
StK	Statsansattes Kartel (Association of Danish State Employee Organisations)
TFU	StatsTjenestemændenes Fællesudvalg (Danish Central Federation of Public and Civil Servants)
TIB	Træ, Industri, Byg (Union of Joiners, Carpenters and Wood Industry Workers)
TKF	Telekommunikationsforbundet (Union of Danish Telecommunications Workers)

Towards a New Form
of German Trade Unionism?

Jeremy WADDINGTON and Jürgen HOFFMANN

Throughout the 1990s calls for reform of German trade union struc-ture came from far and wide. From within, Hermann Rappe, the then Chair of IG CPK (Chemical, Paper and Ceramic Workers' Union), advocated the formation by mergers of a number of multi-industry unions of sufficient, yet roughly equal, size to ensure the delivery of a wider range of services to members (Rappe, 1992). Central to Rappe's approach was the limited extension of union recruitment bases to incorporate contiguous industries, an assessment that small unions were no longer viable as a means to provide services to members and a belief that mergers among affiliated unions would stimulate reform of the DGB (German Trade Union Confederation). A competing programme of reform was advocated from within a group of public sector unions. Instead of mergers, this programme was based on the establishment of a federation of unions, within which each union could maintain its inde-pendence and share services. This programme owed much to the cartels of unions, which characterise developments in Nordic countries (see Chapters 4, 7 and 9). It was also supported from within the DGB, as the role of the DGB was secure as a provider of services to affiliated unions. From outside the trade union movement, the research institute of the BDA (Confederation of German Employers' Associations) also joined the fray and recommended restructuring around seven multi-industry unions, each of which should represent contiguous trades or industries (Niedenhoff and Wilke, 1991).

This chapter examines why these calls for reform were made, and charts their impact on the German trade union merger process in the context of the historical development of the German trade union move-ment. It argues that defensive adjustments to adverse membership and financial developments, coming to a head through the problems arising from the unification process after 1990, and the mismatch between union structure and industrial structure were the primary reasons for merger activity. Two implications arising from the merger process for the future development of German trade unionism are also assessed: the future of the DGB, and the possibilities for extending recruitment, participation and organisation into hitherto unorganised sectors of the economy by post-merger unions. We argue that if the merger process is to facilitate the extension of union organisation, more wide-ranging internal reforms are necessary.

This chapter addresses these issues in five sections. The first section briefly reviews the history of industrial organisation among German trade unions. The second section identifies the characteristics of union structure between 1949 and 1989. The third section charts the merger process among German trade unions, while the fourth section isolates the factors that have promoted the merger process. The final section examines the implications of the merger process in terms of inter-union relations and prospects for recruitment and participation. From the outset, it should be noted that German industrial relations legislation provides no specific means of regulating trade union mergers. In consequence, a variety of different methods have been applied, including the use company mergers' legislation (for details, Koopmann, 2000; Waddington *et al.*, 2003)

German Industrial Unionism in Historical Context

Both the Christian and liberal tendencies within the German trade union movement were initially organised in craft or occupational unions. All trade unions were repressed between 1878 and 1890 under the Bismarckian *Sozialistengesetz* (Anti-Socialist Law). The *Sozialistenesetz* was repealed in 1890 and later in the same year, following a wave of strikes that had commenced in 1889, the *Generalkommission der Freien Gewerkschaften Deutschlands* (General Commission of Free German Trade Unions) was established. At the Halberstadt Congress of 1890, there was an overwhelming majority in favour of strong centralised unions as the means to oppose the authoritarian state and the interests of capital. The Congress also made the *Beruf* (occupation) the decisive criteria for trade union organisation and emphasised the role of craft unions. Simultaneously, delegates recommended that cartels of craft unions should be established within industries and did not exclude the possibility of organising industrial unions. Moreover, in a response to the authoritarian state led by Bismarck, the Congress rejected local and direct democratic forms of organisation (*Lokalisten*) in favour of centralised organisational principles, hence underpinning the bureaucratic and authoritarian organisational form. Only the metalworkers and woodworkers organised industrial federations, in part, reflecting the expansion of factory work and the division of labour in these industries.

The industrial union, however, became more dominant. On the eve of World War I seven industrial unions existed: in metal, wood, construction, textiles, transport and mining industries and the general factory workers federation, which organised skilled and unskilled workers in the chemicals, rubber, margarine and coffee industries. These industrial unions organised more than two-thirds of all union members. In addition, there were 39 other unions, the majority of which were craft unions (Tenfelde *et al.*, 1987: 180-185; 228).

After World War I, German trade union structure remained fairly stable. The principle of industrial unionism was endorsed by delegates at the 1923 Congress of the renamed ADGB (All German Trade Union Confederation) held at Essen. Although there was widespread acceptance of the principle of industrial unionism, the number of unions in 1923 was forty-four, even though there had been many amalgamations and acquisitions, together with several union formations. More than 50 per cent of membership of the free trade union movement was organised in the five largest unions of metal, factory, textile, transport and agricultural workers (Tenfelde *et al.*, 1987: 310). In 1930 thirty-one unions were affiliated to the ADGB. In addition, rival communist and Christian union confederations, together with several independent union federations of public and civil servants that advocated a nationalist political position, competed for membership with the ADGB.

The lessons learned by the German trade union leaders from the period of Nazism, resistance and exile was that strong, top-down, centralised and politically unified unions (*zentralistische Einheits-gewerkschaften*) were required to challenge capitalists, the majority of whom had supported the Nazis, and the state. The view of the American and British officers responsible for the establishment of new unions was quite the opposite. They wanted to establish bottom-up trade unions, thus implicitly favouring the British model of craft unionism (Fichter, 1990: 35ff.). The outcome of this struggle was not a single model, but seventeen strong and centralised unions, comprising industrial, craft and company unions.

Features of German Trade Union Structure

The formation of the DGB in 1949 with sixteen affiliated unions laid down the basic trade union structure. The only significant change to this initial structure was the affiliation of the GdP (Union for Police Officers) in 1977-78. The seventeen unions affiliated to the DGB from 1978 maintained a wide range of recruitment bases. The GdP and the GEW

(Education and Science Union) are essentially occupational unions, which make little attempt to recruit support and ancillary workers in policing and education. Similarly, ÖTV (Public Services, Transport and Traffic Sectors Union) organised on a sectoral basis, rather than within a single industry. A further variant is represented by the DPG (Postal Workers' Union) and the GdED (Railway Workers' Union) which were, in practice, company unions. All unions affiliated to the DGB, however, subscribe to the principle of 'one plant-one union', the outcome of which was that disputes between unions for members were usually conducted in terms of gaining access to sites rather than within the plant. This principle was also contravened, however, as the occupational unions do not organise ancillary workers to policing and teaching, such as caretakers.

The DAG (Union of Salaried Employees) and the DBB (Union of Civil Servants) remained apart from the DGB. The DAG organised primarily white-collar workers across a range of industries[1] whereas the DBB organises civil servants. More white-collar workers and civil servants are organised by DGB-affiliated unions than by either the DAG or the DBB. Attempts by the DAG to affiliate to the DGB in 1949 and during the early 1970s were rejected on the grounds that it operated in contravention of the principle of industrial unionism.

Christian (primarily catholic) unions affiliate to the CGB (Christian Trade Union Confederation), which broke away from the DGB in 1956. Compared to the DGB, this is a small confederation (306,000 members in 2001) and does not figure in the examination that follows. A relatively large number of independent professional associations (*Berufsverbände*) also exist, with the object of furthering the interests of specific professions. These associations do not claim trade union status, although they have been involved in trade union restructuring.

The adoption of the one plant-one union principle contributed to the stability of the German trade union movement between 1949 and 1989. Also contributing to this stability was the structure of capitalism in Germany, which, since the 1890s, was a model of an "organised" or "co-ordinated" capitalism with strong and well-organised or cartelised companies and capitalist factions. Moreover, German "corporatism", which was embedded in the structure and practices of capital, demanded strong and centralised unions able to commit membership to the outcomes of bargaining. This model was further stabilised by the political

---

[1] The DAG claims members among the following occupations and industries: managers, commercial employees, technicians, mining, engineering, banking and insurance, public services, and media.

system of regulating labour relations and the successes achieved through the quasi-fordist production regime after 1950.

Since 1989 this structure has been profoundly reformed. The number of unions affiliated to the DGB fell from 17 in 1988 to 8 by 2001 and the DAG became part of a trade union affiliated to the DGB. Trade union mergers have also led, in practice, to a further movement away from the principle of industrial organisation towards sectoral orga- nisation.

Charting the Pattern of Merger Activity

This section charts the merger process since 1989. It demonstrates that mergers have not followed any single specific industrial or political 'logic', whereby mergers involve only unions that organise contiguous industries or advocate a similar political programme. Instead, a wide range of combinations is in evidence, as unions adjust to changing circumstances and attempt to secure or retain political influence. The merger process is 'mapped' in Figure 1.5.

The period of stability in German trade union structure was broken by the merger to form IG Medien (Media Workers' Union) in 1989. The DGB-affiliated unions involved in this formation were the craft-oriented IG Drupa (Printing and Paper Workers) and GK (Artists' Union), which operated as a cartel after 1985. Traditionally, but especially from the mid-1970s, IG Drupa had adopted a militant stance against employers as it was threatened by the imminent loss of traditional typesetting jobs due to new computer-aided technologies. This was marked by large-scale strikes from 1976 onwards, initially concerning demarcation between printers and journalists in the operation of new technology, and latterly in pursuit of the 35-hour working week. The cost to the union of these strikes, coupled to concurrent membership decline, resulted in a parlous financial position. At the time of the merger the GK was the smallest of the DGB affiliates, with less than 30,000 members, the majority of whom were not artists, but crafts and auxiliary workers. The merger was presented as furthering the principle of industrial unionism as it unified contiguous trades. This position was strengthened by the involvement in the merger of several smaller *Berufsverbände* (professional associ- ations), which were not affiliated to the DGB. Prominent among these were the DJU (German Journalists' Union), VS (Writers' Association) and the RFFU (Radio, Television and Film Union). These organisations maintained loose connections with IG Drupa or GK before the merger. Their involvement in the merger thus formalised such arrangements and brought these organisations within the constitutional authority of the new union.[2] However, the DJV (German Journalists' Association), another organisation that was not affiliated to the DGB, remained independent of IG Medien, thus preventing the unification of journalists' organisations.

Three strands of the merger process after 1989 involve the consolidation of union organisation around the three largest private sector unions affiliated to the DGB: namely, IG CPK, IG BSE (Construction Workers' Union) and IG Metall (Engineering Workers' Union). A fourth strand of the merger process involved five unions that represented members in both the public and private sectors. Examining these four strands reveals the extent of the shift in the character of union organisation in Germany.

IG CPK was at the core of the first strand of merger activity in the private sector, much prompted by the initiative of Hermann Rappe. IG CPK acquired the small GL (Leatherworkers' Union) in 1996-1997 and, in a more wide-ranging amalgamation, combined with IG BE (Mining and Energy Union). At the time of its acquisition the GL was the smallest affiliated union of the DGB and was unable to support its membership. The GL had relied heavily on support services provided by the DGB prior to the merger, such as the training of *Betriebsratmitglieder* (works councillors) and the provision of legal services. Furthermore, the leather industry was contracting under the pressure of international competition, thus resulting in a declining number of potential members. The GL was also the only affiliate of the DGB that failed to secure significant additional members after unification (see Table 5.1).

The IG BE was also locked into a declining industrial recruitment base with little opportunity to break out. The IG BE was a membership beneficiary from unification, albeit only for the short-term. In attempting to abandon the straitjacket of a mining recruitment base, IG BE encountered strong opposition from ÖTV in the recruitment of energy workers in the new *Länder*. The IG CPK supported IG BE in its opposition to ÖTV within the DGB. This support, coupled to the moderate alignment of both unions within the DGB and their advocacy of 'social partnership' based approaches to industrial relations, was the basis on which merger negotiations were built. The long-term future of the IG BE, however, was open to question due to the decline of the mining industry.

---

[2] The sections of the *Verband der Schriftsteller* (VS) with communist affiliation encouraged the entire association to join in the merger to form IG Medien. However, a substantial proportion of the VS refused to take part in the merger and established another professional association with the intention of furthering professional interests, which were viewed as differing from trade union interests.

A large and growing proportion of its membership comprised retired mineworkers, which also suggests a long-term diminution of influence and income from membership contributions. More important to the merger was the prospect of establishing a moderate influence to counterbalance that of the left-led IG Metall within inter-union bargaining institutions. In order to promote such a development, IG CPK had attempted to build an alliance with IG BSE in 1991, with the objective of moving from the closer working agreement signed by the two unions towards a merger (IRS, 1992). Although this initiative went into abeyance, it seems likely that it may be resuscitated in the light of further membership decline and the acquisitions made later by IG Metall.

As the two unions were organised on different principles, the merger process involving IG CPK and IG BE is of special relevance. The IG CPK was based on the industry, especially in the larger chemicals companies, where works councils were very influential on trade union politics. Workplace organisation in the chemicals industry was strengthened by the *Vertrauensleutekörper* (representatives' committees) of IG CPK. In contrast, the IG BE was one of the few German unions organised on a local or district basis. Both principles still exist in parallel in the structure of the post-merger IG BCE.

The second strand of private sector merger activity centred on IG BSE. Bruno Köbele, the then Chair of IG BSE had endorsed the views towards mergers of Hermann Rappe during the early 1990s, but had been unable to develop the closer working arrangements between IG BSE and IG CPK into a merger. The membership of the GGLF (Horticulture, Agriculture and Forestry Workers) had remained at less than 50,000 before unification and, after the initial post-unification surge, had fallen away steeply. The wide geographical distribution of the agriculture and forestry industries, coupled to the small average size of workplaces and the anti-union culture of many rural communities, militated against dense union organisation. The relatively small size of the GGLF also limited the range of services available to members. The 'prize' from the merger for the IG BSE was the opportunity to incorporate the word '*Umwelt*' (environment) in the title of the post-merger union and, hence, claim recruitment preference in an expanding area of the economy. Earlier attempts to change the name of the IG BSE and adopt *Umwelt* had met with fierce resistance from IG Metall, IG CPK and ÖTV, which also claimed recruitment access in the area. This opposition resulted in a decision within the DGB to reject the proposed name change. The name change from the IG BSE to IG BAU (Construction, Agriculture and Environment Union) was thus not the result of an amalgamation of equal parties, but the preference to situate the post-merger union in an area of potential membership growth. In practice, IG BSE acquired the GGLF, which was the minor party in the merger.

Table 5.1: Trade Union Membership, 1975-2001

	1975	1980	1985	1990	1991[1]	1992	1994	1998	2001
IG Bau-Steine-Erden	509,442	533,054	507,528	462,751	776,781	695,712	652,964		
Gew. Gartenbau, Land und Forstwirtschaft	39,309	42,196	42,450	44,054	134,980	120,190	90,281		
IG Bauen-Agrar-Umwelt								614,500	510,000
IG Bergbau und Energie	378,369	367,718	356,706	322,820	506,640	457,239	390,000		
IG Chemie-Papier-Keramik	644,271	660,973	649,569	675,949	876,674	818,832	742,367		
Gew. Leder	56,458	55,689	48,725	42,615	41,718	31,890	25,043		
IG Bergbau, Chemie, Energie								955,734	862,000
IG Metall	2,556,184	2,622,267	2,553,041	2,726,705	3,624,380	3,394,282	2,995,738	2,752,226	2,710,000
Gew. Textil-Bekleidung	283,324	293,766	258,846	248,880	348,095	288,198	234,240		
Gew Holz und Kunststoff	132,054	157,142	144,653	152,731	239,472	204,763	179,678		
Gew. Nahrung, Genuss, Gaststätten	247,724	253,001	267,158	275,203	431,211	394,686	336,239	282,521	251,000
Gew. Erziehung und Wissenschaft	139,294	183,793	194,028	189,155	359,852	346,040	316,196	281,236	268,000
Gew. Der Eisenbahner Deutschlands	447,914	406,588	354,180	312,353	527,478	474,530	423,163	353,161	306,000
Gew. der Polizei		165,900	163,590	162,780	200,997	197,451	197,482	193,578	186,000
IG Druck und Papier	157,985	143,970	140,725						
Gew. Kunst	36,461	45,252	27,019						
IG Medien				184,720	244,774	236,306	215,155	184,656	
Gew. Öffentliche, Dienste, Transport und Verkehr	1,058,525	1,149,689	1,179,396	1,252,599	2,138,316	2,114,522	1,877,651	1,582,776	
Deutsche Post-gewerkschaft	419,585	450,201	460,626	478,913	611,969	611,244	546,906	474,094	
Gew. Handel, Banken und Versicherungen	257,123	351,328	371,228	404,695	737,075	629,727	546,270	471,333	
Deutsche Angestellten-Gewerkschaft	470,446	494,874	500,922	573,398	584,775	578,352	520,709	480,225	
Vereinte Dienstleistungsgewerk-schaft									2,806,000

[1] From 1991 data include membership from the former East Germany.
Sources: Quelle, Statistical Yearbook, DGB.

After 1949 IG Metall was the largest union in Germany. Mergers involving other unions threatened this position and prompted the union to consolidate by acquiring the GTB (Textile and Clothing Workers'

Union) and the GHK (Wood and Plastics Workers' Union) after 1998. By acquiring these unions IG Metall precluded their involvement in mergers with other competitor unions. The GTB organised in a contracting industry and had searched for merger partners since the late 1980s. Merger discussions with both IG CPK and NGG (Food and Restaurant Workers' Union) failed to produce a satisfactory merger agreement. Politically, IG CPK and NGG would have been a more 'natural' home for the GTB, as all three unions were aligned with the moderate wing of the DGB. Furthermore, the industrial linkages between the chemical and textile industries are wide-ranging, particularly in the area of artificial fibres. Both IG Metall and GTB, however, cited industrial linkages between the memberships following the announcement of their merger agreement. In particular, the links between textile workers engaged in the production of car seats, safety belts and automobile upholstery and the metal workers that assemble the cars were emphasised. While these may be contiguous processes, the two unions also acknowledged that separate collective agreements would be maintained after the merger. Working in contiguous processes thus does not necessarily lead to mutual support. Indeed, the maintenance of separate collective agreements suggests that logistic support rather than collective support is the likely outcome. The choice of IG Metall by the GTB was also influenced by the relatively high rates of pay paid to full-time officers in IG Metall, which would be available to officers from the GTB after the merger (Streeck and Visser, 1998: 26).

IG Metall acquired the GHK during 1999. Again, representatives of the unions stressed the industrial linkages between the two memberships. Both unions organised the car components industry, and in bus and coach manufacturing the same company was organised by different unions in different *Länder* (IRS, 1996). In addition, both unions were on the left-wing of the DGB. The capacity of the post-merger union to improve the quality of services available to members was cited by Gisbert Schlemmer, Chair of GHK. This reflected the internal difficulties faced by the GHK of a declining membership, 145,128 at the time of the merger from a peak of 239,472 in 1991, and rising internal costs mainly due to the unification process. In other words, acquisition by IG Metall represented a means of maintaining services for GHK members. Apart from the additional votes gained by IG Metall for deployment within DGB institutions, the direct benefits of the merger to metal workers remain unclear.

A further prompt to IG Metall to consolidate its position was the proposal to amalgamate five unions to form a union that would straddle the public and private sectors. In addition to four affiliates of the DGB, ÖTV, IG Medien, DPG and HBV (Banking and Commerce Union), the proposal included DAG. Each of the unions subsequently ratified the proposal and a new union was formed in 2001 with the title ver.di (Unified Services Union).

A complex series of alliances and pacts preceded the merger proposal. Two principal avenues of development can be identified. The first of these was set in motion during 1994 when the ÖTV and DAG announced a programme of co-operation at the centre of which was the co-ordination of wage demands. Prior to this announcement, ÖTV had pursued disproportionate increases for its lower-paid members, whereas DAG, with a significant number of higher paid members, had advocated across-the-board percentage increases. The two unions amended these initial positions in order to co-ordinate their bargaining strategy. Co-ordination of wage demands facilitated the development of a federation for bargaining purposes (*Tarifgemeinschaft*) of unions in the public sector, which included ÖTV and DAG, together with GdP, DPG and GdED.

Principal parties in the second avenue of development included the left-led IG Medien and HBV, together with the DPG. During October 1996 these unions announced a package of closer co-operation arrangements and invited other unions to participate. This invitation was made in the hope of attracting more financially stable unions into the alliance, as the three participating unions were not financially robust. NGG was interested in the alliance for a period and entered into preliminary merger discussions with the HBV before electing to maintain its independence. The telling development, however, was the interest, and subsequent involvement, of ÖTV and DAG. Initially the GEW and GdED also participated in the discussions. These two unions declined to further the merger negotiations that arose from the initial co-operation arrangements and dropped out of the formal merger proposal, thus leaving five unions organised into two distinct alliances.

Two alliances were thus key to the period of pre-merger positioning: the alliance involving two unions in the political centre, ÖTV and DAG, and the left-of-centre alliance comprising IG Medien, HBV and DPG. Integral to bringing these two alliances together were the positions taken by DAG and HBV. Consistent with the dominant political perspective within the union, DAG had entered into alliance with ÖTV. Membership competition with HBV, however, was fierce, particularly in finance and retail. The prospect of two unions emerging in services, one occupying the political centre and the other on the left-of-centre, would not have addressed this membership competition and, indeed, may have exacerbated it by infusing it with an overt political dimension. These points were acknowledged within HBV, but HBV was reluctant to merge with the ÖTV-DAG alliance because it would become a minority left-of-centre enclave within a politically central union. Representatives of HBV thus insisted that IG Medien and DPG should also be involved in the merger to bolster the left-of-centre within the proposed union. This position was accepted, albeit reluctantly in some quarters, within ÖTV and DAG. Hence, ver.di came into being as a union of five constituent parts.

The decision to form ver.di represented a significant shift away from the original federal restructuring arrangements suggested by ÖTV. Furthermore, the formation of ver.di introduced, on a much larger scale than earlier mergers, issues of post-merger integration. The organisational solution agreed by representatives of the five unions at the founding conference in Berlin in 2001 was a matrix organisation comprising thirteen *Fachbereiche* (sections), which are responsible for bargaining policies in specific trades or industries. The head office organisation is responsible for political policy and relationships, together with the establishment of bargaining principles. When differences occur, a *Gewerkschaftsrat* (union council) is elected by delegates at the Congress with the authority to act in a clearing capacity through an arbitration award. Each horizontal department comprises three vertical layers: county – *Bezirk*, regional – *Landesbezirk* – and central – *Bundesvorstand*. By these means it was anticipated that ver.di will be able to articulate the challenge of economic and social diversity.

In summary, the German trade union merger process has followed neither a political nor an industrial logic. Unions aligned with the moderate wing of the DGB have merged with their left-led counterparts and *vice-versa*. Similarly, some opportunities to merge unions of contiguous industries were rejected, as the terms of an alternative merger agreement were viewed as superior. Mergers, however, have resulted in a significant shift further away from industrial unionism. Indeed, three of the four unions that have not been involved in a merger are either occupational- (GdP and GEW) or company-based (GdED). Furthermore, the plans for restructuring formulated during the early 1990s were rejected in practice. The initiatives launched from within acquiring unions were often opportunistic, while the smaller unions were prepared to listen to merger offers from several unions before selecting a merger partner. An additional characteristic of the merger process is that it tends to be initiated at head-office level. Although members or delegates may be involved in pre-merger conferences and working parties and in ratifying the final agreement, there is no concerted pressure for merger exerted by members on union leaderships.

What Are the Reasons for Merger Activity?

The reasons that underpin trade union merger activity are wide in scope and irregular in their effect (Waddington, 1995; Chaison, 1996). In Germany three inter-linked factors were particularly influential and account for the clustering of merger activity within a relatively narrow time frame: membership change and shifts in the composition of potential membership; financial shortfalls, as a result of the financial involvement in eastern Germany after unification, and membership demands for improved services; and the effect of the erosion of industrial boundaries on a union structure where vertical organisation is prominent. The impact of these factors on the four merger strands are examined below.

The impact of membership change can be usefully differentiated into three discrete categories. The first of these is membership decline. Reference to Table 5.1 shows that the period since 1975 is divided into pre- and post-unification developments. Between 1975 and 1990 there was a mixed pattern of development among unions affiliated to the DGB, with eight unions sustaining membership losses and nine unions achieving membership growth. Both IG DruPa and GK, which merged before 1990, lost members. Immediately after unification all unions except the GL increased members as large numbers of workers from the new *Länder* transferred allegiance to unions based in the west. Membership peaked in 1991 for most unions and fell sharply thereafter. With the exception of the GdP, all unions lost a substantial number of members after 1991. Thus, for some unions membership loss was a long-term phenomenon stretching back beyond 1975, although interrupted by the sharp increase associated with unification, whereas for other unions decline was relatively short-term and was linked directly with members lost from the new *Länder*.

A second, and long-term issue, related to membership change is the changing composition of the German labour force, which shifted away from primary industries and manufacturing towards private sector services. Within the context of overall economic growth between 1957 and 1994, employment in agriculture, forestry and fishing and in energy, water and mining declined markedly. Furthermore, the rate of decline in manufacturing accelerated during the 1990s. In other words, where union organisation was concentrated, employment declined. The impact of the decline of specific industries is particularly hard-felt where unions adhere to the principle of industrial unionism. For example, it was not possible for GGLF, GTB or GL to extend their recruitment bases into expanding areas of employment, yet the contraction of employment within these recruitment bases prevented these unions from sustaining sufficient members to retain their independence. Similarly, the efforts of IG BE to extend recruitment activities into the energy sector met with fierce resistance and thus limited opportunities to move into an area of large potential membership. Another issue that should be mentioned in this context is the process of 'tertiarisation'. This parallels the process of modernisation of society and implies the erosion of traditional socio-cultural milieus where the culture of industrial working class was pre-served (Vester *et al.*, 1993). Tertiarisation thus weakens the capacity of unions to recruit new members using traditional methods. Furthermore, the pluralisation of society means that the near automatic integration of young workers into the culture and organisation of the industrial work-force has diminished.

A third influence on the merger process arising from membership change is relative union size. The impact of changing union size is accentuated by the constitution of the DGB, which confers voting rights to affiliated unions on the basis of membership size. IG Metall, for example, has maintained a pre-eminent position within the DGB on the basis of its membership size (Markovits, 1986). The formation of ver.di has put greater pressure on the unions in manufacturing on at least two counts. First, in the short-term ver.di will organise 35.5 per cent of the membership of the DGB compared to 34.3 per cent in IG Metall and 10.9 per cent in IG BCE (based on 2001 data, see Table 5.1). Second, the potential membership of ver.di has grown over recent years, a pat-tern that is likely to continue, whereas that of the manufacturing unions is more likely to contract. The relative size of ver.di is, therefore, likely to increase in the medium- or long-term, unless the unions in manufac-turing can complete more mergers or extend their recruitment bases. Preliminary discussions towards the first of these options between IG Metall and GdED and between IG BCE and IG BAU may thus consti-tute initial steps in a further phase of restructuring. Pursuit of the second option is also underway as unions in manufacturing attempt to recruit service sector workers employed on outsourced work at manufacturing sites, such as catering, laundry and cleaning. Policies directed towards this second option have already led to disputes with ver.di.

Financial shortfalls and rising membership demands for improved services have also promoted merger activity. In particular, IG BE, GL, DAG, HBV and IG Medien encountered severe pre-merger financial difficulties in the IG BCE and ver.di merger processes (Waddington *et al.*, 2003) and it is likely that GTB and GGLF were also in financial trouble. The parlous financial position of several unions was adversely affected by the policies adopted to accommodate German unification. Trade unions were obliged to set up office and communication networks throughout the new *Länder* in order to support the vast numbers of new members they had recruited. This proved extremely expensive. Even though unions in manufacturing tended to opt for skeleton networks in anticipation of the subsequent decline, they opted for arrangements that proved to be too extensive. Unions that organised the public sector and private sector services established more extensive office communication networks in anticipation of sustaining the membership gains secured between 1990 and 1991. They were thus more hard-hit than the manufacturing unions when the collapse in membership took effect. ÖTV, HBV, DAG and DPG, in particular, were forced to adopt austerity measures in order to address financial shortfalls. These took the form of transferring money from strike to operating funds, introducing voluntary retirement schemes for paid officials, imposing freezes on the hiring of new staff and closing offices. A slower than expected rate of wage increases for workers in the new *Länder* compounded financial difficulties. Union contributions are based on a percentage of wages. The slow rate of wage increases thus slowed the rate of increase in membership contributions.

Financial difficulties were also exacerbated by the impact of bargaining decentralisation and union attempts to adjust. Decentralisation in Germany has taken the form of a rising number of company agreements; a decline in the membership of employers' associations; and a decline in the coverage of collective agreements, particularly at small sites (Hassel, 1999; Flecker and Schulten, 1999). For example, recent estimates indicate that 38.4 per cent of workplaces are not covered by collective agreements (Kohaut and Bellmann, 1997). As collective bargaining coverage and plant size are inversely related, and future employment growth will be concentrated at smaller plants, coverage is likely to decline still further. The rise in the number of company agreements increased organising costs, as it necessitated that unions support members or officers in the conduct of a larger number of negotiations. Furthermore, following an extensive review published in 1990, several unions embarked on a strategy of promoting decentralised and participatory institutions with the intention of generating more members from under-represented groups (Hoffmann *et al.*, 1990). The outcome of both of these developments was rising internal union costs, which encouraged unions, particularly the smaller ones, to seek a merger.

A third influence on the merger process is the restructuring of the German economy. The stability of trade union structure resulted from the system of exclusive jurisdiction established by trade unions during the late 1940s and the apparatus administered by the DGB to 'police' these jurisdictions. While inter-union disputes over membership have always characterised trade union relations, they have tended to become more intractable due to three developments.

Firstly, the industrial boundaries on which trade union structure was initially founded are disappearing or no longer exist. In particular, companies have diversified, privatisation has shifted the industrial location of companies and outsourcing has undermined the distinction between manufacturing and services (Hoffmann, 2001). Where diversification involved company mergers or acquisitions, it has often resulted in two unions organising different plants within the same company. When one company acquires a second with different bargaining arrangements, the union in the acquired company may have to abandon its members. Similarly, where a company diversifies by establishing a separate enterprise, the union in the parent company has often recruited members in the new enterprise, thereby, further breaking down the structure of union jurisdiction. Privatisation has clouded the issue still further in that it has shifted companies from the public to the private sector and has often been accompanied by additional companies entering the market of the original public sector enterprise. *Deutsche Telekom*, for example, now competes with several other companies for telephone services, including *Mannesmann*, which was founded on the steel industry. The DPG, which traditionally was the union for uniformed postal workers, organises *Deutsche Telekom*, was thus brought into recruitment competition with other unions in order to maintain jurisdiction over telephone services. The response of unions to outsourcing has also contributed to the erosion of industrial jurisdictions. Where manufacturing companies have outsourced catering, cleaning or laundry services, the union that organises the manufacturing plant has often claimed the service workers as potential members and sought to recruit them. Through this approach, unions with contracting recruitment bases in manufacturing have extended their recruitment opportunities. This extension, however, is at the expense of unions from private sector services.

Secondly, new industries established after the original jurisdictions were laid down have been a source of dispute throughout the period since 1949. Earlier disputes between unions concerned the allocation of companies involved in the then new industries of photographic processing and artificial fibres. Recently these disputes have become more frequent as a whole range of industries associated with micro-chip technologies have developed. Jurisdiction over data-processing and computer-software enterprises, for example, is hard fought, as unions within the contracting manufacturing sector attempt to extend their jurisdiction. Unification heightened this tension, as industry in the new *Länder* was not organised on the same basis as that in the west and resulted in a further series of jurisdiction disputes.

A final element of restructuring that impacts on the merger process is the decline of the traditional training-employment-retirement career path and its replacement with periods of employment interspersed with repeated periods of retraining. A result of this development is that the allegiance of a worker to a single industry is likely to be more temporary than in the past. In these circumstances vertical union organisation does not offer the worker long-term protection unless s/he transfers from union to union with each change of employment. Furthermore, in many service sector occupations where there are low level qualification re-quirements, transfers between companies and industries are common-place, particularly among the young. An industrial union offers nothing more than short-term security for such workers.

The German trade union merger process is thus primarily a defensive reaction to shifts in membership, union finances and industrial restruc-turing. Although merger activity has been concentrated within a short period of time, the reasons that promoted it were present for much of the period after about 1970. The impact of German unification accentuated existing trends insofar as it promised false hope, in the form of extra members, only for this to be dashed as these members lost their jobs. In consequence, unions were left with an infrastructure to support in the new *Länder*, but insufficient members to pay for it. The merger process is unlikely to conclude with the formation of ver.di. With a rising size threshold of union viability, the remaining smaller unions will come under increasing pressure to merge unless they improve on their current rates of recruitment. Whatever the case, a keen interest in further merg-ers will be sustained within the larger unions as part of a response to the new politics of relative membership size.

Post-Merger Questions

In common with merger processes elsewhere, German union restruc-turing is a defensive adjustment. Three key questions arise from the nature of the union response. First, what is the future of the DGB in circumstances of eight or fewer affiliated unions? Second, are post-merger unions equipped to extend higher levels of membership, partici-pation and organisation into hitherto unorganised sectors of the econ-omy? Associated with this second question is a third: what is the impact of the merger process on union government? How trade unionists address these questions will determine the future of German trade unionism and whether defensive mergers may be turned to long-term strategic advantage. Issues associated with these questions are now considered.

Traditionally the DGB has provided services to, and performed co-ordination functions on behalf of, affiliated unions. The services provided by the DGB include training and legal support and the adjudication of inter-union disputes. To facilitate co-ordination the DGB convenes *Ortskartelle* (local trade councils),[3] fosters links with, and lobbies, the SPD (Social Democratic Party), lobbies the governments of the *Länder* and the federal state on social affairs and labour market policy, and has represented German trade unions within the European Trade Union Confederation (ETUC). The reduction in the number of affiliated unions raises questions about the future of the DGB, which has led to its role in each of these areas being subject to detailed scrutiny from within post-merger unions. The uncertainty surrounding the DGB has been compounded by the absence of direct constitutional authority held by the DGB over affiliated trade unions, coupled to the cut-backs that it has been forced to introduce to offset a marked decline in income.[4]

The role of the DGB in the provision of services is being curtailed. The larger post-merger unions are increasingly trying to provide support services to their own members, rather than outsource such provision to the DGB. The larger post-merger unions, for example, now provide legal services directly to members. In this context the DGB tends towards being a support service for the smaller affiliated unions. As these smaller unions are acquired by larger affiliates, so the role of the DGB diminishes. The future of the DGB as a provider of services to all affiliated unions is thus very much open to question.

The impact of merger activity on the DGB's role in the adjudication of inter-union disputes is more difficult to assess. It is clear, for example, that mergers have not eliminated inter-union tensions concerning recruitment, but merely shifted their location. In the case of ver.di long-running disputes between HBV, ÖTV and DAG will become issues for intra-union resolution. The acceptance of the DAG into the DGB, however, will bring a raft of new inter-union tensions over recruitment on to the agenda of the DGB. It is also questionable whether a smaller

---

3 *Ortskartelle* are local trades councils comprising representatives of the different DGB-affiliated unions at the level of a *Kreis* (region) or town. Issues of concern to the locality are discussed, such as local levels of unemployment and employment, environment, cultural events (including solidarity campaigns, concerts, car boot sales, etc.), and the servicing and recruitment of members. Recent estimates put the total number of *Ortskartelle* at between 1,200 and 1,300 (Mielke *et al.*, 1994).

4 Affiliated unions are the principal source of income for the DGB. The sharp decline in membership among affiliates after 1991 thus led to a similarly sharp decline in the income of the DGB, which was forced into a wide-ranging austerity programme that involved the closure of complete departments.

number of larger unions will be prepared to accept the decisions of the DGB *Schiedskommission* (Disputes Committee). An increasing number of these decisions have been questioned subsequently by unions in the Labour Courts, thus bringing the mandate of the *Schiedskommission* into question. Furthermore, if the DGB *Schiedskommission* adheres to current practice by adjudicating in favour of the established union, it would effectively consolidate the horizontal structure of the DAG within ver.di. This would curtail recruitment opportunities for each of the unions in manufacturing and thus, repeatedly, bring them into conflict with ver.di. Whatever the case, it appears that, at the very least, current practices will need to be reformed if the allegiance of all affiliated unions is to be secured.

The DGB is also under similar pressure regarding its co-ordination activities. Although the *Ortskartelle* were already under considerable pressure, post-merger unions are engaged in discussions to take over their functions, not least because taking over these functions would 'bring the union closer to the members'. In pursuit of policies attached to the *Neue Mitte* programme, relations between the unions and the SPD have been conducted at 'arms length'. The authority attained by the DGB in lobbying the SPD on behalf of affiliated unions has thus been dissipated. Furthermore, as membership becomes more concentrated in larger unions, the opportunities for direct relations between unions and the SPD become more widespread. The support facilities required to promote such relations, including research and communication departments, are available within the larger unions.

The position of the DGB is strengthened by its role within the ETUC. Furthermore, a recent review within the ETUC ratified existing arrangements, insofar as national confederations retained their dominant position and European Industry Federations (EIFs) were prevented from securing wider influence. The separate affiliation of DAG to the ETUC, however, was rescinded once the ver.di merger was ratified. On the surface, therefore, the position of the DGB appears secure. Three points, however, suggest that this security may not be long-lasting. Firstly, affiliated unions have fairly successfully prevented the DGB from assuming a direct role in negotiations through the ETUC. Although some framework agreements have been concluded, these have not eroded the dominant position of the sectoral unions. Secondly, in recent years affiliated unions have raised their profile within EIFs. In several EIFs German unions are the largest affiliates. Furthermore, the merger to form IG BCE followed the corresponding merger in 1996 between the two EIFs in the same industries (European Federation of Chemical and General Workers' Unions and the Miners' European Federation) to form the European Mine, Chemical and Energy Workers' Federation

(EMCEF). In other words, the merger to form IG BCE strengthened the position of the post-merger union with EMCEF.

Thirdly, there is a range of initiatives launched by individual unions that by-pass the DGB and offer the possibility of offering direct working links between German unions and their European counterparts. IG BCE, for example, concluded joint recognition of membership cards agreements with the GMB from the UK and the Services, Industrial, Professional and Technical Union (SIPTU) from Ireland. Representatives from these unions now convene regular meetings with the objective of deepening working relationships. Similarly, both IG Metall and IG BAU are engaged in cross-border bargaining initiatives with unions from the Netherlands, Belgium and Luxembourg. In the case of the Doorn initiative, the DGB observed the discussions leading to the joint declaration but, as it has no direct bargaining role, representatives of affiliated unions were the major participants. European works councils have also fostered relations between representatives of individual unions and their counterparts from other countries to the exclusion of the DGB. Of course, this is not to argue that European wide collective bargaining is on the immediate horizon, but to point out that the days are over when international relationships were conducted exclusively through the DGB. A complex network of direct linkages is being established between individual unions from different countries. Those that involve German unions weaken the position of the DGB. The DGB is thus a major 'loser' from the merger process. Each of the functions that it performs on behalf of affiliated unions is threatened by the activities of post-merger organisations.

A second key question that arises from the merger process concerns the capacity of post-merger unions to extend recruitment, organisation and participation into the unorganised sectors of the economy. Aggregate membership continues to fall and union density is declining towards 20 per cent. Young, women and foreign workers, employed at small workplaces primarily in private sector services, are under-represented among existing members. Will the merger process provide the opportunities to reverse these trends? A positive answer to this question would enable advocates of the merger process to argue that unions were able to transform a defensive reaction into a strategic gain. Concurrently, post-merger unions will also have to retain traditional members. In order words, measures will have to be taken to ensure that traditional members sustain their links with extant organisational cultures (*organisatorische Heimat*) in larger, and perhaps more centralised, post-merger unions.

As is evident from Table 5.1, post-merger rates of membership decline are comparable with those sustained before the mergers, suggesting that mergers have had little impact in arresting the rate of membership decline. Advocates of mergers would argue, however, that most of the mergers to date involved unions from contracting areas of employment, where relatively few young and women workers were employed. The acquisitions of GTB and GHK by IG Metall, of GGLF by IG BSE and, arguably, of GL within the IG BCE merger were never likely to result in large numbers of new unionists due to the long-term contraction of the industries from which the acquired unions drew their memberships. Similarly, the long-term decline in mining employment, coupled to the high levels of density achieved by IG BE, means that IG BCE is unlikely to increase membership in the short- or medium-term. Indeed, in each of these cases the maintenance of support services was a priority. Membership decline arising from employment contraction meant that these unions were unable to sustain an appropriate level of support services.

The ver.di merger is thus the acid test, as the intention is to spread union organisation throughout private sector services.[5] Ver.di covers most of the services sector. It can thus offer long-term protection to workers employed in the service sector, even if they transfer employment between different service industries. The ver.di merger certainly consolidated recruitment initiatives that had been launched before the merger by constituent unions acting together. The pre-merger co-operation between ÖTV and DAG around IPSO (International Public Servants Organisation), intended to recruit in European level organisations based in Germany,[6] continues within ver.di. Similarly, the connexx.av project was adopted by ver.di from IG Medien, HBV and DPG, with the intention of recruiting potential members in radio, film and audio-visual media.[7] What is not certain is how the manufacturing unions will respond, particularly if ver.di extends recruitment initiatives directed towards outsourced workers employed in service occupations, such as catering or cleaning, but located within manufacturing plants. It is also unclear whether ver.di will be able to counter the membership

---

[5] Any future merger involving NGG would also fit into this category, as it has members located in private sector services and represents a basis upon which wider organisation might be established.

[6] Among the institutions targeted by IPSO are the European Central Bank, the European Patent Office and the European Shipping Law Courts.

[7] The connexx.av project was set up by IG Medien, HBV and DPG in 1996 and offered legal assistance, support in establishing works councils, training and literature for workers employed in the 'new' media sectors, particularly to freelance workers. The project was not, however, a membership project in so far as members did not join connexx.av, but remained in membership of one of the constituent unions.

growth recorded by professional associations, dedicated to the representation of narrow occupational interests. The membership heterogeneity
of ver.di, for example, raises a range of issues concerning the post-
merger representation of occupational interests, which have yet to be
addressed.

Central to these issues is the development of more extensive links
between unions and existing members at organised workplaces. The
decentralisation of bargaining has shifted the settlement of a wider range
of issues to the workplace. Unions need to develop their support networks for members engaged in these negotiations. In broad terms, these
two issues focus on the articulation and co-ordination of union organisation. That is, can mechanisms be introduced to ensure that activities
conducted at different levels of union organisation are interdependent,
thereby precluding the isolation of local unionists, and, in the multi-
industry unions, can activities within different industries be co-ordinated
as part of a process to develop a coherent union identity? There is
limited evidence to suggest that mergers have provided the opportunity
for some shift in resources towards the localities, but this is far from
convincing as yet (Waddington *et al.*, 2003).

A third, and associated, question concerning post-merger organisation asks about the impact of the merger process on internal union
government. As the German merger process involves both acquisitions
and amalgamations, there is no single answer to this question. The
acquisitions of GTB and GHK by IG Metall and of GGLF by IG BSE
effectively involved the extension of existing systems of internal sectional representation, as new sections were created to accommodate the
acquisitions.

The two amalgamations, however, differ substantively in terms of the
intended degrees of post-merger integration. In the case of IG BCE, the
post-merger union comprises eleven industrial groups (*Industrie-
gruppen*), five of which originate exclusively from IG CPK and five that
originate in IG BE. Members from GL were accommodated within a
single industrial group, plastics and leather, that otherwise contains only
ex-IG CPK members. In other words, the post-merger structure of IG
BCE minimised the integration of members from the constituent unions.
Furthermore, responsibility for the six post-merger industrial groups
comprising ex-IG CPK members rested with the Chair of IG BCE, an
ex-IG CPK officer, while responsibility for the five industrial groups
into which IG BE members were organised rested with the Deputy Chair
of IG BCE, an ex-IG BE officer. The IG BCE merger negotiations also
failed to implement far-reaching reforms on the representation of
women. Although the rulebook provides for a special representation
channel for women and insists on the 'adequate' representation of

women on all union bodies, it does not specify what this means in practice. Horizontal structures, however, were established for white-collar workers, but these were subdivided into nine substructures, which again tended to minimise the integration of ex-IG CPK with ex-IG BE members.

The ver.di merger envisages greater degrees of integration of members from the different constituent unions. The central features of the post-merger matrix organisation were thirteen sections (*Fachbereiche*) and three geographical tiers (national, regional and county levels). Each section represents the interests of a particular industrial group. Although members from one or other of the post-merger unions dominate specific sections, most of the sections comprise members from at least two pre-merger unions. Notably, some sections also combine members from areas of acute pre-merger membership competition, such as in financial services and commerce (Waddington *et al.*, 2003). The post-merger structure of ver.di thus necessitates a degree of integration of members from the constituent unions.

In addition, a series of horizontal structures of representation were established for specific interest groups including youth, women, pensioners, civil servants and freelancers. Members eligible for these horizontal structures are found in a range of the sections, thus further contributing to post-merger integration. Associated with the horizontal structure for women are gender policies based on two pillars. First, the representation of women in all positions is guaranteed in proportion to the share of women in the membership group that is represented. Second, ver.di was the first German trade union to attempt to integrate systematically gender mainstreaming into all levels of organisation and policy development. To assist these developments the rulebook envisages the establishment of women's committees at each of the three geographical tiers.

The extent of constitutional reform and membership integration is thus more wide-ranging in the ver.di merger than in the other German mergers. A consequence of the scale of the merger and the complexity of the post-merger structure is that there is considerable disquiet regarding the post-merger operation of ver.di and post-merger finances are in a state of disrepair. This is exacerbated by an absence of informal relations, as new relationships have to be established. The extent to which these issues will inhibit the development of the proposed post-merger system of government is open to question. What is beyond doubt, however, is that the post-merger structure intended for ver.di constitutes the most-wide-ranging reform of German union government to arise from the merger process.

Conclusions and Prospects

In the course of the last ten years the German merger process has transformed a trade union structure that had remained virtually unchanged since 1949. With the ratification of the ver.di merger, the number of unions has been halved and the principle of industrial unionism abandoned in practice. Inter-union politics are also likely to be fundamentally changed as the pre-eminent position of IG Metall is under threat. Furthermore, it seems likely that additional mergers will be completed before the current wave of activity dissipates.

Whether the trade union movement is stronger or better equipped to address its policy agenda as a result of these mergers is a moot point. It is certain that the position of the DGB is more precarious than hitherto, and is likely to become more so. There is no convincing evidence to indicate that post-merger unions are delivering economies of scale, nor have post-merger unions proved more attractive to non-members. A key question for the future is, can post-merger unions achieve higher rates of unionisation in private sector services and, in particular, attract more young, women and foreign workers into membership? If this question can be answered in the affirmative over the coming years, German unions will have transformed a defensive reaction to adverse change to their strategic advantage. In contrast, a negative response to the question points to a long period of decline with membership remaining concentrated in the contracting sectors of the economy.

List of Abbreviations

ADGB   Allgemeiner Deutscher Gewerkschaftsbund (All German Trade Union Confederation)

BDA   Bundesvereinigung der Deutschen Arbeitgeberverbände (Confederation of German Employers' Associations)

CGB   Christlicher Gewerkschaftsbund Deutschlands (Christian Trade Union Confederation)

DAG   Deutsche Angestellte-Gewerkschaft (Union of Salaried Employees)

DBB   Deutscher Beamtenbund (Union of Civil Servants)

DGB   Deutsche Gewerkschaftsbund (German Trade Union Confederation)

DJU   Deutsche Journalisten Union (German Journalists' Union)

DJV   Deutscher Journalisten Verband (German Journalists' Association)

DPG   Deutsche Postgewerkschaft (Postal Workers' Union)

EIF   European Industry Federation

EMCEF   European Mine, Chemical and Energy Workers' Federation

ETUC   European Trade Union Confederation

GdED   Gewerkschaft der Eisenbahner Deutschlands (Railway Workers' Union)

GdP   Gewerkschaft der Polizei (Union for Police Officers)

GEW   Gewerkschaft Erziehung und Wissenschaft (Education and Science Union)

GGLF   Gewerkschaft Gartenbau, Land und Forstwirtschaft (Agriculture and Forestry Workers)

GHK   Gewerkschaft Holz und Kunststoff (Wood and Plastics Workers' Union)

GK   Gewerkschaft Kunst (Artists' Union)

GL   Gewerkschaft Leder (Leatherworkers' Union)

GTB   Gewerkschaft Textil-Bekleidung (Textile and Clothing Workers' Union)

HBV   Gewerkschaft Handel, Banken und Versicherungen (Banking and Commerce Union)

IG BAU   Industriegewerkschaft Bauen-Agrar-Umwelt (Construction, Agriculture and Environment Union)

IG BCE   Industriegewerkschaft Bergbau, Chemie, Energie, Mining, Chemical and Energy Workers' Union

IG BE   Industriegewerkschaft Bergbau und Energie (Mining and Energy Union)

IG BSE   Industriegewerkschaft Bau-Steine-Erden (Construction Workers' Union)

IG CPK   Industriegewerkschaft Chemie-Papier-Keramik (Chemical, Paper and Ceramic Workers' Union)

IG Drupa Industriegewerkschaft Druck und Papier (Printing and Paper Workers' Union)

IG Medien Industriegewerkschaft Medien (Media Workers' Union)

IG Metall Industriegewerkschaft Metall (Engineering Workers' Union)

IPSO   International Public Servants Organisation

NGG   Gewerkschaft Nahrung, Genuß, Gaststätten (Food and Restaurant Workers' Union)

ÖTV   Gewerkschaft Öffentliche, Dienste, Transport und Verkehr (Public Services, Transport and Traffic Sectors Union)

RFFU   Rundfunk-Fernseh-Film Union (Radio, Television and Film Union)

SIPTU	Services, Industrial, Professional and Technical Union
SPD	Sozialdemokratische Partei Deutschlands (Social Democratic Party)
ver.di	Vereinte Dienstleistungsgewerkschaft (Unified Services Union)
VS	Verband der Schriftsteller (Writers' Association)

CHAPTER 6. GREECE

From Divided "Quangos"
to Fragmented "Social Partners"
Explaining the Absence of Mergers

Christos A. IOANNOU

At the end of the twentieth century Greek trade unionism comprised two confederations, 114 federations and 3,611 primary level unions. More than 680,000 members voted in the 1998 union elections. As the labour market comprised 2,245,000 salary and wage earners in a total labour force of 3,967,000, this represents a density among salary- and wage-earners of more than 30 per cent. Trade union structure is extremely fragmented. The average size of a federation is 5,996 members and the average size of a union is 189 members. Trade unions affiliate to either the GSEE (General Confederation of Workers of Greece), or ADEDY (Supreme Administration of Civil Servants' Trade Unions). Both GSEE and ADEDY have three levels of operation, which are supported by legislation on trade union rights: primary-level trade unions (company, occupation, regional or craft unions), secondary-level federations (in addition, GSEE comprises Local Labour Centres at this level), and tertiary-level confederations.

Excessive state regulation of trade union recognition, bargaining processes and trade union finances resulted in trade unions taking the form of quangos from 1950, when the civil war ended, until the return to parliamentary democracy in 1974. During this period trade unions were autonomous entities in neither the polity nor the labour market. After 1975, social mobilisation resulted in unparalleled levels of strike activity, the emergence of new forms of workers' organisation at company level, and the democratic reform of trade union legislation. From the late 1970s until the mid-1980s these developments gradually resulted in the present structure of Greek unionism. Since the early 1990s, trade unions have exhibited elements of a transition from 'quangos' to becoming more autonomous 'social partners' (Ioannou, 1996; 2000).

The increasing autonomy and changing practices of trade unions have not been coupled to major changes in union structure. The need for mergers has been recognised since the early 1980s and encompasses the three levels of union structure. At the confederal level a merger of GSEE and ADEDY is envisaged. Among the federations there are 75 GSEE-affiliated federations and 52 ADEDY-affiliated federations. At the primary level more than 2,347 trade unions affiliate to the GSEE federations and 1,264 trade unions affiliate to ADEDY federations. Trade union mergers have, however, remained rare. At the level of the federations, only two mergers have been recorded during the last decade, and these took place under exceptional and specific circumstances. At the primary level, the wave of company mergers and acquisitions since the mid-1990s has raised the need for trade union mergers. Trade unionists, however, have failed to co-ordinate their activities, let alone merge their organisations, with the result that inter-union conflicts over jurisdiction, recognition rights and membership are commonplace.

This chapter examines the experience of Hellenic trade unions with mergers. The analysis suggests that the lack of mergers is associated with the particular stage of trade union development in Greece, the effects of long-lasting state intervention in union activities, the absence of trade union financial autonomy, the impact of party politics on trade union activities, and the impact of bargaining structure. In a nutshell, industrialisation and political factors underpinned the expansion of trade unions at the primary and the secondary level, but institutional factors linked to political cleavages have buttressed the fragmented structure of trade unionism. Implicit in this fragmentation is the preservation and predominance of 'micro' trade unions. As a result, trade union bargaining power is weak and there is unequal development of trade unions in the public and private sectors. The analysis questions whether trade unionists will abandon these fragmented and ossified structures, and restructure through mergers, even when confronted by membership decline.

To these ends, the first section identifies the sources and the degree of fragmentation in Greek union structure. The second section analyses the exogenous and endogenous factors that restrict or enhance the opportunities for mergers. The third section assesses the prospects for trade union mergers in Greece, given the recent restructuring of the labour market.

Persisting Fragmentation

This section examines the reasons that underpin the fragmentation of Greek trade unionism by reference to the structure of GSEE and ADEDY.

The Structure of the General Confederation of Workers of Greece

The present structure of GSEE resulted from decisions taken after the end of the Civil War (1945-49) at the GSEE Congress of 1950. The Congress decided that national federations[1] (occupational/craft and sectoral), along with the Labour Centres,[2] would form the two-fold organisational structure of GSEE. Reforms to this effect took place over the period until the GSEE Congress in 1953. Whereas 1,664 primary-level unions and 63 Labour Centres participated at the Congress in 1950, 17 federations and 52 Labour Centres participated at the Congress in 1953. The present structure of GSEE comprises 2,347 primary-level trade unions, which are subsumed within 62 federations and 75 Labour Centres.[3]

The numerical evolution of the structure of the GSEE can only be outlined and assessed for the period after the mid-1980s. For the preceding period, trade union statistics are not reliable and may only be used as indicators of GSEE structure, rather than as measures of membership and the population of unions. The reason is that over the post-war period until the early 1980s organisational problems, inter-union conflicts and extensive state interference plagued the functioning of Greek trade unionism.[4] Furthermore, before 1975 there were also four

---

[1]   In theory, federations comprise primary-level trade unions organised on an industry, sectoral or occupational basis.

[2]   Labour Centres are organisations at the local or regional level. They normally follow the division of the country in Prefectures, and comprise the unions of the region concerned. They are the oldest secondary-level structure in national industrial relations (for details, see Mitsou, 1992: 30).

[3]   Calculations based on data released at the GSEE Congress of March 1998. These federations and Labour Centres represent the interests of 442,852 voting members, of whom 269,095 voted via federations, 147,372 via Labour Centres and 26,385 were pensioners that voted via federations for pensioners.

[4]   Quite often electoral malpractice dominated the internal 'democracy' of trade unions (Jechinis, 1967; Katsanevas, 1984: 194-198). Inter-union conflicts were coupled with political rivalries, since most trade unions were run with significant political interference (Katsanevas, 1984: 227-248) and industrial relations were dominated by a strong adversarial tradition directly linked to political developments and divisions (Fakiolas, 1978: 340-392; Ioannou, 1989: 54-68).

small 'autonomous', breakaway confederations acting at the tertiary level.[5] At the secondary level, even after the return to parliamentary democracy in 1974, many major federations were excluded from the GSEE (Katsanevas, 1984: 137-167). At all levels, and contrary to the provisions of the ILO Convention No. 87,[6] the internal life of trade unions was heavily regulated by state legislation that shaped electoral systems, voting rights and trade union activities (Koukiadis, 1981: 376-383). Things started to change after 1982 with the adoption of Law 1264 on trade union rights by the then newly elected PASOK (socialist) government.

Law 1264 consolidated the structure of federations and Labour Centres, the three tiers of GSEE and stipulated that these organisations had to enrol all unions that applied to join, regardless of their political orientation. Proportional representation was introduced and the representation of primary-level unions at higher levels of union structure was reformed. Each primary-level union was allowed membership of only one federation and only one Labour Centre. Furthermore, federations and Labour Centres were entitled to be members of only one confederation. Thus, GSEE became *de facto* the only national confederation. To avoid double voting[7] when representatives for GSEE congresses are elected, Law 1264 entitles members to choose only one route for electing their representatives; either via federations or via Labour Centres.

Since 1953 the GSEE has thus rested on a structure of federations and Labour Centres. But, as indicated by Table 6.1, the number of federations and Labour Centres has changed over time. Between 1953 and 1986 there was an increasing number of federations, because trade unionism developed rapidly during the mid-1970s and the 1980s as a result of the return to parliamentary democracy and rapid economic growth (Ioannou, 1989; 1999). The period after 1974 was marked by the emergence of new labour movements, such as the 'factory movement' in manufacturing that promoted the sectoral industry federations; and the 'federations movement' in the state-owned public sector utilities, where strong company federations were formed.

---

[5] Breakaway confederations were established in 1954, New GSEE; in 1960, Christian GSEE; in 1963, Panhellenic Confederation of Orthodox Christian Trade Unions; and in 1971, Hellenic Confederation of Greek Labour. All these breakaway confederations comprised between 2 and 11 federations and between 4 and 9 Labour Centres (Fakiolas, 1978: 161).

[6] Convention concerning Freedom of Association and Protection of the Right to Organise.

[7] Double voting was widespread during the period 1950-81. This practice made any statistics on trade union membership for that period unreliable.

As far as employees working under private law contracts are concerned, it is not surprising that the mid-1980s are considered as the peak in the expansion of Greek unionism. Union density peaked at 43.3 per cent in 1986. Table 6.1 indicates this in terms of the number of GSEE-affiliated federations (a total of 67), the number of primary-level unions (3,045) and the members that voted in union elections (593,487). Concurrently, this peak illustrates the fragmentation of union structure. The average size of a federation was 8,858 voting members, while the average size of a primary-level trade union was 195 voting members.

Table 6.1: GSEE Congress Structure and Membership, 1953-1998

Year	LABOUR CENTRES		FEDERATIONS			Average Size of Federations	Average Size of Unions	Density[2] %
	Unions	Voting Members	Unions	Voting Members				
1953	52	–	–	17	–	–			
1965	54	–	–	41	–	–			
1976	77	–	330402	43	n.a.	260623			
1986	70	1545	390849	67	1500	203638	8858	195	43.3
1995	66	1275	147962	53	1043	281526	8103	185	26.9
1998	68	1248	145562	57	1047	268281	7851	181	23.5
	(75)[1]	(1285)	(147372)	(62)	(1062)	(295480)	(7142)	(189)	

For the years 1953 to 1976 the numbers of unions and of members that voted in union elections are not reliable, as there was extensive double (or multiple) voting. The numbers of federations and Labour Centres are indicative of the evolution of the trade unions structure at the secondary level of the GSEE structure.

[1] The numbers in brackets include the unions that did not qualify for participation in the GSEE Congress because they had not the required minimum of members that have to vote in union elections to elect representatives for the GSEE Congress. The provision states that a minimum of 500 voting members is required to elect at least one representative to the GSEE Congress.

[2] Union density refers to employees (salary and wage-earners) employed under private law contracts and organised in corresponding GSEE-affiliated trade unions.

Source: GSEE and author's calculations.

Between 1986 and 1998 this fragmentation persisted, although membership of the GSEE declined by 25.4 per cent and union density for employees working under private law contacts fell to 23.5 per cent. The number of GSEE-affiliated federations fell from 67 to 62, and the number of primary level trade unions fell by 22.9 per cent from 3,045 to 2,347. The number of Labour Centres, however, increased to return to the level of 1976. Labour Centres are supposed to organise primary-level unions within each prefecture. Although there are 52 prefectures in

Greece, in several two or more Labour Centres operate, usually based on different cities.

Persistent fragmentation, particularly in a context of falling membership, suggests that union mergers play only a very marginal role in shaping union structure. The decreasing number of primary-level unions between 1986 and 1998 is mainly associated with the dissolution of trade unions at the workplace level, rather than merger activity. The case of OBES (Federation of Industrial Factory Unions) is indicative of the mechanism through which the number of primary-level trade unions fell after the mid-1980s. In 1985 there were 135 company trade unions affiliated to OBES. Subsequently, no fewer than 76 of these were dissolved due to the closure of the enterprises within which they organised (Ioannou, 1997: 27). Following its formation in 1979 and its expansion during the early 1980s, when it challenged the established craft and sectoral unions in manufacturing, OBES was clearly discouraged by these closures and failed to consolidate its presence. OBES thus gradually disappeared from the list of influential federations.[8] The slight decrease in the number of federations is associated, first, with minor harmonisation of trade union structures based on the provisions of Law 1264; and, second, with the dissolution of 'phantom' federations. The impact of mergers is restricted to only one merger of three federations that took place in 1993.

A small number of sectoral federations and a larger number of small, craft-based federations affiliate to the GSEE,[9] but the most influential (in terms of voting members) of the 62 affiliated federations that elect representatives to GSEE congresses are the company federations of the public sector utilities. In 1998 the ten largest federations accounted for 41.9 per cent of the total GSEE membership and for 64.8 per cent of the union members that voted via federations. The ten largest federations comprise five company federations that organise public sector utilities and five sectoral federations. The company federations include GENOP-DEH (General Federation of DEH Personnel), where DEH is the Public Electricity Corporation;[10] OME-OTE (Federation of OTE Employees),

---

[8]   At the GSEE Congress in 2002, OBES only just ensured its presence by electing one representative (from a total of 552 voting members).

[9]   A full list of the 62 federations that form the GSEE is available in Ioannou (1999). Federations have not been strictly organised according to industrial and occupational divisions of the labour force. Many federations incorporate primary unions from a variety of industries and occupations.

[10]   A further indication of fragmentation is that in the Public Electricity Corporation there are two smaller federations, OME-DEH with 7 unions and 1,785 voting members in 1998, and NOP-DEH with 8 unions and 1,004 voting members in 1998.

where OTE is the Hellenic Telecommunications Organisation; POS (Panhellenic Federation of Railways), which is the federation of the Hellenic Railways Organisation (OSE); OSPA (Federation of Olympic Airways Employees); and POE-ELTA (Federation of the Hellenic Post Office Employees). Each of these federations covers only a single public sector utility, thus they are company federations. Each federation comprises primary-sector unions that are usually based on occupation, but may also have a regional component. For instance GENOP-DEH comprises 90 primary level unions, while OME-OTE organises 60 primary level unions (Mitsou, 1992: 27).

Table 6.2: The Ten Largest GSEE Federations (by Membership), 1998

FEDERATION	Member Unions	Voting Members	Share of the total voting membership of Federations %	Average Size of Unions
OTOE (Bank employees)	45	46,143	17.1	1,025
OOSE (Construction Workers)	72	34,856	13.0	484
GENOP – DEH (Electricity Board Employees)	20	19,137	7.0	957
OME-OTE (Hellenic Telecommunications Organisation)	12	18,603	6.9	1,550
POS (Railway employees)	18	10,791	4.0	600
OIYE (Private-sector Employees' Federation)	46	9,714	3.6	211
POEM (Metalworkers)	19	9,553	3.6	503
OSPA (Civil Aviation Employees)	18	9,107	3.4	506
POE-ELTA (Post Office Employees)	63	8,953	3.3	142
POETE (Tourist industry employees)	38	7,642	2.8	201
Share of 10 Federations in All Federations (per cent)	33.1	64.8	64.8	
Share of 10 Federations in All Federations and Labour Centres (per cent)	15.0	41.9		

Source: GSEE, Register of the 1998 Congress.

Beyond the company federations, OTOE (Federation of Banking Sector Trade Unions of Greece) organises private and public sector banks. In terms of membership, OTOE is the largest federation. In 1998 OTOE registered 46,143 voting members and attained a density of 82.1 per cent. OTOE organises 45 primary-level unions, which have an average size of 1,025 members (Table 6.2). This fragmentation is associated with the division of the banking sector into many small banks. It remains to be seen whether this fragmentation is appropriate, given the wave of company mergers and acquisitions in the banking sector since 1998.

As indicated in Table 6.2, fragmentation also dominates the other major private sector federations. The POEM (Metalworkers Federation), the OOSEE (Federation of Construction Workers) and the OIYE (Federation of Private Sector Employees) organise unions with an average size varying between 211 members to 503 members.

Structure of the Supreme Administration of the Civil Servants' Trade Unions

ADEDY was founded in 1947,[11] but had been preceded by SDYE (Confederation of Greek Civil Servants), which had been repeatedly banned by the government during the political instability of the inter-war years. Throughout the post-war period, ADEDY suffered direct governmental interference and experienced electoral malpractice. The decisive step towards democracy within ADEDY was taken at the 1983 Congress when it was decided that the election of representatives should be conducted on the basis of proportional representation and ADEDY was re-organised in a three-tier structure similar to that of GSEE. A total of 54 federations participated at the Congress of 1995.[12] The present structure of ADEDY includes 1,264 primary-level unions, organised in 52 federations.[13]

The federations and the primary-level unions affiliated to ADEDY are mostly products of the 1970s and the 1980s. Of the 53 federations that participated at the 1989 Congress, only 8 had been founded before 1974 and 29 were founded after 1983. Furthermore, 41 of the 53 federations that participated at the 1989 Congress had affiliated to ADEDY after 1983. Union density of ADEDY started from a low of 26.9 per cent in 1983 and peaked at 51.3 per cent in 1992. As is indicated in Table 6.3, density fell slightly after 1992 to 49.4 per cent in 1998. The structure of ADEDY at the primary and secondary levels is fragmented. Despite adopting the principle that each Ministry should be organised by a single federation, there are cases where in the same Ministry civil servants are organised in two or more different federations; for example, the Ministry of Finance and Ministry of Agriculture. The number of primary-level unions is also increasing. Between 1986 and 1998 the number more than doubled from 607 primary level unions to 1,264 (see

---

[11] The initiative was taken by the DOE (Greek Teachers' Federation of Primary Education), ODYE (Judicial Clerks Federation), TTT (Panhellenic Telephony, Telegraphy, Postal Service Federation) and 15 other unions of civil servants.

[12] Representing about 226,000 voting members.

[13] Data taken from those released at the 30th Congress held in November 1998, at which 240,709 voting members were represented.

Table 6.3). Despite increases in membership, the average size of AD-EDY-affiliated unions fell from 272 voting members to 190 voting members.

**Table 6.3: ADEDY Structure: Federations,
Unions and Voting Members, 1950-1998**

Year	Primary level Unions	Federations	Voting Members	Average Size of Unions	Average Size of Federations	Density[2] %
1950	n.a	33[1]	n.a	n.a	n.a	n.a
1961	n.a	42[1]	n.a	n.a	n.a	n.a
1975	n.a	44[1]	n.a	n.a	n.a	n.a
1983	n.a	25	96,000	n.a	3,840	26.9
1986	607	46	165,000	272	3,587	41.7
1989	834	53	202,000	242	3,811	45.2
1992	1,090	55	235,533	216	4,282	51.3
1995	1,258	54	226,177	178	4,188	48.6
1998	1,264	52	240,709	190	4,629	49.4

[1] The number includes both primary-level unions and federations participating in ADEDY Congresses. Therefore, the data for 1950, 1961, 1975 are not comparable with the 1983-1998 data.

[2] Union density refers to employees under public law contracts (civil servants) that are entitled to organise in ADEDY-affiliated unions.

Source: ADEDY.

The structure of ADEDY can be illustrated by reference to the larger affiliated federations (see Table 6.4). Even the four largest federations are fragmented, however, as the average size of affiliated primary unions varies from 161 voting members in POEDHN (Public Hospitals Personnel) to 374 voting members in OLME (Federation of Secondary Education Teachers). The ten largest federations of the 52 that affiliate to ADEDY account for 69.2 per cent of the primary-level unions and for 78.2 per cent of the ADEDY total membership. Not surprisingly, at the 1998 ADEDY Congress the DOE (Federation of Primary School Teachers), POEDHN and OLME elected 52.1 per cent of the elected representatives, while the ten largest federations controlled 79 per cent of elected representatives. Similarly to the GSEE, membership increases since the mid-1980s are coupled to declines in the average size of primary-level unions, although the average size of federation has remained fairly constant at about 4,500 voting members.

Table 6.4: The Ten Largest ADEDY Federations
by Membership, 1998

FEDERATION	Member Unions	Voting Members	Share of the total voting membership of Federations %	Average Size of Unions
DOE (Primary School Teachers)	146	45,777	19.0	314
POEDHN (Public Hospitals)	266	42,874	17.8	161
OLME (High-school teachers)	86	32,186	13.4	374
POE – OTA (Local Government)	162	27,458	11.4	169
POE – DOY (Taxation services employees)	26	11,643	4.8	448
POE – YETHA (Ministry of Defence employees)	64	9,120	3.8	143
POSE – IKA (Social Security Fund employees)	27	6,668	2.8	247
POSYPPO (Ministry of Culture employees)	15	4,279	1.8	285
ODYE (Ministry of Justice employees)	55	4,134	1.7	75
POSE – YPECHODE (Ministry of Public Works & Environment employees)	28	4,100	1.7	146
Share of 10 Federations in All Federations (per cent)	69.2	78.2		

Source: ADEDY, Register of the 1998 Congress.

From Over-regulation to Ossification?

The fragmentation of trade union structure has been openly ac-knowledged as a barrier to trade union efficiency by the GSEE and reform has been attempted in several instances. Two GSEE Congresses, in 1983 and in 1992, resolved that trade union structure at the level of the federations should be harmonised through mergers. The 1983 Con-gress agreed that trade union mergers should lead to a structure based on between 22 and 25 federations. As there was no progress towards this goal, the 1992 Congress again resolved to proceed with the rationalisa-tion of the GSEE structure at the level of federations through mergers to create a GSEE structure of 21 federations. The sectoral coverage of the planned new federations was outlined, together with a blueprint of the mergers that were recommended. The issue of mergers was also raised in the 1995 GSEE Congress, when the GSEE Administrative Board issued guidelines for the federations that were to merge and proposed that Sectoral Committees for Mergers be set up in order to streamline merger activities (GSEE, 1995). The 53 federations that participated in the GSEE Congress (together with another seven federations that had not achieved the required threshold of 500 voting members) had, according to the GSEE guidelines, to form Sectoral Committees for Mergers to prepare and manage the merger process.

The pattern of considering, announcing and deciding on restructuring through mergers was reproduced at the GSEE Congress in November 2002. This Congress was intended to discuss merger policy and the restructuring of Greek trade unionism. Again, proposals to move towards a structure comprising 20-25 federations and 52 Labour Centres were agreed. The scepticism of many representatives, particularly those that held posts in the federations and Labour Centres, resulted in a further decision for a transition period, Prefectural Co-ordination Councils for the Labour Centres within the same prefecture, and Sectoral Co-ordination Councils for federations. In other words, the new resolution merely replicates the decisions taken in 1992 and 1995.

Despite these GSEE resolutions, there has been no important merger activity among the federations. In practice, GSEE has no real authority over the affiliated federations and thus cannot impose a merger blueprint. There are, however, two exceptions, which arose from specific circumstances. Following the decisions of, and guidelines issued by, the 1992 GSEE Congress, three sectoral federations covering textiles, clothing and leather processing merged in 1993 and formed OEKIDE (Federation of Textile, Clothing, and Leather Workers of Greece). Another merger of two federations organising chemical and oil products was concluded in 2000. The POPEEP (Oil Trade Federation), which had been created in 1955, and the POEPDXB (Refineries Federation), which was founded in 1970, merged to form the OEPDXB (Federation of Oil, Refineries and Chemical Industries). These two mergers illustrate the meagre level of merger activity at the secondary level of the GSEE. Among the civil servants within ADEDY, there has been no merger activity at any level (primary or secondary).

How we can explain the absence of mergers? Although the requirement for mergers is acknowledged and successive decisions made by GSEE Congresses support restructuring through mergers, their impact has been marginal. The absence of mergers at the level of the federations may be explained by reference to two sets of questions. First, are there exogenous barriers to mergers, which overcome the endogenous support for mergers? Second, how strong is the endogenous support?

Exogenous Barriers to Mergers

The limited number of mergers and the persistence of fragmentation may be associated with legal, financial, political, 'idiosyncratic' and bargaining structure factors that operate at the present stage of trade union development in Greece.

As legal regulation is prevalent throughout the Greek system, it is no surprise that mergers are also legally regulated. Trade unions are 'recognised' through the judiciary and are subject to 'state supervision'.[14] Over the post-war period, mergers have been subject to the provisions of the Civil Code (CC), which also stipulates the minimum contents of trade union statutes (CC Article 80). Decisions on mergers can only be made by the General Assembly of a trade union (CC Articles 94, 99, 100 and 103), irrespective of the trade union rulebook. According to the Civil Code (CC Article 99) a decision to merge required 75 per cent of those voting at a General Assembly to vote in favour and stipulated that a minimum of 50 per cent of those eligible to vote do so. The two or more unions intending to merge had each to hold a General Assembly. These provisions made the process of mergers very bureaucratic and extremely difficult to ratify. For example, two unions, each with 1,000 members, had to call a General Assembly where at least 500 members were present. At each General Assembly a minimum of 375 members had to vote for the merger for it to be successful.

Law 1264/82, which was intended to promote the rationalisation of trade union structure, added special provisions for mergers in order to relax the Civil Code requirements. Thus, since 1982, merger decisions could be made by a 75 per cent vote at a General Assembly at which between 20 per cent and 33 per cent of union members that had paid their dues were present.[15] Under these requirements, if from the total of

---

[14]   The formal recognition of trade unions occurred for the first time in 1914 by Law 281. This Law distinguished between 'recognised' and 'not recognised' trade unions, the former being those founded by judicial decision and the latter being those founded with the simple declaration of their members. 'Recognised' unions were subject to 'state supervision'. The Civil Code (as adopted in the early 1940s) maintained this distinction and, indeed, favoured the 'recognised' unions, as those with bargaining and industrial action rights (Vlastos, 1996: 2-3, 128-135). In 1964, under a centre-liberal government, Law 4316 halted the 'state supervision' of trade unions in order to fulfil obligations *vis-à-vis* International Labour Convention No. 87, which was ratified by Parliament in 1961. Under the military regime between 1967 and 1974 trade union rights ceased. Law 4316 came into force again in 1974 together with Law 42/74, but ceased again in 1976 with the adoption of Law 330, which was voted by referring to reservations with regard to ILO Convention No. 87. In other words, the Law recognises that the provisions of ILO Convention No. 87 are not fully met.

[15]   Article 8 of Law 1264/82 provides, in paragraph 2, special provisions for decision-making on mergers with another union by the General Assembly of a trade union. According to the law the decision to decide to call a General Assembly to debate a merger must be taken by the Administrative Board or 10 per cent of the membership. At the General Assembly a merger proposal is ratified if a minimum of 33 per cent of the members that have paid their dues are present and 75 per cent of those present

1,000 members only 800 have paid their annual dues, the General Assembly is valid if 160 members are present and 120 of them vote for the merger. This measure thus eased the merger process. Current legislation, therefore, cannot be singled out as the major barrier to mergers.

The failed attempts to complete mergers in banking illustrate that legislation still forms a barrier to mergers. OTOE (Banking Sector Employees' Federation) initiated several attempts to merge with OASE (Federation of Insurance Sector Employees). Stimulated by mergers and acquisitions between banking and insurance companies, OTOE twice voted in favour of a merger with OASE, but both times failed to obtain the required 75 per cent majority in favour of the proposal.

Another factor accounting for the absence of mergers was the legal control of bargaining structures and processes, in place until 1990. Law 3239/1955 provided for legal regulation of bargaining levels and units, the qualification of organisations as trade unions, their recognition for bargaining, the coverage of collective agreements, and the substantive contents of collective agreements and arbitration awards. Law 3239 also prohibited sectoral and company agreements. Collective agreements at the sectoral and the company level only became legal after 1990, with the adoption of Law 1876/90 on 'free collective bargaining'. The regulation of collective bargaining via compulsory arbitration between 1955 and 1990 had a 'freezing' effect on collective bargaining and trade union structure (Ioannou, 1994). The growth of trade unions in the decade 1975-1985 and the expansion of informal company and sectoral agreements comprised an attempt to reshape the over-regulated bargaining structure. The legal reform of 1990 (Law, 1876) consolidated the trend towards company and sectoral collective agreements by legalising them and by dismantling the state-controlled compulsory arbitration system. Legal regulation and collective bargaining practices were thus harmonised, although bargaining structure remained relatively centralised. In the area 'covered' by GSEE, for example, bargaining structure comprises a total of approximately 350 collective agreements, nearly 150 of which are company agreements where federations are not involved; 115 are sectoral agreements; and 90 are craft or occupational agreements. It appears that while the existence of the 62 federations may

vote for the proposal. If a sufficient majority is not achieved at the first General Assembly, the presence of at least 25 per cent of the members that have paid their dues is required at a subsequent Assembly. If a third Assembly is required at least 20 per cent of the members that have paid their dues are required to attend. At both the second and thirds attempts to secure the merger a majority of 75 per cent of those present must vote in favour of the proposal. This provision was supposed to make mergers far easier.

be attributed to the ossified bargaining structure, which is reproduced by the existing bargaining processes, the presence of 2,347 primary-level unions is independent of formal collective bargaining structure at company level. Given the extremely weak information and consultation processes at company level, the large number of primary level unions can only be attributed to the bureaucratic needs of the three-tier structure.

Another important influence of the bargaining process on trade union structure may stem from the provisions of collective bargaining qualification, together with the availability of legal or administrative ways to obtain collective agreements or arbitration awards and to extend their coverage to non-members. Qualifying bargaining units were confined to the 'recognised' trade unions, and in each employment sector (occupation or region), only 'representative' trade unions could qualify.[16] In 1969, Law 186 allowed two, instead of the previous one, 'representative' trade unions to be recognised. In 1990 collective bargaining reform (Law, 1876) re-instated the provision for the single 'most representative' trade union (Mitsou, 1992: 45-48). Frictions emerge where more than two trade unions claim 'representation' of the same section of the labour force. These inter-union frictions and conflicts are normally linked to party political rivalries. The provision regarding the 'most representative' union excludes cartel practices, enhances inter-union conflict for membership and provides no incentives for co-operation and mergers. The lack of mergers is thus not associated with cartel practices acting as a substitute for mergers. The absence of mergers, however, is associated with the ability of federations with weak bargaining power to obtain state-controlled compulsory arbitration awards until 1992, or to turn to quasi-compulsory arbitration through the use of mediation services after 1992. The widely used provisions in legislation that permit, with a decision of the Ministry of Labour, the extension of the terms of collective agreements and arbitration awards to other employers and employees which were not party to them, has also contributed to the reproduction of the existing bargaining structure. Contrary to the terms of the law regarding private sector collective bargaining, collective bargaining regulations for civil servants laid down in Law 2738/99 allow all trade unions to participate in bargaining where there is more than one trade

---

[16] Until 1990 the Ministry of Labour was empowered to determine, via the arbitration court, the 'representative' trade unions in each jurisdiction and thus to settle any inter-union and intra-union disputes over recognition rights and qualification for contracting collective agreements. Typically, membership was the single major criterion, but this was not always a sound base for determining which union was 'representative'. In many cases, 'declared' membership was false. In consequence, Law 1264 introduced the voting members as a criterion, rather than 'declared' membership.

union, provided they have jointly-agreed bargaining positions. In other words, since 1999 the collective bargaining system for civil servants allows and enhances co-operation and cartel practices.[17]

A third factor that has acted as a barrier to mergers comprises political interference, rivalries, cleavages and the lack of political autonomy of trade unions *vis-à-vis* political parties. Trade union mergers reshape political influence, which is not favoured by the competing political factions. A major factor that facilitated the mergers to form OEKIDE and OEPDXB was that there were no repercussions regarding the relative power of political factions. Both the pre- and post-merger federations were under the control of the same political factions. In other words, political cleavages and conflicts within the trade unions may also have a freezing effect on structure.

The lack of financial autonomy of trade unions is another factor that may act as a barrier to mergers. Trade unions are not dependent on members' subscriptions, which, in the majority of cases, are symbolic and act as a prerequisite for voting in trade union elections, but rely on compulsory contributions from the state institution OEE (House of Labour Organisation). From the *Metaxas* dictatorship (1936-40), the three tiers of trade union organisation were funded through a compulsory system, which was funded by the social security contributions of employers and employees (Koukoules, 1984).[18] In 1990, Law 1915 abolished trade union funding through the compulsory contribution system. This resulted in the collapse of unions. In 1992, after extensive campaigning by GSEE, Law 2091 reinstated the previous regime and strengthened its 'tripartite administration',[19] in the sense that GSEE and

---

[17]   This system is based on Law 2738/99, which was effective from 2000. The first bargaining round was not successful and it remains to be seen whether cartel practices operate as a substitute for mergers among trade unions of civil servants.

[18]   Despite minor reforms in the system brought about either by governmental initiative or in answer to trade unions demands, the OEE remains the principal source of funding for trade unions. Employers and employees forward, by means of social security contributions, 0.25 per cent of the latter's salaries to IKA (Social Security Fund) on behalf of OEE. Part of this sum is allotted to trade unions for their operation.

[19]   In 1992 GSEE announced that it would take measures to enhance the financial autonomy of trade unions. Today GSEE is mainly funded by OEE. For instance, from 1st April 1995 until 31st December 1997, 88.02 per cent out of gross revenues of 3.2 billion drachmas came through the subsidy from OEE, and only a mere 1.42 per cent from members' contributions. The remainder comprised proceeds from interest and, primarily, EU subsidies. The funding of secondary-level organisations is comparable. For instance, the 70 Labour Centres and 68 federations that participated in the process of electing representatives for the GSEE congress (in March 2001) received their funding by OEE, which, incidentally, also provided funds for the Congress.

employer representatives were incorporated on the board that administered trade union funding, although overall control remained with the Ministry of Labour. In the case of federations in banking and the state-owned public utilities, trade union contributions are deducted from employees' salaries by the company and handed over to the appropriate federation.[20] Although the same system could be applied in the private sector by means of collective agreements, it is extremely limited in coverage.

In the main, trade unions in the private sector depend on compulsory contributions collected and administered by the OEE, which only finances minimal functions.[21] The GSEE Congress in November 2002 debated the lack of trade union financial autonomy and the reliance on OEE funds. With falling GSEE-affiliated membership, increasing difficulties in collecting contributions, and the reluctance of members to sanction any increases in their contributions, the GSEE Congress demanded that the government increase the OEE funding from the current level of 25 per cent of its annual budget to 30 per cent, to meet increasing costs and falling revenues from members. The amount paid to trade unions in 2002 was 6.2 billion Drachmas (18,195 billion Euro).

Vested interests of elected trade union officials also act as barriers to mergers. Since the early 1950s in Greece, elected members of a trade union board were awarded supplementary pension rights.[22] Furthermore, participation on the board of a primary-level union is an informal prerequisite for further career development to higher levels of the three-tiered union structure. Mergers may result in severe cuts to the number of these 'privileged' posts, although recent experiences suggest that accommodations can be found. The new OEPDXB federation, with a total of 29 primary-level unions, has an elected administrative board of 33 members, which comprises the members of the boards of the pre-merger federations.

Funding is provided on the basis of each organisation's membership and in accordance with a Ministry of Labour and Social Security resolution, which specifies the prerequisites and conditions of distribution and payment of funds.

[20] Federations in the banking sector and public sector utilities are also able to finance their activities by negotiating lump-sum payments from employers in the annual collective agreements.

[21] Many unions attempt to develop research activities and services for their registered or potential members through EU programmes, training and community initiatives.

[22] These 'privileges' have been strongly criticised by many trade unionists, as they foster 'clientelism' and the manipulation of trade unions by the government in office.

Weak Endogenous Support for Mergers: Character, Reasons and Outcomes

The set of factors outlined in the previous section act as barriers to mergers. Some of these factors are also indicative of a lack of endogenous support for mergers at both the primary and the secondary level. For a long period, state regulation of trade union affairs was a barrier to autonomous trade union development and re-structuring. The easing of the legal requirements for mergers indicates that the state is now prepared to encourage mergers more than in the past. Furthermore, mergers were encouraged after 1983 when the GSEE decided in favour of trade union re-structuring by merger. So, the question then arises, why have more mergers not occurred?

Employers' attitudes towards mergers do not exert any negative or significant influence on mergers. For instance, in the case of the OEPDXB merger, the attitude of SEB (Federation of Greek Industry, the main employers Confederation) was positive, as it considered it easier to deal with one federation rather than two. In the OEKIDE merger in the textile industry, the employers' associations were so fragmented that they appeared completely indifferent towards the merger.

Marginal merger activity also suggests that endogenous support for mergers is weak. This is often due to the political balance of power within trade unions between the different party-affiliated factions. It is also associated with the large number of the fragmented sectoral or craft-based federations, which generally follow the EGSSE (National General Collective Agreements) guidelines agreed at the centralised level between GSEE and the three employers' Confederations (SEB, ESEE, GSEBEE). Within the bargaining structure, federations merely act as transmission belts for agreements or guidelines. As such, there is no advantage to be gained by merging. Furthermore, the mechanism available to extend the coverage of any sectoral or occupational (craft) agreement provides additional disincentives for cartel practices and mergers. Having obtained 'recognition' and the right to conclude a collective agreement, the 'most representative' federation also has the right to 'regulate' industrial relations in its jurisdiction. No room is left for either co-operative or antagonistic unions to intervene.

The two successful mergers were underpinned by a need to harmonise agreements within a sector and to maintain bargaining power when trade union density was declining. The OEKIDE merger resulted in a new federation, which at the GSEE Congress in 1998 comprised twenty-five primary level unions and 5,441 voting members.[23] A similar consolidation of forces was observed in the OEPDXB merger. In these two mergers trade union staffing levels remained minimal, as the majority of unions employed only one or two secretarial staff.[24] In both cases, post-merger federations appear in relatively better positions to support members at their workplaces. This is more important in the OEKIDE federation, as many of the affiliated primary-level unions have regional coverage and, hence, organise many workplaces. By contrast, primary-level unions in OEPDXB are mainly company unions and thus the merger merely united different primary unions organising at different sites. In both mergers, however, it is impossible to identify the introduction of new forms of representation or new forms of trade union government. Indeed, the post-merger experience of OEKIDE indicates two types of problem in the operation of the new structure. First, in order to establish a more representative administrative board based on sectoral and regional coverage, and meeting the implicit aim of accommodating all pre-merger board members of the new administrative board, it was decided to form a board of thirty-five members. This board proved very costly to operate and very difficult to assemble. Second, an upper limit of two terms was stipulated for membership of the new administrative board. Falling union density and participation rates have created major problems in filling vacant posts on the administrative board. In other words, although the pre-merger rationale revolved around sectoral harmonisation, increased membership and the maintenance of bargaining power, idiosyncratic factors that act as barriers to merger still cause problems to the effective operation of the post-merger federations.

Long-term Perspectives for Mergers

Although mergers have been marginal to Greek trade union structural development to date, a series of labour-market-related developments set the scene for more merger activity. Included among these developments are the privatisation of public sector utilities, company restructuring in the banking sector, declining trade union density and mounting pressure from the GSEE. This is not to say that an extensive merger process will develop regardless of changes in the attitudes, ideas and roles of trade unionists. Instead, it is to argue that labour market

---

[23] As some primary-level unions opted to be represented via the Labour Centres, the merger may have resulted, at best, in the creation of a federation with fifty primary level unions and 10,000 voting members.

[24] Company federations of the public utilities and the banking sector federation employ more than one or two functionaries. Normally, under the system of trade union funding, the salaries of staff are paid directly by the OEE fund.

developments coupled to the changing role of trade unions *vis-à-vis* the state and polity, provide new challenges for trade unions in Greece to which they must adapt during the first decades of the new century.

Mergers at Confederal Level

Since the early 1990s, the consequences of economic restructuring and de-industrialisation have adversely affected GSEE. Union density in the areas covered by GSEE peaked in 1986 at 43.3 per cent. Throughout the 1990s, however, density fell to 23.5 per cent in 1998 (see Table 6.5). During the same period, density in areas organised by ADEDY, which had peaked in 1992 at 51.3 per cent, remained relatively stable. Thus, while GSEE has secured its place as the leading national organisation of salary- and wage-earners employed under private law contracts, it has been weakened by labour market developments. In view of these developments, and in the general context of the need for harmonisation of trade union structures, the leaderships of GSEE and ADEDY started to discuss the merger of the two national confederations in 1999. The first step in this direction was closer co-operation, marked in 1999 by the creation of a joint Labour Institute, which incorporated the pre-existing GSEE Labour Institute (INE-GSEE). Next steps included a joint Congress, which was to discuss issues relating to the GSEE-ADEDY merger. The GSEE-ADEDY merger proposal was discussed at the GSEE Congress in November 2002. Prior to the Congress the Chairs and Executive Committees of both confederations agreed to restart the merger processes by forming a 'National Trade Union Council' in early 2003, which was to act as a co-ordination body of the two Executive Committees. This Council also decided to develop a five-year plan, which outlined a framework for the proposed merger. The initial stages of this framework required the joint running of secretariats on industrial relations, employment, development, social policy, culture and sports activities.

Table 6.5: Trade Union Voting Members and Trade Union Density, 1983-1998

Year	GSEE (000s)	ADEDY (000s)	Salary- & Wage-Earners (SWE) in Employment (000s)	SWE Density (%)	GSEE Density (%)	ADEDY Density (%)
1983	571	96	1,697	39.3	42.6	26.9
1986	596	165	1,774	42.9	43.3	41.7
1989	564	202	1,882	40.7	39.3	45.2
1992	482	236	1,938	41.3	32.6	51.3
1995	430	226	2,060	31.8	26.9	48.6
1998	442	241	2,245	30.4	23.5	49.4

Source: GSEE, ADEDY and Labour Force Surveys.

The experience of the period 1999-2002 suggests that the GSEE-ADEDY merger initiative had its origins in the politics of bargaining with the state (the government and political parties), rather than in collective bargaining and industrial relations. Since the announcement of the plan for a confederal merger, the two confederations have increasingly acted as a cartel in political bargaining with the government on national issues, such as social security reform. In organisation terms, there have been no other moves towards outlining the form of the proposed merger. Given that the two confederations act in distinct areas of the collective bargaining system and in different sub-systems of national industrial relations, basic questions remain unanswered. For example, a merger that combines the federations affiliated to the GSEE with those affiliated to ADEDY has no real meaning, to the extent that the fragmented trade union structure at the secondary and primary levels would remain unchanged. It is only at the level of the federations and the primary unions that mergers will have a real impact in transforming the fragmented trade union structure in Greece.

It remains an open question whether there is real intention to drive towards a GSEE-ADEDY merger. If closer co-operation is aimed at securing political objectives, and this is based on the existing balance of power between the various political factions in the GSEE and ADEDY boards, small changes in the balance of power may cause centrifugal tendencies. Political factions are determined by political party affiliations. In both GSEE and ADEDY boards there are currently small majorities in favour of PASOK, which may allow the closer co-operation of the two national confederations. Marginal changes in the balance of power between the political factions, however, may cast serious doubts on the continuity of closer co-operation between GSEE and ADEDY.

Another important factor that may influence trade union mergers in Greece, and especially the prospects of closer co-operation between GSEE and ADEDY, is the changing relationship between the two major political parties (PASOK and Nea Dimokratia) and their political factions within the trade union movement. Trade union political factions are party political organisations, with the result that trade unionists are able to adopt two positions depending on tactical and political calculations; either as a member of a political faction and party, or as a trade union official. This has often caused friction within political parties. Recently, however, PASOK and Nea Dimokratia have indicated that they seek greater distance from the trade unions. In the case of the PASOK, this has taken the form of proposals to dissolve its distinct trade union organisation. This means that the model of control and operation of the past twenty-five years, through the triple relationship

'state-political party-trade union', is to change, and that political resources will be reduced. The greater distance of the political parties may
lead to more autonomous trade unions. In the present context of declining union membership, the greater distance of the political parties from
trade unions may result in a serious lack of political resources that later
could be followed by the withdrawal of financial resources on which
trade unions survive. In such a situation, a 'collapse' of confederal trade
union structures should not be dismissed.

Trade union leaders also appear to be losing political influence and
acceptance. The GSEE Congress in November 2002 decided to extend
the upper time limits for terms of office served on the GSEE administrative board from two to three terms (of three years). This reform allowed
current office holders to prolong their term of office. A reason for this
reform was the failure to renew cadres in the hierarchy of the unions, as
young people, in particular, decline to participate. Another reason for
this reform was the increasing difficulty faced by leading trade unionists
in finding political positions or election to parliament. The trend of trade
unionists moving into political positions was dominant during the 1980s
and 1990s.

Federations in Public Sector Utilities Seek New Roles

The deregulation and privatisation of public sector utilities has
forced the strongholds of Greek trade unionism to develop a proactive
approach. Thus, the OME-OTE (telecommunications), GENOP-DEH
(electricity) and OME ELTA (Post Office) federations have declared
their intention to broaden their scope and to shift from being company
federations to becoming sectoral federations. The intention is to organise employees of entire sectors, including those enterprises that are
currently union-free, such as the mobile phone companies Panafon and
Telestet. Concurrently, within the federations that organise the public
sector utilities centrifugal tendencies are developing, particularly among
the more skilled segments of the labour force. Engineers and telecommunications scientists of the Hellenic Telecommunication Organisation,
which were members of the company federation OME-OTE, for example, decided to leave the federation in 1999, because they considered
that it had failed to pursue their interests in collective bargaining. These
scientists opted for separate bargaining arrangements

Although employment has expanded in the recently deregulated sectors of telecommunications and civil aviation, there have been no real
membership campaigns from the federations that organise the public
sector utilities. They remain inward-looking and there are very few
opportunities to expand their coverage to embrace the new entrants to

the sector, particularly as employers are hostile towards unions. To transform these company federations into sectoral federations requires enormous change, the will for which does not appear to exist. Not surprisingly, the GSEE Congress in 2002 encouraged affiliated company federations within public sector utilities to change their statutes to enable them to organise private sector employees where deregulation had occurred, as in telecommunications, electricity and postal services.

Mergers of Company Unions

Although at the primary level of the GSEE structure signs of merging activity have been marginal,[25] the wave of company mergers and acquisitions in the banking sector stimulated the search for mergers among primary level unions. One would expect company mergers and acquisitions to have mobilised company trade unions to seek their own re-organisation through mergers. The experience of two major mergers in the banking sector, however, demonstrates the pathology of fragmentation among Greek trade unions.

In 1999 EFG Eurobank acquired, after an offensive take-over, the majority of Ergobank. EFG Eurobank and Ergobank shareholders decided to merge and, in July 2000, created a new bank with 7,500 employees and 330 branches. The company trade unions in both banks announced their plans to merge in January 2000 with the intention of establishing a unified structure and playing an active role in the company merger process. Both unions also invited the personnel of other smaller banks controlled by EFG Eurobank[26] to join the new union, so that a single trade union would represent employees throughout the EFG Eurobank group of companies. The trade union merger process never took off, however, and currently there are three different and competing trade unions.[27] In the context of the legislation that favours the 'most representative' trade union for collective bargaining and excludes any other, legal measures were taken by the competing unions against each other to secure the position of being the 'most representative'. Amid this legal conflict, the banking sector Federation OTOE was not very influential in its aim to create a single united company trade union.

---

[25] For instance, the Cooks' Trade Union of Athens decided to merge with the Waiters' Trade Union of Athens to form a new trade union.

[26] Interbank, Euroinvestment, Athens Bank and Bank of Crete.

[27] The three trade unions are EFG Eurobank (Association of Employees of Ergo Bank and EFG Eurobank) with 2,850 members; EFG Eurobank (Association of Banking Company EFG Eurobank) with 3,150 members; and EFG Eurobank (Association of EFG Eurobank Personnel) with 350 members.

Another case that would normally have led to a merger of company trade unions was the acquisition of Ionian Bank by the Alpha Credit Bank to form the Alpha Bank in May 2000. For months there was no sign of a merger initiative from the trade union side. When the company merger was completed, however, conflict erupted between the company trade unions that required legal intervention. The Ionian Bank company union sought legal redress against the Alpha Credit Bank trade union and the Alpha Bank management, and claimed that management and union had exerted pressure on Ionian Bank trade union members to abandon their own union and join the Alpha Credit Bank trade union. Alpha Bank thus represented a case where the Alpha Credit Bank trade union attempted to poach members from the Ionian Bank trade union. This inter-union conflict illustrates the endogenous constraints on trade union mergers in the most developed sector of trade unionism in Greece. Provisions on the bargaining rights of the 'most representative' trade union and the exclusion of any other company trade union, coupled to the existing political divisions of trade unionists in a situation where employers can also exert an influence, tend to promote inter-union conflict rather than mergers. Ossified trade union structures containing micro-unions are thus preserved or, after the poaching of members, the 'losing' union is driven out of existence.

Conclusions

Since the early 1950s trade union structure in Greece has remained stable and has tended towards fragmentation, rather than consolidation through mergers. This pattern is associated with the historical cycle of development of trade unionism, which occurred after the return to parliamentary democracy in 1974. The present structure of two national confederations is the product of the developments during the 1980s and is fragmented at the level of the federations and at the primary level. Union structure is dominated by 'micro' trade unions and union co-ordination is organised through a three-tier structure. During the 1990s there were only two cases of mergers between federations.

Restructuring representation is becoming an issue of increasing interest, promoted by the restructuring of major sectors of the economy and the decline in union density in the private sector. The planned merger of GSEE and ADEDY was announced in 1999, but remains an extremely difficult task and is currently restricted to the objective of closer co-operation in the achievement of political objectives. Long-standing principles of organisation established around occupation- and sector-based trade unions and the three-tier structure of unionism, however, are not challenged.

Factors that explain the inertia of trade union structure are related to the historical development of occupation-based trade unions, which were organised at the secondary level through a dual structure of federations and Labour Centres during the post-war period. Extensive legal regulation of trade unions, together with a lack of financial autonomy and the impact of political rivalries, contributed to structural stability. Moves towards democratic re-organisation of trade unions during the early 1980s and the emergence of new movements in the industry sector and in the public sector utilities since the return to parliamentary democracy, changed the locus of Greek trade unionism, but failed to initiate restructuring. Declining trade union density has reiterated the requirement for mergers throughout the three tiers of union structure. Support for mergers, however, is weak. Reforming trade unions from being quangos to becoming social partners is thus thwarted by the fragmentation of union structure, with the result that trade union attempts to move towards social partnership, in the sense commonplace throughout the European Union, are undermined.

Despite the long-lasting ossification of trade union structures and the weak endogenous support for trade union mergers, existing structures may become the subject of emergency restructuring if and when two cornerstones of the existing structures are withdrawn. Such a withdrawal depends on government policy. The first cornerstone relates to the funding of trade union activities through compulsory contributions administered by the state-controlled OEE. A withdrawal of such funding may lead to the immediate collapse of trade union activities, with the exception of those in banking and in public sector utilities. The second cornerstone concerns the availability of mediation and quasi-compulsory arbitration services that enable weak unions to conclude collective agreements or obtain arbitration awards that are then extended to cover non-members. A reform of this mechanism would necessitate weak unions reconsidering their alliances in the private sector, which, in turn, may lead to mergers.

List of Abbreviations

ADEDY	Supreme Administration of Civil Servants' Trade Unions
DOE	Federation of Primary Education Teachers
GENOP – DEH	General Federation of Public Electricity Corporation Employees.
GSEE	General Confederation of Greek Labour
INE-GSEE	Labour Institute of GSEE

NOP-DEH	New Federation of Public Electricity Corporation Employees
OASE	Federation of Insurance Sector Employees
OBES	Federation of Industrial Factory Unions
ODYE	Federation of Ministry of Justice Employees
OEE	House of Labour Organisation
OEKIDE	Federation of Textile, Clothing, and Leather Workers of Greece
OEPDXB	Federation of Employees in Oil, Refineries and Chemical Industries
OIYE	Federation of Private Sector Employees
OLME	Federation of Secondary Education Teachers
OME-DEH	Federationof Public Electricity Corporation Employees
OME-OTE	Federation of Hellenic Telecommunications Organisation Employees
OOSE	Federation of Construction Workers
OSPA	Federation of Civil Aviation Employees
OTOE	Federation of Banking Sector Employees
PASOK	Panhellenic Socialist Movement
POE-ELTA	Federation of the Hellenic Post Office Employees
POEDHN	Federation of Public Hospital Employees
POE-DOY	Federation of Taxation Services Employees
POE-OTA	Federation of Local Government Employees
POEM	Federation of Metalworkers
POEPDXB	Federation of Employees in Refineries and Chemical Industry
POETE	Federation of Tourist Industry and Restaurants Employees
POE-YETHA	Federation of Ministry of Defence Employees
POPEEP	Federation of Employees in Oil Trade Companies
POS	Federation of the Hellenic Railways Organisation Employees
POSE-IKA	Federation of Social Security Fund Employees
POSE-YPECHODE	Federation of Ministry of Public Works and Environment Employees
POSYPPO	Federation of Ministry of Culture Employees
SDYE	Confederation of Greek Civil Servants
SEB	Federation of Greek Industry

CHAPTER 7. NORWAY

Adapting Slowly

Kristine NERGAARD[1]

This chapter examines, in three sections, the Norwegian merger process. The first section briefly identifies the key characteristics of the Norwegian industrial relations system. The second charts the dimensions of the merger process, attention being paid to the different merger trajectories among unions within the different confederations. The third section identifies the key influences on the merger process. The argument throughout is that, in comparison with several other countries examined in this volume, the rate of trade union structural change in Norway has been modest. Where such change has been implemented, however, it has led to the formation of multi-industry unions in manufacturing and the consolidation of union organisation among the professions.

Trade Union Organisation and the Bargaining System

Industrialisation came late to Norway. Though the first national trade union – for printworkers – was founded in 1882, national unions did not proliferate until the 1890s. Although the majority of these were craft unions, the traditional distinction between skilled and unskilled workers never dominated the Norwegian labour movement. During the same period, confederations for employees and employers within manufacturing were also formed. LO (Norwegian Confederation of Trade Unions) was established in 1899, followed shortly afterwards by the creation of a confederation for employers in 1900. The first sectoral collective agree-

[1] I take this opportunity to thank Line Eldring, Dag Olberg and Torgeir Aarvaag Stokke, of Fafo, for helpful comments on earlier drafts. Håvard Lismoen translated the text into English, and contributed to this process with useful comments and some well-placed question marks. Thanks also to Jeremy Waddington, whose editorial work considerably strengthened the final result.

ment was concluded in 1908 in manufacturing, and was soon followed by other sectors. These developments contributed to the gradual institutionalisation of a national bargaining system, in which the central level played an important role. Norway has never experienced periods of significant decentralisation and weakening of the central organisations and, for most of the period since World War II, the relationship between the main actors in the labour market has been characterised by mutual respect and co-operation.

Trade Unions and the Confederations

There were approximately 95 trade unions in Norway in 2001.[2] They varied considerably in size from the smallest with fewer than 100 members, to the largest with more than 235,000 members. Many of these unions organise – or aim to organise – all employees within specific industries and sectors or public services and enterprises. There are also a number of unions that organise only specific professions/occupations or employees with a particular level of higher education. Within manufacturing, it is customary to have separate unions for blue- and white-collar workers.[3] There are some unions that deviate from the mainstream characteristics outlined above, but their share of unionised employees is not significant.

A majority of trade unions affiliate to one of the four union confederations, which share approximately 95 per cent of all unionised employees. The LO is by far the largest with approximately 800,000 members, almost 600,000 of whom are employed. YS (Confederation of Vocational Unions) and AF (Confederation of Norwegian Professional Associations) were both established during the 1970s, and their coverage includes a large number of previously independent unions. AF was dissolved on 7 July 2001 after a long period of internal tension during the 1990s. Two new confederations were formed, *Akademikerne* (Fed-

---

[2]   There are no requirements regarding the approval or registration of trade unions in Norway, for either collective agreements or in the legal framework. The implication of this is that there is uncertainty attached to surveys and data on the number of trade unions in existence, despite Statistics Norway's considerable efforts in keeping track of unions and union members in Norwegian working life. The deficiencies with regards to available figures are most evident early in the period 1945-2000.

[3]   The LO union NOPEF (Norwegian Oil and Petrochemical Workers Union) organises vertically, thus incorporating both blue- and white-collar workers. The YS union PRIFO (traditionally a blue-collar workers union) has introduced a vertical organisational principle. Another example is YS-union KFO which was a white-collar union that in the 1960s decided to open up membership also to blue-collar workers (Thue 1986).

eration of Norwegian Professional Associations) and UHO (Confederation of Higher Education Unions). *Akademikerne* organises employees with an academic education, classified as at least 3-4 years of education at university level. The affiliates of UHO include the unions for police, teachers and nurses.

Union organisation in Norway is not divided between confederations in the same way as in the other Nordic countries. Both LO and YS organise across all industries and occupations. Whereas lower- and medium-level white-collar workers make up the majority of YS members, LO members in the private sector are drawn mainly from blue-collar workers. LO is also deeply involved in the public sector, recruiting members among lower- and medium-level white-collar workers. Although both LO and YS aim to unionise groups with higher education, most of these groups are affiliated to the other two confederations. Traditionally, the relationship between LO and YS has been tense, as many of the unions affiliated to YS are in direct competition for members with LO unions.

Union density in Norway is lower than in other Nordic countries. In 2000, 53 per cent of wage-earners were union members. Unlike the other Nordic countries, the Norwegian unemployment benefit scheme is not administered by trade unions, a factor that explains much of the variation in union density. Private sector services in Norway are characterised by low union density. Exceptions, however, are banking and insurance and – to a lesser degree – private transport. There is a wide range of unions within the municipal sector. The dominant unions within this sector are NKF (Norwegian Union of Municipal Employees) which is affiliated to LO, and the professional unions within the health sector, which affiliate to UHO or *Akademikerne*. In the state sector, there is a variety of unions and confederations. The larger, state-owned enterprises, however, are dominated by LO unions.

Bargaining System and Legal Framework

The Norwegian bargaining system is centralised. Most collective agreements are national-level agreements that cover a whole sector or industry. The parties to these agreements are national unions and employers' associations. The central arena for collective bargaining in Norway is the so-called LO/NHO agreement area, which covers manufacturing, construction, private transportation and hotels and restaurants. NHO (Confederation of Norwegian Business and Industry) is also party to agreements with YS within these sectors. In the LO/NHO agreement area, the confederations play a major role in the negotiations, and the agreements are often negotiated together. There are also a number of other agreements in the private sector of which the largest are located in banking and insurance and the wholesale and retail trade. Here the employer side is represented by organisations outside the NHO. In the public sector there is one collective agreement for the state sector and, in effect, one agreement for the municipal sector. The confederations and/or the bargaining cartels associated with the main confederations thus play an important role in collective bargaining in the public sector.

Trade Union Mergers in Norway

No survey of trade union mergers had previously been conducted in Norway. Original data and information have thus been collected for this study. There are no complete data series or surveys on the number of trade unions and mergers in Norway. The only sources of data available are the trade unions' own reports and registers, and Statistics Norway's *Statistisk Årbok* (Statistical Yearbook of Norway) which includes listings on the number of unions in existence and their membership. The annual reports of LO provide insight into developments within the confederation since 1945. With regard to developments in union organisation outside LO, the establishment of AF and YS in the 1970s also provides reliable data from that period.

The first survey from Statistics Norway to include unions outside the LO was the 1956 *Statistisk Årbok*. The information available for the early years of this study is thus incomplete. There are three areas of ambiguity regarding the data. First, there is some uncertainty concerning the formal status of some of the smaller unions during the early period. Second, a number of smaller unions in the state sector are not listed in the *Statistisk Årbok*, because in membership reports from the EL (Association of Civil Service Employees) unions with less than 100 members are excluded.[4] This type of under-reporting of very small unions is present throughout the period until 1980. Where it was possible to identify them, some of these unions (and mergers) have been included in this survey.

---

[4] There are, in all likelihood, at any given time between 20 and 30 such small organisations that are not listed in the membership reports of EL. All of these have less than 100 members and a majority have less than 50 members. When AF is established in 1975 many of these unions are listed as member unions of AF. Then many disappear again, and we are not able to determine whether their disappearance may be attributed to mergers or dissolutions. The smallest AF unions are also left out of the Yearbook in the first few years of AF's existence, and we have therefore chosen not to include them in our survey.

A third problem is that of dealing with groups of trade unions whose status is somewhere between a trade union and a confederation. The STAFO (Union of Civil Servants in Norway) and BFO (Military Officers' Association), for example, originally functioned as confederations, in which affiliated associations/unions retained some independence and could choose to re-establish themselves as an independent union. Both STAFO and BFO joined YS as ordinary trade unions when it was established in 1977. There is little doubt that these groups of trade unions should be treated as single trade unions today, as their affiliated units or associations do not enjoy the status of independent unions. The matter may be debated, however, for the period prior to the establishment of YS. For the purposes of this chapter STAFO and BFO are treated as independent unions throughout, due to their gradual development towards becoming 'ordinary' trade unions.

All in all, these data ambiguities have led to an underestimation of the number of mergers outside LO and of the total number of unions in existence. This under-reporting applies to the period 1956 to 1980, and is primarily a problem in relation to the smaller unions.

Overview

Developments in the Number of Trade Unions from 1945 to 2000

Table 7.1 shows that there have not been significant changes in the number of trade unions in Norway since 1945. For large segments of the period 1945 to 2000 the total number of unions remained relatively stable, at just above 100. It is important to bear in mind the uncertainty surrounding figures and data concerning the number of trade unions outside LO before the late 1970s. Had a less strict definition of 'trade union' been adopted, the number of unions in this period would have been significantly higher. Bearing these points in mind, Table 7.1 shows that there has been a continual, albeit slight, decline in the number of unions from 1980. This is the case both outside and within LO. Mergers, formations and breakaways influence the number of trade unions. Neither formations nor breakaways have had an important effect on trade union structure in the period since 1945. The great majority of today's trade unions existed in some form before the 1950s.[5]

---

5   The data indicate that a substantial number of new trade unions have emerged throughout the period (approximately fifty). Some of these are newly established unions. Others are old unions that have probably existed throughout the period, but that have not been registered. Some unions emerge in the statistics because they breakaway from federal unions/confederations like BFO, STAFO or KFL/KFO, where they have enjoyed a fairly autonomous status.

Table 7.1: The Number of Trade Unions
by Confederation and Independent Unions

	LO	YS	AF	AKADE-MIKERNE	UHO	INDE-PENDENT	TOTAL
1945	37						
1950	39						
1955/1956	45					68[1]	109
1960	43					69	108
1965	43					68	110
1970	38					64	103
1975	38					68	106
1980	35	15	41			24	115
1985	32	15	40			26	113
1990	29	17	39			23	108
1995	28	18	35			19	100
2000	26	17	18	15		18	94
2002[2]	25	21	–	15	5	24	90

[1] The figures for independent unions are based on information from 1956.
[2] October 2002.

Source: Statistical Yearbook; LO Annual reports 1945-1999; YS Annual Reports 1977-1999; AF Annual Reports 1975-1999.

Mergers in the Period 1945 to 2000

With the exception of the immediate post-war years, trade union mergers have taken place during most of the period. Information about the type of mergers that have taken place stems from two sources, namely, reports issued by trade unions, and literature on the history of the trade union movement or on the history of specific trade unions. In addition we draw upon a regular survey on Norwegian organisations/ associations (Moren, 1966; Moren *et al.*, 1972; Hallenstvedt *et al.*, 1983).

Table 7.2 shows the mergers we have been able to register. In total there have been roughly seventy mergers, an average of little more than one union disappearing each year. There are, however, variations over time. Within LO there was only one merger in the period 1945 to 1959. During the 1960s, however, several mergers took place within LO resulting in the disappearance of eight unions. The second half of the 1980s was also a period during which a significant number of mergers took place within LO. Among the trade unions outside the LO, the 1960s and the 1990s were periods of relatively intense merger activity.

Table 7.2: Number of Trade Union Mergers

	LO	OTHERS	TOTAL
1945-1949	1	0	1
1950-1954	0	0	0
1955-1959[1]	0	1	1
1960-1964	4	8	12
1965-1969	4	8	12
1970-1974	2	1	3
1975-1979	3	4	7
1980-1984	1	2	3
1985-1989	6	3	9
1990-1994	2	8	10
1995-1999	1	5	6
2000-2002[2]	3	6	9
1945-2002[2]	27	46	73
1956-2002[2]	26	46	72

[1] The time-series for other organisations starts at 1956.

[2] October 2002.

Amalgamations and Acquisitions

The distinction between amalgamations and acquisitions is not always clear-cut in Norway because unions tend to stress that a new union has been set up even where the merging unions are of different size. Another problem is that there is little information on some of the earlier mergers, especially those involving small unions, which leaves the classification subject to substantial discretion. When in doubt, we have tended to classify such mergers as an amalgamation. Table 7.3 shows that there have been more amalgamations than acquisitions, but that both kinds of merger occur over most of the period. Since the 1990s, however, the number of amalgamations has been high, both in absolute terms and relative to the total number of acquisitions. Most of these have taken place in the public sector or in the private sector services. The same is true of the 1960s, when many of the changes took place in the manufacturing sector.

Table 7.3: Amalgamations and Acquisitions, 1945-2000

	AMALGAMATIONS	ACQUISITIONS	TOTAL
1945-1955[1]	1	0	1
1956-1959	0	1	1
1960-1969	15	9	24
1970-1979	4	5	9
1980-1989	6	7	13
1990-1999	11	5	16
2000-2002[2]	6	3	8
Whole period	43	30	73

[1] LO only.

[2] October 2002.

The Principal Characteristics of Mergers within LO

The LO Congressional Resolution of 1923

LO approved the principle of industrial unionism as early as 1923. The implication was that LO abandoned the so-called craft or occupational unions. At the 1923 LO Congress it was decided that member unions were to carry out wide-ranging organisational changes such as mergers, dissolutions and transfer of members.[6] The main objective of these changes was to reduce the number of affiliated unions from 30 to between 10 and 12 (AFL, 1923). This proved difficult to accomplish. Several unions chose to leave the LO rather than comply with the resolution. Others managed to ignore the decision. The LO debated its structure on several occasions after 1923. The 1957 LO Congress reaffirmed the resolution to merge unions in those industries where two or more unions were active, although it abandoned the requirement to merge with the objective of achieving stronger trade unions. Despite the emphasis on the industrial union principle, LO has never made any attempt to unify white-collar and blue-collar workers in the private sector.

---

[6] The LO Congress may, in principle, make far-reaching decisions on its internal organisational structure. The Congress has on earlier occasions made decisions that would imply mergers among its members. However, LO has never succeeded in forcing member unions to merge against their wish, and have never actually put force behind such decisions. Today LO would probably not make any imperative decisions on a merger that is not supported by the unions involved. Decisions on which trade union does have the right to conclude an agreement for a certain sector lies, without doubt, within the authority of the LO.

Although the all-encompassing principles of 1923 were never properly implemented, the resolution has nevertheless been influential on the structure of LO by virtue of being a norm, with which most unions agree or which, in principle at least, they accept. The principles have thus influenced the long-term adaptation of LO structure, insofar as they have had a bearing on the inclusion of new affiliates. LO has, however, abandoned the absolutist requirement of the principle of industrial unionism in order to attract new groups. Several unions with members in the municipal sector, for example, have affiliated and have been able to keep their status as independent unions instead of joining the NKF. This was the case in relation to the three unions organising advanced college-educated personnel within the social care sector. On other occasions this has not been possible.

Mergers among LO-Affiliated Unions in Manufacturing: Towards a Multi-Industry Union

The structure of LO during the 1960s and the first half of the 1970s was marked by a number of mergers of unions within manufacturing. Most of these mergers were industry-based amalgamations. A few were also characterised by craft unions joining or establishing industrial unions.

Within the textile industry there were four unions in 1945. During the immediate post-war period the membership of these unions fell and their financial situation deteriorated. A new union was established in 1968 through an amalgamation of three of the unions. The fourth, and the smallest of the unions, joined four years later. An industrial textile union was thus established almost fifty years after LO had resolved to move towards this objective (Kamsvåg, 1990).

There were also originally four unions within the food manufacturing industry, and these later merged into a single union NNN (Norwegian Union of Food and Allied Workers). The merger took place in two phases, in 1962 *Norsk Tobakksarbeiderforbund* (Tobacco Workers), *Norsk Baker og Konditorforbund* (Bakery Workers) and NNN merged. In 1970 the remaining *Norsk Kjøttindustriarbeiderforbund* (Union of Meat Industry Workers) also joined (NNN, 1998).

The merger of the three graphical unions also took place almost fifty years after the LO resolution of 1923. The unions were craft-based and co-existed in many enterprises, but had established some kind of system for co-ordination through a joint graphical cartel. The national conventions of the three unions approved the merger in 1966, and the NGF (Norwegian Graphical Union) was established (Andersen, 1999).

Figure 7.1: Mergers 1945-2000, LO Unions in Manufacturing, Construction and Primary Sector

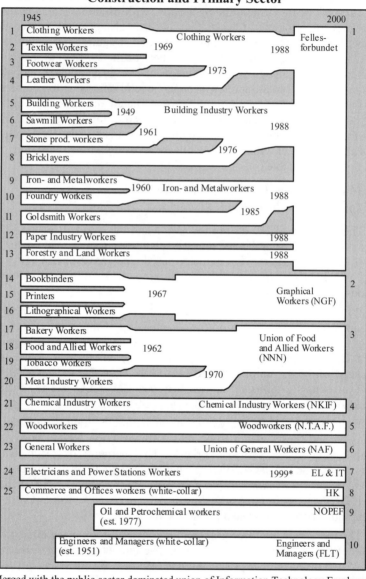

* Merged with the public sector dominated union of Information Technology Employees.

Within the building sector, the dominant union was the *Norsk Bygningsarbeiderforbund* (Building Workers' Union), which recruited both skilled and unskilled workers. In addition, there were separate unions for bricklayers and electricians, as well as unions for contiguous trades such as stone and wood manufacturing and production. By 1970 all the unions with the exception of the craft-conscious electricians had merged (Hansen, 1949; Berntsen, 1993). The new union was named NBIF (Norwegian Union of Building Industry Workers).

Two LO unions competed within the metal industry, the dominant NJM (Iron and Metalworkers' Union) and much smaller *Norsk Former-forbund* (Union of Foundry Workers). In this sector there was also a long-standing LO decision to merge, which had not been implemented. The fact that *Norsk Formerforbund* eventually joined the NJM, owes a lot to 'a more disenchanted view with regard to the viability of standing alone' (Halvorsen, 1990: 259). The small *Norsk Gullsmedarbeiderfor-bund* (Goldsmiths' Union) joined NJM in 1985, as it no longer had enough members to survive independently.

Within a time span of 10 to 15 years during the 1960s and 1970s much of the plan launched at the LO Congress of 1923 was thus carried out. There is little evidence to suggest that these developments were controlled from above. Although the resolution of 1923 did not directly effect a significant number of mergers, the principle of industrial union-ism was agreed and many minor changes were accomplished, such as the transfer of groups of members from one union to another. In addi-tion, the 1923 resolution contributed to the establishment of broad industrial unions within the textiles, chemical, food and construction industries. The establishment of broader, but industry-based, unions meant that the more specialist unions, most of which were not pure craft unions, were prevented from extending their coverage towards new industries.

Mergers among the unions in manufacturing came in a period when a significant number of unions were losing members. It was also a period in which increasing state involvement in industrial policy-making meant that it was important to increase efforts to exert influence on this process. Size was also seen as an advantage in relation to bargaining, although the traditional collective agreements based on the old trade union areas were retained. Large size was also seen as an advantage with regard to influence within the LO, especially for the smaller unions. It was also argued that there were no longer any 'natural' boundaries separating trade unions, because there was a high degree of blurring between traditional industries. This was the certainly the case in printing and in textiles.

Many of the smaller unions organised substantial numbers of skilled workers and maintained strong craft traditions, which generated some reluctance towards merging with larger unions of unskilled workers.

When the old craft traditions disappeared, mergers were usually more readily accomplished. Despite a variety of good reasons for bringing unions together, a merger was not always an easy decision to take. In most cases, mergers were based on long negotiation processes at the end of which membership ballots were usually held.

The next major organisational development of LO in the private sector came with the establishment of *Fellesforbundet* (Norwegian United Federation of Trade Unions) in 1988. *Fellesforbundet* was the result of a merger between five unions: BAF (Norwegian Union of Clothing Workers), NBIF, NJM, NPF (Norwegian Union of Paper Industry Workers), and NSLF (Norwegian Union of Forestry and Land Workers). Whereas most mergers during the 1960s and 1970s involved several unions within the same industry, *Fellesforbundet* incorporated members from different industries and sectors, thus accommodating very different traditions regarding wage systems, employer relationships and local union structures. The establishment of *Fellesforbundet* in 1988 was the most recent merger within the industry section of LO. Since 1945 the number of blue-collar unions in manufacturing and construction has dropped from 24 to 8 (see Figure 7.1). *Fellesforbundet* alone comprises what in 1945 were 13 LO unions.

What was the rationale behind the amalgamation of such a diverse blend of unions? As was the case for most other mergers, the financial aspect and a general wish to increase organisational efficiency with regard to the utilisation of resources were important to many of the unions involved. Furthermore, *Fellesforbundet* became the largest union affiliated to LO, which allows greater influence both within, as well as outside, LO. This, however, was not the decisive factor. The NJM was already the second largest union affiliated to LO, and NBIF was the third largest, and, as such, both were already powerful actors. Traditionally, the private sector unions have held a strong position within LO, although public sector unions have steadily increased their share of membership.

The establishment of *Fellesforbundet* may partly be seen as a response to another unsuccessful organisational project within LO. Both the NJM and the NBIF wanted to transform LO into a confederation without trade unions, but with cartels/sections for the main sectors. The leaders of the two unions decided to continue talks on organisational change, despite the fact that neither the public sector unions nor a substantial number of private sector unions wanted to take part.

There are two unions for white-collar industry workers within LO, namely, HK (Norwegian Union of Employees in Commerce and Offices) and FLT (Norwegian Engineers and Managers Association). They are both subject to significant competition over members from other unions with similar membership profiles outside LO. Although the issue has been raised on several occasions, LO has never attempted to dissolve the structural distinction between blue- and white-collar worker unions.

Public Sector: Unifying Blue- and White-collar Workers

In the public sector there have been fewer changes to union structure than in the private sector. At the 1923 LO Congress it was decided that there should be only one union for the municipal sector and one for the state sector. With the exception of the electricians in municipal electricity power plants, which were never persuaded to join the NKF, this goal had been achieved in the municipal sector by the mid-1920s.

In the state sector a single large union never saw the light of day. Here, unions already organised within particular departments/enterprises. Even if LO wanted one union for the state sector, one union per department/enterprise was, after a while, seen as acceptable according to the industrial union principle. This policy was managed pragmatically with, for example, the establishment of 'joint organisations' within telecommunications and postal services. Originally a blue-collar dominated union affiliated to LO, while white-collar dominated unions were outside.[7] When the white-collar unions joined LO, practical solutions were sought to safeguard the autonomous position of all unions.

The first mergers among unions in the state sector took place during the 1970s. These mergers comprised the combining of unions within the same department/enterprise: the three postal unions became one in mergers during 1977 and 2001; the two unions within telecommunications merged in 1988; and a single union was created from the two unions within the armed forces in 1978. There are still two unions within the railways, one for railway employees and a small union for engine drivers. The merger of these unions is the only recommendation of the 1957 LO Congress that has not been implemented.

In the municipal sector, NKF has been the dominant union and – since the mid-1970s – Norway's largest union. A merger between NKF and the former YS-union NHS (Norwegian Association of Practical

---

[7] The differences between the various unions for postal workers (and telecommunication workers) within and outside LO were originally based on type of work and partly on educational background/recruitment practice and thereby social class. However, the blue-collar/white-collar distinction seems less obvious than in the manufacturing sector (Bergh, 1985; 1989).

Nurses) took place in 2003. In 1993 the three LO-unions for professions within the social care sector merged.

With one exception, there have neither been mergers between public and private sector unions, nor between unions in the municipal and state sectors. The exception is the EL&IT (Electricians and Information Technology Workers' Union), which was formed in 1999 by the merger between NEKF (Norwegian Union of Electricians and Power Station Workers) and TD (Norwegian Union of Information Technology Employees).

Mergers and Trade Union Structure outside LO: Organisation Building and Consolidation

Mergers that have taken place outside of the LO involved a variety of trade unions. Some were specialised professional unions, while others were small with limited resources, often covering a very restricted category of employees. Furthermore, several mergers involve two small unions joining forces, but then continuing to lead a rather shadowy existence. What is noteworthy about several of these mergers, however, is that they started to multiply, and that many of them may be regarded as a form of organisation building culminating in modern unions enjoying strong positions within their own respective areas.

Teachers: From Twelve to One

In 2001 the two largest teachers' unions – NL (Norwegian Union of Teachers) and *Lærerforbundet* – made a final decision to merge, resulting in the creation of *Utdanningsforbundet* (Union of Education), Norway's third largest trade union with approximately 130,000 members. *Utdanningsforbundet* emerged through a series of mergers, involving what were twelve teachers' unions during the 1950s. These unions either competed with each other or organised teachers in different types of schools. Two separate strategic mergers form the basis of this development: the unification of teachers within the primary and lower secondary school system during the 1960s, and the combining of teachers within the upper and secondary school system that took place during the 1990s.

There are a number of historical reasons why the primary and lower secondary school system was divided between four unions until the mid-1950s. Teachers were initially unionised in *Norges Lærerlag*, but were split in 1911 when female teachers broke away to form a separate union as a protest against the undermining of the union's constitution relating to gender quotas. The new union, *Norges Lærerindeforbund*, was one of the few female trade unions in Norway. A further division came when the Oslo branches of both unions broke away after a dispute over wages in 1953. There were also a number of smaller unions for teachers in other types of school (Hagemann, 1992).

The split between the two unions for women did not last for long, however, and by 1959 the Oslo branch had re-joined *Norges Lærerinde-forbund*. The further amalgamation of teachers' unions came about gradually. During the 1960s five unions merged to form NL. Further-more, the union for nursery teachers had already joined NL, and was allowed separate systems of representation within the new organisation to cater for their special interests (Greve, 1995).

Outside the primary and lower secondary school system there were also a variety of unions within different types of school. The largest, *Norsk Lektorlag*, organised only university-educated upper and secon-dary school teachers (*lektorer*) until the 1970s. After an enduring inter-nal debate the union decided to open membership to groups with other kinds of teachers' education (Seip, 1990). The introduction of a joint upper secondary school for both vocational and common-core subjects, as well as changes in the membership base, led to a merger between teachers from the more traditional subjects and teachers from the com-mon-core subjects. The new union was named *Lærerforbundet*.

Unity among Legal Practitioners, Agricultural Academics, and Researchers: The Growth of Modern Trade Unions

Three other merger processes account for the majority of mergers outside the LO; these are the amalgamation of legal practitioners, agri-cultural academics, and researchers/university teachers. At the end of the 1950s these groups were organised in many, relatively fragmented, small unions. Through mergers and the gradual extension of their re-cruitment bases, they developed into modern trade unions. The nature and character of these unions vary markedly.[8]

A number of smaller unions for legal practitioners joined forces in 1969 and formed NJ (Association of Norwegian Lawyers). Prior to this merger there was a large number of local unions in a wide range of governmental departments. In addition, there were eight or nine smaller unions in the state sector, as well as at least one union in the municipal

---

[8] We might have included another merger, from the late 1950s in this section. In the period 1956-1957 several smaller unions established a union for military officers. We have not included this in our survey (data on unions outside LO starts in 1956 and most of these organisations were not included in this list).

sector (Moren *et al.*, 1972; Norges Juristforbund, 2000; Farner, 1991).[9] Following the merger in 1969, two other unions joined the amalgamation; DND (Norwegian Judges' Association) and DNA (Norwegian Bar Association).

Another group that came together during the 1960s was agricultural academics. In the beginning the number of unions was consistent with the number of subject areas within higher agricultural education. In 1961 the first merger took place, and later more groups followed (NaFo 1995). Today the membership base of the union is relatively broad, encompassing all groups with higher agricultural education and within the related natural sciences.

Norsk Forskerforbund (Norwegian Association of Research Workers) is a union for personnel within research and higher education. The merger of a large number of local unions created a union for scientific personnel at universities in 1959. Soon other smaller unions followed, including university librarians and teachers' organisations from advanced colleges. The union has gradually extended to include employees at research and educational institutions outside the national university system. The membership base has thus been transformed from a select group of employees within the university/advanced college sector to comprise a wider selection of research personnel and personnel within higher education.

The creation and consolidation of these three unions reveal the variety of paths that the development of modern trade unions may take. The NJ brought together all those with higher legal qualifications within a professional union. The unions for agricultural academics and researchers are relatively broad organisations, created through the amalgamation of smaller unions, which then gradually extended their membership coverage outside their traditional professions. This has been achieved by recruiting among new groups of employees, but also through mergers. All three unions have retained the original focus on professional and educational interests by allowing acquired unions to retain some decision-making autonomy within the post-merger union.

Sector and Branch-Based Consolidation: Traditional Mergers

A majority of mergers that have taken place in the LO have attempted to establish either broader industry-based unions in the private sector, or to unify unions within the same department or public enterprise in the state sector. A similar pattern of mergers is found outside the

---

[9]   Only two of these unions were registered in Statistical Yearbook, and this merger is therefore only registered as one merger.

LO. The former type was seen in connection with the merger between three YS unions within the insurance and banking sector, which in 2000 formed *Finansforbundet* (Finance Sector Union). The merger of NPF (Norwegian Police Federation) and LEL (National Association of Rural Police Officers) was the culmination of a long period of co-operation. Sector-based mergers also occurred when the unions for police officers, customs officers and (maritime) pilots left LO during the 1970s and established new unions by merging with the unions for the same groups outside LO. All these groups both joined and left LO during the post-war period.

The four unions for seafarers, including an LO affiliate, traditionally organised different occupations. The unions for mates and shipmasters merged in 1994 (Bakka, 1994). In 2001 the ship engineers decided not to join after the members voted against the proposed merger.

Summing Up

About seventy trade union mergers have been identified in the period 1945 – 2000, which on average constitute 1.3 mergers per year. In some areas these mergers have generated considerable changes to trade union structure.

- LO structure within manufacturing has been significantly changed through industry-based mergers and the creation of *Fellesforbundet*;
- Over a period of forty years, teachers' unions have unified;
- Several mergers have enabled small and, often, nascent unions to develop into modern trade unions (legal practitioners, researchers and agricultural academics);
- Within the state sector mergers have led to the bringing together of unions within the same public department or enterprise (police, maritime pilots, customs officers, the postal service, telecommunications and the armed services).

Detailed and complete information about merger process procedures, and choice of organisational solutions is scarce. It is possible, however, to identify certain principal characteristics. Most mergers are subject to thorough debate within the unions involved, and more often than not they proceed through some form of joint merger bodies. Unionists also devote considerable time and discussions to mergers in their representative bodies. Often member ballots are held, but there also a significant number of mergers in which such ballots are not held. In such cases, merger decisions are left to the representative bodies. Mergers are time-consuming. Several years may elapse between a proposal and the final decision to merge. The idea of a merger has also often been through a process of maturation within the unions concerned before the issue is placed on the agenda. Furthermore, several cases draw on previous merger experiences that did not materialise, and which are revitalised after some years.

Another observation is that mergers – or planned mergers – create internal conflicts and meet with opposition. There are many examples of failed mergers. Some of these ended as a proposition that was never put forward formally. But several were thoroughly deliberated and even presented to members or an assembly for a vote before the idea was set aside. As is seen with many other organisations, trade union members are hesitant before dismantling their organisations. Members within the smaller partner are often the most hesitant.

There are significant variations with regard to the structural solutions chosen for new trade unions. In many cases, merging unions are allowed representation in decision-making bodies and in the leadership of the new union, at least for a transitory period. This is especially the case where a smaller union merges with a larger union. In cases where professional/educational unions merge into larger and broader unions, it is common to establish specific structures to safeguard professional interests. Such structures may exist on a permanent basis.

Most mergers also trigger a fusion of the local or company level branches of the trade unions concerned, or at least a thorough review of the local structure. There are significant variations as to how unions chose to organise their local union branches, some have local union branches connected to the workplace, while others have geographically based branches in, for example, cities or counties. There is little information available as to what happens to the local or company-level organisation in the case of mergers. An impression is that many unions try to encourage voluntary local mergers where appropriate, but that they are generally cautious where the local branch structures differ between unions.

A final question relates to the extent to which mergers have generated increased centralisation in the form of fewer and larger unions. There is a case to be made for answering 'yes' to this question. Both within manufacturing and the school system, mergers have created large unions from what was previously a collection of medium-sized and small unions. Generally speaking, the number of unions has decreased. The decline in the number of unions is moderate, however, compared to most other countries covered in this volume. Nor is there any strong tendency towards membership concentration: the twenty largest unions organise approximately 75 per cent of all union members, and the ten

largest unions organise almost 60 per cent. These proportions were more
or less the same both twenty and forty years ago.

What Influences Trade Union Structures and Trade Union Mergers?

There are a variety of reasons why trade unionists decide to merge or
choose to remain independent. A merger may result from a strategic
decision, based on expectations about increased bargaining strength or
improved recruitment opportunities. Mergers may also be seen as a more
defensive reaction to internal or external developments, such as financial difficulties or declining membership. Changes to the industrial
relations system or bargaining structures may also promote union mergers. This section assesses the impact of these different factors on the
Norwegian merger process.

Impact of Confederations

Most unions today are affiliated to a confederation. There was, and
still is, an ideological division between LO and unions outside LO.
There have not been many mergers across confederal boundaries. There
are, however, some examples of unions leaving LO, thus enabling them
to merge with unions outside LO. There are also a few examples of the
opposite. Another way in which confederations may influence mergers
is through policies on internal structure. Such policies may influence
trade union structure in two ways: through entrance requirements with
regard to size or availability of resources; and through the regulation of
recruitment bases and internal competition. LO has the greatest capacity
to control the structure of affiliated unions. Despite LO willingness to
control its own unions, it is difficult to link the mergers taking place
within LO to this tendency. The policy of LO has been more influential
in structuring developments in the membership coverage of existing
unions, and to some extent regulating the entrance of new unions.

Both YS and AF initially wanted to prevent the emergence of too
many small unions and, as such, encouraged the creation of larger units.
Within YS smaller unions were not allowed the status of independent
unions, but instead were asked to join one of the several federal trade
unions in YS, which allow considerable autonomy. AF had no formal
requirements with regard to the size of member unions. Modest pressure
was exerted towards larger unions in the form of higher affiliation fees
for smaller unions. *Akademikerne*, the confederation for academics with
higher education, does not pursue a strict policy with regard to membership size, with the exception of the requirement that affiliates must be
large enough to have a secretariat and to be able to place sufficient

resources at the disposal of the confederation. One of the reasons for this practice is that *Akademikerne* does not plan to set up a large secretariat at confederal level. The confederal requirements with regard to educational level within its member unions also have practical implications for mergers, in that they allow member unions to merge only with other unions that meet these requirements. Much of the same implies to UHO. Indications suggest that UHO will pursue a strict entrance requirement policy, and also keep a relatively hard-line policy in relation to the size of affiliates. Trade unions that compete with one of existing unions in the confederation will not be allowed to join, but may be encouraged to merge with the relevant union.

Internal Driving Forces: Finance and Membership Development

Decreasing or stagnating membership, with subsequent financial hardship, is, beyond doubt, an important contributory factor to many mergers. This is particularly the case for mergers within manufacturing. Unions losing out in competition over members with other organisations may also prompt mergers. The NL, for example, experienced more favourable membership developments than the Union of Women Teachers in the period prior to their merger in 1965, which prompted the latter to seek a merger.

Bargaining Structure

Bargaining structure influences trade union structural development, although Norwegian bargaining structure cannot be said to have brought about mergers. Generally speaking, bargaining structures both in the private and public sector favour the larger actors, but do not prevent the smaller actors operating within the shade of the larger actors. The bargaining systems in the state and municipal sectors force unions into bargaining cartels or federations, but do not compel unions to merge. On the contrary, bargaining cartels make it easier for smaller trade unions to maintain their independence, as in Denmark and Sweden (Chapters 4 and 9). Exceptions to this can be found. Over the period 1956-2000 several smaller unions chose to join a larger union – such as STAFO or KFL (Union of Municipal Employees), later KFO (Union of Municipal Employees) – to secure their bargaining position within the public sector. This approach applies primarily to unions that have not had the option to join AF or its predecessor EL, both of which accepted very small unions as affiliates.

The basic agreements between NHO and LO/YS stipulate rules for when a member company should enter into a collective agreement.

Unions may demand a collective agreement when they organise 10 per cent of employees within a given enterprise.[10] This means that it is possible for a 'number two' union to recruit enough members to demand inclusion in a collective agreement. Smaller unions in competition with larger unions will usually have to make do with replica agreements; that is, to accept the agreement achieved by the largest union. Variations with regard to degree of influence in such negotiations, however, do not seem to have led to mergers between the largest unions and the second largest unions (or third largest union, *etc.*).

Employers' Structure and Strategies

There are no suggestions that the structure and strategies of employers are a driving force in trade union mergers, other than through their influence on bargaining structure. The large-scale restructuring of the trade unions within the manufacturing industries, in the 1960s and in the first half of the 1970s, took place during a period of relative organisational and structural stability on the employer side. In the last decade, however, the employer side in the private sector has been subject to significant change, which involves the establishment of NHO and the restructuring of its affiliated sectoral federations. During the same period trade union structure in manufacturing has remained relatively stable.

A significant development in recent years that may, in principle, have an effect on the structure of trade unions is de-regulation or privatisation of public enterprises. This implies a transfer from one collective agreement to another, which, in turn, may lead to questions concerning the transfer of members from one union to another. State-sector unions have been able to maintain both members and bargaining responsibility in the privatised state enterprises. The challenges of privatisation are greater in the municipal sector. Here some privatised municipal enterprises have joined NHO, and thus have become party to collective agreements that are traditionally handled by private sector unions within LO. The question of who has the right to unionise these employees has given rise to a controversial debate within LO. Thus far it seems that privatisation is more likely to lead to internal struggles over members and member coverage areas, rather than to mergers of unions.

---

[10] The 10 per cent limit applies only to companies with more than 25 employees. The 10 per cent rule does not apply to vertical agreements or to individually applicable agreements (i.e. agreements for white-collar workers). In the retail and wholesale sector, a union must organise 50 per cent of the employees in order to be able to demand an agreement.

Changes in Employment Structure

Significant industrial and occupational shifts in the labour market between 1945 and 2000 have blurred traditional divisions between trade unions and, as such, have promoted mergers. The gradual introduction of thirteen years of schooling for the majority of Norwegian youngsters through a series of educational reforms, for example, contributed to the mergers of teachers' unions. Moreover, the merger to form EL&IT was grounded in technological developments. An important driving force behind the merger of the unions within the banking and insurance sector, in 2000, was the growing collaboration among banks and insurance companies. Mergers among LO unions in manufacturing during the 1960s and 1970s indicated that industrial shifts in employment were an important factor. Such changes are associated with financial factors (decreasing membership base) and strategic considerations.

Strategic Considerations: Future Union Structures

Most mergers have within them a strategic element. When the smaller LO unions in manufacturing merged during the 1960s and 1970s, it was very much due to a general wish to become larger and stronger in facing employers, the government, and, indeed, within LO. The same argument may be applied to the mergers that paved the way for trade unions of legal practitioners and researchers. In some mergers the strategic elements seem to be more important than in others. The creation of *Fellesforbundet* was a strategic response from some unions to the resistance to change within LO. Through this, a new type of union was established within LO, which deviated from all earlier Norwegian trade union structures and had no direct counterparts in other Nordic countries. However, *Fellesforbundet* was not just a response to changes in industrial and occupational structures but, more importantly, was an attempt to create a stronger actor able to compete with the fast growing unions in the public sector. In addition, there was a widespread desire within the unions involved to employ economic resources more efficiently.

Conclusion: Further Changes to the Union Structure

Further changes to trade union structure in Norway are expected in the years to come. It is possible to identify a number of motivating factors:

- A number of unions are experiencing stagnating or shrinking memberships, which will make them financially weaker and undermine their influence;

- Developments in working and industrial life make it significantly harder to maintain traditional union boundaries. This is the case both with regard to industry and occupation. In addition, the traditional distinction between blue- and white-collar workers is increasingly being questioned;
- Changes in ownership structure, such as privatisation and deregulation, outsourcing of functions, and company mergers and acquisitions, challenge the traditional forms of industrial activity. Today one may find employees with different employers in the same workplace and employees in different industries but with the same owner;
- Changes in traditional conflicts between confederations may open up opportunities for mergers that were previously politically and ideologically impossible;
- Several unions for academics have ambitions to increase their membership base by mergers and/or by allowing in new groups as members.

It is evident that organisational changes take time. Some processes have, however, been initiated. Firstly, efforts have been made to examine the possibilities of establishing a service union within LO, which involves unions within the sectors of transport, hotels and restaurants, and the wholesale and retail trades. If such a merger takes place, it will be the most significant alteration to the structure of LO in private and public services for seventy years. Another alternative is also mooted, comprising a more limited transport industry union that unites railway transport, postal services and private transportation. A new LO-union within the service sector will most probably not include any groups from the municipal sector.

Another issue likely to appear on the LO agenda is an increasing emphasis on vertical organisation and/or vertical collective agreements, in other words, the abandonment of the traditional distinction between blue- and white-collar workers. Thirdly, there has been recent turmoil among the confederations. The central question in the years to come centres on the type of alliance established amongst the four confederations. Although, traditionally the majority of mergers have taken place within confederations, changes in these structures may open up opportunities for new trade union alliances and for mergers that today may not seem viable.

List of Abbreviations

AF   Akademikernes Fellesorganisasjon (Confederation of Norwegian Professional Associations)

BAF   Bekledningsarbeiderforbundet (Norwegian Union of Clothing Workers)

BFO   Befalets Fellesorganisasjon (Military Officers' Association)

DNA   Den Norske Advokatforening (Norwegian Bar Association)

DND   Den Norske Dommerforening (Norwegian Judges Association)

EL   Embetsmennenes Landsforbund (Association of Civil Service Employees)

EL&IT   EL & IT Forbundet (Electricians and Information Technology Workers' Union)

FLT   Forbundet for Ledelse og Teknikk (Norwegian Engineers and Managers' Association)

HK   Handel og Kontor i Norge (Norwegian Union of Employees in Commerce and Offices)

KFL   Kommunal Funksjonærenes Landsforbund – changed name to KFO in 1985 (Union of Municipal Employees)

KFO   Kommunalansattes Fellesorganisasjon (Municipal Employees' Federation)

LEL   Lensmannsetatens Landslag (National Association of Rural Police Officers)

LO   Landsorganisasjonen i Norge (Norwegian Confederation of Trade Unions)

NAF   Norsk Arbeidsmandsforbund (Norwegian Union of Manual Workers)

NBIF   Norsk Bygningsindustriarbeiderforbund (Norwegian Union of Building Industry Workers)

NEKF   Norsk Elektriker og Kraftstasjonsforbund (Norwegian Union of Electricians and Power Station Workers)

NHO   Næringslivets Hovedorganisasjon (Confederation of Norwegian Business and Industry)

NHS   Norsk Helse- og Sosialforbund (Norwegian Association of Practical Nurses)

NJ   Norsk Juristforbund (Association of Norwegian Lawyers)

NJM   Norsk Jern- og Metallarbeiderforbund (Iron and Metalworkers' Union)

NKF   Norsk Kommuneforbund (Norwegian Union of Municipal Employees)

NKIF   Norsk Kjemisk Industriarbeiderforbund (Norwegian Union of Chemical Industry Workers)

NL   Norsk Lærerlag – before 1967 Norges Lærerlag (Norwegian Union of Teachers)

NNN   Norsk Nærings- og Nytelsesmiddelarbeiderforbund (Norwegian Union of Food and Allied Workers)

NOPEF   Norsk Olje- og Petrokjemisk Fagforbund (Norwegian Union of Oil and Petrochemical Workers)

NPF   Norsk Papirarbeiderforbund (Norwegian Union of Paper Industry Workers)

NPF   Norsk Politiforbund (Norwegian Police Federation)

NSLF   Norsk Skog og landarbeiderforbund (Norwegian Union of Forestry and Land Workers)

PRIFO   Privatansattes Fellesorganisasjon (Private Sector Employees Federation)

STAFO   Statstjenestemannsforbundet (Union of Civil Servants in Norway)

TD   Tele- og Dataforbundet (Norwegian Union of Information Technology Employees)

UHO   Utdanningsgruppenes Hovedorganisasjon (Confederation of Higher Education Unions)

YS   Yrkesorganisasjonenes Sentralforbund (Confederation of Vocational Unions)

CHAPTER 8. PORTUGAL

Mergers within a Fragmented Union Structure, 1974-2000

Alan STOLEROFF

The starting point for this chapter is the fragmented union structure imposed by the dictatorship of 1933 to 1974. This self-proclaimed 'corporatist' dictatorship enforced a system of labour 'representation' based upon *sindicatos nacionais* (national unions).[1] The only national characteristic of these unions, however, was their ideological disposition. Union structure was divided by territory, sector, craft and occupation in order to inhibit class action. As a result, there were some 326 unions in 1973, the year before the change in regime. These corporatist unions were present in most industries throughout the period of the dictatorship, although prohibited in agriculture, fishing, public administration, education and domestic services.[2] Where unions existed, membership was mandatory, although a distinction existed between full, effective members and merely contributing members.[3]

The revolution of 1974-75 and the advent of constitutional democracy freed Portuguese unions from the constraints of dictatorship, but the established structure was largely carried over to the new regime. Although the fragmented union structure did not 'fit' with industrial collective bargaining, for political and ideological reasons union re-

---

[1] For background on the corporatist system and unions under the dictatorship, see Lucena (1976a; 1976b), Patriarca (1994; 1995) and Barreto (1994).

[2] In various phases of the dictatorship, opposition trade unionists were able to work within these organisations in order to achieve some degree of class representation. From the 1960s, opposition slates actually won leadership elections in important sectors, transforming these corporatist institutions into embryonic trade unions.

[3] A full member of the union joined the union, paid dues, obtained a union card and voting rights. A contributing member assumed only the minimum duty of paying union dues.

organisation was not the priority of the emerging union leadership during the early phases of democratisation. Union structure was thus not dismantled during the revolution, as were many other institutions of the old regime. The majority faction of the emerging leadership, closely associated with the PCP (Portuguese Communist Party), initially placed greater emphasis on securing leadership of the existing unions and ensuring unity at the confederal level rather than on union restructuring. The orientation of the Communist union leadership and its allies was 'political' in that it sought to strengthen the class struggle against *revanchisme*, rather than to strengthen the bargaining power of unions within capitalism. In accordance with this shared orientation, the revolutionary government in 1975 passed a law to regulate trade unions, which imposed a single confederal structure upon the emerging labour movement. This confederation was known as CGTP-IN (General Confederation of Portuguese Workers).[4]

For the most part, existing unions were taken over by new leaderships, who left the inherited structures largely intact, while changing their constitutions and statutes according to the new 'democratic' rules of trade unionism.[5] As a result, the structure of the *sindicatos nacionais* was basically passed on to the new regime. The formation of new unions frequently complied with this pattern. In 1975 no fewer than 282 unions were formally constituted following the new legal regulations. Thus a union structure based upon fragmented territorial and occupational jurisdictions was carried over from one regime to another and accentuated by the extension of labour organisation.[6]

In the context of the acute and irreconcilable political conflicts of democratisation,[7] the introduction through legislation of a single con-

---

[4] *Intersindical* originated in 1970 under the dictatorship as a coalition of opposition trade unions. It was transformed in the democratic transition into the CGTP-IN confederation. For the history of *Intersindical* see Barreto (1992).

[5] After the passage of the basic law on trade unions in 1975 most of the existing unions held assemblies in which new statutes were adopted and leadership bodies were elected. While almost universally convened according to formal requirements, these assemblies varied in the degree to which the revolutionary atmosphere affected their proceedings.

[6] The new unions of teachers and public employees were formed on a regional, rather than district, basis following the North, Centre, South pattern, with specific unions for the autonomous regions (Azores and Madeira).

[7] It should be appreciated that the democratisation process in Portugal led to a situation of incipient civil war throughout much of 1975, culminating in the 'hot summer' of 1975.

federation promoted opposition rather than unity.[8] As a result, an ideological and political split took place within the labour movement. When the non-revolutionary government repealed the law on confederal unity in 1976, a reformist-led union confederation was thus created as a breakaway from the CGTP-IN, by a group of important unions with leadership from the Socialist and Social-Democratic factions. In 1978 the UGT (General Union of Workers) was founded as an alternative confederation to the CGTP-IN. The creation of the UGT inaugurated a period of competitive pluralism within the Portuguese union movement (Optenhogel and Stoleroff, 1985; Stoleroff, 1988).

In an attempt to compete for members with existing unions affiliated to the CGTP-IN, the UGT sought to create a parallel structure in the form of a network of national 'vertical' unions. This initiated a process of organisational duplication and provided an impetus for the proliferation of unions on the basis of competing party allegiance, which undermined inclusiveness. The successful resistance of 'horizontally-organised' white-collar workers to integration within 'vertical' industrial unions added to the fragmentation. The permanent schism at confederal level meant that the structure of the Portuguese labour movement became divided between the two ideologically and politically opposed confederations, the CGTP-IN and the UGT, to which a cohort of non-aligned unions were added.

Within each of the two confederations, mechanisms were developed to compensate for defects of structure, but these often stopped short of fundamental structural change. The CGTP-IN, for example, resorted to 'Inter-Union Commissions' at company level and 'federations' of unions in collective bargaining as pragmatic solutions to the co-ordination of union activity. There were thus only limited restraints on the centrifugal tendencies towards occupational and professional exclusivism (Stoleroff, 2000). Exclusive occupational interests, frequently promoted by politi-

---

[8]   *Intersindical* was a primary vehicle of revolutionary mobilisation during the most turbulent initial phase of the democratic transition. Although various factions vied for influence, the Communist Party was clearly dominant and the Communists used their influence to tie the emerging confederation to the new state and to concretely support the revolutionary governments of the 'hot summer' of 1975. (Whereas the revolutionary forces were a clear minority within the society as a whole, they were a majority within the leadership of the unions.) The single confederation law facilitated the consolidation of the organisational predominance of the Communist faction over the labour movement as a whole. This led to a responsive politicisation of the labour movement by the non-revolutionary forces. This political alliance had consequences within labour relations as *Intersindical* sided with the government in its opposition to a number of strike movements in important enterprises.

cal incentives, and the incapacity of existing unions to expand their constituencies, led to the freeing of such centrifugal forces, resulting in a proliferation of very small unions.

This trend was very influential throughout the 1980s and until the mid-1990s. At that point, structural changes in employment and the labour force began to take their toll, and the decline in unionisation and union influence began to have an impact upon union structure. Many small unions were no longer viable, some became virtually inactive and some dissolved.[9] In 1995 the CGTP-IN adopted a general policy of rationalising union structure and signs of progress in this endeavour have recently begun to appear.

Change and continuity in the evolution of Portuguese union organisation, therefore, are evaluated in this chapter by reference to the legacy of the fragmented union structure of the old regime and the proliferation of unions during the democratic period. Mergers have played an important role in this evolution but, at crucial stages in Portuguese union development, they have been overshadowed by the formation of new unions. The most recent merger wave within the CGTP-IN, therefore, is a major break in the development of Portuguese trade union structure. For this reason, it will receive particular attention in this chapter.

It is difficult to explain the inertia of the union movement in other than strategic and political terms. In spite of numerous mergers, there has been no fundamental structural re-organisation throughout twenty-five years of democracy, but only incremental change. In short, the evolution of Portuguese union structure over the last quarter century demonstrates just how resistant institutionalised structures can be, and how difficult it is to rationalise such structures.

---

[9]   There is evidence of significant and consistent decline in union membership since the crisis of the mid-1980s. At its VII Congress (1993) the CGTP-IN presented a sober analysis of union evolution highlighting various tendencies: an increase in unionisation in public administration, a decline in unionisation in sectors affected by the economic crisis, and a decline of unionisation in commerce and other expanding services. The overall tendency was a decline in unionisation, which had serious repercussions upon union stability. CGTP-IN unions suffered a consistent decrease in dues collection between 1987 and 1990. If we look at the figures claimed by the CGTP-IN at its Congresses since 1983 there was a loss of almost 43 per cent, that is, 672,000 members from the unions in its orbit. According to Cerdeira (1997) total unionisation declined to an average of 44 per cent in the period 1985-90 and an average of 36 per cent in the period 1991-95. She speculates that at present it may be less than 30 per cent. The ILO, for its part, has recently reported a rate of unionisation of 25.6 per cent for Portugal in 1995, a drop of 50 per cent in relation to the figure it quotes for ten years earlier (ILO, 1997).

Politics in the form of the struggle between ideological coalitions and parties for influence within unionism is the key explanatory variable of the merger process. Two confederations allied to antagonistic political coalitions emerged from the intense conflicts of democratisation, and have since constituted the framework within which distinct processes of structural development have occurred. Union structure has followed the rules of the coalitions that constitute each camp. The result is that it is necessary to refer separately to the processes of restructuring within the two confederations. In addition, independent unions are examined separately.

Portuguese trade union structural development also involves the fragmentation of professional and occupational interests. In contrast to the trends found in several of the countries covered in this volume, numerous occupations have created and maintained their own exclusive unions, in practice rejecting any search for economies of scale. Explanations for this tendency must take into account the strong corporatist influences within Portuguese society as a whole and the major role of the state as an employer of professional workers. The explanation must also acknowledge the influence of industrial relations factors, such as the legal possibility for a union to participate in collective bargaining independently of any measure of its representation, and the federal character of representation in bargaining, which permits the participation of many unions in one negotiating process.

Over the last quarter century, the Portuguese economy has suffered several major shifts in its development. Since the mid-1980s there has been a pronounced contraction of industrial employment and an increase of uncertainty due to flexible employment in the services. This has exerted significant pressure on trade union structure, as decreasing membership and income from dues have jeopardised the survival of many unions.

Portuguese Union Structure

Portuguese union structure is characterised by fragmentation, overlapping and duplication of jurisdictions, and occupational atomisation. Territorial fragmentation continues to influence union structure, although, over time, the merger process has attenuated this dispersion, as has the formation of exclusive unions for particular occupations. Since 1978, Portuguese union structure has reflected the division at the confederal level between the two ideologically and politically distinct confederations. The majority of Portuguese unions are associated with one of these political blocks, although a significant number of unions are independent and associated within the loose USI (Union of Independent Trade Unions). In addition, unions of managerial and supervisory personnel are organised in the FENSIQ (National Federation of Managerial Unions). Table 8.1 presents the distribution of unions according to their affiliation.[10]

Table 8.1: Distribution of Unions by Affiliation (1998)

Affiliation	Number of Unions
CGTP-IN-MSU	184 (116 affiliated to the CGTP-IN, 68 non-affiliated)
UGT	61
Independents	87
Total	332

Sources: CGTP-IN, UGT.

The CGTP-IN

The CGTP-IN is a composite of individual trade unions, federations and local inter-union associations (*uniões*). Additionally, within the orbit of the CGTP-IN, there are a significant number of unaffiliated, yet closely allied, unions, which are referred to as the MSU (Unitary Union Movement). In 1998 the CGTP-IN-MSU comprised 184 unions (116 affiliated, 68 non-affiliated) within practically all industries with the exception of banking and insurance.[11] In industry, the union structure of the CGTP-IN-MSU continues to be influenced by jurisdictions based upon districts, although the merger movement has made a significant impact on this structure. Regional (North, Centre, and South and Islands), as well as national jurisdictions, have become increasingly important.

Within the industrial sector, the CGTP-IN unions are composites of closely related industries (for example, paper and printing or construction, carpentry, ceramics, cement and marble quarries) or sector-based (food and beverages or metallurgy and engineering). Most industries also comprise district and regionally based unions. For example, of the eight metallurgical and engineering unions in the CGTP-IN, two are still based upon single districts (Braga, and Viana do Castelo), three

---

[10] At the time of this writing the number of unions in each grouping has decreased as extinct unions continue to be deleted from the rosters of the confederations. At present the UGT, for example, lists only fifty-seven unions – and two federations – as its members.

[11] The financial sector, in which the established unions went over entirely to the UGT, is an exception to parallel unionism.

are multi-district (Aveiro-Viseu-Guarda, Coimbra-Leiria and Lisboa-Santarem-Castelo Branco), two are regional (North, South) and one covers the island of Madeira. The structure of the textile, woollens and garment industries' unions is more heterogeneous and encompasses four unions that are multi-district or 'provincial' (provinces of Minho and Trás-Os-Montes, Beira Baixa, and Beira Alta, the joint districts of Porto and Aveiro), two regional unions (Centre and South), and two district-based unions (Aveiro and Oporto).

The unions in the shoe and leather industries are regional- or district-based (and mainly located in the north of the country), although two leather industry unions overlap in national jurisdictions. The same pattern basically holds for the CGTP-IN unions which cover construction, carpentry, ceramics, cement and marble quarries, although in some cases these industries are together in one union, while in others separate unions exist for construction as opposed to ceramics or cement. In the food industry, there are several unions, which are general food and beverage unions, as well as meat-packing, bakery and canning unions. The food and beverage unions are now mostly multi-district or regional. The tobacco workers were integrated into the food industry union of the southern region. Two industries are composed entirely of regional-based unions: electronics where there are three regional unions (North, Centre, and South and Islands) and chemicals and pharmaceuticals where there are two regional unions (North and Centre, and South and Islands). Finally, the union in the paper and printing industries is a national union created by mergers in 1996.

In transportation, the unions affiliated to the CGTP-IN organise road, rail, sea and air separately. The bus drivers' (urban and inter-city) unions are still predominantly district-based, though there are three regional unions (Centre, North and South). Two of the district unions are actually general transport unions of the two largest cities, Lisbon and Porto. The railway workers union affiliated to the CGTP-IN is now national, which distinguishes it from the myriad of UGT and independent general and occupational unions existing on the railways. There are several unions in the merchant marine but, of necessity, they are demarcated by category and not by spatial jurisdictions. Only one of the many unions in aviation is affiliated to the CGTP-IN and it is a general union.

There is a vast array of public service unions within the CGTP-IN-MSU. The civil service is divided into regional unions, while municipal employees, apart from those of the Lisbon municipality, are organised within a national union. Other public employees are grouped into either professional or sectoral unions; such as for magistrates, tax employees, police or prison guards. Apart from the large Lisbon teachers' union, the teachers' unions affiliated to the CGTP-IN are all regional (South,

Centre, North, Azores and Madeira). The CGTP-IN-MSU also comprises many unions of public service health professionals, which are regional (doctors) or national (nurses and veterinarians).

There are a number of regional and national professional and occupational unions in private sector services. The hotel and restaurant workers unions are organised by region (South, Centre, North, and Azores and Madeira). The union affiliated to the CGTP-IN, which organises commercial, office and service workers, is now a national union, following mergers of district unions in 1998. Finally, in the primary sector, the unions in the fishing industry are now also mainly, but not exclusively, regional, while there is one national union for agriculture and forestry.

Thus far the picture drawn of the organisation of the CGTP-IN continues to show signs of territorial fragmentation within fairly tightly defined industries. This fragmentation is nevertheless mitigated by the existence of federal structures within the CGTP-IN. These are coalitions of autonomous unions, usually of contiguous trades, from within the MSU. These federations cannot be considered as unions in themselves in that they are strictly associations of unions, with leadership bodies composed of representatives of the member unions, generally on a proportional basis. They do, however, perform many of the functions performed by integrated vertical unions in other countries. In collective bargaining the local unions affiliated to the CGTP-IN generally obtain their voice through such federations. In industry, the largest federations are the coalition of the unions in textile, garment and footwear industries and that of the very recently merged sectors of metallurgy, engineering and mining and chemicals, pharmaceuticals, oil and gas. Other federations combine unions in the ceramics and glass industries, and in the electrical and power industries. As a result of the recent efforts towards restructuring in the CGTP-IN, the federation in the printing and paper industries – which combined regional unions – was dissolved and substituted by one union with a national scope. The federation of unions in the food and beverage industry also very recently merged with the federation encompassing hotels, catering and tourism to form a new organisation. Unions in the construction industry are united in a federation, which also includes woodworking, cork and marble quarries. The federation in the secondary and tertiary sector organises all categories of workers in commerce and in various services as well as office employees in all industrial and service sectors, except for those preferring to belong to the CGTP-IN's industrial unions.[12] In the transport sector there is a federation of bus and public transportation unions and a federation of maritime unions. There is a federation of civil service employees unions and another of teachers' unions and still another for doctors' unions. In the primary sector, there is a federation for unions in the fishing industry.

The structure of the CGTP-IN also includes *uniões* (unions), which are associations of CGTP-IN-MSU trade unions of all activities in a district or county. These territorial groupings were created at around the same time as the federations (1975-81) in all districts and, like the federations, have their own leadership bodies. Although the *uniões* with the highest membership figures are those in the largest urban areas (Lisbon and Porto), they have their most significant role in the more remote regions, because the organisational weakness of the local sectoral unions forces them to pool their limited resources.

The UGT

Although it also includes two federations of unions, in education and the ports, the structural foundation of the UGT comprises a combination of both 'vertical' and 'horizontal' unions. The fifty-eight UGT unions span much of the labour market but do not cover it entirely. The most developed union is in the financial sector of banking and insurance where there are no CGTP-IN unions. The UGT is much less complete in its industrial organisation.[13]

The core of the UGT comprises white-collar unions of bank, insurance and office workers.[14] There are three regional unions of bank workers (South and Islands, Centre and North)[15] and two regional insurance unions (South and Autonomous Regions, and North). These are inclusive unions and there are no additional UGT unions in the financial sector. There is some overlapping of jurisdictions in the area of office workers, since there are several horizontal office workers' unions

---

[12] This federation is likely to be dissolved in the future since the unions within it have merged into a national union. This is what happened in the paper and printing industry and on the railways, as a result of the mergers of unions into one national union.

[13] Its weakness in industry has very recently been compounded by the exit of the metal workers' union (SIMA) from the confederation. There is now no UGT union representing metallurgical and engineering workers.

[14] In 1990 the Bank Employees' Union of Southern Portugal (SBSI) alone contributed over half the UGT's total membership dues.

[15] These three regional bank employee unions are presently engaged in the process of forming a federation.

that organise administrative and office personnel across a range of industries. One of these office workers' unions is national in scope, one is district-based, and two are regional. In addition, there are three very local office and commercial workers' unions. There is a federation of office workers' unions, which includes a union of sales people.[16]

The UGT also contains a number of manual and industrial unions, which claim national and vertical jurisdictions, although some are of only local significance. There is a union in agriculture and forestry, two in fishing and there are separate unions in most of industry and construction: ceramics-cement-glass, cork, paper and printing, electricity-electronics, textiles, energy-chemicals-diverse industries,[17] food-beverage-kindred workers, construction-public works. There is a national bus drivers' union and one for airline flight attendants. In rail, one national vertical union co-exists with three occupational UGT-unions. There are also national unions in civil service-public administration, and education.

There are three dozen or so other unions with varying geographical and sectoral coverage. In education, there are several unions of teachers of regional scope besides the national union mentioned above. Education is one of the sectors in which UGT has a federation. Apart from the national vertical unions in transport, there are a number of occupational unions in transport (road, rail, sea and air). There is a federation of port workers' unions that affiliates to the UGT, but whose member unions strangely enough are not affiliated to the UGT. Finally, there are a number of professional unions for economists, engineers, football coaches, casino workers and nurses; as well as unions in diverse areas of services, including domestic employees.

Independent Unions

There are somewhere between one hundred and one hundred and fifty unions which are independent of the two confederations. The number of independent unions is hard to calculate since they constitute an indeterminate group of small and very small unions,[18] a considerable

---

[16] In an acquisition the UGT hotel and restaurant union was integrated within one of the office workers' unions.

[17] The UGT miners' union was integrated within the chemicals union. The unions in Chemicals, Paper and Printing, Ceramic, Glass, Wood and Mining are allied in a federation.

[18] The CGTP-IN recently claimed that the large union of local authority employees (STAL, Union of Local Administration Workers) has more members than all of the independent unions put together.

proportion of which no longer have any internal life or active members. Many of these unions are in the service sector, particularly in the public services. Among these are a small number of representative unions of highly specialised occupations.[19] Political, as well as occupational, factors have motivated the emergence of a wide range of such independent unions. Among these are a group of unions whose leadership is aligned with the PSD (Social Democratic Party) and whose creation was politically motivated.[20] New unions have also organised very specific categories of public sector workers, such as the various associations of auxiliary personnel in schools.

The Evolution of Portuguese Union Structure, 1974-2000

The total number of unions has varied widely since the revolution of 1974 (see Table 8.2). The number of unions increased from 331 to 407 between 1976 and 1992. There was a break in this trend from 1979 to 1984, but after 1984 a continuous rise in the number of unions led to the peak of 407 in 1992. Although there was a temporary increase in the number of unions from 1996 to 1997, since 1992 the number of unions has been steadily decreasing, falling to 381 in 2000.[21]

---

[19] Amongst state employees the independent unions of magistrates (attorneys in the court system and the Interior Ministry) as well as of tax department employees, doctors and some teachers are highly representative. The unions of journalists, airline pilots, railroad locomotive engineers and some of the workers of the public electricity utility are other highly representative independent unions.

[20] At the end of the 1980s, the labour faction of the PSD (TSD, Social Democratic Workers) adopted a line, which resulted in the break-up of the alliance with the UGT's majority socialist tendency. With the aim of founding a third confederation, the TSD promoted the creation of a number of unions formed from splinter groups of existing UGT unions. These came together in the CSI [Convention of Independent Trade Unions], now the USI).

[21] These totals incorporate of course a significant number of tiny, frequently redundant, unions existing in the island regions outside of mainland Portugal.

Table 8.2: Unions by Jurisdiction, 1970-2000

Year	Total Number of Unions	Total Mainland	National[1]	Continental	Autonomous Regions (islands)	Multi-district	Single District	Multi-county	Single County
1970	326	296							
1971	326	296							
1972	326	296							
1973	326	296							
1974	308	279							
1975	316	286							
1976	331	298							
1977	X	X							
1978	376	336							
1979	375	336							
1980	366	326	86	1	40	96	137	1	5
1981	356	316	96	1	40	96	116	3	4
1982	351	312	102		39	96	109	2	3
1983	361	319	105		42	102	107	2	3
1984	352	313	105		39	99	104	2	3
1985	354	315	109		39	99	101	3	3
1986	365	322	118		43	99	99	3	3
1987	368	324	122		44	98	97	3	4
1988	370	326	131		44	95	93	3	4
1989	377	333	135		44	97	94	3	4
1990	396	352	150		44	99	96	3	4
1991	406	362	156		44	100	98	4	4
1992	407	363	164		44	100	98	4	4
1993	396	352	164		44	85	95		8
1994	390	346	166		44	82	90		8
1995	390	346	166		44	82	90		8
1996	383	339	161		44	81	88		9
1997	387	343	168		44	81	85		9
1998	386	342	176		44	80	77		9
1999	380	336	178		44	74	74		10
2000	381	337	184		44	73	70		10

[1] From 1984-1988 includes five unions with headquarters in Lisbon, but with jurisdiction outside of the country. Since 1988 includes five unions with headquarters in Lisbon and one in Oporto, but with jurisdiction outside of the country.

Source: Instituto Nacional de Estatística.

The main factors responsible for the increase in the number of unions until the early 1980s were: first, the creation of unions in the areas where they had been prohibited or severely impeded, such as in the public sector, including the postal service and telecommunications; and, second, the creation of new unions for the professions and specific occupations. An additional multiplier was the establishment of parallel union structures, due to the competition for membership between the UGT and the CGTP-IN.[22]

Due largely to the restructuring efforts of the CGTP-IN, there was a temporary brake on the increasing trend between 1979 and 1984 when the number of unions declined from 375 to 352. This was still significantly more than had existed in 1974. Since some restructuring, entailing amalgamations, acquisitions and the dissolution of numerous tiny unions, had been initiated during the second half of the 1970s, the formation of new unions between 1974 and 1984 was actually more significant than appears. Table 8.3 shows this clearly in the balance between union formations and union dissolutions. Between 1979 and 1984 the balance between union formations and dissolutions was negative, but the balance was consistently positive after 1984.

In 1979 many district and craft unions merged to form regional industrial unions. However, as many unions were formed in 1979 as were dissolved. In 1980 mergers began to produce regional unions from some of the CGTP-IN's district unions in paper and printing, baked goods, bus transport, hotel and restaurant, metal working and engineering, commerce and office workers, and in the food industry. For the first time more unions dissolved than were formed. In 1981 this restructuring wave reached its height with a net decrease of 10 in the total number of unions, as 31 unions were involved in a record number of 10 mergers for a single year. This restructuring continued throughout 1982 when, once again, the net balance of total unions was negative. By 1983 the rate of restructuring began to decline and it came to a halt in 1984. Although more unions dissappeared in mergers in 1979, 1980, 1981 and 1982 than were formed, substantial numbers of unions were formed in these years. The vertical unions of the UGT in industry were formed during this period. In each year between 1985 and 1992, more unions were formed than dissolved or dissappeared in mergers. The formation wave reached its peak in 1989 when 17 new unions were constituted, making for a net increase of 16 unions. This does not mean

---

[22] Following 1979 many of the basic industrial unions of the UGT were created and constituted formally (in metallurgy, hotel and foods, construction and woodworking, chemicals, electricity); in all of these branches, unions were already in existence.

that there were no amalgamations or acquisitions in this period, but they were no longer sufficient to bring about a decrease in the total number of unions.

Table 8.3: Formations, Dissolutions and Mergers, 1975-2000

Year	Formations	Dissolutions	Balance	Amalgamations	Total Number of Unions Merged by Amalgamation	Acquisitions	Total Mergers (Amalgamations + Acquisitions)
1975	282		282				
1976	37	5	32			3	3
1977	17	2	15	1	2		1
1978	15	5	10	1	3	2	3
1979	14	14	0	1	6	6	7
1980	11	18	-7	4	14	3	7
1981	21	31	-10	10	23	5	15
1982	13	26	-13	7	21	3	10
1983	7	8	-1	2	4	3	5
1984	4	9	-5			8	8
1985	7	1	6			1	1
1986	9	3	6	1	2	1	2
1987	4		4				
1988	5	2	3	1	2		1
1989	17	1	16			1	1
1990	10	6	4	2	6		2
1991	6	3	3	1	2	1	2
1992	5	2	3			2	2
1993	3	5	-2	2	5		2
1994	3	5	-2	2	4	1	3
1995	7	9	-2	3	7	2	5
1996	5	18	-13	5	12	7	12
1997	10	7	3	3	6	1	4
1998	7	9	-2	1	8	1	2
1999	5	10	-5	2	5	5	7
2000	1	4	-3				1

Source: Data obtained from Direcção General das Relações Colectivas.

Since 1992 there has been a consistent and substantial decrease in the number of unions. According to official statistics from INE (the National Institute of Statistics) in 1998 there were 386 unions, but, in a recent document analysing the structure of Portuguese unions, the CGTP-IN estimated that less than 300 unions were in operation. Much of the reduction can be attributed to a process of union restructuring inside the CGTP-IN that has been going on in recent years, due to both dissolution and planned efforts at merger and acquisition.[23]

According to the data of INE, of the 366 unions in existence in 1980 (the year in which INE began to publish disaggregated statistics on union jurisdictions), 137 unions were limited to only one district, another 96 were multi-district, and 86 were national in scope. From 1980 the number of unions with national jurisdiction began to increase steadily from 86 in 1980 to 166 in 1994 and by 2000 the number had reached 184. The number of unions with district-based jurisdictions decreased from 137 in 1980 to 70 in 2000. In 1980 unions with a national scope represented only 23 per cent of the total number of unions. In 1992, when the number of unions was at its peak, national unions constituted 40 per cent of all unions. In 2000 they represented 45 per cent of all unions. Contrary to what might be expected, the increase in unions of national scope has not always been a sign of structural rationalisation. During the 1980s the trend results from fragmentation in the form of the creation of national parallel unions of the UGT and occupational unions that established national jurisdictions. After 1994 the merger movement within the CGTP-IN produced several national unions, but just as important was the formation of regional and multi-district unions from unions of more local scope.

In spite of the significant merger activity that has taken place throughout the democratic period, Portuguese trade unionism remains fragmented. There were still 184 national unions, 73 multi-district unions and 70 district unions in 2000. A large proportion of the national unions are industrial 'vertical' unions of the UGT or occupationally exclusive unions. The CGTP-IN's overall structure remains strongly influenced by local constituencies. This pattern is only viable due to the CGTP-IN's federations that aggregate unions within similar industries for the purposes of collective bargaining. In practice, union federations in Portugal perform a similar function to union cartels in Nordic countries (see Chapters 4, 9 and 7). Parallel unionism is a product of political division and is very unlikely to be overcome in the short term,

---

[23] The CGTP-IN in 1995 set itself specific objectives for a reorganisation of its structures and has accomplished a great deal in this sense, most notably in agriculture, fishing, printing, chemicals, food, metallurgy and mining, and commerce and services. Besides acknowledging and formalising the extinction of numerous inactive unions, it promoted numerous mergers of smaller unions into broader and less spatially-restricted unions.

but the continuing reduction of territorial demarcations is feasible throughout the CGTP-IN, and in the financial sector and in offices, in particular, within the UGT. Fragmentation is also strongly influenced by the dynamics of occupational and professional particularism. Professional unions serve the twin functions of union represention of economic interests and of a professional association (Freire, 2000). These unions are also frequently affected by regional demarcations.[24]

Structural Change and the Role of Mergers

The structure of unions inherited from the pre-revolution period left a great deal of room for restructuring. Nevertheless, the schism in the labour movement and the proliferation of mostly unaffiliated occupational unions made it politically impossible to implement a single process of rationalisation. The structure of the UGT was, for the most part, not conducive to rationalisation on a sectoral basis, as it comprised industrial unions and in the major service sectors, banks and insurance, regional unions predominated. The greatest fragmentation in the UGT structure is among the unions of office employees. Furthermore, the UGT does not assign the structure of its member unions a major policy concern. On the other hand, the structure of the unions within the CGTP-IN remained most strongly influenced by the fragmented structure inherited from the old regime; it was, therefore, the basic space within which restructuring could take place. Although the CGTP-IN does not have statutory powers to decree or to enforce structural change of its member unions, it has had a very strong influence at specific moments. Following decisions made at crucial national congresses, this influence has been particularly effective and has acted as a mandate for structural change. Mention has already been made of the rationalisation efforts in the initial phase of democracy and the restructuring in the CGTP-IN between 1979 and 1984. These efforts to restructure continued to be at the centre of policy discussion within the CGTP-IN. In 1995, the CGTP-IN officially launched a campaign to restructure affiliated unions.[25]

---

[24] Two useful examples of this tendency are doctors' unions in the public sector and teachers' unions, which are divided between the rival confederations and by region.

[25] The member unions of the CGTP-IN are sovereign and, in general, any decision regarding changes in union statutes must be submitted to membership ratification and voted upon in a duly convened General Assembly. However, the leadership of the CGTP unions generally participates in their respective federations (or unions), the leadership of which also participate in the leadership of the Confederation. Through this overlapping of levels of decision-making the Confederation level is able to obtain significant influence.

The first important form of restructuring was the integation of declining categories of workers or of isolated craft workers into larger, functionally more adequate constituencies, in accordance with changes in the structure of enterprises, labour force and collective bargaining. This would generally lead to the dissolution of these unions. By 1976 the first efforts at rationalisation took place with the acquisition of several unions, which, in a number of cases, required the distribution of members throughout a number of 'vertical' unions. This process was termed 'verticalisation'. The attempt was made to bring all the unionised workers of an enterprise into one union, which would generally be an industrial union. In this manner, for example, the employees of the airline company would become members of one 'vertical' union of airline employees, regardless of their craft or occupation. Similarly, the employees of an engineering firm would become members of the union of metal workers, regardless of whether they were electricians or welders. This trend was illustrated by several cases of the members of shipyard craft and occupational unions being transferred to metal workers' unions. The merger of construction crafts into a general, but district-based, union of construction workers was also typical of this rationalisation. This type of restructuring has also resulted in the distribution of the members of unions in some occupations, for example garage employees, into a range of unions dependent on whether they were employed by transportation firms or auto repair shops.

A second important type of restructuring has been the merger of closely related categories of workers or industries into a unified structure with a broader occupational or industrial jurisdiction. An example of this type of restructuring was the creation in 1975 of a regional textile, woollen goods and clothing workers' union in the south, which coincided with the passing of the new law on trade unions. This important union rapidly became a pole of attraction for unions within this field. In 1976 it succeeded in acquiring two more district-based textile workers' unions. This union certainly influenced the merger process among district-based unions with the same coverage in the centre of the country in 1980 to form a regional union. Similar mergers also took place without necessarily expanding significantly territorial jurisdictions. In the same year, such a process took place on a strictly district basis in Aveiro, creating a general textile workers' union out of rug-makers, hat-makers, woollen goods workers and assorted clothing workers. The case of textiles and clothing demonstrates how a process, which could have been developed more profoundly, was held back by various types of resistance, including political division. In spite of the success in organising the two regional unions in the merger process of textile and clothing workers' unions, the sector continues to include district-based unions, some of which are limited to specific sub-industries, such as woollen goods. Much of the resistance to wider restructuring in this sector has to do with the local concentration of sections of the textile and woollen goods industries in the northern districts of the country and the desires of local union leaders to keep things local. Within the CGTP-IN, this situation is administered through a wide-ranging federation, which has not been able to bring about further mergers. Only in 1996 was a further merger completed with the acquisition by the southern textile union of a shoe and glove workers' union. Keeping to the pattern of emulation of form, the shoe and glove workers' union in question was a union that had been created in the revolutionary period on a broad geographical basis.

The third and most evident form of restructuring has been the fusion of similar unions from single districts into larger, multi-district, regional and, eventually, national unions of the same category of workers. Over the course of the entire democratic period, this form of restructuring has had a significant impact in many industries and sectors.

The example of the metal working and engineering, and the chemical and pharmaceutical sectors, illustrates the progress of restructuring (Tables 8.4 and 8.5). The interest in considering these two broad sectors together derives from the subsequent merger of the two federations affiliated to the CGTP-IN in 1998, as an integral part of the restructuring efforts. In 1976, still in the initial phase of democracy, seventeen unions of metal workers were demarcated by their inherited single-district jurisdictions, but were united in one federation. There were also two regional jewelry workers unions and several craft unions of shipyard workers. The unions of chemical and pharmaceutical industry workers, however, were much less fragmented. By 1976, following the process of reconstitution of unions in accordance with the union legislation of 1975, a regionally-based structure had emerged within the chemical industries. In addition, a national level union comprised both the production and commercial workers of the pharmaceutical industry, as well as the match industry workers. By 1985, within metal working and engineering, the dissolution of the craft unions in the shipyards and the unions of jewelry workers had taken place as part of their integration within metal workers' unions. A merger of several district unions from the south had also produced a regional union. Thus, until the mid-1980s, the structure of the sector within the CGTP-IN remained largely fragmented among thirteen district unions and the regional union. These were nevertheless associated through an important federation of metal workers and miners unions. A 'vertical' union of the UGT had also emerged. By 1985, in the chemical and pharmaceutical sector, the regional structure within the CGTP-IN had been consolidated with the acquisition of the match workers' union by the southern chemical workers' union. The three regional unions and the national pharmaceutical union were affiliated to the same federation. The union structure of the sector had also been altered by the creation of the vertical chemical workers' union affiliated to the UGT.

Table 8.4: Evolution of Union Structure in the Metalworking and Engineering Industries

1976	1985	2000
STIMMDL (District Lisbon)	STIMMDL (District Lisbon)	STIMMDLSCB (Districts Lisbon, Santarem e Castelo Branco) (i)
STIMMDS (District Santarem)	STIMMDS (District Santarem)	
SMDCB (Distrito de Castelo Branco)	SMDCB (District de Castelo Branco)	
SIMDP (District Oporto)	SIMDP (District Oporto)	SIMDP (District Oporto)
SMB (District Braga)	SMB (District Braga)	SMB (District Braga)
SNOMDB (District Bragança)	STICCMMMTMAD (Trás-Os-Montes and Alto Douro) (f)	(j)
SMDVC (District Viana do Castelo)	SMDVC (District Viana do Castelo)	SMDVC (District Viana do Castelo)
SMV (District Viseu)	SMV (District Viseu)	STIMMDAVG (Districts Aveiro, Viseu e Guarda) (k)
SMA (District Aveiro)	SMA (District Aveiro)	
STIMMDG (District Guarda)	STIMMDG (District Guarda)	
STIMDC (District Coimbra)	STIMDC (District Coimbra)	STIMMDCL (Districts Coimbra e Leiria) (l)
SMDL (District Leiria)	SMDL (District Leiria)	
SMDS (District Setubal)		STIMMS (Sul)
SMDP (District Portalegre)	STIMMS (South) (g)	
SNTOMMDF (District Faro)		
STMA (Alentejo)		
SCNCOCMMVPECNF (Carpenters, Sail Makers, Polishers, etc. in Ship Building) (a)		
SPCRN (Painters in Ship Building) (b)		
STCRNDPBVC (Ship Building Districts Oporto, Braga, Viana do Castelo) (c)		
SIORCS (Jewelry South) (d)		
SPOROCN (Jewelry North) (e)		
SMOCDF (District Funchal)	SMOCDF (District Funchal)	SMOCDF (District Funchal)
	SIMA – UGT (h)	SIMA – UGT (m)
		SIM (n)

Notes to Table 8.4:

a) Union dissolved in 1976 and members transferred to other unions of metal workers in the 'verticalisation' process.

b) Union dissolved in 1976 and members transferred to unions of metal workers based in Lisbon and Setubal in the 'verticalisation' process.

c) Union dissolved in 1979 and members transferred to unions of metal workers based in Porto, Braga and Viana do Castelo in the 'verticalisation' process.

d) Union dissolved in 1979 and members transferred to unions of metal workers based in Lisbon and Setubal.

e) Union dissolved in 1980 and members transferred to the union of metal workers based in Porto and the union of commerce workers based in Coimbra.

f) Formed in 1982 by the merger of SNOMDB; SOCCOCC (Construction and Kindred Trades District Chaves); and SOCCOCDVR (Construction and Kindred Trades District Vila Real).

g) Formed between 1981 and 1983 from mergers of STMA; SMDS; SNTOMMDF, and SMDP.

h) Formed in 1978.

i) Formed in 2000 by the merger of STIMMDL, STIMMDS, and SMDCB.

j) STICCMMMTMAD acquired by STCMMPCMCNV (Union of Construction, Wood, Marble, Quarry Ceramic and Construction Materials of the North and Viseu) in 1997.

k) Formed by the merger of SMV with SMA in 1995; which was followed by the merger of STIMMDAV with STIMMDG in 1998.

l) Formed by the merger of STIMDC and SMDL in 1995.

m) Left the UGT in 2001.

n) Formed in 1989.

Table 8.5: Evolution of Union Structure in Chemicals and Pharmaceuticals

1976	1985	2000
STIFDL (Match Workers District Lisbon) 1975		
STIQCSIAMCS (Chemicals and Mill Workers Centre, South & Islands) 1975	STIQS (Chemical Industries South) 1975, 1978	
STIQCI (Chemical Industries Centre & Islands) 1975	STIQCI (Chemical Industries Centre & Islands)	STQFPGCSI (Chemicals, Pharmaceuticals, Oil & Gas Centre, South & Islands) 1996
STICF (Pharmaceutical Workers Industry & Commerce) 1975	STICF (Pharmaceutical Workers Industry & Commerce)	
STIQPGN (Chemicals, Oil & Gas North) 1975	STIQPGN (Chemicals, Oil & Gas North)	STQFPGN (Chemicals, Pharmaceuticals, Oil & Gas North) 1996
	SINDEQ (Democratic-Chemicals) – UGT 1979	SINDEQ (Democratic-Chemicals) – UGT

By the year 2000, major changes had taken place and union structure in metal working and engineering and in chemicals and pharmaceuticals was significantly more concentrated. A co-ordinated process involving mergers among several CGTP-IN district-based unions of metal workers, the restructuring of the chemical and pharmaceutical unions affiliated to the CGTP-IN, and the merger of the two federations affiliated to the CGTP-IN for metal working and engineering and for chemicals and pharmaceuticals had been successfully completed. The CGTP-IN in metals was reduced to five multi-district and three district unions, which co-existed with the national union affiliated to the UGT. In chemicals and pharmaceuticals two regional unions affiliated to the CGTP-IN, and the one industrial union affiliated to the UGT remained. Within the CGTP-IN there is now only one federal structure for the two industries. Reforms in metal and chemicals highlight the extent of the changes that have taken place in union structure, particularly within the orbit of the CGTP-IN, as these are industries that are heavily influenced by tradition and are politically very polarised.

Since about 1994 merger processes among CGTP-IN unions, similar to those of the metal workers' unions, have culminated in several industrial structures composed entirely of either national or regional unions. Of particular note is the formation of one national CGTP-IN union for the paper and publishing industries from three regional unions (Table 8.6). The three regional unions that merged in 1996 had been previously formed by mergers in 1980 and 1982 involving combinations of regional, district and national unions of printers, paper, other printing and publishing workers. The unions that merged in 1980-1982 were divided geographically and by occupation. Thus, the formation of the regional unions was a continuation of the 'verticalisation' process in this sector. Union structure in this industry now consists of only two competing unions: STICPGI (Cellulose, Paper, Graphics and Printing Workers Union) affiliated to the CGTP-IN, and SDGPA (Democratic Union of Graphics, Paper and Kindred Workers) affiliated to the UGT. As a consequence of the creation of the national union, the federation affiliated to the CGTP-IN in this sector was dissolved. As can be seen from a comparison of the evolution of structure in these industries with that of the metal workers (Tables 8.4 and 8.6), the starting point in 1975-76 for the reform of the unions was qualitatively different. Whereas the unions of metal workers emerged in the new regime with a structure inherited from the old regime, the unions in all the paper industry and printing trades had already been largely restructured into regional and national organisations, with little emphasis placed on district-based structures.

Table 8.6: Evolution of Union Structure in Paper and Printing

1976	1985	2000
STICPCAZS (Cellulose, Paper, Cardboard and Kindred South)		
STICPCAZC (Cellulose, Paper, Cardboard Centre)	STICFGISI (Cellulose, Paper, Typographical and Printers South and Islands) 1980	
STGSIA (Typographical South and Islands)		
STI (Printers) (a)		
STGA (Typographical and Kindred Minho)		
STICPCAZN (Cellulose, Paper, Cardboard and Kindred North)	STICFTGIN (Cellulose, Paper, Typographical and Printers North)	STICPGI (Cellulose, Paper, Graphics, Press)
STGDPBVR (Typographical Districts Oporto, Bragança and Vila Real)		
STI (Printers) (a)		
STCPCCSPADABV (Cellulose, Paper, Cardboard and Kindred Districts Aveiro, Braga and Viseu)		
SGTPDA (Typographical and Paper District Aveiro)	STICFTGIC (Cellulose, Paper, Typographical and Printers Centre) 1982	
STGC (Typographical Centre)		
SOPOCDC (Paper and Kindred District Coimbra)		
	SDGA (Democratic Graphics and Kindred) – UGT 1982	SDGA (Democratic Graphics and Kindred) – UGT

a) one union dissolved and members integrated within the two unions established in the simultaneous merger processes of the northern and southern regional unions.

A similar gradual process of merger resulted in the creation during 2000 of a single national CGTP-IN union for commerce, office and service workers (Table 8.7). The creation of the national union was the result of a long process of restructuring of the CGTP-IN unions in this sector. In the aftermath of democratisation, this sector still consisted of a multiplicity of district-based unions. Several of these unions went over to the UGT in the early 1980s. In 1982, four district unions merged to form a regional union for the South. In 1996 several of the district-based unions in the North merged to form another regional union. Thus in 1998 a national union, STCESP (Commerce, Office and Service Workers' Union of Portugal), was formed out of the southern regional union and all the remaining CGTP-IN district unions in the sector. This national union still co-exists with the northern regional union and a multi-district union of the Minho zone (north).

Table 8.7: Evolution of Union Structure in the Sector of Commerce, Offices and Services

1976	1985	2000
SPECDG (Office and Commerce District Guarda)	SPECDG (Office and Commerce District Guarda)	
STECDV (Office and Commerce District Viseu)	STECDV (Office and Commerce District Viseu)	
STCEDCB (Commerce and Office District Castelo Branco)	STCEDCB (Commerce and Office District Castelo Branco)	CESP (Commerce, Office and Services District Portugal) (1998)
STCSDSa (Commerce and Services District Santarem)	STCSDSa (Commerce and Services District Santarem)	
STCDC (Commerce District Coimbra)	STCESDC (Commerce, Office and Services District Coimbra) (1981)	
STEDC (Office District Coimbra)		
STCEDL (Commerce and Office District Leiria)	STCEDL (Commerce and Office District Leiria)	
STCESDL (Commerce, Office and Services District Lisbon)	STCESDL (Commerce, Office and Services District Lisbon)	
STCSDBe (Commerce and Services District Beja)	STCESS (Commerce, Office and Services South) (1982)	
STCSDE (Commerce and Services District Evora)		
SLEECDF (Office and Cashiers District Faro)		
STCSDSe (Commerce and Services District Setubal)		
STCSDP (Commerce and Services District Oporto)	STCSDP (Commerce and Services District Oporto)	CESNORTE (Commerce, Office and Services North) (1996)
SESN (Office and Services North)	SESN (Office and Services North)	
STECDVC (Office and Commerce District Viana do Castelo)	STECDVC (Office and Commerce District Viana do Castelo)	
STCSDBr (Commerce and Services District Braga)	STESCDB (Office, Services and Commerce District Braga)	STESCM (Office, Services and Commerce Minho)
STEDB (Office District Braga)		
STECDA (Office and Commerce District Aveiro)		
STECSDP (Office, Commerce and Services District Portalegre)	STESC (Office, Serives and Commerce) – UGT (1984)	STESC (Office, Services and Commerce) – UGT
SES (Office Setubal)	STEISRS (Office, Computer, Services South) – UGT	STEISRS (Office, Computer, Services South) – UGT
SITESE (Office, Commerce and Services)	SITESE (Office, Commerce and Services) – UGT	SITECHS (Office, Commerce, Hotel and Services) – UGT
STECDVRB (Office and Commerce Districts Vila Real and Bragança)	STECDVRB (Office and Commerce Districts Vila Real and Bragança) – UGT	STECDVRB (Office and Commerce Districts Vila Real and Bragança) – UGT
STECAH (Office and Commerce District Angra do Heroismo)	STECAH (Office and Commerce District Angra do Heroismo) – UGT	STECAH (Office and Commerce District Angra do Heroismo) – UGT
SPECITSCISMSM (Office, Commerce, Tourism, Services Islands of S. Miguel and S. Maria)	SPECITSCISMSM (Office, Commerce, Tourism, Services Islands of S. Miguel and S. Maria) – UGT	SPECITSCISMSM (Office, Commerce, Tourism, Services Islands of S. Miguel and S. Maria) – UGT

Within the CGTP-IN federation in this sector, the national and the northern union already operate virtually as one union, and the federation has adopted a policy of merging these unions in order to form one national union for the sector. On the whole, this sector maintains a unique type of fragmentation due to the continuing existence of a multiplicity of UGT unions covering similar groups of workers, several of which have jurisdictional overlaps. Some of the UGT unions are district-based and have maintained the jurisdictions inherited from the old regime.

Additionally, three regional railway workers unions from the CGTP-IN merged in 1999 to complete the process of forging a national railway workers' union. The overall union structure in rail is now characterised by one national railway workers' union of the CGTP-IN, numerous UGT unions and several independent occupational unions.

Merger as Process

The CGTP-IN has thus experienced various phases of concerted restructuring in which mergers have been the basic vehicle. Many leaders of the CGTP-IN envisage further structural evolution. The cases of paper/printing and commerce/office are examples of completed processes of structural rationalisation through the creation of the national union. The reduction of multiple local unions into two or three regional unions are also significant transformations and, in the case of some industries, this may be the limit of restructuring possibilities in the present framework.

In all these processes a fundamental role has been played by the federations and the CGTP-IN confederation. The federations were created by the CGTP-IN in the initial phases of institutionalised trade unionism specifically to deal with the problem of co-ordination of fragmented unions in collective bargaining. Even in the relatively fragmented structure of Portuguese collective bargaining, centralisation takes place at the level of specific industries or sub-sectors. The existence of many unions that frequently separated workers employed in the same enterprise made even marginally centralised processes of bargaining unworkable without a complementary union. Thus, the federations became important as a means to bring together leaders of unions from around the country in a forum with a perspective that permitted them to see beyond local problems and to view the problems of their sector or industry as a whole.

Decision-making within the federations rests primarily with representative bodies comprising members of the affiliated unions. Through these regular and, often, charged meetings of the federations, the leaders of the individual trade unions are confronted with sectoral realities and with the necessity of evaluating relations between unions and the processes of collective bargaining. Similarly, the meetings of the national leadership of the CGTP-IN bring together the federation and union representatives and oblige assessments of the state of the labour movement from an overall perspective, rather than that based on a specific sector. This 'holistic' view of the labour movement is certainly facilitated by the 'class' ideology that commonly orients the leadership of the confederations and federations, whether the leaders espouse a Communist, left Catholic, Socialist or far-left standpoint.[26]

The federations have frequently initiated the merger process, while the CGTP-IN has played an orienting role. Since the leaderships of the federations and the confederation are closely articulated, these roles have often been fused. Nevertheless the CGTP-IN, as a confederation, has continually sought to rationalise union structure throughout the democratic period. In the early phases of democratisation, it played a much stronger orienting role, perhaps even what is colloquially called a 'strong-arm' role. Many CGTP-IN union leaders arrived at the conclusion, after much damage was done in inter-union relations in certain sectors, that mergers, together with the dissolution of unions, could best be achieved as a gradual process of consensus-building. As a result, in all of the sectors analysed above, three or four phases of restructuring can be observed. A first phase, from 1975 to 1979, frequently quite problematic, was the initial verticalisation. A second phase was the merger of district-based unions into multi-district or regional unions. This may or may not have involved all the unions of a sector or federation. In some sectors this phase took place in the early 1980s, while in others it was only accomplished during the 1990s. The third phase was the creation of a national union, either as a pole of attraction for remaining unions or as an end result, integrating all the CGTP-IN unions in the field. This achievement has been very recent in most cases and is incomplete, as many federations remain in the second phase of the process.

In the course of the restructuring process within the CGTP-IN the structure of the federations was altered. There have been several mergers of federations. The federation of food and beverage industries merged with the federation of hotel and restaurant unions. With the development of integrated enterprises, frequently multi-nationals, in the field of catering and hotels, new and obvious affinities emerged between food workers and hotel workers. It is a clear advantage to associate such

---

[26] It is nevertheless difficult to underplay the role of Communist Party links in these leadership organs.

unions in collective bargaining. There was also a merger of the federations of metal working and engineering and chemical and pharmaceutical unions. The mergers of federations have generally promoted further mergers among the unions belonging to the post-merger federation. In the cases of sectors where national unions have been created, the federation has lost its significance. In the paper and printing trades sector, the federation was dissolved with the national union taking on all of the functions of the federation. In commerce and offices the federation continues to exist, but, in practice, there has been a fusion between the structure of the new national union and the federation.

In all the cases analysed, the passage from the second to the third phases of restructuring involved consolidation of previous mergers, prolonged negotiations within the federation, proposals to the diverse memberships, plenaries and voting assemblies of the memberships, restructuring in the federation, and transformation in the federation. Integral to this process was a consensus constructed within the CGTP-IN confederation regarding the objectives of the systematic restructuring.

Conclusions

Mergers have had a profound impact upon the Portuguese union structure that was inherited from dictatorship. For the most part, this has been through the rationalisation of the structure of the CGTP-IN. The most advanced merger processes have produced national unions. The structure of the CGTP-IN, therefore, is significantly different today than it was a quarter of a century ago. Equally important have been the mergers within the CGTP-IN at the level of the federations. Since federations, as opposed to individual unions, are the organisations that play the most active role in collective bargaining, they actually have a function similar to that of a union or a cartel of unions in many other countries. When the merger process has advanced to its furthest degree, the federations have been dissolved, leaving a national union to conduct collective bargaining.

Much of the merger movement has been motivated by efforts to strengthen union intervention in collective bargaining. The combination of weaker unions with stronger unions, even when this has involved the merging of district-level unions, has increased the resources at the disposal of the weaker union. On the other hand, it is difficult to find an association between the character of mergers and transformation of collective bargaining structures. An exception to this point is in the area of commerce. The increase in employment in large distribution chains and hyper-markets is opening up the possibility of enterprise-specific agreements. In consequence, the new national union of commercial workers has reformed its internal structures to facilitate local and company representation. Apart from this example, the achievement of 'verticalisation' has been more typical of the attempt to make union structures correspond more effectively to existing bargaining structures. Thus, there have not been changes in bargaining structure that have spurred the changes in union jurisdictions, but adaptation to existing bargaining structure. Mergers have also resulted from rationalisation in the light of decreasing union resources in declining sectors.

The structure of the UGT has been fairly static since the creation of the industrial unions. In certain industries industrial unions affiliated to the UGT may lack members and resources, but they are sustained through their participation in collective bargaining. This is only viable because the norms of bargaining in Portugal permit the autonomous negotiation of agreements, even by unions whose representation in the sector is not the majority. For example, rather than construct a national union in such a strongly consolidated sector as banking, the three regional unions have contemplated the establishment of a federation. These three unions are strongly institutionalised and have sufficient resources to preclude a merger, hence their interest in a federation.

List of Abbreviations

CESNORTE	Sindicato dos Trabalhadores do Comércio, Escritório e Serviços do Norte (Commerce, Office and Services Workers Union North)
CESP	Sindicato dos Trabalhadores do Comércio, Escritórios e Serviços de Portugal (Commerce, Office and Services Workers' Union Portugal)
CGTP	Confederação Geral dos Trabalhadores Portugueses-Intersindical Nacional (General Confederation of Portuguese Workers)
CSI	Convenção de Sindicatos Independentes (Convention of Independent Trade Unions)
FENSIQ	Federação Nacional de Sindicatos de Quadros (National Federation of Managerial Unions)
INE	Instituto Nacional de Estatística (National Institute of Statistics)
MSU	Movimento Sindical Unitário (Unitary Union Movement)
PCP	Partido Comunista Português (Portuguese Communist Party)

PSD   Partido Social Democrata (Social Democratic Party)

SCNCOCMMVPECNF   Sindicato dos Carpinteiros Navais, Calafates e Ofícios Correlativos, Mecânicos e De Madeiras, Veleiros, Polidores, Estufadores e Construção Naval de Fibras (Union of Carpenters, Wood Mechanics, Sail Makers, Polishers, and Kindred in Shipbuilding)

SDGA   Sindicato Democrático dos Gráficos e Afins (Democratic Graphical and Kindred Workers' Union)

SES   Sindicato Escritórios Setúbal (Office Workers' Union Setubal)

SESN   Sindicato dos Escritórios e Serviços do Norte (Office and Services Workers Union North)

SGTPDA   Sindicato dos Gráficos e Transformadores de Papel do Distrito de Aveiro (Typographical and Paper Workers Union District Aveiro)

SIM   Sindicatos das Indústrias Metalúrgicas – UGT (Metalworking Industries Union)

SIMDP   Sindicato da Indústrias Metalúrgicas do Distrito do Porto (Metalworkers Union District Oporto)

SINDEQ   Sindicato Democrático da Química – UGT (Democratic Union of Chemicals)

SIORCS   Sindicato das Indústrias de Ourivesaria, Relojoaria e Correlativos do Sul (Jewelry, Watchmakers and Kindred Professions Union South)

SITECHS   Sindicato dos Trabalhadores de Escritório, Comércio, Hotelaria e Serviços – UGT (Office, Commerce, Hotel and Services Workers' Union)

SITESE   Sindicato dos Trabalhadores de Escritório, Comércio e Serviços (Office, Commerce and Services Workers' Union)

SLEECDF   Sindicato Livre dos Empregados de Escritório e Caixeiros do Distrito de Faro (Office and Cashiers Workers' Union District Faro)

SMA   Sindicato dos Metalúrgicos de Aveiro (Metalworkers Union District Aveiro)

SMB   Sindicato dos Metalúrgicos de Braga (Metalworkers Union District Braga)

SMDCB   Sindicato dos Metalurgicos do Distrito de Castelo Branco (Metalworkers Union District Castelo Branco)

SMDL	Sindicato dos Metalúrgicos do Distrito de Leiria (Metalworkers Union District Leiria)
SMDP	Sindicato dos Metalúrgicos do Distrito de Portalegre (Metalworkers Union District Portalegre)
SMDS	Sindicato dos Metalúrgicos do Distrito de Setúbal (Metalworkers Union District Setubal)
SMDVC	Sindicato dos Metalúrgicos do Distrito de Viana do Castelo (Metalworkers Union District Viana do Castelo)
SMOCDF	Sindicato dos Metalúrgicos e Ofícios Correlativos do Distrito do Funchal (Metalworkers and Kindred Union District Funchal)
SMV	Sindicato dos Metalúrgicos de Viseu (Metalworkers Union District Viseu)
SNOMDB	Sindicato Nacional dos Operários Metalúrgicos do Distrito de Bragança (Metalworkers Union District Bragança)
SNTOMMDF	Sindicato Nacional dos Técnicos e Operários Metalúrgicos e Metalomecânicos do Distrito de Faro (National Union of Technicians and Workers in Metal and Engineering Industires District Faro)
SOCCOCC	Sindicato dos Operários da Construção Civil e Ofícios Correlativos de Chaves (Union of Construction and Kindred Trades Chaves)
SOCCOCDVR	Sindicato dos Operários da Construção Civil e Ofícios Correlativos do Dist. de Vila Real (Union of Construction and Kindred Trades District Vila Real)
SOPOCDC	Sindicato dos Operários Papeleiros e Ofícios Correlativos do Distrito de Coimbra (Paper and Kindred Workers' Union District Coimbra)
SPCRN	Sindicato dos Pintores da Construção e Reparação Naval (Union of Naval Painters)
SPECDG	Sindicato dos Profissionais de Escritório e Comércio do Distrito da Guarda (Office and Commerce Workers Union District Guarda)
SPECITSCISMSM	Sindicato dos Profissionais de Escritório, Comércio, Indústria, Turismo, Serviços e Correlativos das Ilhas de S. Miguel e Santa Maria (Office, Commerce, Tourism, Services Workers' Union Islands of S. Miguel and Santa Maria)

SPOROCN	Sindicato dos Profissionais de Ourivesaria, Relojoaria e Ofícios Correlativos do Norte (Jewelry, Watchmakers and Kindred Professions Union North)
STAL	Sindicato dos Trabalhadores da Administração Local (Union of Local Administration Workers)
STCDC	Sindicato dos Trabalhadores do Comércio do Distrito de Coimbra (Commerce Workers' Union District Coimbra)
STCEDCB	Sindicato dos Trabalhadores do Comércio e Escritório do Distrito de Castelo Branco (Commerce and Office Workers' Union District Castelo Branco)
STCEDL	Sindicato dos Trabalhadores do Comércio e Escritório do Distrito de Leiria (Commerce and Office Workers' Union District Leiria)
STCESDC	Sindicato dos Trabalhadores do Comércio, Escritório e Serviços do Distrito de Coimbra (Commerce, Office and Services Workers' Union District Coimbra)
STCESDL	Sindicato dos Trabalhadores do Comércio, Escritórios e Serviços do Distrito de Lisboa (Commerce, Office and Services Workers' Union District Lisbon)
STCESS	Sindicato dos Trabalhadores de Comércio, Escritórios e Serviços do Sul (Commerce, Office and Services Workers' Union South)
STCMMPCMCNV	Sindicato dos Trabalhadores da Construção, Madeiras, Mármores, Pedreiras, Cerâmica e Materiais de Construção do Norte e Viseu (Union of Construction, Wood, Marble, Quarry Ceramic and Construction Materials of the North and Viseu)
STCPCCSPADABV	Sindicato dos Trabalhadores de Celulose, Papel, Cartão Canelado, Sacos de Papel e Afins dos Distritos de Aveiro, Braga e Viseu (Union of Cellulose, Paper, Cardboard and Kindred Workers Districts Aveiro, Braga and Viseu)
STCRNDPBVC	Sindicato dos Trabalhadores da Construção e Reparação Naval dos Distritos do Porto, Braga e Viana do Castelo (Union of Shipyard Workers Districts Oporto, Braga, Viana do Castelo)

STCSDBe	Sindicato dos Trabalhadores do Comércio e Serviços do Distrito de Beja (Commerce and Services Workers' Union District Beja)
STCSDBr	Sindicato dos Trabalhadores do Comércio e Serviços do Distrito de Braga (Commerce and Services Workers' Union District Braga)
STCSDE	Sindicato dos Trabalhadores do Comércio e Serviços do Distrito de Évora (Commerce and Services Workers Union District Evora)
STCSDP	Sindicato dos Trabalhadores do Comércio e Serviços do Distrito do Porto (Commerce and Services Workers Union District Oporto)
STCSDSe	Sindicato dos Trabalhadores do Comércio e Serviços do Distrito de Setúbal (Commerce and Services Workers' Union District Setubal)
STCSDSa	Sindicato dos Trabalhadores de Comércio e Serviços do Distrito de Santarem (Commerce and Services Workers' Union District Santarem)
STECAH	Sindicato Trabalhadores Escritório Comércio Distrito Angra do Heroismo (Office and Commerce Workers' Union District Angra do Heroismo)
STECDA	Sindicato dos Trabalhadores de Escritório e de Comércio do Distrito de Aveiro (Office and Commerce Workers' Union District Aveiro)
STECDV	Sindicato dos Trabalhadores de Escritório e Comércio do Distrito de Viseu (Office and Commerce Workers' Union District Viseu)
STECDVC	Sindicato dos Trabalhadores de Escritório e Comércio do Distrito de Viana do Castelo (Office and Commerce Workers' Union District Viana do Castelo)
STECDVRB	Sindicato dos Trabalhadores de Escritório e Comércio dos Distritos de Vila Real e Bragança (Office and Commerce Workers' Union Districts Vila Real and Bragança)
STECSDP	Sindicato dos Trabalhadores de Escritório, Comércio e Serviços do Distrito de Portalegre (Office, Commerce and Services Workers' Union District Portalegre)
STEDB	Sindicato dos Trabalhadores de Escritório do Distrito de Braga (Office Workers' Union District Braga)

STEDC	Sindicato dos Trabalhadores de Escritórios do Distrito de Coimbra (Office Workers Union District Coimbra)
STEISRS	Sindicato dos Trabalhadores de Escritório, Informática e Serviços da Região Sul – UGT (Office, Computer, Services Workers' Union South)
STESC	Sindicato dos Trabalhadores de Escritório, Serviços, Comércio (Office, Services and Commerce Workers' Union)
STESCDB	Sindicato dos Trabalhadores de Escritório, Serviços e Comércio do Distrito de Braga (Office, Services and Commerce Workers' Union District Braga)
STESCM	Sindicato dos Trabalhadores de Escritório, Serviços e Comércio do Minho (Office, Services and Commerce Workers' Union Minho)
STGA	Sindicato dos Trabalhadores Gráficos e Afins do Minho (Typographical and Kindred Workers Union, Minho)
STGC	Sindicato dos Trabalhadores Gráfico do Centro (Typographical Workers' Union Center)
STGDPBVR	Sindicato dos Trabalhadores Gráficos dos Distritos do Porto, Bragança e Vila Real (Union of Typographical Workers Districts Oporto, Bragança and Vila Real)
STGSIA	Sindicato dos Trabalhadores Gráficos de Sul e Ilhas Adjacentes (Typographical Workers Union South and Islands)
STI	Sindicato dos Trabalhadores na Imprensa (Union of Workers in the Press)
STICCMMMTMAD	Sindicato dos Trabalhadores das Indústrias da Construção Civil, Madeiras, Metalurgia e Metalomecânica de Trás-Os-Montes e Alto Douro (Union of Construction, Wood, Metalworkers and Engineering Union of Trás-Os-Montes and Alto Douro)
STICF	Sindicato dos Trabalhadores da Indústria e Comércio Farmacêuticos (Union of Pharmaceutical Workers in Industry and Commerce)
STICFGISI	Sindicato dos Trabalhadores das Indústrias de Celulose, Fabricação e Transformação do Papel, Gráfica e Imprensa do Sul e Ilhas (Union of Cellulose,

Paper, Typographical and Printers South and Islands)

STICFTGIC	Sindicato dos Trabalhadores das Indústrias de Celulose, Fabricação e Transformação do Papel, Gráfica e Imprensa do Centro (Cellulose, Paper, Typographical and Printers Union Center)
STICFTGIN	Sindicato dos Trabalhadores das Indústrias de Celulose, Fabricação e Transformação de Papel, Gráfica e Imprensa do Norte (Cellulose, Paper, Typographical and Printers Union North)
STICPCAZC	Sindicato dos Trabalhadores da Indústria de Celulose, Papel, Cartonagem e Afins – Zona Centro (Union of Cellulose, Paper, Cardboard Workers Center)
STICPCAZN	Sindicato dos Trabalhadores das Indústrias de Celulose, Papel, Cartonagem e Afins Zona Norte (Cellulose, Paper, Cardboard Workers Union North)
STICPCAZS	Sindicato dos Trabalhadores das Indústrias de Celulose, Papel, Cartonagem e Afins – Zona Sul (Union of Cellulose, Paper, Cardboard Workers South)
STICPGI	Sindicato dos Trabalhadores das Indústrias de Celulose, Papel, Gráfica e Imprensa (Union of Cellulose, Paper, Graphical and Press Workers)
STIFDL	Sindicato dos Trabalhadores da Indústria de Fósforos do Distrito de Lisboa (Match Workers Union District Lisbon)
STIMDC	Sindicato dos Trabalhadores das Indústrias Metalúrgicas do Distrito de Coimbra (Metalworkers Union District Coimbra)
STIMMDAVG	Sindicato dos Trabalhadores das Indústrias Metalúrgicas e Metalomecânicas dos Distritos de Aveiro, Viseu e Guarda (Metalworkers and Engineering Districts Aveiro, Viseu and Guarda)
STIMMDCL	Sindicato dos Trabalhadores das Indústrias Metalúrgicas e Metalomecânicas dos Distritos de Coimbra e Leiria (Metalworkers and Engineering Districts Coimbra and Leiria)
STIMMDG	Sindicato dos Trabalhadores das Indústrias Metalúrgica e Metalomecânica do Distrito da Guarda (Metalworkers and Engineering District Guarda)

STIMMDL	Sindicato dos Trabalhadores das Indústrias Metalúrgica e Metalomecânica do Distrito de Lisboa (Metalworkers and Engineering Union District Lisbon)
STIMMDLSCB	Sindicato dos Trabalhadores das Indústrias Metalúrgica e Metalomecânica dos Distritos de Lisboa, Santarem e Castelo Branco (Metalworkers and Engineering Union Districts Lisbon, Santarem and Castelo Branco)
STIMMDS	Sindicato dos Trabalhadores das Indústrias Metalúrgicas e Metalomecanicas do Distrito de Santarem (Metalworkers and Engineering Union District Santarem)
STIMMS	Sindicato dos Trabalhadores das Indústrias Metalúrgicas e Metalomecânicas do Sul (Metalworkers and Engineering Union South)
STIQCI	Sindicato dos Trabalhadores das Indústrias Quimicas do Centro e Ilhas (Chemical Industries Union Centre and Islands)
STIQCSIAMCS	Sindicato dos Trabalhadores das Indústrias Quimicas do Centro Sul e Ilhas Adjacentes e das Moagens do Centro e Sul (Chemicals and Mill Workers Union Center, South & Islands)
STIQPGN	Sindicato dos Trabalhadores das Indústrias Químicas, Petróleo e Gás do Norte (Union of Chemicals, Oil and Gas Workers North)
STIQS	Sindicato dos Trabalhadores das Indústrias Quimicas do Sul (Chemical Industries Union South)
STMA	Sindicato dos Trabalhadores Metalúrgicos do Alentejo (Metalworkers Union Alentejo)
STQFPGCSI	Sindicato dos Trabalhadores da Química, Farmacêutica, Petróleo e Gás do Centro, Sul E Ilhas (Chemicals, Pharmaceuticals, Oil and Gas Workers Union Centre, South and Islands)
TSD	Trabalhadores Sociais-Democratas (Social Democratic Workers)
UGT	União Geral dos Trabalhadores (General Union of Workers)
USI	União dos Sindicatos Independentes (Union of Independent Trade Unions)

CHAPTER 9. SWEDEN

Mergers in a Class-segmented Trade Union System[1]

Anders KJELLBERG

It is a paradox that the Nordic countries, known as welfare societies with comparatively far-reaching equality, contain the most class-segmented union movements. The blue-collar/white-collar divide and the division between university graduates and other white-collar workers have had a profound impact on union structure (Kjellberg, 2000a: 610-16). As a consequence, in Sweden separate union confederations exist for blue-collar workers, university-educated professionals and other white-collar workers: LO (Swedish Confederation of Trade Unions), SACO (Swedish Confederation of Professional Associations) and TCO (Swedish Confederation of Professional Employees). In 1974, SACO acquired a small confederation, SR (National Association of Civil Servants).

To assess the impact of this segmentation on the Swedish trade union merger process, this chapter comprises two sections. The first section reviews the pattern of structural development since 1950. The second section examines the merger process by reference to the different segments of union organisation. As several of the mergers ratified after 1950 were proposed earlier, both sections refer to events before 1950. From the outset, it should be noted that there is no legislation, nor has there been, to regulate the merger process. The LO unions have provisions in their constitutions that allow a merger if a majority of congress delegates consents. In several cases, opponents of industrial unionism proposed membership ballots that resulted in the rejection of mergers, which strengthened the negative attitude of LO towards ballots. What would have been the largest union amalgamation in Swedish history was

[1] This chapter was written with financial support from the Swedish Bank of Tercentenary Foundation.

prevented by a few votes, which led to a failure to attain the required two-thirds of council delegates of one of the three TCO unions concerned.

Swedish Trade Union Structure

All three confederations contain private and public sector unions. In SACO each affiliate recruits in both sectors. From a Nordic perspective, Sweden has the most far-reaching separation of national unions and confederations along the blue-collar/white-collar divide and with respect to university graduates versus other white-collar workers. In recent decades, the divisions between SACO and TCO and between TCO and LO have been diluted and shared interests accentuated. Within manufacturing industry, unions from the three confederations co-operate closely in collective bargaining, among them the largest TCO and SACO unions and the largest LO private sector union.

Another major change is that the majority of trade union members are now white-collar workers rather than blue-collar workers. This shift reflects the expanding employment share of white-collar workers and a long period of increasing union density. Today about 80 per cent of both white-collar and blue-collar workers are unionised. This development is reflected in considerable shifts between union confederations. LO's membership share declined from 79 to 52 per cent between 1945 and 2002, while the share organised by TCO and SACO grew. Of the ten largest unions in 2000, five each were LO and TCO affiliates. Seven out of ten Swedish unions are white-collar unions, almost all of which affiliate to TCO or SACO. The total number of unions with at least 150 members declined from 165 in 1945 to 66 in 2003 (Table 9.1). Today only half as many LO and TCO unions exist as in 1950.

Table 9.1: Number of National Unions in Sweden, 1945-2003 (with at least 150 members)

	LO	TCO	SACO*	SYACO**	SR	SAC	INDEPENDENT	ALL
1945	46	35	–	7	14	1	65	165
1946	45	34	–	8	15	1	54	157
1947	45	45	18		16	1	43	168
1948	45	43	17***		16	1	40	162
1949	44	41	16		18	1	34	154
1950	44	42	17		20	1	27	151
1951	44	44	24		19	1	19	151
1952	44	44	26		19	1	17	151
1953	44	41	27***		16	1	16	145
1954	44	41	22		15	1	17	140
1955	44	41	22		11	1	18	137
1956	44	40	23		11	1	17	136
1957	44	36	25		12	1	16	134
1958	44	36	25***		13	1	17	136
1959	44	36	25		15	1	17	138
1960	44	35	27		14	1	17	138
1961	43	35	25		16	1	16	136
1962	41	33	25		15	1	14	129
1963	41	32	25		15	1	13	127
1964	39	32	24		14	1	15	125
1965	38	31	26		13	1	11	120
1966	38	30	26		13	1	10	118
1967	37	26	28		12	1	11	115
1968	37	25	28		12	1	11	114
1969	37	23	27		11	1	10	109
1970	29	23	28		10	1	7	98
1971	29	22	28		8	1	7	95
1972	27	22	25		8	1	8	91
1973	25	22	24		7	1	8	87
1974	25	22	26		7	1	7	88
1975	25	24	26			1	7	83
1976	25	24	25			1	7	82
1977	25	24	24			1	5	79
1978	25	24	25			1	5	80
1979	25	22	25			1	6	79
1980	25	21	25			1	6	78
1981	24	20	25			1	7	77
1982	24	20	25			1	6	76
1983	24	19	25			1	6	75
1984	24	19	24			1	7	75
1985	24	21	24			1	5	75
1986	24	20	24			1	4	73
1987	24	20	24			1	4	73
1988	24	20	24			1	4	73
1989	23	20	24			1	4	72
1990	23	20	24			1	4	72
1991	23	19	24			1	4	71
1992	23	19	24			1	4	71

	LO	TCO	SACO*	SYACO**	SR	SAC	INDEPENDENT	All
1993	22	19	24			1	4	70
1994	21	20	24			1	4	70
1995	21	19	23			1	5	69
1996	20	19	23			1	5	68
1997	20	18	24			1	7	70
1998	19	18	25			1	6	69
1999	19	18	25			1	6	69
2000	18	18	25			1	6	68
2001	18	18	25			1	6	68
2002	16	19	25			1	6	67
2003	16	18	25			1	6	66

*   Reserve Officers Association excluded as it has no employed members.
**   SYACO was a precursor of SACO.
*** Estimated.

Major Changes among the Largest 40 Unions, 1950-2000

Of the largest 40 unions in 1950 (Table 9.2) no fewer than nine had their origin in breakaways, four of them from Grov & Fabriks (Union of Labourers and Factory Workers). They organised municipal workers, transport workers, paper workers and road workers. Before 1950, a total of 26 unions (with at least 150 members) were founded through breakaways. Most breakaways occurred between 1906 and 1924 (19 unions) with a peak recorded between 1914 and 1920 (11 unions). During this period, many categories of workers considered the founding of separate unions with their own identities as a more efficient means of raising union density than remaining in a large conglomerate union such as Grov & Fabriks. LO opposed breakaways, except if they facilitated moves towards industrial unionism. Hostile breakaways from LO unions were refused affiliation.

Among the largest 40 unions in 1950, almost the same number of unions resulted from breakaways (nine) as from amalgamations (eight). While all breakaways occurred before 1925, all but one amalgamation took place after 1920. This indicates a clear transition from breakaways to amalgamations after 1920. The majority (23) of the largest 40 unions in 1950, however, were founded as single unions without involvement of others.

Of the largest 40 unions in 2000 only six were founded by breakaways, but 18 had been formed by amalgamations (Table 9.3). Seven of the nine white-collar unions among the largest 20 unions originated from amalgamations. Exceptions were the largest TCO union (SIF) and the second largest SACO union, LR (National Union of Teachers in Sweden), although the latter had acquired several unions. Furthermore, none of the two largest LO unions were formed by amalgamations. Of the largest 40 unions in 1950 about half still existed in 2000. As many as

15 unions had amalgamated, six of which were involved in two successive amalgamations. Another six unions were acquired by other unions.

Table 9.2: The 40 Largest National Unions in Sweden, 31 December 1950 (excl. SAC)

(1)	(2)	(3)	(4)	(5)	(6)	(7)	(8)	(9)	(10)	(11)	(12)	(13)
1	Metall	211,800	15,200	M	M	M	BC	V	LO		1888	X
2	Byggnads/ Building	111,100	1,200	M	M	M	BC	V	LO	AMALG	1949	X
3	Kommunal/ Municip.	85,900	35,800	M	G	S	BC	V	LO	BREAK	1910	X
4	Järnvägs/ Railways	69,100	3,000	M	G	S	BC/ WC	V	LO		1899	AM1
5	Handels/ Commercial	66,600	28,400	M	M	S	BC/ WC	V	LO		1906	X
6	Fabriks/ Factory	60,100	12,300	M	M	M	BC	V	LO		1891	AM1
7	SIF/Clerical	59,700	15,200	M	M	M	WC	V	TCO		1920	X
8	Träind/ Wood Ind*	56,300	1,400	M	M	M	BC	V	LO	BREAK	1924	X*
9	Textil	47,400	24,200	W/M	M	M	BC	V	LO		1898	AM2
10	Lant/Agricult.	42,900	2,900	M	M	M	BC	V	LO		1918	X**
11	Transport	39,700	3,700	M	M	S	BC	V	LO	BREAK	1897	X
12	Pappers/Paper	37,900	2,300	M	M	M	BC	V	LO	BREAK	1920	X
13	Livs/Food	37,900	10,400	M	M	M	BC	V	LO	AMALG	1922	X
14	Bekläd.arb./ Garment	35,400	28,800	W	M	M	BC	V	LO		1889	AM2
15	Skogs/Forest	30,800	0	M	M	M	BC	V	LO		1918	AC*
16	Ledarna/ Supervis.	30,400	500	M	M/ G	M	WC	C	TCO	AMALG	1928	X
17	HRF/Hotel & Rest.	22,000	17,300	W	M	S	BC	V	LO		1918	X
18	SKTF/ Municipal wc	21,000	10,200	M/W	G	S	WC	V	TCO	AMALG	1936	X
19	Fastighets/ Maint.	20,200	6,100	M	M	S	BC	V	LO		1936	X
20	SvT/Tele	19,700	8,800	M/W	G	S	BC	V	LO		1901	AM1
21	Försvars/ Defence	19,300	3,200	M	G	S	BC	V	LO		1917	AM1
22	Elektriker/ Electr.	18,600	0	M	M	M	BC	C	LO	BREAK	1906	X
23	Målare/Painters	17,900	0	M	M	M	BC	C	LO		1887	X
24	SPF/Post	17,000	3,600	M	G	S	BC/ WC	V	LO		1886	AM1
25	Väg/Road	15,300	0	M	G	M	BC	C	LO	BREAK	1914	AM1
26	DFF/ United Unions	15,100	4,200	M	M	M	BC	V	LO	AMALG	1905	AC
27	Typograf	13,800	500	M	M	M	BC	C	LO		1886	AM1
28	Musiker/ Musicians	13,800	900	M	M	S	WC	C	LO		1907	X
29	Sjöfolks/ Seamen	13,600	0	M	M	S	BC	V	LO	AMALG	1932	AC
30	Murare/ Bricklayers	13,100	0	M	M	M	BC	V	LO		1890	AC
31	HFT/ Commercial wc	12,600	5,600	M/W	M	S	WC	V	TCO	AMALG	1937	X

229

(1)	(2)	(3)	(4)	(5)	(6)	(7)	(8)	(9)	(10)	(11)	(12)	(13)
32	ST/Civil Servants	12,600	6,100	M/W	G	S	WC	V	TCO	AMALG	1938	X
33	Gjutare/ Foundry	12,300	100	M	M	M	BC	C	LO	BREAK	1893	AC
34	SSF/Nurses	12,000	12,000	W	G	S	WC	C/P	TCO		1910	AM1
35	Sko & Läder Shoe	12,000	4,400	M	M	M	BC	V	LO		1888	AM2
36	POF/Mil. Officers	11,000	0	M	G	S	WC	C	TCO		1918	AM2
37	Bokbind/ Bookbind.	10,800	6,100	W/M	M	M	BC	C	LO		1893	AM1
38	SSLF/Inf. Sch.Mistr.	10,800	10,800	W	G	S	WC	C	TCO	BREAK	1918	AM2
39	Folkskol/ El. School	9,900	0	M	G	S	WC	C	TCO	BREAK	1920	AM2
40	Gruv/Miners	9,600	100	M	M	M	BC	V	LO		1895	AC

* From 1998 Skogsträ, after acquisition of No. 15 Skogs.
** Acquired by No. 3 in 2002.

(1) Rank by size.
(2) Abbreviated name.
(3) Number of 'active' union members. Unemployed included. Pensioners, self-employed and students excluded.
(4) Women members.
(5) Membership dominated by men (M), by women (W).
(6) Most members in government sector (G), in market sector (M).
(7) Membership in predominantly manufacturing, construction and agriculture/forestry (M), in service sector (S).
(8) Blue-collar union (BC), white-collar union (WC).
(9) Vertical (industrial) union (V), craft (occupational) union (C), professional union (P).
(10) Affiliated to confederation. Ind = Independent.
(11) Founded by amalgamation or breakaway.
(12) Year of foundation.
(13) X = still existed in 2000; AM1 = amalgamated with other union(s); AM2 = amalgamated with other union(s), which subsequently amalgamated again; AC = acquired by other union.

The number of LO unions among the largest forty unions almost halved between 1950 and 2000, even though all but one of the eighteen LO unions were included in the 2000 list. Mergers among LO unions thus created space for white-collar unions on the list. TCO is now represented by more than half of its unions, compared to less than 20 per cent in 1950. The big winner is SACO, with half of its unions on the 2000 list, but none in 1950. Another indication of how far the merger process has proceeded is that 111 national unions in 1950 fell outside the list of the largest forty unions, while the corresponding figure in 2000 was just twenty-eight.

Of the 20 largest unions in 2000 no less than fifteen were vertical (industrial unions), but just twenty-one among the largest forty, a clear decline since 1950. Conversely, a large number of professional unions, among them twelve SACO unions, appeared on the 2000 list. A TCO union of journalists had been transformed to a professional union. Another two TCO unions, *Lärarförbundet* (Swedish Teachers' Union) and *Vårdförbundet* (Swedish Association of Health Professionals), might also be characterised as professional. The largest twenty unions in 2000 comprised about 90 per cent of all LO and TCO members, but only every third SACO member. Most SACO unions are relatively small. The largest are CF (Swedish Association of Graduate Engineers), LR and *Jusek* (Federation of Lawyers, Social Scientists and Economists). Several SR civil servants' associations were very small. As no SR or SACO union exceeded 5,000 members in 1950 their absence from the list of the largest forty unions is not surprising.

Manufacturing (including construction and agriculture/forestry) was represented by less than half as many unions among the largest forty in 2000 compared to 1950. Another four unions recruit within both manufacturing and services. The remaining twenty-five are service sector unions, indicating the growth of the 'service society'. The border between public and private services is being blurred. No fewer than twelve unions among the largest forty unions recruit in both sectors, reflecting the rise of professional unions. Since 1950 the number of unions with a majority of women members among the largest forty unions has increased from three to thirteen, including six of the largest ten unions, while seven unions contain about as many women as men.

Table 9.3: The 40 Largest National Unions in Sweden, 31 December 2000

(1)	(2)	(3)	(4)	(5)	(6)	(7)	(8)	(9)	(10)	(11)	(12)
1	Kommunal/ Municip.	595,200	483,400	W	G/M	S	BC	V	LO	BREAK	1910
2	Metall	314,300	62,900	M	M	M	BC	V	LO		1888
3	SIF/Clerical	298,600	117,000	M	M	M	WC	V	TCO		1920
4	Lärarförb/ Teachers	176,100	143,400	W	G	S	WC	C/P	TCO	AMALG	1991
5	HTF/ Commerc. wc	151,800	95,500	W	M	S	WC	V	TCO	AMALG	1937
6	Handels/ Commerc.	147,800	102,100	W	M	S	BC/ WC	V	LO		1906
7	SKTF/ Municip. wc	145,100	107,400	W	G	S	WC	V	TCO	AMALG	1936
8	SEKO/ Communic.	120,700	39,600	M	M/G	S	BC/ WC	V	LO	AMALG	1970
9	Byggnads/ Building	100,400	700	M	M	M	BC	V	LO	AMALG	1949
10	Vårdförb/ Nurses	97,700	90,500	W	G/M	S	WC	C/P	TCO	AMALG	1965
11	Industri-facket	80,300	30,500	M	M	M	BC	V	LO	AMALG	1993
12	ST/Civil servants	72,900	48,200	W	G	S	WC	V	TCO	AMALG	1938
13	Transport	67,000	10,500	M	M	S	BC	V	LO	BREAK	1897
14	CF/Civil Engineers	63,600	11,800	M	M/G	M	WC	P	SACO	AMALG	1954
15	Ledarna/ Supervis.	60,600	6,600	M	M/G	M/S	WC	C	Ind	AMALG	1928
16	HRF/Hotel & Rest.	59,400	40,700	W	M	S	BC	V	LO		1918
17	Skogsträ/ ForestWood	56,400	9,500	M	M	M	BC	V	LO	BREAK	1924
18	LR/Second. Teachers	52,100	33,300	W	G	S	WC	P	SACO		1912
19	Livs/Food	46,800	18,500	M	M	M	BC	V	LO	AMALG	1922
20	Fastighets/ Maint.	40,800	19,700	M/W	M	S	BC	V	LO		1936
21	Jusek/ Lawyers	38,900	18,700	M/W	G/M	S	WC	P	SACO		1940
22	Finans/ Finance	34,000	22,100	W	M	S	WC	V	TCO		1887
23	SSR/Social Science	30,100	23,300	W	G/M	S	WC	P	SACO	BREAK	1958
24	GF/ Graphical	29,500	8,700	M	M	M	BC	V	LO	AMALG	1973
25	Pappers/ Paper	26,500	4,700	M	M	M	BC	V	LO	BREAK	1920
26	Läkarf/ Physicians	25,800	10,400	M	G	S	WC	P	SACO		1902
27	Elektrik/ Electr.	22,900	150	M	M	M	BC	C	LO	BREAK	1906
28	Polis/Police	16,400	2,900	M	G	S	WC	C	TCO		1903
29	SULF/Univ. Teach.	16,200	6,600	M	G	S	WC	P	SACO	AMALG	1984
30	Civilekon/ Econ.	15,900	7,600	M/W	M	M/S	WC	P	SACO		1942

(1)	(2)	(3)	(4)	(5)	(6)	(7)	(8)	(9)	(10)	(11)	(12)
31	Målare/ Painters	14,800	500	M	M	M	BC	C	LO	AMALG	1887
32	SJF/ Journalist	14,600	6,900	M/W	M	S	WC	P	TCO		1901
33	DIK/ Document	14,200	10,800	W	G/M	S	WC	P	SACO	AMALG	1972
34	FF/Social Insur.*	13,000	10,500	W	G	S	WC	V	LO*	AMALG	1918
35	Lant/ Agricultural**	12,800	5,400	M	M/G	M/S	BC	V	LO		1918
36	FTF/ Insurance	12,700	7,500	W/M	M	S	WC	V	TCO	AMALG	1940
37	Officers/Mil. Off.	12,400	300	M	G	S	WC	P	SACO	AMALG	1995
38	SN/Scientists	10,500	4,800	M/W	G/M	S	WC	P	SACO		1945
39	SRAT/General Group	9,100	5,300	W/M	G/M	S	WC	P	SACO	AMALG	1968
40	Ingenjörs/ Engineers	8,800	900	M	G/M	S/M	WC	P	SACO		1941

*   Acquired by No. 12 in 2003.
**   Acquired by No. 1 in 2002.
(1) – (12): see Table 9.2.

The Swedish Merger Process

The timing of rapid industrialisation and emergence of socialism caused industrial workers to define themselves in class rather than craft terms, and prevented liberal or religious currents from having a decisive impact upon structure and ideology of the Swedish union movement. Together with the ethnic and religious homogeneity of the Swedish population, it prevented the emergence of competing political or religious confederations, as in much of continental Europe. The close ties between LO and the SAP (Social Democratic Labour Party), however, promoted the formation of separate white-collar unions and confederations.

Employers' associations came into being only after the founding of LO. Within a few years several large lockouts or threats thereof occurred, often ending in compromises such as the Engineering Agreement of 1905 and the 1906 December Compromise between LO and SAF (Swedish Employers' Confederation), which acknowledged the right to organise. Almost from the outset SAF and VF (Swedish Engineering Employers' Association) advocated nation-wide collective agreements within each industry, with the objective of taking wages out of competition and minimising the impact of union tactics, which involved singling out particular companies and campaigning against them before moving to the next company. Thirty years later LO and SAF concluded a basic agreement, the *Saltsjöbaden* agreement (1938). This was followed by the centralisation of LO in 1941, which moved much decision-making from affiliated unions to LO. The timing and rate of industrialisation, the emergence of socialism and the bargaining strategies of employers' organisations combined to have a profound influence on Swedish trade union structure and the merger process.

Craft versus Industrial Unionism

In addition to unions in the public sector, three types of union existed around 1900: craft unions, industrial unions and general unions of unskilled workers. In engineering, for example, there were a number of unions. Almost all occupations directly related to metal manufacturing, however, fell within the recruitment area of *Metall* (Swedish Metalworkers' Union). The union was a conglomerate of trades with the common denominator that the members directly worked with metals (Lindgren, 1938: 87). Consequently *Metall* was neither an industrial union nor a craft union, but a 'work-material union' (Westerståhl, 1945: 42; Fulcher, 1991: 47). Only two small craft unions preferred to stand apart: *Gjutare* (Swedish Foundry Workers' Union) and *Bleck & Plåt* (Swedish Sheet Metal Workers' Union), both of which were breakaways from *Metall* in 1893. In contrast to the skilled artisan trades, the local *Metall* branches had no competence requirements for entry (Lindgren, 1938: 92). The absence of sharp borderlines between skilled and unskilled metal workers in Sweden can be attributed to the late but very rapid industrialisation, implying a distinct break with the guild system.

Similarly, *Träarb* (Swedish Wood Workers' Union) embraced all kinds of workers within the wood trades (Hansson, 1938: 30ff., 57ff.). This very special form of organisation applied by the dominant unions in the metal and wood industries blocked the development of the craft unions. As late as 1900, development towards British craft-*cum*-general unions was a possible alternative. The leading general union, *Grov & Fabriks*, was LO's largest union in 1906-08. From 1910, however, its expansion was retarded by several breakaways. The development of this union was also curbed by the growth of many other unions of unskilled workers. By preventing all unskilled workers going to *Grov & Fabriks*, the work-material principle facilitated a transition to industrial unionism. During the mid-1920s most unskilled metalworkers in *Grov & Fabriks* were transferred to *Metall*, in accordance with the decision at the 1922 LO Congress to complete the transition to industrial unions within the next three years. Some membership transfers, but no mergers, occurred during these years, which clearly illustrates that decisions to be made by individual unions can not be ordered from above. This was the only time that an LO Congress tried to force unions to merge, but LO has never had any constitutional right to dissolve or merge affiliated unions. Among others, the Chair of LO opposed this controversial *Metall* initiative, fearing that a number of unions would leave LO rather than merge. This, however, did not happen.

The impetus towards industrial unionism did not stem only from within the labour movement, but also from the strategy of employers to centralise collective bargaining (Westerståhl, 1945: 58). The resolute behaviour of the engineering employers in 1908 was a decisive turning-point. From a half-hearted or even negative stance towards industrial unionism, *Metall* from this juncture argued strongly that all workers within an industry should belong to the same union. The 1905 Engineering Agreement had been signed by four unions. Two of them, *Metall* and *Träarb*, applied the work-material principle, while *Gjutare* was a craft union and *Grov & Fabriks* a union of unskilled workers. During the negotiations for a new agreement in 1908, the engineering employers in VF insisted upon the participation of another four unions to make the agreement effective, making eight unions in all (Lindgren *et al.*, 1948: 188ff.). The argument was that a number of disputes, each with the potential to escalate into large conflicts, had been caused by unions other than the parties to the 1905 agreement. These additional four unions organised sheet metal workers, painters, bricklayers and transport workers. Despite intense pressure from both *Metall* and LO, the painters refused to participate in any negotiations. As a consequence, VF refused to negotiate with the other seven unions. A union representing just 0.5 per cent of union members in engineering thus prevented *Metall* from entering into negotiations. VF threatened a lockout if the old agreement was not prolonged for another five years and supplemented by some new paragraphs. Taking into consideration the unfavourable business cycle, the unions had to accept these poor terms.

The growing practical difficulties with a multitude of unions in engineering led *Metall* to propose a transition to industrial unionism at the 1909 LO Congress. Both in engineering and steel, *Metall* had to deal with employers' associations organised by industry. The union risked being involved in conflicts where it had only a few members (in non-metal industries) or where other unions had very few members. Up to the great 1909 conflict, mergers were increasingly considered as a means to strengthen the LO unions against offensive employers' organisations. The magnitude of the 1909 conflict resulted in the active involvement of LO, but this could not prevent the defeat. The authority of LO, therefore, was seriously weakened. Furthermore, the syndicalist confederation SAC (Central Organisation of Swedish Workers) was founded in 1910 by disappointed LO members.

The 1912 Congress adopted a radical plan to halve the total number of unions, including those outside LO. It was based on two principles: only one union should sign each collective agreement (the principle of collective agreement area); and unions in contiguous or dependent industries should merge, even if they were the sole union signing an agreement (the principle of industry). As the implementation of the plan was completely voluntary, not many mergers occurred during the first decade. On the contrary, the number of unions not affiliated to LO, but with membership among manual workers, grew rapidly.

As can be seen from Table 9.4 (part A) the frequency of amalgamations and acquisitions during the period 1890-1929 was relatively low. Most of the activity was concentrated in the years 1900-10 and 1916-24 (Table 9.4-part B). Both these periods were characterised by rapid union growth followed by severe setbacks for unions during recessions. In addition, the first period ended in the 1909 strike/lockout defeat. The second period, to a large extent, coincided with a high frequency of breakaways.

It took several decades to reorganise the trade union movement along industrial lines. Not until the mid-1920s did it begin to leave clear tracks. To increase bargaining power, it was proposed that all workers at a workplace should belong to the same union (Westerståhl, 1945: 44-51). In the 1920s, *Metall* was fully transformed from a union of metal workers to an industrial union comprising all blue-collar workers in engineering and steel works (except foundry workers). This important step towards industrial unionism was implemented by transfers of groups of members between unions, rather than by mergers.

LO: From 46 Unions to 16 between 1945 and 2002

The number of LO unions reached its maximum, 46 unions, in 1940-45. A marked decline occurred in the 1960s: from 44 to 37 unions. A large amalgamation of public sector unions in 1970 reduced the number to 29. After further mergers, 25 unions were left in 1973. Then the development slowed considerably with the result that there were still 24 affiliates in 1988. After a new wave of mergers the number was down to 16 in 2002.

Table 9.4: Number of Acquisitions and Amalgamations in Sweden 1890-2003 involving unions with at least 150 members

	ACQUISITIONS			AMALGAMATIONS			SUM ACQUIS. + AMALG.		
	Blue-Collar	White-Collar	All	Blue-Collar	White-Collar	All	Blue-Collar	White-Collar	All
A. Per decade									
1890-99	0	0	0	0	0	0	0	0	0
1900-09	7	0	7	6	0	6	13	0	13
1910-19	5	1	6	1	3	4	6	4	10
1920-29	7	1	8	2	3	5	9	4	13
1930-39	5	5	10	4	14	18	9	19	28
1940-49	8	21	29	1	13	14	9	34	43
1950-59	3	22	25	0	7	7	3	29	32
1960-69	7	16	23	0	8	8	7	24	31
1970-79	2	13	15	12	9	21	14	22	36
1980-89	2	5	7	0	2	2	2	7	9
1990-99	3	0	3	1	2	3	4	2	6
B. Per period									
1890-99	0	0	0	0	0	0	0	0	0
1900-10	8	0	8	6	0	6	14	0	14
1911-15	0	0	0	0	1	1	0	1	1
1916-24	10	2	12	3	4	7	13	6	19
1925-31	2	0	2	0	1	1	2	1	3
1932-39	4	5	9	4	14	18	8	19	27
1940-49	8	21	29	1	13	14	9	34	43
1950-59	3	22	25	0	7	7	3	29	32
1960-69	7	16	23	0	8	8	7	24	31
1970-73	2	6	8	12	8	20	14	14	28
1974-79	0	7	7	0	1	1	0	8	8
1980-89	2	5	7	0	2	2	2	7	9
1990-99	3	0	3	1	2	3	4	2	6
Sum	49	84	133	27	61	88	76	145	221
2000-2003	2	1	3	0	0	0	2	1	3

The low rate of mergers during long periods can be attributed to the pragmatic attitude of LO described above, combined with hesitation, particularly within craft unions. Among the driving forces for mergers since 1945 were:

- structural shifts of employment, which undermined the membership base of many unions;
- technological changes that diluted borders between unions;
- increased demands for improved services;
- growing necessity to avoid, or at least restrict, rising membership dues, which were and are considerably higher among LO unions, compared to TCO and SACO unions;
- administrative rationalisation required by the two preceding points;
- mergers may be a means of increasing bargaining strength and political influence *vis-à-vis* employers and the state;
- the state and employers may encourage mergers or intensified cooperation between unions through their insistence on specific bargaining structures.

A classic example of employment changes affecting union structure is the heavy losses of jobs within textile and garment industries. From 1950 to 1970 *Textil* (Swedish Textile Workers' Union) lost more than half its members. The LO unions of garment workers and shoe and leather workers were also severely hit. In 1972 all three unions amalgamated to form *Beklädnads* (Swedish Textile, Garment and Leather Workers' Union), but soon the decline of members accelerated. In 1993 *Beklädnads* and *Fabriks* (Swedish Factory Workers' Union)[2] amalgamated to form *Industrifacket* (Industrial Workers' Union). A third union, *Livs* (Swedish Food Workers' Union) initially participated, but backed out due to membership opposition. In contrast to *Beklädnads*, *Livs* was much less exposed to membership losses.

In some cases, the transition to industrial unions was a lengthy process. *Träarb* split in 1924 into two unions: the building carpenters established *Byggnadsträ* (Building Wood Workers' Union), while the remaining members founded *Träind* (Swedish Wood Industry Workers' Union). As the latter union adopted the principle of industrial unionism, its members in the metal industry were transferred to *Metall* from 1926. On the other hand, *Byggnadsträ* was a new craft union, reflecting the resistance among building workers towards industrial unionism. Strong craft cultures explain why no fewer than 13 unions signed the 1908 national building agreement (Åmark, 1998: 168). The 1912 LO blue-

---

[2] Fabriks, originally known as Grov & Fabriks, was hit by a series of breakaways. In 1949 the building labourers broke away reducing Grov & Fabriks from 104,000 to 59,000 members. It thus was transformed from a general union of unskilled workers and factory workers, to an industrial union of factory workers.

print proposed a single union for all building workers. Despite pressure from LO and the existence of a single wage agreement, the building labourers in *Grov & Fabriks* and the skilled building workers in the unions of wood workers and bricklayers refused to merge for several decades. The absence of co-ordination during the building conflict 1933-34, however, made the unions more inclined to merge (*ibid.*: 171ff.), but it was only in 1949 that *Byggnadsträ* and the building labourers in *Grov & Fabriks* amalgamated to form *Byggnads*. The origin of *Byggnads* thus was two breakaways, one from *Grov & Fabriks* (in 1949), the other stemming from the split of *Träarb* in 1924.

Murare (Swedish Bricklayers' Union) initially feared that a minority position in the new *Byggnads* would result in wage equalisation *vis-à-vis* unskilled workers and make opposition to the centralisation of LO more difficult (*ibid.*: 178ff.). Later, technological development forced the union to change its view. The blurred border between bricklaying and concreting, which was performed by labourers, threatened to exclude bricklayers from new jobs, which *Byggnads* aspired to monopolise for its members (*ibid.*: 184ff.). In 1961 *Murare* was acquired by *Byggnads* to protect its members from such exclusion. Another union of skilled building workers, *Bleck & Plåt*, did not abandon its independence until 2000, while the LO unions of painters and electricians still exist. Not by chance, small, independent employers' associations negotiate separate agreements with these unions.

An example of a large union acquiring a small, contracting union is *Metall*'s acquisition in 1993 of *Gruv* (Swedish Miners' Union). During the 1980s the membership of *Gruv* almost halved due to rationalisation and the closure of mines. While *Gruv* was a vertical union in a trade close to the metal industry, *Gjutare* was a craft union within the same area as *Metall*. Its existence was in direct opposition to the principle of industrial unionism advocated by LO. After decades of pressure from LO and *Metall*, in 1964 the foundry workers, almost exactly seventy years after their breakaway, returned to *Metall* (*ibid.*: 205ff.). As *Gjutare* lacked its own collective agreement, they were reliant on the *Metall* agreement, which they implemented at local level for their members. Opposition to the solidaristic wage policy of LO and *Metall* was one of many disagreements between *Gjutare* and *Metall*. Furthermore, the membership of *Gjutare* was stable, albeit relatively small, which also deterred the search for a merger.

The breakthrough for industrial unionism in the printing industry occurred in 1973 when three craft unions amalgamated to form GF (Graphic Workers' Union). They organised typographers, bookbinders and lithographers. The motive for the merger was not declining membership, but small size, resulting in weak finances, limited membership services and difficulties in exerting influence, within as well as outside LO. Like the building workers, the printing unions had opposed industrial unionism for several decades. To forestall LO demands for a merger, the three craft unions in the mid-1920s founded a cartel (Björklund, 1965: 31-62). From the mid-1930s it served as a bargaining cartel to fulfil employer demands for a single agreement. Among bookbinders and typographers, the dilution of demarcation due to technological change appeared as a major argument for a merger (Åmark, 1998: 286-298). In the 1960s, rising administration costs was another argument among bookbinders in favour of a merger. A third argument, the merger of the printing employers' associations was presented at the 1965 typographers' Congress. The weakest, although not the smallest union, the union of bookbinders, was dominated by relatively unskilled workers and was the driving force in the merger process (*ibid.*: 300). Fearing isolation if the two other printing unions merged, the lithographers finally gave up and participated in the 1973 amalgamation.

In 1970 no fewer than eight LO unions of government employees amalgamated to form SEKO (Union of Service and Communication Employees, known as SF from 1970 to 1994). The founding unions organised workers within railways, post, telecom, road construction, defence forces, civil administration, prisons, and state power stations. Like several other cases, the process from the first initiative to the final decision was lengthy. As long as government workers had no right to strike, the need for unified action was limited. Furthermore, the state as an employer appeared with many faces, reflected in varying strategies, policies and cultures among the unions. A first step towards closer co-operation was taken in 1937 when the Cartel of State Servants was founded.

From the early 1950s wage negotiations were transferred from individual government agencies to the Department of Public Administration. Unionists argued for a unified union with which to confront a shared employer (*ibid.*: 304). In particular, small unions had problems maintaining acceptable levels of service. From the 1950s rank-and-file members generally were less willing to spend leisure time on union activities, while more knowledge was required to undertake union duties. As many local branches were too small to hire an official, they often merged into regional 'big branches'.

A significant step forward was taken when government employees in 1966 obtained full bargaining rights and the right to strike. Employers and unions in the public sector had a shared interest in bargaining rights monopolised by a few bargaining cartels or large unions. Such a centralised system would obstruct breakaways and independent unions, and 'rationalise' the very fragmented union structure, which comprised about 110 unions within central government in 1964. Although the Cartel of State Servants fulfilled the requirements of the basic agreement within the government sector, a merger between the eight LO unions of 'state servants' was realised in 1970. Administrative rationalisation was necessary, as dues were low in these unions and a strike fund had to be established, rather than relying on eight separate funds (*ibid.*: 321). Without another development, however, the merger might not have been achieved. In contrast to the early 1950s, the membership of the largest union in the group, *Järnvägs* (Swedish Railway Employees' Union), was declining due to the rationalisation of railways, while that of the post and telecom unions expanded. Faced with the prospect of declining influence, *Järnvägs* now preferred a merger to a cartel. It is remarkable that LO did not act as a driving force for the largest amalgamation in its history – the founding of SEKO/SF in 1970. LO was considerably more active the next time SF was involved in a merger.

Deregulation and privatisation resulted in SEKO adopting its present name in 1995, the year preceding the acquisition of *Sjöfolks* (Swedish Seamen's Union). Exposed to long-term membership decline *Sjöfolks* had no other alternative than merging. At the end of the 1980s a merger had been planned with *Transport*, but the seafarers' leadership was divided. The 1991 LO Congress proposed a merger between *Transport*, SF/SEKO and *Sjöfolks* to form a communication workers' union. Since *Transport* left the deliberations, the other two unions decided to merge in 1996. The acquisition of *Sjöfolks* by SEKO was motivated by too few seafarers to sustain an acceptable membership service (Johnsson, 1998: 217).

The Rise of Swedish White-collar Trade Unionism

Sweden probably has the most marked separation along the blue-collar/white-collar divide regarding unions and confederations. The labour movement's success in the industrial and political arenas narrowed income inequalities, which, in turn, encouraged the organisation of status groups. By restricting the admission of white-collar employees and promoting openness towards unskilled workers, LO accentuated working class solidarity and strength. In order not to 'fall behind', white-collar employees transformed their status associations into unions or formed new unions. LO's close links to social democrats encouraged the formation of separate, politically independent white-collar unions.

The first large-scale white-collar confederation emerged in the private sector. DACO (Central Organisation of Employees) was founded in 1931 by eight white-collar unions. The principal motive was lobbying for bargaining rights, which were secured by law in 1936. Local government employees won restricted bargaining rights in 1937 and central government employees in 1940. This encouraged the founding of a peak association of white-collar public sector workers, 'old' TCO. Founded in 1937, it merged with DACO in 1944, keeping the name TCO.

Another status divide cuts across the white-collar salariat. The associations of university graduates and other higher white-collar employees have their origin primarily in the public sector. The higher civil servants formed a peak association (1917), which merged in 1946 with a small federation of transport and communication unions. The result was SR, comprising many very small staff associations with members concentrated in particular government branches. In addition, it contained a few larger unions of secondary school teachers and military officers. A parallel confederation SACO was founded in 1947, described as 'the world's oldest professional peak association' (Heidenheimer, 1976: 50). In 1974/75 SR joined SACO, thus uniting higher government employees and professionals within the same confederation. In contrast to LO and TCO, all SACO unions are organised along occupational lines, open to all persons practising a profession, irrespective of sector, branch or employer.

DACO and TCO Initiatives to 'Rationalise' White-collar Unionism

When DACO was founded it comprised occupational as well as industrial unions. The leading industrial union, *Finans* (Union of Financial Sector Employees), was soon surpassed by another vertical union, the rapidly expanding SIF (Swedish Union of Clerical and Technical Employees in Industry), which would become Sweden's largest white-collar union. Only a small share of the new members was added by the sole acquisition made by SIF in 1940. SIF's recruitment of all kinds of white-collar workers within manufacturing industry has restricted the need for mergers, although it is not the sole union within this segment. CF, which is affiliated to SACO, organises considerably more graduate engineers than SIF. Similarly, *Ledarna* (Association of Managerial and Professional Staff) recruits supervisors. At an early stage of Swedish trade union history, the position of supervisors in the white-collar/blue-collar dichotomy was not obvious. After the defeat in the 1909 general strike LO had to accept the employers' demand that supervisors should not be members of blue-collar unions.

Several initiatives were taken by DACO to 'rationalise' white-collar union structure within the categories of trade and transportation, hotels and restaurants, insurance, and agriculture. The hiring of a union officer was a salient feature when white-collar associations with a 'weak' union orientation were transformed into trade unions. Often a merger was a precondition to such a step. DACO's most important reorganisation initiative was the process that ended in the formation of HTF (Union of Commercial Salaried Employees) in 1937. From 1932 clerks in manufacturing industry were organised exclusively by SIF. DACO aimed to found a union with similar scope for clerks in private services, including retail employees. These plans clashed with the ambitions of the LO union *Handels* (Commercial Employees' Union), which had sales personnel within its recruitment area and also wished to recruit office employees. Engineering, however, had been closed to *Handels* since the 1920s, when the union lost a struggle within LO. In practice, the victorious union, *Metall*, had left the field open for white-collar unions. DACO first tried to persuade a non-affiliated association of clerks to extend its recruitment area to retail clerks, but without success. In the mid-1930s this association was transformed from a predominantly social association to a trade union and hired an officer. After a merger with a small union of shop assistants, HTF was formed. Soon two unions, organising ironmongers' assistants and book-sellers' assistants respectively, were acquired. In Sweden these occupations are classified as white-collar workers, in contrast to shop assistants in other trades, which are classified as blue-collar workers and, hence, are organised by *Handels*. Starting as a vertical white-collar union in the trade and transport sectors, HTF gradually extended its recruitment area to all private services through a series of acquisitions.

The leadership of 'old TCO' spent much energy trying to recruit new unions in the public sector, but were less successful in bringing about mergers between unions (Wallén, 1989: 59). Both local government officers and civil servants founded vertical unions by amalgamations, SKTF (Swedish Union of Local Government Officers) and ST (Union of Civil Servants), before their affiliation to 'old TCO'. After the formation of the modern TCO no fewer than seventeen unions of government employees were successively acquired by ST.

The prevalence of a large number of government agencies with diverging employment policies and the division of employees into different categories, in combination with the relatively loose character of the 'white-collar movement', left plenty of scope for a multitude of unions and staff associations among government employees. The sharp division of labour between the sexes accentuated the number of unions of specialised state employees, many of which organised only women. The largest of the unions acquired by ST was a TCO-affiliated union of women telephone employees, itself founded by amalgamation of two unions of women. By joining ST or other TCO unions, unions exclusively catering for female memberships gradually disappeared. Both the efforts to create large, powerful TCO unions and the vertical principle of organisation worked against the continued existence of separate unions of women. From the outset in 1944, TCO assigned a high priority to the establishment of clear borderlines between affiliated unions and to merge its many small affiliates into larger unions (TCO, 1944: 33). According to the first TCO blueprint a number of small unions were re-commended to join ST, SKTF or HTF (TCO, 1946: 41ff.). Many female trade union leaders opposed mergers with male-dominated unions, but the forces of centralisation were stronger (Östberg, 1997: 160). In particular, from the early 1950s the state demanded co-ordinated bar-gaining, which, when introduced, encouraged centralisation and mergers. In 1953 KST (Association of Female Civil Servants) joined ST, but not voluntarily. It was rather a combination of coercive measures on the part of TCO and ST, insufficient resources, and a failure to strengthen its position within TCO that promoted the merger (Nilsson, 1996: 251ff., 294).

Acquisitions played a prominent role in ST's growth during the 1950s and 1960s, but had no part in the exceptionally rapid growth during the 1970s. The relatively large numbers of members joining ST through acquisitions in the 1980s, however, did not prevent a decline. No acquisitions took place in the 1990s, despite the urgency for a sub-stantial influx to balance the considerable loss of members due to the end of public sector growth, cuts in public expenditure and the privatisa-tion of public agencies (Kjellberg, 2000a: 619). As all employees in privatised or state-owned companies are contractually classified as private sector workers, and ST continued to restrict its membership to public sector employees, heavy membership losses were unavoidable. The same applies to SKTF, which grew rapidly until the mid-1980s after which it contracted markedly.

Rationalisation of office work, combined with increased demands on higher education, changed the labour force composition within public administration. Like other vertical TCO unions, SKTF and ST saw some of their traditional membership groups dwindle, while concurrently SACO unions of university graduates expanded markedly. As there are hardly any more small unions left for SKTF and ST to acquire, a merger of a radically different scale was planned between these two unions and HTF, which would cross the border between the public and private sectors. In contrast to SKTF and ST, HTF has expanded considerably, although its density is relatively low due to its concentration on private services. A former LO union, FF (Swedish Social Insurance Employees' Union), also joined the 'Trio project'. An important motive behind Trio joining was obtaining a stronger voice in public debate and lobbying. Membership dues were also to be kept down and services to members improved. The amalgamation between the four unions, however, was cancelled, as a two-thirds majority among delegates was not attained at the decisive HTF conference. Instead FF joined ST in 2003.

Many of the largest TCO unions are vertical unions; in the public sector SKTF and ST, in the private sector SIF, HTF, *Finans* and FTF (Union of Insurance Employees). Also organising public sector employees are a number of occupational TCO unions that represent teachers, nurses, police officers, and journalists. The former TCO union *Ledarna* is also an occupational union. Due to its opposition to TCO's organisational plan and its aggressive membership competition with other affiliated unions, *Ledarna* was expelled from TCO in 1997.

The two largest TCO affiliates are SIF and *Lärarförbundet*. While SIF has been almost completely unaffected by mergers, the opposite is the case among teachers' unions, which emerged much earlier, were all occupational unions and were soon split by gender. Their early history is characterised by breakaways rather than amalgamations. Three unions broke away from SAF (Swedish General Union of Teachers): *Folkskollärarinne* (Swedish Union of Elementary School Mistresses; 1906), SSLF (Swedish Union of Infant School Mistresses; 1918) and *Folkskol* (Swedish Union of Elementary School Teachers; 1920). The reason for the breakaway of women teachers was deep discontent with the decision of the state around the turn of the nineteenth century to abandon equal wages between the sexes, which was supported by male teachers (Florin, 1987). From 1947, SAF was reconstructed as a federation to foster co-operation between the unions of primary school teachers. As a federation, rather than as a union, no individuals could be members of SAF. SAF also left TCO in 1947. The next step was a merger between the unions of primary school teachers, initiated at the 1952 TCO Congress.

Between 1945 and 1991, no fewer than sixteen teachers' unions successively merged into the giant *Lärarförbundet*. One of the two unions participating in the final 1991 amalgamation was SL (Swedish Union of Teachers), which had been formed when the unions of male and female primary school teachers amalgamated in 1963. After acquiring SSLF in 1967, the three breakaways from SAF were re-united in SL. Another path of mergers took place among specialist teachers. In 1946 TCO had declared it desirable to unite all unions recruiting this category of teachers. After TCO-initiated deliberations, six unions, two of which were for women, amalgamated in 1948 to form SFL (Swedish Union of Specialist Teachers). Another five unions were acquired by SFL between 1949 and 1953. Finally, in 1991 the two unions stemming from the large amalgamations in 1948 (SFL) and 1963 (SL) merged to form *Lärarförbundet*.

Among military officers, two TCO unions amalgamated in 1981 to form ORF (Officers' National Association). Due to cuts and restructuring of military personnel, however, the new union sustained heavy membership losses. For the first time in Sweden, a major union affiliated to a confederation merged with a union from another confederation. The TCO-affiliated union ORF amalgamated in 1995 with the SACO union of military officers. The post-merger union, *Officersförbundet* (Association of Military Officers), remained independent for some years before affiliating to SACO in 1998.

SACO: Around Twenty-five Unions since the 1950s

Although there have been several mergers involving SACO affiliates, the number of SACO unions has remained about twenty-five for decades. Most of these mergers occurred before the confederal merger between SACO and SR in 1974/75. Like the largest TCO union (SIF), its SACO equivalent (CF) has its stronghold within manufacturing industry. When CF was founded in 1954 by a merger of eight unions of graduate engineers, about half of its members worked in the public sector. Since 1957 CF has increased its membership six-fold without acquiring any union. In 1990 it replaced LR as largest SACO union. Another SACO union stemming from a large number of unions is DIK (Swedish Association of Graduates in Documentation, Information and Culture), founded in 1972 by five SACO unions amalgamating into a multi-professional union within the cultural sphere (libraries, museums and archives).

As we have seen, a large number of teachers' unions within the TCO sphere successively merged into one big union. In SACO there were two groups of teachers' unions, one recruiting secondary school teachers and the other university teachers. Within each group, a series of mergers took place. Among the secondary school teachers mergers took the form of acquisitions by LR. In 1949-51 six unions were acquired and became sections within LR, which was transformed to a modern union with hired officers (Carle *et al.*, 2000: 117-132). The equivalent to LR among university teachers is SULF (Swedish Association of University Teachers), founded in 1984 by an amalgamation of two unions, one of which had been formed by an amalgamation in 1961.

The Rise and Fall of Bargaining Cartels: New Cross-confederal Bargaining Constellations

The large number of mergers among public sector unions in the second half of the 1960s and early 1970s (see Figure 1.8) can partly be attributed to the policy of Swedish government to centralise public sector negotiations. The formation of bargaining cartels among white-collar workers also accelerated as a result of this development. Government employees won full bargaining and strike rights in 1966, but individual unions, in general, were refused the right to negotiate. The number of union negotiators was limited to the bargaining cartels within TCO and SACO, or large unions such as SEKO. Bargaining rights were also conceded to the confederation SR. In the municipal sector, bargaining rights were granted to TCO and SACO cartels and the large LO union *Kommunal* (Swedish Municipal Workers' Union).

The past decades of bargaining decentralisation have diminished the role of cartels in both public and private sectors. New *cross-confederal* bargaining constellations have emerged. In 1997 eight unions formed FI (Unions within Manufacturing), which besides SIF (TCO) and CF (SACO) comprises all LO unions in manufacturing. This process was facilitated by the reduction of LO unions in manufacturing from fifteen in 1950 to five in 1998 (excluding the printers). Another facilitating factor was that both SIF and CF cover all manufacturing industries. By 1992 SIF, CF and *Metall* had formed a common front to block the engineering employers' plans on completely decentralised bargaining. Union alliances based upon class were thus replaced by constellations based upon sector. The emergence of FI also encouraged unions within services to strengthen their position. The collapsed white-collar project 'Trio' fits into this category, as it was aimed at assigning the service sector a more prominent position in wage formation and public debate. Another cross-confederal bargaining organisation, OFR (Public Employees' Negotiation Council), was formed in 1991 by a merger of two TCO bargaining cartels of public sector unions. Since 2002 ORF has also incorporated two SACO unions.

Conclusions

Very few, if any, union mergers in Sweden have been dictated by confederations. Instead, the confederal role has been the pragmatic implementation of blueprints and the initiation of negotiations between unions. In some cases LO has exerted pressure on individual unions, but never forced a union to merge. Even under intense pressure, mergers tend to be lengthy processes, sometimes extending over several decades. The primary aim has not been increased size, but a union structure well adapted for collective bargaining, membership services and minimising demarcation disputes. Membership transfers fulfil similar functions without affecting the number of unions. In contrast to the limited authority of LO on merger issues, decisions on border conflicts and transfers are imperative. Another important means is the power to concede or deny unions' confederal affiliation. Since LO adopted the principle of industrial unionism early in the twentieth century only unions that comply with this principle have been accepted as affiliates, otherwise they have been recommended to merge with an existing LO union.

In general, a combination of factors has convinced unionists of the desirability of mergers. Such factors include: contracting employment within their recruitment area, technological changes diluting borders with other unions, increased administrative costs, growing member demands for services, and resistance towards increased dues. Mergers have also resulted from employer demands for co-ordinated bargaining and serve as a means of strengthening unions in the industrial and political arenas, including strengthening versus competitor unions, but also towards unions in other sectors. Probably, the absence of protracted membership decline in Sweden has restrained the urgency for mergers. In contrast to most other countries, union density expanded for long periods.

Three waves of mergers can be discerned in Sweden: 1900-1910 (14 mergers), 1916-24 (19) and, above all, 1932-73 (161) with peaks in the 1940s (43) and early 1970s (28). It is open to debate whether about 1.5 mergers per year in the first period is enough to label it a wave. In the second merger wave, no fewer than eleven breakaways also occurred, which underlines it as a period of rapid union restructuring. While blue-collar unions dominated the first waves, three-quarters of mergers between 1932 and 1973 exclusively involved white-collar unions. Furthermore, all major white-collar confederations were founded and merged during the third wave: DACO (founded in 1931) and 'old TCO' (1937) amalgamated into modern TCO in 1944; SACO, founded in 1947, acquired SR in 1974/75.

Industrial relations underwent important institutional changes in the first and third waves. Centralised employers' associations concluded pioneering compromises with blue-collar unions (1905-06). After the defeat in 1909, blue-collar unions lost ground, but a strong recovery followed after 1915. Another period of major institutional change and union growth began in the 1930s. All categories of white-collar workers now obtained bargaining rights, although public sector workers still had to wait for full rights. The *Saltsjöbaden* agreement was followed by a considerable centralisation within LO in 1941, and the introduction of centralised bargaining during the 1950s. It should be noted, however, that centralisation of decision-making, not mergers, played the crucial role in the implementation of centralised negotiations (Hadenius, 1976: 159). On the contrary, centralised bargaining and solidaristic wage policy raised doubts about mergers among LO craft unions. Things were different among the public sector LO unions. As public sector employers centralised their organisations at the end of the 1960s, they demanded co-ordinated unions before conceding full negotiating and strike rights, which impelled LO unions of government workers to merge. Almost all LO mergers in the third wave were concentrated in the 1960s and early 1970s. Among blue-collar manufacturing workers, mergers often were motivated by shifts of employment and technology, coupled to rapid increases in administration costs, caused by the duplication of officials within LO unions.

To sum up, the first and third waves of mergers were associated with major institutional changes of industrial relations. The character of Swedish industrialisation, shifts of employment and technological change also played prominent roles. This does not mean that institutional and economic/technological factors had an equal influence on each merger case. Internal factors, such as demands for improved services without rising dues, were also of great importance.

It is remarkable that none of the three largest unions in Sweden were founded by amalgamations. Neither have acquisitions played any significant role in their membership development. The leading public sector union, *Kommunal*, in 1977 surpassed *Metall* as Sweden's largest union. In 2001 white-collar SIF replaced *Metall* as second largest union. Together with *Industrifacket*, *Metall* will recapture this position if the planned amalgamation of the two unions is realised. Membership decline explains this step to be decided at earliest in 2004.

What are the outcomes of mergers? Most post-merger unions are probably in better positions compared to a continued independent existence, with or without an influx of members from acquired unions. Growing membership heterogeneity, however, implies increased bureaucratisation, declining membership participation and more diversified interests among members (Offe and Wiesenthal, 1985: 185). Some features of Swedish union structure tend to offset such developments. First, the strong class-segmentation of the union movement allows different social categories to keep their own unions and identities. Second, the breakthrough of industrial unionism prevented the American and British development of heterogeneous conglomerates. Third, as a consequence of well-developed workplace organisation, mergers have limited effects at the level closest to members. For example, when the unions of factory and garment workers amalgamated, workplace 'clubs' of both unions were left intact. A study of participation rates two years later demonstrates fairly stable levels (Chaison *et al.*, 2001).

On the other hand, the membership of some vertical TCO unions is very diversified. The largest white-collar union, SIF, recruits all kinds of white-collar workers within manufacturing, from clerical employees to civil engineers and managers. In contrast to white-collar unions like ST and *Ledarna*, SIF has never participated in mergers, apart from a minor acquisition in 1940. Also in contrast to ST and *Ledarna*, it does not contain occupational associations or other sub-units designed for different membership groups. Consequently, SIF lacks mechanisms for dealing with membership heterogeneity (Huzzard, 2000; Kjellberg, 2001). SIF also contrasts with the LO union SEKO in this regard. Of the eight unions amalgamating to form SF/SEKO in 1970, most were preserved as 'sections'.

A large number of unions, however, still are relatively homogenous occupational/professional unions: all 25 SACO unions, 10 of 18 TCO unions, 5 of 16 LO unions and 5 of the 7 independent unions, in all 43 of 66 unions (2003). Furthermore, union growth is now concentrated among professional SACO unions. Most, if not all, LO and SACO unions are more homogenous than the vertical TCO unions. Three of the latter (HTF, SKTF and ST) recently planned, albeit without success, a giant amalgamation. The proposed union would have been very heterogeneous and would have required increased space for membership sub-units.

Workplace organisations and occupational sub-units are the primary faces of unions for members. The Swedish union system can be characterised as simultaneously centralised and decentralised (Kjellberg, 1983; Kjellberg, 1998: 75, Kjellberg, 2000b: 531). The high priority given the workplace organisation was manifested in the 1960s when LO unions with many members dispersed at small workplaces established 'big branches', but kept workplace units intact. The dominant motive behind the new branches was improved services to workplace activists. Since the 1970s, the significance of workplace clubs has increased due to new laws on co-determination, increased union efforts for 'good work', and decentralisation of bargaining.

Of course, mergers between occupational unions or between an occupational and a vertical union might result in merged workplace organisations. If only industrial LO or TCO unions are involved, workplace mergers do not occur, as only one LO/TCO union is present in each industry and workplace (except within construction). Secondly, the strongly class-segmented union system in Sweden militates against the merging of workplace union organisations, but future cross-confederal mergers might, for example, involve *Metall*, SIF and CF workplace clubs within engineering. Alternatively, mergers between national unions will be combined with continued separate, but closely cooperating, workplace units.

List of Abbreviations

Bekläd.arb. Svenska Beklädnadsarbetareförbundet (Swedish Garment Workers' Union)

Beklädnads Beklädnadsarbetarnas förbund (Swedish Textile, Garment and Leather Workers' Union)

Bleck & Plåt Svenska Bleck- och Plåtarbetareförbundet (Swedish Sheet Metal Workers' Union)

Bokbinderi Svenska Bokbindareförbundet (Swedish Bookbinders' Union)

Byggnads Svenska Byggnadsarbetareförbundet (Swedish Building Workers' Union)

Byggnadsträ Byggnadsträarbetareförbundet (Swedish Building Wood Workers' Union)

CF Civilingenjörsförbundet (Swedish Association of Graduate Engineers)

Civilekon Civilekonomerna (Swedish Association of Graduates in Business Administration and Economics)

DACO De anställdas centralorganisation (Central Organisation of Employees)

DFF De Förenade Förbunden (United Unions)

DIK DIK-förbundet (Swedish Association of Graduates in Documentation, Information and Culture)

Elektriker Svenska Elektrikerförbundet (Swedish Electricians' Union)

Fabriks Fabriksarbetareförbundet (Swedish Factory Workers' Union)

Fastighets Fastighetsanställdas förbund (Swedish Building Maintenance Workers' Union)

FF Försäkringsanställdas förbund (Swedish Social Insurance Employees' Union)

FI Facken inom industrin (Unions within Manufacturing)

Finans Finansförbundet (Union of Finance Sector Employees)

Folkskol Sveriges Folkskollärarförbund (Swedish Union of Elementary School Teachers)

Folkskollärarinne Sveriges Folkskollärarinneförbund (Swedish Union of Elementary School Mistresses)

FTF	Försäkringstjänstemannaförbundet (Union of Insurance Employees)
Försvars	Försvarsverkens Civila Personals Förbund (Swedish Defence Forces Civilian Employees' Union)
GF	Grafiska Fackförbundet (Swedish Graphic Workers' Union)
Gjutare	Svenska Gjutareförbundet (Swedish Foundry Workers' Union)
Grov & Fabriks	Grov- och Fabriksarbetareförbundet (Union of Labourers and Factory Workers)
Gruv	Svenska Gruvindustriarbetareförbundet (Swedish Miners' Union)
Handels	Handelsanställdas förbund (Commercial Employees' Union)
HRF	Hotell- och restauranganställdas förbund (Hotel and Restaurant Workers' Union)
HTF	Handelstjänstemannaförbundet (Union of Commercial Salaried Employees)
Industrifacket	Industrial Workers' Union
Ingenjörs	Ingenjörsförbundet (Swedish Society of College Engineers)
Jusek	Jusek (Federation of Lawyers, Social Scientists and Economists)
Järnvägs	Svenska Järnvägsmannaförbundet (Swedish Railway Employees' Union)
Kommunal	Svenska Kommunalarbetareförbundet (Swedish Municipal Workers' Union)
KST	Föreningen Kvinnor i Statens Tjänst (Association of Female Civil Servants)
Lant	Svenska Lantarbetareförbundet (Swedish Agricultural Workers' Union)
Ledarna	Ledarna (Association of Supervisors and Foremen; later Association of Managerial and Professional Staff)
Livs	Svenska Livsmedelsarbetareförbundet (Swedish Food Workers' Union)
LO	Landsorganisationen (Swedish Confederation of Trade Unions)
LR	Lärarnas Riksförbund (National Union of Teachers)

Läkarförb	Sveriges Läkarförbund (Swedish Medical Association)
Lärarförbundet	Lärarförbundet (Swedish Teachers' Union)
Metall	Svenska Metallindustriarbetareförbundet (Swedish Metalworkers' Union)
Murare	Svenska Murareförbundet (Swedish Bricklayers' Union)
Musiker	Svenska Musikerförbundet (Swedish Musicians' Union)
Målare	Svenska Målareförbundet (Swedish Painters' Union)
Officers	Officersförbundet (Association of Military Officers)
OFR	Offentliganställdas Förhandlingsråd (Public Employees' Negotiation Council)
ORF	Officerarnas Riksförbund (Officers' National Association)
Pappers	Svenska Pappersindustriarbetareförbundet (Swedish Paper Workers' Union)
POF	Plutonofficersförbundet (Union of Non-Commissioned Officers in the Defence Forces)
Polis	Svenska Polisförbundet (Union of Swedish Police Officers)
SAC	Sveriges Arbetares Centralorganisation (Central Organisation of Swedish Workers)
SACO	Sveriges Akademikers Centralorganisation (Swedish Confederation of Professional Associations)
SAF	Svenska Arbetsgivareföreningen (Swedish Employers' Confederation)
SAF	Sveriges Allmänna Folkskollärarförening (Swedish General Union of Teachers)
SAP	Sveriges socialdemokratiska arbetareparti (Swedish Social Democratic Labour Party)
SEKO	Facket för service och kommunikation (Union of Service and Communication Employees)
SF	Statsanställdas Förbund (Swedish State Employees' Union)
SFL	Svenska Facklärarförbundet (Swedish Union of Specialist Teachers)
SIF	Svenska Industritjänstemannaförbundet (Swedish Union of Clerical and Technical Employees in Industry)

SJF	Svenska Jornalistförbundet (Swedish Union of Journalists)
Sjöfolks	Svenska Sjöfolksförbundet (Swedish Seamen's Union)
Sko & Läder	Svenska Sko- och Läderarbetareförbundet (Swedish Shoe and Leather Workers' Union)
Skogsträ	Svenska Skogs- och Träfacket (Swedish Forest and Wood Workers' Union)
SKTF	Sveriges Kommunaltjänstemannaförbund (Swedish Union of Local Government Officers)
SL	Sveriges Lärarförbund (Swedish Union of Teachers)
SN	Sveriges Naturvetareförbund (Swedish Association of Scientists)
SPF	Svenska Postförbundet (Swedish Post Union)
SR	Statstjänstemännens Riksförbund (National Association of Civil Servants)
SRAT	SACOS:s Tjänstemannaförbund SRAT (SACO General Group)
SSF	Svensk Sjuksköterskeförening (Swedish Nurses' Union)
SSLF	Sveriges Småskollärarinneförbund (Swedish Union of Infant School Mistresses)
SSR	Akademikerförbundet SSR (Swedish Association of Graduates in Social Science, Personnel and Public Administration, Economics and Social Work)
ST	Statstjänstemannaförbundet (Union of Civil Servants)
SULF	Sveriges Universitetslärarförbund (Swedish Association of University Teachers)
SvT	Svenska Teleförbundet (Swedish Tele Union)
SYACO	Sveriges Yngre Akademikers Centralorganisation (Swedish Confederation of Younger Professionals)
TCO	Tjänstemännens Centralorganisation (Swedish Confederation of Professional Employees)
Textil	Svenska Textilarbetareförbundet (Swedish Textile Workers' Union)
Transport	Svenska Transportarbetareförbundet (Swedish Transport Workers' Union)
Träarb	Svenska Träarbetareförbundet (Swedish Wood Workers' Union)

Träind	Svenska Träindustriarbetareförbundet (Swedish Wood Industry Workers' Union)
Typograf	Svenska Typografförbundet (Swedish Typographers' Union)
VF	Sveriges Verkstadsförening (Swedish Engineering Employers' Association)
Vårdförb	Vårdförbundet (Swedish Association of Health Professionals)
Väg	Svenska Vägarbetareförbundet (Swedish Road Workers' Union)

CHAPTER 10. UNITED KINGDOM

Merge, Merge and Merge Again

Jeremy WADDINGTON

Trade union structure in the United Kingdom (UK) is notoriously complex. Throughout the twentieth century no single structural form of union organisation was predominant. Overlapping recruitment bases, a large number of unions that adhere to a variety of principles of organisation, and diversity in the origin of trade unions, contribute to this structural complexity. Structural reform to create a more 'logical' or 'simple' structure has been on the agenda for UK unions almost since the inception of unionism. Trade union mergers have been the primary means of structural reform since the early nineteenth century. Each of the principal trade union 'types' was formed by mergers. The 'new model' of craft organisation was initiated by the formation by merger of the Amalgamated Society of Engineers in 1851. Similarly, the National Union of Railwaymen and the National Union of Mineworkers, which both adhered to the principle of industrial unionism, and the archetypal general unions, the Transport and General Workers' Union (TGWU) and the National Union of General and Municipal Workers (NUGMW), were formed by mergers in the first half of the twentieth century. Rather than simplify trade union structure in the UK, however, mergers have added to its complexity in that they have crossed industrial, occupational and political lines of demarcation between unions.

This chapter traces the pattern of influence of the merger process on trade union structure, organisation and activity in the UK since 1950. It argues that;

- in the context of a comparative study of trade union mergers, the sheer scale of merger activity in the UK is a distinguishing feature;
- mergers have not markedly 'simplified' the notoriously complex structure of trade unionism in the UK, but have consolidated a

trend towards increasing membership heterogeneity among the larger unions;

- issues of internal union representation have become increasingly complex as unionists have introduced systems of representation designed to maintain union cohesion in the face of more diverse memberships;

- mergers in the UK are associated with changes in union government. In particular, mergers have been the occasion on which central control of union finances and decisions over industrial action was introduced or consolidated. In contrast, bargaining autonomy has often remained located within some sub-section of the post-merger union's membership;

- larger unions sought mergers to gain more influence within the Trades Union Congress (TUC), where voting strength is determined by membership size. At various times the TUC attempted to influence the structure of trade unionism in the UK by advocating mergers within specific frames of reference, such as the pursuit of industrial unionism. These approaches have had very little direct effect on the merger process, although the TUC remains influential in facilitating merger negotiations.

To develop these arguments the chapter comprises two sections. The first section charts the pattern of the merger process after 1950 and identifies the influences on its development. The second section examines the merger activity undertaken by specific unions and its impact on the development of forms of internal representation. It thus assesses how developments in the external shape or structure of unionism influence reform of internal systems of union government.

Extent and Causation of the Merger Process

This section establishes the dimensions of the aggregate merger process and its causation since 1950. No attempt is made here to examine the merger policies of specific unions, which are addressed in the next section. In charting the dimensions of the merger process, two themes are evident. First, the sheer scale of the merger process in the UK distinguishes it from elsewhere. Second, the period after 1950 can be usefully considered in terms of two distinct sub-periods: 1950-1965, when merger activity was relatively sparse; and 1966 to date, during which the merger process intensified (see Figure 1.9). Four influences on merger activity are reviewed: trade union finances; legislation; the impact of employers; and the TUC. Each of these influences is shown to have stimulated merger activity, albeit to different degrees and with varying intensity since 1950.

Charting the Dimensions of the Merger Process

Between 1950 and 2000 there were 461 mergers in which 543 unions and 3,983,476 members were absorbed (see Table 10.1). A total of 68 unions was formed by mergers in the same period. Although the fall in the number of unions from 691 in 1950 to 228 in 2000 was influenced by the merger process, two other trade union structural events were also prominent in their effect.[1] First, the number of union formations rose throughout the 1960s, remained relatively high during the 1970s, before falling sharply during the 1980s and 1990s. Between 1966 and 1979, for example, no fewer than 266 unions were formed. The impact of the high formation rate of unions slowed the rate of decline in the total number of unions. Second, during the late 1970s and early 1980s the dissolution rate of unions rose sharply. The combined effect of union dissolutions and mergers accelerated the rate of decline of the number of unions after 1980.

The distribution of merger activity after 1950 was uneven. Between 1950 and the mid-1960s merger activity was relatively sparse. After the mid-1960s the number of mergers, unions absorbed, members absorbed and the number of unions formed by merger increased and remained relatively high. It is also clear from Table 10.1 that the post-1966 peak in merger activity is not the sole result of declining aggregate membership. Between the mid-1960s and 1979 aggregate membership rose in the UK, followed by the longest continuous period of annual membership decline on record between 1980 and 1998. In other words, merger activity was intense during periods of membership growth and membership decline.

---

[1] A third structural event is also influential: the breakaway, where a section of one union secedes to form an independent union. In practice a breakaway is the reversal of a merger. Breakaways are not considered explicitly, as their numbers are relatively small compared to dissolutions, formations and mergers. It is acknowledged, however, that breakaways have reduced the rate of decline in the number of trade unions.

Table 10.1: the Scale of the Merger Process, 1950-2000

Year	Trade union membership (000s)	Number of mergers[3]	Number of unions absorbed[1]	Number of members absorbed	Number of unions formed by mergers
1950	9,289	5	5	1,700	1
1951	9,530	2	2	496	0
1952	9,578	6	9	15,774	2
1953	9,518	3	3	1,706	0
1954	9,551	4	4	293	0
1955	9,720	5	5	7,049	2
1956	9,778	8	8	8,385	1
1957	9,829	2	2	839	1
1958	9,639	2	2	1,241	1
1959	9,623	2	2	7,623	1
1960	9,835	1	1	1,000	0
1961	9,916	7	9	1,166	2
1962	10,014	8	8	12,555	3
1963	10,067	9	9	48,013	2
1964	10,218	6	6	20,639	1
1965	10,325	12	12	14,900	0
1966	10,259	8	8	54,318	1
1967	10,188	8	9	99,144	2
1968	10,200	21	21	122,207	2
1969	10,479	12	14	33,435	3
1970	11,187	20	26	101,406	3
1971	11,135	14	16	139,783	5
1972	11,359	21	37	95,588	7
1973	11,456	14	14	32,023	0
1974	11,764	15	19	66,507	0
1975	12,026	23	23	38,717	1
1976	12,386	13	16	60,033	1
1977	12,846	9	9	14,998	0
1978	13,112	12	12	67,856	1
1979	13,289	13	13	13,660	1
1980	12,947	13	14	77,048	0
1981	12,106	4	4	7,690	1
1982	11,593	12	21	300,452	4
1983	11,236	10	10	75,413	1
1984	10,994	15	19	105,026	4
1985	10,821	10	112	42,355	0
1986	10,539	5	31	50,211	1
1987	10,475	5	5	37,611	0
1988	10,376	11	11	271,963	2
1989	10,158	10	10	77,953	0

1990	9,947	16	16	71,539	3
1991	9,585	8	8	227,232	2
1992	9,048	4	4	362,780	1
1993	8,700	10	11	758,088	1
1994	8,278	1	1	150	0
1995	8,031	4	4	120,408	1
1996	7,935	6	6	59,028	1
1997	7,795	7	7	14,695	0
1998	7,852	5	5	127,874	1
1999[4]	7,898	10	11	97,678	1
2000[4]	7,779	10	10	15,228	0
Total	/	461	543	3,983,476	68

[1] Number of unions and number of members absorbed includes unions/members absorbed in acquisitions and in amalgamations.

[2] This figure excludes the Colliery Trades and Allied Workers' Association (CTAWA), which merged into the Union of Democratic Mineworkers. The CTAWA was formed in the same year as the merger with the consequence that no annual membership returns were submitted on behalf of the union. No membership figures are thus available. For the purposes of this chapter, therefore, the CTAWA is excluded from the statistical analysis.

[3] Mergers involving the different section of the National Union of Mineworkers and the National Association of Colliery Overmen, Deputies and Shotfirers are excluded from the merger data for the reason that these are administrative re-alignments within existing unions, rather than formal mergers. Only because of the peculiarities of the constitutions of these unions has it been necessary to go through the legal procedure.

[4] The periods covered by the Annual Report of the Certification Officer were 1st January 1999 to 31st March 2000 and 1st April 2000 to 31st March 2001. These changes reflected a shift to reporting on the basis of the financial, rather than the calendar, year.

Sources: Trade union membership data, Ministry of Labour Gazette or its successors; number of mergers, number of members absorbed, number of unions absorbed and number of unions formed by merger, union membership and structure series maintained by the author.

The membership size of the unions engaged in the merger process between 1966 and 2000 is illustrated in Table 10.2. The table is divided into two sections to identify differences in the merger process between 1966-1979, when membership increased, and 1980-2000, when aggregate membership declined.

The merger process primarily comprises the absorption of smaller unions. In both sub-periods about 80 per cent of the unions absorbed organised fewer than 5,000 members. In terms of membership absorbed, however, the contribution of smaller unions was marginal, particularly after 1979. There are some differences between the two sub-periods. Unions with more than 25,000 members were relatively infrequently engaged in the merger process before 1980: only seven unions of this size were absorbed. Between 1980 and 2000, in contrast, 24 unions with more than 25,000 members were absorbed, no fewer than eight of which organised more than 100,000 members. The merger process during the period of membership decline was thus more likely to involve larger unions as absorbed unions than between 1966 and 1979, suggesting that some larger unions were unable to resist the adverse effects arising from long-term membership decline.

Table 10.2: Number of Trade Unions and Membership absorbed by Size, 1966-2000

	UNIONS ORGANISING A MEMBERSHIP OF										
	Under 100	100-500	501-1,000	1,001-2,500	2,501-5,000	5,001-10,000	10,001-15,000	15,001-25,000	25,001-50,000	50,001-100,000	100,001 and over
1966-1979											
Unions Absorbed	45	45	42	47	21	14	7	9	2	5	0
Cumulative percentage	19.0	38.0	55.7	75.5	84.4	90.3	93.2	97.0	97.9	100	
Membership absorbed	2,201	10,731	29,571	73,728	73,530	96,255	89,364	171,305	85,056	307,304	0
Cumulative percentage	0.23	1.28	4.85	12.38	20.21	30.46	39.97	58.22	67.27	100	
1980-2000											
Unions absorbed	22	57	41	34	25	5	4	7	10	6	8
Cumulative percentage	10.3	36.1	54.7	70.3	81.7	84.0	85.8	89.0	93.6	96.3	100
Membership absorbed	1,049	14,031	28,686	49,291	80,387	33,162	48,786	134,170	341,022	368,864	1,800,974
Cumulative percentage	0.04	0.52	1.50	3.20	5.97	7.12	8.81	13.4	25.14	37.91	100

Source: Data series maintained by the author.

Influences on the Merger Process

A range of measures has influenced the merger process in the UK since 1950. This section identifies some of the principal influences. It is acknowledged that different aspects of membership change influence the merger process. Membership decline may promote financial insolvency, for example, and increases in relative membership of one union may secure greater influence within voting forums based on membership size. This section focuses on some of the effects arising from membership change, rather than on membership directly. As such, it highlights two key relationships: the bargaining position of unions relative to employers and the state; and a union's bargaining position relative to its competitor unions. The argument is that these relationships are central to both the rate and the character of the merger process.

Finances

The financial position of unions since 1950 is illustrated in Table 10.3. Throughout the period 1950-1965 the key indicators suggest financial well-being. In particular, rises in income per member were broadly commensurate with increases in prices until 1960, after which they rose more steeply. Similarly, income was about 20 per cent greater than expenditure and unions were able to service extant membership with income from members with an excess of 60 per cent. Union funds were also more than three times greater than total annual expenditure. In short, the aggregate financial position of unionism before 1965 was one of relative stability and solvency, and was not a widespread pressure towards merger activity.

Although membership grew by 2.62 million members or 25.4 per cent between 1965 and 1980, the aggregate financial position of unions deteriorated markedly. Contribution income per member and total income were both 6.9 times greater in 1980 than in 1965. Total expenditure increased 7.7 times in the same period and expenditure on administration 9.5 times. In other words, growth in expenditure outstripped growth in income by some margin. Income from members, however, continued to exceed administrative expenditure by more than 20 per cent and total income exceeded total expenditure by about 15 per cent. The ratio of union funds to expenditure declined continuously between 1965 and 1980 to reach a low of 1.25 by 1980, suggesting the use of funds to offset the growth in expenditure.

Between 1965 and 1980 contribution income per member rose at a slightly faster rate than retail prices. In other words, higher levels of income resulting from rising membership obviated any need for substantial real increases in contributions per member. Although a variety of measures were introduced with the intention of reducing subscription dependency (Latta, 1972), they had no long term effect insofar as contribution income from members comprised 85.2 per cent of total income in both 1965 and 1980.

Annual membership declines were recorded for every year between 1980 and 1998. No fewer than 5,434,000 members (40.1 per cent) were lost between 1980 and 1998. The impact of this decline on union finances was profound. Total income increased by 2.9 times between 1980 and 2000. Total expenditure increased by 3.0 times in the same period, while administrative expenditure rose by 2.9 times between 1980 and 1996. Dependency on subscription income fell from 85.2 per cent in 1980 to 80.3 per cent in 2000, reflecting the combined effects of investment income and the marked decline in membership. Throughout the 1980s and 1990s unions tried to recoup some of the income lost through membership decline by raising contributions at a higher rate than retail prices. The real cost of unionism thus rose after 1980. Although during the early 1980s, when the initial large-scale membership losses were sustained, unions managed to maintain the income/expenditure ratio at about 1.10, it fell sharply during the late 1980s and did not recover during the 1990s. Similarly, the ratio of union funds to expenditure declined during the late 1980s to less than 1.20. Furthermore, income from members was less than expenditure on administration from 1988 onwards. Trade unions were thus unable to service their existing membership from the contribution income that they received throughout the 1990s.

Table 10.3: Trade Union Finances in the UK, 1950-2000

Year	Income from members £000s	Contribution income per member (1950=100)	Retail price index (1950=100)	Total income £000s	Total Expenditure £000s	Expenditure on administration[1] £000s	Union funds at year end £000s	Income/Expenditure ratio	Union funds/ Expenditure	Income from members/administrative expenditure
1950	15,721	100	100	17,624	14,026	8,266	62,150	1.26	4.43	1.90
1955	19,347	115	131	22,093	19,390	11,319	76,565	1.14	3.95	1.71
1960	25,076	148	142	28,631	24,710	14,881	90,267	1.16	3.65	1.69
1965	33,301	194	169	39,069	32,852	20,619	117,572	1.19	3.58	1.62
1970	43,784	238	211	52,225	50,402	30,222	134,599	1.04	2.67	1.45
1975	100,800	437	389	121,716	105,728	79,449	190,231	1.15	1.80	1.27
1976	130,243	542	453	151,501	125,001	94,194	216,459	1.21	1.73	1.38
1977	151,637	602	525	176,931	146,909	111,734	245,214	1.20	1.67	1.36
1978	170,993	662	569	197,714	176,486	128,716	269,969	1.12	1.53	1.33
1979	198,025	757	645	234,643	212,483	156,763	295,228	1.10	1.39	1.26
1980	230,719	922	761	270,657	252,202	195,097	316,034	1.07	1.25	1.18
1981	284,457	1167	851	335,946	303,159	223,630	351,106	1.11	1.16	1.27
1982	298,114	1282	924	369,565	310,413	235,112	431,117	1.19	1.39	1.27
1983	310,223	1443	967	387,200	340,700	250,712	468,455	1.14	1.37	1.24
1984	322,134	1495	1015	394,736	353,598	264,793	498,419	1.12	1.41	1.22
1985	358,588	1674	1076	447,919	418,503	363,838	528,016	1.07	1.26	0.99
1986	383,981	1830	1113	476,532	428,761	377,792	577,998	1.11	1.35	1.02
1987	407,737	1965	1160	498,326	467,510	407,693	604,118	1.07	1.29	1.00
1988	429,639	2089	1216	522,590	499,799	442,035	619,655	1.05	1.24	0.97
1989	442,614	2225	1311	539,398	525,770	468,663	630,774	1.03	1.20	0.94
1990	462,746	2382	1435	561,760	554,940	489,153	635,911	1.01	1.15	0.95
1991	505,089	2688	1519	619,568	597,888	526,552	661,800	1.04	1.11	0.96
1992	517,825	2929	1576	622,975	601,065	529,080	693,215	1.04	1.15	0.98
1993	498,801	2907	1601	615,984	602,330	530,648	688,692	1.02	1.14	0.94
1994	551,916[3]	3387	1640	669,761	654,026	585,155	700,661	1.02	1.07	0.94
1995	548,502	3449	1697	666,533	653,477	575,473	705,420	1.02	1.08	0.95
1996	560,676	3567	1738	683,922	650,013	571,089	736,997	1.05	1.13	0.98
1997	576,638	3733	1792	724,089	682,121	NA[2]	777,963	1.06	1.14	NA
1998	588,327	3784	1852	737,792	703,756	NA	811,506	1.05	1.15	NA
1999	593,246	3767	1894	754,131	722,178	NA	839,443	1.04	1.11	NA
2000	631,093	3921	1928	785,743	755,038	NA	892,805	1.04	1.14	NA

[1] Administrative costs are the sum required to provide support and services to members. These costs exclude the direct costs of benefits provided to union members. The ratio of income from members and administrative expenditure thus indicates whether unions are supporting and servicing extant members from the income they receive from them.

[2] The expenditure on administration series was discontinued in 1997.

[3] The figures sent by UNISON to the Certification Officer for 1994 cover a period of 18 months rather than one year. The UNISON figures for one year were estimated by subtracting a third of the union's submission from the UNISON data and from the aggregated data. The 1994 data should, therefore, be treated with some caution.

Sources: 1950-1970 data, Ministry of Labour Gazette. The data refer to registered unions in Great Britain. 1975-2000 data, Certification Officer, Annual Reports. The data refer to the UK.

Throughout the period of intense merger activity, administrative expenditure as a proportion of total expenditure rose from 62.8 per cent in 1965 to 77.4 per cent in 1980 and further to 87.9 per cent in 1996. There are four principal reasons that underpin this increase. First, after the report of the Donovan Commission in 1968, a series of measures were introduced to strengthen the procedural aspects of industrial relations. These necessitated a growth in the number of shop stewards with commensurate increases in trade union education and training. Second, a large number of unions established support departments to handle the rising demand for research, legal, health and safety, and equality advice and information. This was particularly the case during the 1960s and 1970s when the dilute forms of corporatism that characterised industrial relations in the UK required senior union officers to be briefed on a wide range of policy matters. Third, the decentralisation of collective bargaining, particularly after 1980, placed rising demands on the union support function, as larger numbers of collective agreements were required to cover a declining number of members. Fourth, lax financial controls within some unions led to inadequate countermeasures to rising costs and thus compounded their effects (Willman and Morris, 1988).

The impact of these rising costs influenced a wide variety of merger policies. Two general effects are usefully noted at this juncture. Firstly, the impact of the procedural changes in industrial relations were particularly hard-felt by smaller unions. Such unions were unable to finance legal, research or other support departments and, in many instances, had insufficient funds to contract-in such expertise. Furthermore, many small unions were unable to sustain an adequate cohort of workplace representatives. The inadequacy of the member support available within small unions thus acted as a prompt to mergers. Second, the presence of large numbers of competing unions often resulted in the withholding of increases in membership contributions in order that competitor unions did not gain an advantage. The scope for increasing income from members was thus constrained by the competition arising from the peculiarities of union structure. Concurrently, advocates of mergers suggested that they would lead to economies of scale in union operations and, hence, might ameliorate some of the adverse effects arising from a deteriorating financial position.

Legislation

The merger process in Britain has been regulated since 1876. Successive measures eased the legal requirements for merger in 1917 and 1940. The final legislative measure, the Trade Union (Amalgamation) Act 1964, was passed without debate in Parliament, following lobbying by the TUC. It replaced both the 1917 and 1940 legislation. Although it retained the principles of both the measures it replaced, the 1964 Act further relaxed the requirements and formalised the procedures for mergers into two forms: a transfer of engagements and an amalgamation. For a transfer of engagements to take place the majority of those voting within the transferor union are required to vote in favour. As members of the acquiring union in a transfer of engagements are not required to vote, the direct influence of members on the merger process may be lessened by the transfer of engagements procedure. In an amalgamation the majority of those voting within each amalgamating union are required to vote in favour.

The intensity of merger activity rose sharply immediately after the 1964 legislation was enacted, suggesting that the requirements for merger extant prior to 1964 had acted as a brake on the merger process (see Figure 1.9). After 1964 the transfer of engagements procedure accounted for about 75 per cent of the unions that were absorbed in the merger process, but less than 15 per cent of the membership (Undy *et al.*, 1996: 45). The transfer of engagements procedure is thus essentially a process involving smaller unions. It is not exclusively so, however. Several formations by merger involving larger unions have been achieved using the transfer of engagements procedure. The formation of the Union of Construction, Allied Trades and Technicians (UCATT) in 1971, for example, was completed by three unions transferring their engagements to a fourth union, the Amalgamated Society of Woodworkers (ASW). Adopting this method served two purposes. Firstly, there was no requirement for a costly ballot among the membership of the ASW, to which the three unions transferred their engagements. Secondly, if any single ballot to transfer engagements had failed, it would not have affected the other two transfers of engagements. In contrast, if the members of a single union reject an amalgamation proposal that involves four unions, the entire proposal would fail irrespective of the results of the other ballots.

Impact of Employers on the Merger Process

Employers have both indirect and direct influences on the merger process. A primary function of a trade union is to improve the conditions at work of members. It is, therefore, no surprise that a majority of senior trade union officers reported that an increase in bargaining power is a key objective sought from mergers (Undy *et al.*, 1996: 50). An indirect influence of employers is thus to promote mergers to enable unions to improve their bargaining position. This influence varies dependent upon the character of bargaining. In national multi-employer collective bargaining arrangements, mergers within the union side of the bargaining forum certainly concentrate votes, although it is unclear whether they increase direct bargaining power with employers. For example, mergers between unions affiliated to the Confederation of Shipbuilding and Engineering Unions (CSEU), which negotiated with the Engineering Employers' Federation (EEF) at national level until the mid-1980s, concentrated membership to the extent that the number of affiliated unions fell from 35 in 1950 to 20 in 1980. The bargaining position of acquiring unions within the CSEU improved relative to other affiliated unions on gaining a larger share of the votes. Of course, the concentration of votes does not necessarily mean enhanced bargaining power *vis-à-vis* employers. A wide range of influences affect the development of such bargaining power (Martin, 1992), many of which are not directly altered by mergers. Mergers among unions engaged in national multi-employer bargaining thus may enhance bargaining power in some circumstances, but such an effect is not guaranteed.

Since the mid-1970s, however, the dominant tendency has been towards the decentralisation of bargaining. As was noted above, decentralisation has contributed to rising internal union costs, which promoted some mergers. By decentralising bargaining arrangements employers have thus directly influenced the merger process. Whether mergers strengthen the bargaining power in circumstances of decentralised bargaining is open to question. Where a small union is acquired, additional resources made available through the acquiring union may improve the bargaining position of the members of the acquired union. Similarly, where two unions with overlapping membership merge, a combined membership may have additional bargaining strength. If economies of scale are achieved, the position of a post-merger union may also be improved in terms of resource allocation, but not necessarily regarding bargaining strength. Although a majority of senior trade union officers reported that enhanced bargaining strength was sought from mergers, it is by no means certain that it has been achieved.

Employers also influence the merger process through three further activities. First, where unions organise exclusively within single companies and these companies merge, union mergers often follow. For example, the restructuring of the Alliance Building Society and the Leicester Building Society to form the Alliance and Leicester Building Society was followed by the amalgamation of the Alliance Building Society Staff Association and Leicester Building Society Staff Association to form the Alliance and Leicester Building Society Staff Association. Company restructuring may thus directly promote union mergers.

Second, employers may influence the merger process through their policy on union recognition. In particular, where recently formed unions are unable to secure recognition from employers, they may merge with larger unions in order to press the case for recognition. The example of the Rossendale Union of Boot, Shoe and Slipper Operatives (RUBSSO) illustrates the impact of de-recognition. RUBSSO was formed in 1895 and affiliated to the TUC during the early 1920s. It was able to retain its independence from the dominant union in the industry, the National Union of Boot and Shoe Operatives (NUBSO), as it was the only union recognised by the Lancashire Footwear Manufacturers' Association (LFMA). This recognition effectively prevented NUBSO from competing for members organised by RUBSSO and allowed RUBSSO to pursue an independent bargaining policy. When the NUBSO and three other leather workers' unions elected to merge in 1970 to form the National Union of Footwear, Leather and Allied Trades (NUFLAT), RUBSSO members rejected participation in the merger on a ballot to transfer engagements, electing instead to retain bargaining autonomy. In 1987, however, the employers wound up the LFMA and resorted to local bargaining. This measure effectively de-recognised RUBSSO for regional bargaining. RUBSSO was unable to support local bargaining and transferred its engagements in 1996 to the National Union of Knitwear, Footwear and Apparel Trades, which had been formed by the amalgamation of NUFLAT and the National Union of Hosiery and Knitwear Workers in 1990. Support from employers in the form of recognition thus lengthened the independent existence of RUBSSO. When this support was withdrawn the union was compelled to merge.

A third influence employers have on the merger process concerns their tactics to avoid recognising a union affiliated to the TUC. In part, the rise in the formation rate during the 1970s was due to employers promoting new unions in preference to TUC-affiliated unions. To promote these unions employers offered recognition, financial support and provided a range of facilities. Employers thus encouraged an increase in the number of trade unions. Where these unions established independence from the employer and/or the employer withdrew support, they often merged with TUC-affiliated unions in order to gain access to a wider range of resources and negotiating expertise. The number of unions available for acquisition was thus promoted by the activities of employers.[2]

The Range of TUC Influence

Throughout the period after 1950 the TUC encouraged mergers among affiliated unions and provided arbitrators to facilitate merger negotiations. Within the TUC mergers are viewed as a means to reduce sectionalism, demarcation disputes and inter-union competition for members. The decline in the number of unions affiliated to the TUC from 186 in 1950 to 76 in 2000 almost entirely resulted from mergers, suggesting that TUC encouragement of the merger process had a positive effect. The influence of the TUC was evident in two fields: first, as a conduit to government; and second, through direct measures to promote merger activity.

As an intermediary between affiliated unions and government, the position of the TUC changed markedly during the 1960s and 1970s (Martin, 1980). The shift in authority towards the TUC within trade unionism was promoted by the definition of industrial relations as an area for negotiated reform, increased state intervention, the election of Labour governments and the almost continuous application of some form of wage controls between 1961 and 1979. Before about 1930 union representatives appointed to sit on tripartite institutions were selected directly from individual unions. During the 1960s and 1970s, however, the selection of such representatives rested largely with the TUC. Influence within the TUC thus allowed union representatives some input to government policy formulation concerning collective bargaining and wider economic policy. Influence within the TUC was largely predicated on the size of the membership represented. Mergers were sought as a means of relative increasing membership within the TUC and thus gaining access to influential committees.

The TUC was excluded from any role in macro-economic policy formulation after 1980 by successive Conservative governments. In consequence, the TUC lost authority with affiliated unions. The next section illustrates how this diminution of authority influenced the char-

---

[2] It is also noteworthy that the number of union dissolutions rose during the 1980s, when some employers withdrew their support for some of these staff associations. After 1979 the pressure on employers was lessened as a result of the policies of the Conservative governments with the consequence that they no longer had to support staff associations to keep TUC affiliated unions at bay.

acter of merger activity pursued by some unions. The loss of authority by the TUC, however, did not eliminate a requirement for influence within the TUC. Disputes within the TUC concerning the response to the legislation enacted by the Conservatives, and attempts to promote particular policy positions within TUC and Labour Party forums, sustained a requirement for influence and, hence, mergers to achieve it.

The TUC also sought to influence mergers directly through a variety of mechanisms, including reviews of trade union structure and the manner of operation of the Bridlington Principles. Following a pattern established before 1950, the TUC initiated a review of trade union structure in 1962. Whereas earlier reviews had advocated industrial organisation as the preferred principle of union organisation, by 1963 the emphasis had changed, as industrial unionism was declared to be both undesirable and impractical (TUC, 1963: 162-163). At a series of consultative conferences, convened to examine the results of the review started in 1962, emphasis was placed on the capacity of large unions to provide superior services to members and to act more effectively at national level. In other words, the TUC approach acknowledged the reality of the situation in which membership size was necessary to secure influence within the TUC and other bargaining forums. Few of the eighteen specific recommendations arising from the consultative conferences, however, were implemented by affiliated unions (TUC 1966: 115-121). More than twenty years later, only two of the recommendations had been acted on in full, although several mergers which constituted moves towards the objectives identified by the TUC had also been completed. Most recently, the TUC launched its *Millennial Challenge*, with the objective of achieving a 'more logical' trade union structure comprising fewer unions through which solidarity can be better promoted (TUC, 1999). If this millennial challenge is taken up by unions affiliated to the TUC, a further extensive series of mergers can be expected.

The TUC adopted the TUC Bridlington Principles in 1939 as the means to adjudicate inter-union disputes (for details, see TUC, 1939). The application of these principles effectively promoted merger activity in two ways. First, applications for affiliation were rejected where the recruitment base of the applicant union overlapped with that of a union already affiliated to the TUC. Instead the applicant union was recommended to merge with the affiliated union. Second, where inter-union competition for membership was intense, the TUC attempted to implement spheres of influence agreements, which encouraged mergers in particular directions but not others. Neither of these approaches was universally successful, but they certainly influenced the outcome of the merger process, particularly after 1966.

Divergent Merger Policies and Union Representation

This section shifts the focus of analysis away from the intensity of the merger process to an examination of the variation in the character of merger activity between 1966 and 2000. The character of merger activity refers to the particular form that mergers take. The focus of this section is thus the merger policies of specific trade unions. It argues that engagement in the merger process has accelerated the trend towards increasing membership heterogeneity, which, in turn, has necessitated the development of more complex forms of union government and administration. Unions that allow degrees of post-merger autonomy tended to be more successful as acquiring unions, although concurrently financial control has become more centralised.

These arguments are examined in two different circumstances of membership change: 1966-1979, when membership expanded; and 1980 to 2000, when membership declined. The merger activity of a similar group of large unions is examined for these two periods with the objective of identifying the shifts in merger policies. While mergers undertaken by these larger unions are not representative of all mergers, they illustrate the dominant trends within the merger process. Table 10.4 illustrates the merger process among larger unions during the first period. Recruitment growth is calculated by subtracting acquired membership from membership growth and allows a crude assessment of the relationship between growth by merger and growth by recruitment.

Membership Growth and the Acquisition Process, 1966-1979

The dominant pattern of merger activity among larger unions between 1966 and 1979 was that of acquisition. The listed unions acquired a total of 80 (6.2 per year) unions and 350,446 members. Furthermore, all the listed unions achieved membership growth and recruitment growth, albeit at different rates. White-collar unions with membership concentrated in the private sector achieved higher rates of growth than their predominantly manual counterparts.[3] The Association of Scientific, Technical and Managerial Staffs (ASTMS), Banking, Insurance and Finance Union (BIFU) and Draughtsmen and Allied Technicians Association (DATA), for example, doubled in size between 1965 and 1979. There is, however, no obvious relationship between recruitment growth and membership acquired among these white-collar unions. While ASTMS acquired 29 unions, DATA, BIFU and the

---

[3] The TGWU, AEU, GMWU and the EETPU organised predominantly manual members, but had established white-collar sections with the object of competing with the white-collar unions.

Association of Professional, Executive, Clerical and Computer Staff (APEX) only acquired 9 in combination. Among the manual unions, the two general unions, TGWU and General and Municipal Workers Union (GMWU), were more successful in acquiring unions than their more craft-oriented counterparts, Amalgamated Engineering Union (AEU), Amalgamated Society of Boilermakers, Shipwrights, Blacksmiths and Structural Workers (ASBSBSW) and Electrical, Electronic, Telecommunication and Plumbing Union (EETPU). The four unions with recruitment bases in the public sector, National and Local Government Officers Association (NALGO), National Union of Public Employees (NUPE), Confederation of Health Service Employees (COHSE) and the Royal College of Nursing (RCN), more than doubled their membership between 1965 and 1979. This growth primarily resulted from recruitment, although each union completed at least one acquisition. Examining these data reveals a range of divergent merger policies.

The two general unions were more successful in acquiring unions than the craft-oriented AEU, ASBSBSW and EETPU. Although they both acquired more than ten unions, the pattern of acquisition of the two general unions diverged. Whereas the TGWU acquired several unions with national recruitment bases, the acquisitions completed by the GMWU tended to organise within specific regions of the country, hence the marked difference in the size of the membership acquired by the two unions.

Differences in internal structure underpinned the variation in merger policy. When the TGWU was formed by merger in 1922, it was organised into Trade Groups, each of which represented members in specific industries. Each Trade Group was allowed some bargaining autonomy, although decisions on industrial action and issues of financial control rested with the General Executive Council. Large acquisitions completed by the TGWU formed a new Trade Group with the consequence that the number of Trade Groups had risen from six in 1922 to eleven by 1975. The acquisition of the National Union of Vehicle Builders (NUVB, 74,140 members) in 1972, for example, resulted in the establishment of the Vehicle Building and Automotive Trade Group, into which existing TGWU members employed in the automobile industry were transferred. As the Vehicle Building and Automotive Trade Group, ex-NUVB members were allowed bargaining autonomy, retained many of the same union officers and, through the transfer of members, improved their bargaining position *vis-à-vis* the AEU, the principal competitor union in the industry. In other words, the Trade Group structure of the TGWU facilitated mergers. In contrast, the GMWU was struc-

Jeremy Waddington

tured around Regions.[4] This structure was adopted in 1924 when the GMWU was formed from three unions, which organised regional concentrations of membership. The regional structure thus allowed some degree of post-merger autonomy for the unions that initially formed the GMWU. This regional structure later acted as a barrier to mergers, because it meant that any acquired union would lose all autonomy as its members would have to be allocated to the different Regions of the GMWU. For this reason eight of the unions acquired by the GMWU organised within a specific geographical region.

Table 10.4: The Merger Process of Specific Unions, 1966-1979

Union	Unions acquired	Membership acquired	Membership 1965	Membership 1979	Membership growth	Recruitment growth	Recruitment growth (% of 1965)
TGWU	18	144,539	1,443,738	2,086,281	642,543	498,004	34.5
AEU	4	67,925	1,048,955	1,187,903[5]	138,948	71,023	6.8
GMWU	12	16,479	795,767	967,153	171,386	154,907	19.5
EETPU	2	894	364,929[1]	420,000	55,071	54,177	14.8
NALGO	1	861	348,528	702,566	354,038	353,177	101.3
NUPE	1	800	248,041	691,770	443,729	442,929	178.6
ASTMS	29	78,677	208,121[2]	491,000	282,879	204,202	98.1
ASBSB SW	1	230	122,981	129,712	6,731	6,501	5.3
APEX[4]	4	8,127	82,564	150,611	68,047	59,920	72.6
DATA	0	0	71,707	200,054	128,347	128,347	179.0
COHSE	1	2,020	67,588	212,930	145,342	143,332	212.1
BIFU[3]	5	11,976	58,444	130,691	72,247	60,272	103.1
RCN	2	17,918	39,948	161,962	122,014	104,096	260.6

[1] Membership data are for 1968 when the EETPU was formed by the merger of the Electrical Trades Union and the Plumbing Trades Union.

[2] Membership data are for 1968 when ASTMS was formed from the merger of the Association of Scientific Workers and the Association of Supervisory Staffs, Executives and Technicians.

[3] Before the title BIFU was adopted in 1979, the union was called the National Union of Bank Employees. BIFU is used throughout for reasons of clarity.

[4] Before the title APEX was adopted, the union was called the Clerical and Administrative Workers' Union. APEX is used throughout for reasons of clarity.

[5] Data for 1979 are for the Amalgamated Union of Engineering Workers (Engineering Section).

[4] The GMWU was known as the National Union of General and Municipal Workers (NUGMW) for most of the period before 1979. The title GMWU is used here to avoid overloading the text with different acronyms.

273

Where:

TGWU	Transport and General Workers' Union
AEU	Amalgamated Engineering Union
GMWU	General and Municipal Workers' Union
NALGO	National and Local Government Officers' Association
EETPU	Electrical, Electronic, Telecommunication and Plumbing Union
NUPE	National Union of Public Employees
ASTMS	Association of Scientific, Technical and Managerial Staffs
ASBSBSW	Amalgamated Society of Boilermakers, Shipwrights, Blacksmiths and Structural Workers
APEX	Association of Professional, Executive, Clerical and Computer Staff
DATA	Draughtsmen and Allied Technicians' Association
COHSE	Confederation of Health Service Employees
BIFU	Banking, Insurance and Finance Union
RCN	Royal College of Nursing

Sources: Data taken from various Annual Reports of the Certification Officer and from the data series maintained by the author.

Although the majority of the acquisitions completed by both the TGWU and the GMWU consolidated organisation within areas of existing strength, the Trade Group structure of the TGWU allowed some expansion into areas of relative weakness. Similarly to the NUVB, the acquisition of the National Association of Operative Plasterers (NAOP) in 1968 represented a significant incursion into the construction industry by the TGWU and placed it in competition with UCATT. It is also noteworthy that both the NUVB and the NAOP had long-standing problematic relations with their principal competitor unions. Acquisition by the TGWU thus afforded bargaining autonomy while maintaining independence from unions with which relations were difficult. Such opportunities were not available within the GMWU.

Although the AEU, ASBSBSW and EETPU achieved recruitment growth between 1966 and 1979, the slow rates of growth arising from the contraction of skilled employment and technological change meant that long-term recruitment growth was unlikely. Furthermore, the recruitment activities of the general unions among semi-skilled workers and the white-collar unions among the growing technical grades effectively hemmed in the AEU, ASBSBSW and the EETPU to their traditional recruitment bases. None of the craft unions represented members through trade groups or similar structures, although each established a white-collar or supervisors' section during the 1970s.[5] Opportunities for

---

[5]   The AEU operated sections for different groups of members, based on skill and sex. Separate sections existed for semi-skilled, unskilled and women workers, for example. These sections, however, were not constituted for bargaining purposes, but operated as a means of protecting the craft dominance within the union.

post-merger bargaining autonomy were thus restricted in the craft unions. Mergers completed by the three craft unions primarily comprised the acquisition of small unions, which became post-merger branches within the acquiring union.

The exception to this pattern concerns the acquisition by the AEU of the Amalgamated Union of Foundry Workers (AUFW) in 1967 to form the Amalgamated Union of Engineering and Foundry Workers (AEF). The terms of this merger allowed considerable autonomy for the two pre-merger unions. The reason for this allowance of autonomy was that the AEU and the AUFW were also engaged in merger discussions with the Constructional Engineering Union (CEU) and DATA. These four unions established a federal structure in 1971, the Amalgamated Union of Engineering Workers (AUEW), which was viewed as an intermediary stage towards the establishment of a single organisation for engineering workers, a historic objective of the AEU. Within the AUEW, the constituent unions were allowed considerable autonomy: each union retained its rules, financial autonomy, separate affiliations to the CSEU, TUC and Labour Party, and conducted bargaining independently. Representatives from the four unions met formally only at the Executive Council and at the National Conference.

The four unions were unable to reach agreement on a formal merger for a number of reasons. Prominent among these was an anticipated loss of identity, a view that was held particularly strongly by the white-collar DATA. Within the AUEW the separate identities of the different unions were maintained. Throughout the 1970s, for example, the intended development of joint workplace committees comprising AEU and DATA members failed to materialise. Political differences between the left-oriented DATA officials and the right-led AEU had also hampered earlier merger negotiations. DATA's objection to an alliance with the AEU dissipated, however, when the AEU elected a left-oriented President, who shared much of political platform advocated within DATA.

Several other unions in the engineering industry had rejected merger offers from the AEU on the grounds that they would lose a separate identity within the centralised structure of the AEU (Undy et al., 1981: 194-200). The NUVB, for example, rejected an offer of merger from the AEU, as post-merger autonomy did not form part of the offer. The absence of any form of post-merger autonomy thus weakened the position of the AEU within the engineering industry. By adopting a federal structure, the AEU prevented three further engineering unions from merging with other competitor unions.

Before entering the AUEW federation, DATA had attempted to reach agreement with the Association of Scientific Workers (AScW) and the Association of Supervisory Staffs, Executives and Technicians (ASSET), with the objective of creating a union for white-collar workers in the engineering industry. These discussions failed because both unions already organised workers from other industries and were not prepared to be restricted to engineering. This view was consolidated when AScW and ASSET merged to form ASTMS in 1968. A joint statement issued by the Executives of the two unions stated that a central purpose of the merger was to gain influence within the TUC through membership growth among white-collar workers, irrespective of industry (AScW and ASSET 1967).

The merger policy of ASTMS reflected this policy objective. ASTMS acquired unions from insurance, banking, education, entertainment, health and textiles, as well as consolidating membership within areas of long-standing organisation such as engineering and chemicals. Integral to the success of ASTMS were the terms on which it completed acquisitions. Each acquired union retained its pre-merger organisation as a section of ASTMS, was allowed to opt out of paying the political levy,[6] and retained bargaining autonomy. In addition, ASTMS made bargaining support services available to the acquired membership in the form of full-time officials, research, legal and health and safety advice, and representation at national level.

The offer of these terms was particularly successful in the context of company bargaining, which operated in several of the industries into which ASTMS expanded. In insurance, for example, company level bargaining had promoted an 'internalism' (Blackburn, 1967: 142-148) among the staff associations that resulted in each association restricting recruitment to a single company. Many staff associations thus existed. While the density rates achieved by many of these staff associations was high, recruitment bases restricted to single companies precluded high levels of membership and income, thus limiting the bargaining support services that could be made available. Company level bargaining also undermined attempts to resist the offers for merger from ASTMS. Company-based staff associations in insurance, for example, established federations in 1943 and 1972 to achieve economies of scale and thus provide bargaining support services. Both federations failed when they

---

[6] The political levy is paid by members into a political fund, which is used to fund political activities, notably support of the Labour Party. In most unions members may opt-out of the political levy, but in practice relatively few do so. Most of the staff associations acquired by ASTMS did not have a political fund. ASTMS acquired staff associations on the basis that members may opt-in to the political fund. The assumption was thus that members acquired in staff associations would continue with the same arrangement that operated before the acquisition.

were unable to support more than one full-time officer (Waddington, 1995: 185-190). In other words, the staff associations were unable to provide independently the support required to conduct company-level bargaining, yet ASTMS could offer such support.

APEX and BIFU competed with ASTMS for white-collar members, albeit in different sectors of the economy. Neither union initially offered the autonomy that was available to acquired unions within ASTMS. They were thus less successful in the merger process. During the second half of the 1970s both APEX and BIFU introduced arrangements that allowed degrees of post-merger autonomy which made them more attractive as merger partners. All four acquisitions completed by APEX took place after 1974 and four of the five acquisitions completed by BIFU took place after 1975. By this time, however, the strategic damage had been done. APEX acquired 70,000 fewer members than ASTMS between 1966 and 1979, which led to lower rates of membership growth and a narrower recruitment base from which to expand membership. ASTMS was able to exploit this higher rate of membership growth to establish a more prominent position within the TUC and Labour Party.

BIFU supported the establishment of national bargaining for the banking industry and maintained a geographical branch structure into which members of different banks were allocated. Staff associations in each of the major London clearing banks opposed national bargaining and supported the retention of company bargaining because it ensured that the staff associations held a majority within each company bargaining forum. The goal of national bargaining was achieved by BIFU in 1968. The Midland Bank Staff Association (MBSA) strongly opposed national bargaining, was unable to provide sufficient support to members and was in dispute with BIFU (Morris 1986). In order to retain its independence from BIFU and undertake its obligations within national bargaining, the MBSA voted to transfer engagements to ASTMS in 1974. The absence of any post-merger autonomy within BIFU thus allowed ASTMS to secure a substantial recruitment foothold in banking where previously BIFU was the only TUC-affiliated union. In other words, ASTMS used the merger process to strengthen its position relative to both APEX and BIFU. Only when APEX and BIFU offered similar merger terms to ASTMS were they able to acquire unions.

Merger activity in the public sector was relatively sparse. The rapid rate of recruitment growth achieved by the four public sector unions listed in Table 10.4 indicates that they were under little pressure to merge. Furthermore, some agreed demarcations reduced the impact of competition for membership. Among the TUC affiliated unions, NALGO represented white-collar workers in local government, health and the utilities; NUPE organised manual workers in local government, health and the utilities; and COHSE organised manual workers and some nurses in health. The RCN, which was not affiliated to the TUC, organised primarily qualified nurses and was in competition with both NUPE and COHSE for nurse membership. Acquisitions completed by the TUC-affiliated unions consolidated organisation within existing recruitment bases, while the RCN acquired the National Association of State Enrolled Nurses and the Student Nurses Association, thereby strengthening its recruitment base within nursing. As the following section illustrates, these acquisitions were to form the basis of a rapid expansion of membership throughout the 1980s and 1990s.

In summary, the principal feature of the merger process among the larger unions between 1966 and 1979 was the acquisition of other unions. While there was much variation in the character of merger activity, several features underpinned the process of acquisition. First, unions that allowed some form of post-merger autonomy were more successful in acquiring unions than those with a geographical basis to representation. Second, in order to offer post-merger autonomy and accommodate membership heterogeneity, internal union government was reformed to comprise sectional forms of representation. Third, white-collar and manual unions tended to remain apart in the merger process. The involvement of the white-collar DATA in the primarily manual AUEW was only condoned on the basis of a federal structure, rather than a more centralised constitution. Fourth, the presence of company bargaining coupled to unions with recruitment bases restricted to specific companies ensured a proliferation of small unions, many of which were relatively weak, which facilitated expansion of TUC-affiliates by acquisition.

Membership Decline and Amalgamations among Large Unions, 1980-2000

Table 10.5 illustrates the pattern of merger activity between 1980 and 2000 among the same group of unions as specified in Table 10.4. The extent of acquisition among these unions remains broadly similar to that during the earlier period. A total of 116 (5.5 per year) unions were acquired, which organised 556,981 members. The principal difference between 1966-1979 and 1980-2000 is that amalgamations resulting in the formation of new unions were much more prevalent among the larger unions during the second period. Only two of the listed unions, TGWU and RCN, were not involved in a formation. Two of the unions were involved in two separate formations within the period: the Amalgamated Union of Engineering Workers-Engineering Section (AUEW-ES) became the AEU and later the Amalgamated Engineering and Electrical Union (AEEU); and the GMWU became General, Municipal,

Boilermakers and Allied Trades Union (GMBATU) and later the General, Municipal and Boilermakers Union (GMB). This concentration of union membership by amalgamation accompanied marked and consistent rates of membership loss. Only the RCN increased membership between 1979 and 2000. This increase was achieved entirely by recruitment growth and reflected the growth in nursing employment and the benefits accruing from the acquisitions made by the RCN during the period 1966-1979.

In addition to the prevalence of amalgamations, the general character of merger activity changed in two further regards. First, mergers were more likely to cross the manual/white-collar line of recruitment demarcation, resulting in more heterogeneous memberships and a more pronounced tendency towards general unionism among the larger unions. Second, forms of sectional representation proliferated in order to gain access to the merger process. The form of organisation developed in different styles by the TGWU and ASTMS between 1966 and 1979 thus became almost universal among the larger unions. Within these general tendencies, specific merger policies were enacted. It is to these that we now turn.

The TGWU and the GMWU-GMB sustained massive membership losses after 1979. The acquisitions completed by the TGWU were insufficient to offset the membership losses sustained by the TGWU, but they represented continuity with the policy introduced before 1980 on two counts. First, the acquisitions tended to bolster membership within existing areas of organisation. Second, where relatively large unions were acquired, a new trade group was established to allow some autonomy for the acquired union. Agriculture and Textile Trade Groups were established, for example, on the acquisition of the National Union of Agriculture and Allied Workers and the National Union of Dyers, Bleachers and Textile Workers. An innovation was introduced, however, on the acquisition of the National Association of Licensed House Managers. As this union was relatively small (6,475 members), a national branch was established to ensure some autonomy for the acquired members. Financial difficulties experienced by the TGWU, however, precluded the establishment of new trade groups after 1982, reflecting constraints on an acquisition policy reliant on the establishment of costly post-merger systems of representation.

Table 10.5: The Merger Process of Specific Unions, 1980-2000

Union	Unions acquired	Membership acquired	Membership 1979	Membership (at merger or formation) with date	Membership 2000	Membership growth/loss	Recruitment growth/loss	Recruitment growth/loss (% of 1979 or formation)
UNISON	1	768		1,464,931 (1993)	1,272,470	-192,461	-193,229	-13.2
NALGO	2	6,410	753,226	764,062 (1992)		+10,836	+4,426	+0.6
NUPE	0	0	691,770	527,403 (1992)		-164,367	-164,367	-23.8
COHSE	0	0	212,930	195,519 (1992)		-17,411	-17,411	-8.2
TGWU	13	120,797	2,086,281		858,804	-1,227,477	-1,348,274	-64.6
AEEU	6	4,588		884,463 (1992)	728,211	-156,252	-160,840	-18.2
AEU	0	0		974,904 (1985)	622,622 (1991)	-352,282	-352,282	-36.1
AUEW-ES	3	65,479	1,187,903	1,000,883 (1984)		-187,020	-252,499	-21,3
EETPU	18	35,082	420,000	357,175 (1991)		-62,825	-97,907	-23.3
GMB	6	102,347		865,360 (1990)	683,860	-181,500	-283,847	-32.8
GMBATU	12	42,911		940,312 (1982)	823,176 (1989)	-117,136	-160,047	-17.0
GMWU	0	0	967,153	865,814 (1981)		-62,825	-62,825	-6.5
ASBSBSW	0	0	129,712	119,585 (1981)		-10,127	-10,127	-7.8
APEX	3	1,107	150,611	79,691 (1989)		-70,720	-72,027	-47.8
MSF	29	45,551		653,000 (1988)	350,974	-302,026	-347,577	-53.2
ASTMS	9	9,724	491,000	400,000 (1987)		-91,000	-100,724	-20.5
TASS	5	104,431	200,054	253,000 (1987)		+52,946	-51.485	-25.7
RCN	0	0	161,962		334,414	+172,452	+172,452	+106.5
UNIFI	1	4,214		171,248 (1999)	160,267	-10.981	-15,195	-8.9
BIFU	8	13,572	130,691	106,007 (1998)		-24,684	38,256	-29.3

[1] TASS was formerly the Draughtsmen and Allied Technicians' Association; the title TASS was adopted when the AUEW was formed.

Where:

UNISON	Public Sector Union
NALGO	National and Local Government Officers' Association
NUPE	National Union of Public Employees
COHSE	Confederation of Health Service Employees
TGWU	Transport and General Workers' Union
AEEU	Amalgamated Engineering and Electrical Union
AEU	Amalgamated Engineering Union

AUEW-ES	Amalgamated Union of Engineering Workers- Engineering Section
EETPU	Electrical, Electronic, Telecommunication and Plumbing Union
GMB	General, Municipal and Boilermakers' Union
GMBATU	General, Municipal, Boilermakers and Allied Trades Union
GMWU	General and Municipal Workers' Union
ASBSBSW	Amalgamated Society of Boilermakers, Shipwrights, Blacksmiths and Structural Workers
APEX	Association of Professional, Executive, Clerical and Computer Staff
MSF	Manufacturing, Science and Finance
ASTMS	Association of Technical, Scientific and Technical Staffs
TASS	Technical, Administrative and Supervisory Section
RCN	Royal College of Nursing
UNIFI	Banking Union, formed through the merger of BIFU, National Westminster Bank Staff Association and UNIFI (union of Barclays Bank Staff)
BIFU	Banking, Insurance and Finance Union

Sources: Data taken from various Annual Reports of the Certification Officer and from the data series maintained by the author.

In contrast to the earlier period, the GMWU-GMB was more successful in acquiring unions than the TGWU. The union was transformed in successive formations that extended its recruitment base. What brought about this transformation? The acquisition of the ASBSBSW illustrates the measures introduced to facilitate involvement in the merger process. The ASBSBSW organised a skilled membership, concentrated in areas of engineering such as shipbuilding, and geographically spread throughout much of the country. Traditional hostility between the ASBSBSW and the AEU over dominance in the engineering industry (Mortimer, 1982) made a merger between the two unions unlikely, although both unions were founded on a craft membership. Membership losses and associated financial weaknesses, however, necessitated that the ASBSBSW merge with a better-resourced union. The GMWU had organised some shipyard workers since its formation in 1924. Most of the GMWU members in shipbuilding were semi- or unskilled, whereas those of the ASBSBSW were skilled. In order to complete the acquisition, the GMWU effectively abandoned its exclusive reliance on geographical regions as the basis for organisation. To accommodate the ASBSBSW a set of core rules was agreed, supplemented by separate rules for GMWU and ASBSBSW sections. The rules for the sections provided the ASBSBSW membership with a degree of autonomy within the GMBATU. Representative autonomy was constrained, however, by Rule B26 (section 6) of the Rule Book, which required ASBSBSW delegates to vote in accordance with the policy of the Central Executive Council at the TUC. In other words, at the TUC a single vote of the GMBATU was achieved within a unified decision-making process.

The shift away from the dominance of the regional structure was furthered with the amalgamation between the GMBATU and APEX to form the GMB in 1989. The GMWU had established a white-collar section in 1972, the Managerial, Administrative, Technical and Supervisory Association (MATSA), but this had failed to compete with the white-collar unions in terms of membership growth. As was shown above, ASTMS had outmanoeuvred APEX to the extent that in 1987 ASTMS claimed 400,000 members compared to the 80,000 organised by APEX. Furthermore, membership decline after 1979 weakened the financial position of APEX. As the political positions supported by the GMBATU and APEX were similar and the GMBATU was able to offer the prospect of a transfer of members from MATSA, APEX officials recommended merger with the GMBATU, which was ratified by the membership. APEX and MATSA members formed the APEX Partnership section of the GMB,[7] which, similarly to the ASBSBSW, retained many of the APEX rules for the section, although these were subordinate to the core rules of the GMB.

Amalgamation with APEX thus furthered the development of sections within the GMB. To these sections were added a Clothing and Textile Workers' Section on the acquisition of the Tailors and Garment Workers' Union in 1991 and a Construction, Timber, Furniture and Allied Section when the Furniture, Timber and Allied Trades Union was acquired in 1993. Additional sections were also established by dividing the core membership of the GMB, so that by 2000 the union comprised eight sections. The merger process was thus used within the GMB to break down the reliance on regional organisation. Once mergers had resulted in acceptance of the principle of sections, internal reform of the core membership on a similar basis followed. The structure of the GMB thus moved towards that of the TGWU in order to participate in, and as a result of, the merger process.

The merger of the ASBSBSW and the GMWU signalled the end of any campaign to unite engineering unions and heightened competition for members among the remaining unions within the industry. During the 1980s the AUEW-ES, TASS and the EETPU all made acquisitions. The character of the merger policies pursued within the three unions differed, however, in terms of extension of recruitment bases, the maintenance of political affiliations and the reform of internal government.

---

[7]   Members of the Greater London Staff Association, which had been acquired in 1988 by the GMBATU, were also incorporated in the APEX Partnership section.

During the early 1980s the right regained control within the AUEW-ES and initiated a programme of reform intended to centralise the federal AUEW. The broad left remained powerful within the Technical, Administrative and Supervisory Section (TASS, the renamed DATA) and rejected attempts to centralise the AUEW. Following a long dispute between the two sections of the AUEW that culminated in the courts, TASS withdrew from the AUEW during 1984/85. This withdrawal set in train two distinct courses of merger activity involving the AUEW-ES and TASS.

The AUEW-ES set out to centralise the federal arrangements that had been established in 1971. This was achieved in 1984 when the Construction and Foundry Sections of the AUEW transferred engagements to the AUEW-ES to form the Amalgamated Engineering Union (AEU). This procedure effectively met the objective of the original AEU in 1971, in that in brought together the three engineering unions within a single structure. Although there was some allowance of autonomy within the AEU, the adopted system of government was more centralised than the federal AUEW structure.

TASS, in contrast, implemented a merger policy that provided the basis for a broad left opposition within engineering to the AUEW-ES/AEU. To this end, four engineering unions with broad left-dominated Executives were acquired between 1981 and 1985.[8] Two features of these acquisitions were of note. First, TASS abandoned its centralised structure in favour of separate sections for Pattern Makers, Metal Mechanics, Craft Workers and White-collar Workers.[9] The allowance of sectional representation, coupled to the similarities in the political position expressed by the leaderships of these unions, led to the selection of TASS in preference to the centralised AEU by the acquired unions (Waddington, 1992). Second, these acquisitions involved a predominantly white-collar union absorbing skilled manual members. They thus crossed the line of demarcation between manual and white-collar organisation, which had remained in place within the merger process before 1980.

---

[8]   These acquisitions included the National Union of Gold and Silver Trades (1981); National Union of Sheet Metal Workers, Coppersmiths, Heating and Domestic Engineers (1983); Association of Pattern Makers and Allied Craftsmen (1984); and National Society of Metal Mechanics (1985). TASS also acquired the left-dominated Tobacco Workers' Union in 1986 to consolidate union organisation with leadership drawn from the broad left.

[9]   The Pattern Makers Section, however, was closed to new members, suggesting that the growth of sectional representation within TASS was subject to limits.

The acquisition of the craft unions by TASS was anticipated to form the basis for an expansion of manual membership. The contraction of skilled employment throughout the 1980s thwarted this expectation. Employment among the traditional TASS membership also declined. This decline was compounded by the breakdown of the agreement between TASS and the AUEW-ES, whereby the latter transferred members to TASS when they were promoted into grades organised by TASS. Recruitment into TASS thus contracted rapidly once the split from the AUEW had been finalised. For these reasons TASS sought a further merger.

During the 1980s the members of ASTMS drawn from the engineering industry constituted a decreasing proportion of the union's membership and thus exerted less influence on the policy of the union. In particular, the growing health and insurance sections of ASTMS occupied an increasingly prominent position. The leadership of ASTMS also adhered to much of the broad left position supported within TASS. Furthermore, ASTMS lost 20 per cent of its membership between 1979 and 1987. These issues prompted merger negotiations between the two unions that resulted in the formation of Manufacturing, Science and Finance (MSF) in 1988. In practice, the formation of MSF united unions that had rejected the option of merger twenty-two years earlier (DATA, AScW and ASSET) and consolidated much of the white-collar union membership in the engineering industry.

Similarly to the AEU, the EETPU was initially a craft union, elected a right-of-centre leadership and recruited in a contracting area of employment. The privatisation policies of the Conservative governments during the 1980s accelerated rates of membership decline. In response to membership decline, a policy of expansion was implemented within the EETPU to extend the recruitment base of the union to areas of employment growth. In implementing the expansion policy, the EETPU came into conflict with other unions, the outcome of which was expulsion from the TUC in 1988 for infringements of the Bridlington Principles (Waddington, 1988). After the expulsion, the EETPU continued with its policy of expansion. An element of this policy included the acquisition of small unions, which organised in sectors or occupations where the EETPU was weak. In addition, the EETPU acquired several unions that had earlier broken away from other TUC-affiliated unions.[10]

---

[10] The Prison Service Union and the Institute of Journalists were prominent among these breakaway unions. The Bridlington Principles were operated to preclude a union that had broken away from a TUC-affiliated union from subsequently affiliating to the TUC.

From about 1980 the EETPU was thus able to extend its recruitment base. To accommodate increasing membership heterogeneity, the number of sections was extended. The members gained by these means, however, were insufficient to offset the effects of employment contraction in areas of traditional strength, with the consequence that membership continued to decline. Furthermore, 'distance' from the TUC came to be viewed as a source of political weakness. In 1992 the EETPU and the AEU amalgamated to form the AEEU, thus combining two former craft unions which were led from the right-of-centre and strongly advocated partnerships with employers. Before the EETPU, as part of the AEEU, was readmitted to the TUC, it was compelled to jettison the members from the breakaway unions that it had acquired when it had been expelled from the TUC.

Beyond manufacturing a similar pattern of membership decline underpinned much of the merger activity. As a result of constitutional changes that allowed forms of post-merger sectional representation, BIFU was able to compete with ASTMS/MSF for the acquisition of staff associations from insurance companies, hence the eight acquisitions completed between 1980 and 1998. The majority of BIFU members, however, were employed by the 'big four' London clearing banks. At three of these banks, National Westminster, Barclays and Lloyds-TSB, staff associations competed for membership with BIFU. Although BIFU organised a greater total number of members than these staff associations, each staff association organised more members than BIFU within each of the London clearing banks. Both BIFU and the staff associations sustained membership losses as a result of the 'rationalisation' policies introduced by the clearing banks. While these losses had not resulted in significant financial difficulties, competition between BIFU and the staff associations restricted opportunities to raise membership subscriptions. Changes in personnel at the head of BIFU and the staff associations, coupled to increasing evidence that the banks were the principal beneficiaries of competition for members, formed the basis of the rapprochement between BIFU and two of the staff associations. Furthermore, BIFU representatives highlighted the centrality of company bargaining and downgraded their traditional pursuit of national bargaining for banking, which had been an earlier source of tension between BIFU and the staff associations. Two of the staff associations also took steps towards affiliating to the TUC, hence joining the wider labour movement (Morris *et al.*, 2001). The amalgamation of BIFU with the staff associations from the Barclays and National Westminster Banks thus consolidated union organisation in banking. Within the post-merger UNIFI (Banking Trade Union), company sections were granted considerable autonomy. This degree of autonomy, however, was insufficient to attract the staff association from Lloyds-TSB to join the amalgamation. The leadership of the staff association at Lloyds-TSB rejected involvement in the amalgamation as it had been involved in a series of bitter disputes for members with BIFU and it viewed the new union as being 'too political' (Morris *et al.*, 2001).

The formation of UNISON created the largest union in the UK and unified much of union organisation in local government and health. Underpinning the merger was the failure of the constituent unions to mount concerted resistance to Conservative public sector policies, particularly privatisation, and the membership losses sustained by COHSE and NUPE (Undy, 1999; Waddington *et al.*, 2003). To accommodate a diverse membership, UNISON adopted an innovative system of representation that included Service Groups, self-organised groups and proportionality (McBride, 2001). In other words, the merger presented the opportunity to introduce reforms of internal government, which otherwise would have been more difficult to implement.

In summary, the merger process among the larger unions after 1980 comprised more formations than between 1966 and 1979, as unionists sought to offset membership losses through the consolidation of union structure. In practice, mergers became integral to growth strategies during the 1980s and 1990s when legislation effectively precluded recruitment growth. A consequence of these formations was that the larger unions became more 'general' in so far as they organised increasingly heterogeneous memberships and were organised around more complex forms of internal government. While aspects of these new forms of government allowed hitherto under-represented groups of union members enhanced opportunities to participate in union activities, the increasing complexity of union government mitigated any economies of scale that arose from the merger process.

Conclusions and Future Prospects

The sheer scale of the merger process differentiates the UK from most other countries covered by this volume. The historically large number of trade unions, coupled to the complexity of union structure, has resulted in a widespread expectation that restructuring through mergers should regularly take place. The absence of an overarching principle of organisation, the inability of the TUC to impose a restructuring blueprint, and the manner in which individual unions defend their independence regarding restructuring, combine to ensure that the extensive merger process in the UK has done little to 'simplify' trade union structure.

A larger proportion of members than hitherto are organised by 'general' unions, prepared to recruit workers irrespective of industry or occupation. To accommodate the resultant increasing membership heterogeneity, more complex and costly forms of union government have been developed. The forms of union government that allow some post-merger autonomy have facilitated merger involvement. It is also apparent that the separation between manual and white-collar unions, evident before 1980, largely dissolved thereafter. The involvement of APEX and NALGO in the GMB and UNISON mergers, for example, illustrates the disappearance of multi-industry white-collar unions. At the time of writing, it appears that MSF will amalgamate with the AEEU to further this pattern of development.

The TUC continues to promote mergers as a means of restructuring unionism in the UK. The absence of any direct constitutional authority or the political peculiarities evident in Australia (see Chapter 2) has restricted direct TUC influence over the merger process. There is no evidence, for example, to suggest that the *Millennial Challenge* has influenced either the rate or the character of merger activity. Because the number of unions in the UK remains relatively high, the position of the TUC is not threatened by the merger process, unlike that of the DGB (German Trade Union Confederation).

Further large-scale amalgamations and the continued acquisition of small unions is the likely future of the merger process in the UK. Although the rate of membership decline slowed markedly during the late 1990s, aggregate membership and density continue to decline. Membership decline and financial imperatives are thus likely to 'drive' the merger process. As control of restructuring remains with individual unions, there is little likelihood that the merger process will simplify union structure within an agreed principle of organisation. More likely is the increasing concentration of membership in a relatively small number of large, general unions.

List of Abbreviations

AEEU	Amalgamated Engineering and Electrical Union
AEF	Amalgamated Union of Engineering and Foundry Workers
AEU	Amalgamated Engineering Union
APEX	Association of Professional, Executive, Clerical and Computer Staff
ASBSBSW	Amalgamated Society of Boilermakers, Shipwrights, Blacksmiths and Structural Workers
ASTMS	Association of Scientific, Technical and Managerial Staffs

AScW	Association of Scientific Workers
ASSET	Association of Supervisory Staffs, Executives and Technicians
ASW	Amalgamated Society of Woodworkers
AUEW	Amalgamated Union of Engineering Workers
AUEW-ES	Amalgamated Union of Engineering Workers-Engineering Section
AUFW	Amalgamated Union of Foundry Workers
BIFU	Banking, Insurance and Finance Union
CEU	Constructional Engineering Union
COHSE	Confederation of Health Service Employees
CSEU	Confederation of Shipbuilding and Engineering Unions
CTAWA	Colliery and Allied Workers Association
DATA	Draughtsmen and Allied Technicians Association
DGB	Deutscher Gewerkschaftsbund, German Trade Union Confederation
EEF	Engineering Employers Federation
EETPU	Electrical, Electronic, Telecommunication and Plumbing Union
GMB	General, Municipal and Boilermakers Union
GMBATU	General, Municipal, Boilermakers and Allied Trades Union
GMWU	General and Municipal Workers Union
LFMA	Lancashire Footwear Manufacturers Association
MATSA	Managerial, Administrative, Technical and Supervisory Association
MBSA	Midland Bank Staff Association
MSF	Manufacturing, Science and Finance
NALGO	National and Local Government Officers Association
NAOP	National Association of Operative Plasterers
NUBSO	National Union of Boot and Shoe Operatives
NUFLAT	National Union of footwear, Leather and Allied Trades
NUGMW	National Union of General and Municipal Workers
NUPE	National Union of Public Employees
NUVB	National Union of Vehicle Builders
RCN	Royal College of Nursing
RUBSSO	Rossendale Union of Boot, Shoe and Slipper Operatives
TASS	Technical, Administrative and Supervisory Section
TGWU	Transport and General Workers Union

TUC	Trades Union Congress
UCATT	Union of Construction, Allied Trades and Technicians
UNIFI	Banking Trade Union
UNISON	Public Sector Union

CHAPTER 11. UNITED STATES

Merging in a Hostile Environment

Jeremy WADDINGTON

In the United States trade unionism developed along a rather different trajectory to trade union movements in Western Europe. The practice of 'pure and simple' or business unionism, which became entrenched around the turn of the century, relied on collective bargaining
to secure improvements for members to the exclusion of engagement in
political activity (Perlman, 1928; Taft, 1963). Links with socialist or
social democratic parties were, and are, at best, rudimentary, transient
and informal (Davis, 1980). The Western European notion of a labour
movement comprising trade unions and a political party (or parties) is
thus not applicable to the US. Western European trade unionists debated
the merits and limitations of craft and industrial forms of organisation
within extant confederal boundaries. In contrast, between the mid-1930s
and 1955 US unionism was divided by confederation between the two
principles of union organisation: the American Federation of Labor
(AFL) represented craft unions and the Congress of Industrial Organisations (CIO) advocated industrial unionism. Only with the merger of the
two confederations in 1955, to form the American Federation of Labor-
Congress of Industrial Organisations (AFL-CIO), were the two principles of union organisation institutionally reconciled.

In order to assess how these features impinged upon the trade union
merger process, this chapter comprises three sections. The first section
outlines the principal features of the regulatory regime emanating from
the 'New Deal' and the structure of unionism that was developed within
the context of this regime. The second section outlines the principal
features of the merger process since 1950 by reference to amalgamations, acquisitions and the character of merger activity among the larger
unions. The third section examines merger causation. The conclusion
assesses the outcome of the merger process. Throughout, reference is
made to a data series on mergers and the number of unions that was

compiled by the author and refers only to international and national unions.[1]

The New Deal and Trade Union Structure

This section outlines the regulatory framework set in place during the New Deal and introduces the tensions within US union structure. The section argues that the regulatory framework for unionism was weak compared to those in Western Europe. Furthermore, employers were able to dismantle several of its key elements when economic growth slowed after the mid-1960s. The merger process among US unions has thus taken place in a relatively hostile environment.

The Terms and Context of the New Deal

The activities of modern US trade unionism were regulated in the 'New Deal', a complex of social, legal, economic and political relationships consolidated between the mid-1930s and 1950 (Kochan *et al.*, 1986; Edwards and Podgursky, 1986). With the adverse effects of the Wall Street Crash (1929) and ensuing Great Depression influencing the American polity, and rising militancy among unionists after 1930, a means was sought whereby trade unions could be integrated into US political economy. The legislative centrepiece of this approach was the National Labor Relations Act 1935 (NLRA or Wagner Act).

The NLRA guaranteed non-supervisory workers in the private sector the right to join or organise unions and to bargain collectively with their employer. The NLRA also obliged employers to bargain 'in good faith' and prohibited employers from engaging in unfair labour practices.[2] A

---

[1] In referring to international and national unions, the data series excludes local, state and city central unions. Although they are excluded from the quantitative data, reference is made to the impact of the acquisition of state unions in the second section, which outlines the character of the merger process. The data series was generated from the following sources: Adams, 1984; Chaison, 1996 and 2001; Chitayat, 1979; Dewey, 1971; Fink, 1977; Galenson, 1960; Gifford, various; Janus, 1978; Lorwin, 1933; Troy and Sheflin, 1985; Ulman, 1955; Williamson, 1995; and Wolman, 1936. Data from these sources were supplemented by reference to union web sites, union histories and, in some cases, representatives from unions.

[2] Five practices were initially defined by the NLRA as being 'unfair': interfere, restrain or coerce employees in their union activities; assist or dominate a labour organisation; discriminate in employment or union membership or union activities or lack of them; discriminate for participation in NLRB elections; and refuse to bargain collectively with a certified union (Estey, 1967: 103-104). This list was amended by the terms of the Taft-Hartley Act 1947 and by subsequent decisions of the National Labor Relations Board.

National Labor Relations Board (NLRB) was established to administer and adjudicate certification elections, the method whereby workers choose or reject union representation. Encouraged by the NLRA and the effects of wartime economic growth, union membership rose from 3.6 million members in 1935 to 14.8 million members by 1947, resulting in an increase in union density from 6.8 per cent to 24.9 per cent.[3]

The number of strikes rose during the immediate post-war period as wartime controls were jettisoned. Invoking the rhetoric of 'equalising' the rights of the employer with those accruing to labour from the NLRA, the Labor-Management Relations or Taft-Hartley Act was enacted in 1947 as an amendment to the NLRA. The terms of the Taft-Hartley Act extended the area of government regulation from the process of collective bargaining, as laid down in the NLRA, to the terms of bargaining. In particular, the pre-entry closed shop was deemed unlawful for companies engaged in interstate commerce. The capacity of unionists to picket plants other than their own was also restricted. In practice, these measures restricted union opportunities to extend organisation into Southern states. Furthermore, six categories of unfair union practices were introduced.[4] To these restrictions were added the terms of the Labor-Management Reporting and Disclosure Act 1959, known as the Landrum-Griffin Act, which arose from an investigation into corruption and unethical practices within several unions. This Act further regulated union government by means of a bill of rights for individual union members, which was specifically intended to guarantee due process. The terms of the NLRA, which by comparison with regulations in much of Europe were hardly generous to labour, were thus restricted by subsequent legislation.

The terms of the legislation enacted after 1935 were not the only pertinent feature of the New Deal model. The substantial and sustained rates of economic growth achieved in the US between 1935 and the early 1960s were of particular benefit. These enabled employers to meet many of the union demands. Sustained economic growth, in combination with the practices of the War Labor Board, promoted pattern bargaining in some key industries. Membership and density also increased. Membership rose, albeit unevenly, until 1979 when it peaked at

---

[3] All membership data are taken from the sources listed at Table 11.1.

[4] These practices included: restrain or coerce employees in the exercise of their right to join unions of their own choosing or to refrain from joining a union; cause discrimination for union activities; refuse to bargain with an employer; engage in secondary boycotts; charge excessive or discriminatory initiation fees; and featherbedding, such as when an employer is compelled to pay for services not performed (Estey, 1967: 108-109).

21 million members. Union density, however, peaked during the early 1950s when almost 27 per cent of the labour force was unionised. Membership growth between the early 1950s and late 1970s resulted primarily from the rise in membership in expanding industries and the extension of union organisation into the public sector. Even at its zenith, however, significant groups were excluded from union membership. The failure of unions to engage with the civil rights and women's movements accentuated this tendency and resulted in missed opportunities to recruit new cohorts of trade union activists (Moody, 1988: 249-281).

The New Deal Collapses

Although an immediate post-war employers' counter-offensive forced the introduction of the Taft-Hartley Act, sustained rates of economic growth until the mid-1960s supported the New Deal regime and union activities. From the mid-1960s the economic situation deteriorated as rates of growth slowed (Brenner, 1998: 93-111). Employers further challenged the terms and operation of the New Deal, as they sought to lower the rate of real wage increases and to intensify production with the object of raising output. To these ends, employers embarked on a variety of strategies, each of which threatened the position of business unionism. Massive shifts in the labour market, initially from the Northern (frostbite) states to the South and followed by movements from manufacturing towards private sector services, constituted transfers away from areas of relatively dense unionisation to those of sparse organisation. Initially, unions attempted to follow this relocation, but employer resistance to unionisation increased apace. The percentage of union victories in representation elections fell sharply during the 1960s (Goldfield, 1987: 176-178), as employers stepped up their anti-union campaigns (Kircher, 1968). Employers also resorted to unfair labour practices in ever-increasing numbers. A seven-fold increase in charges against employers occurred between 1955 and 1980 and a six-fold increase in charges against employers who dismissed employees for union activity over the same period (Goldfield, 1987: 195-205). Influencing both of these trends was the increased use of union 'busting' consultants by employers concerned to keep unions at bay. By 1995 employers used anti-union consultants in no fewer than 90 per cent of private sector union organising campaigns (Bronfenbrenner, 1997).

Where unions were able to retain a presence, employers amended the terms of the New Deal. Collective bargaining was decentralised from company to plant level and pattern bargaining was dismantled in most industries. Decentralised bargaining at plant level facilitated the 'whip-sawing' of local unions into conceding new forms of flexibility, such as team working and workplace involvement schemes, which led to further work intensification. These new forms of flexibility were used from the mid-1970s by employers to diminish the commitment of workers to trade unions and enhance that to the goals of the enterprise (Parker and Slaughter 1988). In turn, these led to a diminution of union effectiveness at the workplace where elaborate job classification systems had maintained a degree of workplace control (Brody, 1993).

Attempts by unions to restore lost influence initially focused on legislative change. A Labor-Management Group (LMG) was established by the Carter administration to seek a means of improving, *inter alia*, productivity growth and labour market flexibility. An ensuing growth in confidence among the trade union leadership arising from the LMG soon dissipated, however, when union proposals on the minimum wage were rejected by a Democratic President and in the House, where the Democratic Party held a substantial majority. These failures were compounded by employer successes, particularly in lobbying against the mild Labor Law Reform Bill, which was intended to amend the procedures when employers undertook unfair labour practices during representation campaigns and elections (Clark, 1989).

The defeat and destruction of the Professional Air Traffic Controllers Organisation (PATCO) by the Reagan administration in 1981, coupled to the shift to the right in the composition of the NLRB, further dampened union confidence. By 1980 the peak in union density was 25 years distant and the period of membership decline was to run until the turn of the century. The number of NLRB-supervised representation elections fell precipitously during the early 1980s, reaching 3,241 in 1983, having been maintained at the relatively high average level of 7,788 per year during the 1970s (Goldfield, 1987: 90-91). The capacity of unions to respond to the challenge of the employers' offensive was thus brought into question.

Structure in the Development of US Unions

The AFL was founded in 1886 as an expression of dissatisfaction among craft unionists with the policies of the Knights of Labor. Central to the continuity of the AFL were the principles of 'trade autonomy', whereby affiliated unions retained control over bargaining policy and independence, and 'exclusive jurisdiction', within the terms of which each craft union had sole responsibility to recruit members from within its own designated trade, thus protecting it from competition from other unions. Both of these principles were underpinned by the AFL's steadfast support for craft unionism, its emphasis on economic objectives achieved through collective bargaining, and a reliance on pressure-group politics rather than alliances with political parties (Taft, 1963; Gitelman, 1965). Between 1897 and 1904 no fewer than 92 unions were 'chartered' by the AFL, which took the number of AFL affiliates from 59 to 120, or about 85 per cent of all national unions, and effectively divided the American labour market among them (Bernstein, 1960; Estey, 1967).[5]

As well as protecting affiliates from membership competition, exclusive jurisdiction also precluded the extension of recruitment bases to incorporate areas of employment growth. The spread of mass production, coupled to the opportunities for recruitment presented by the NLRA, opened a division within the AFL. The majority of AFL-affiliated unions argued that principles of craft unionism should underpin recruitment within mass production industries, whereas eight affiliated unions attached to a caucus, the Committee for Industrial Organisation, advocated industrial unionism as the organising principle.[6] This division was consolidated in 1935 when the unions attached to the Committee were suspended, for ignoring a decision of the AFL Convention in favour of craft unionism and for introducing dual unionism. Concurrently, the title Congress was adopted in preference to Committee to reflect independence from the AFL.

CIO-affiliated unions achieved immediate successes in the automobile and steel industries, which were followed by significant recruitment inroads into the electrical, rubber, clothing, textiles and petroleum industries. No fewer than forty-two unions or national organising committees had affiliated to, or were associated with, the CIO by the end of 1937 (see Table 11.1). At this time the CIO claimed more members than the AFL, although more recent data suggests that the AFL was probably

---

[5]   A 'chartered' union was affiliated to the AFL. As well as accepting established unions into affiliation, the AFL also promoted the establishment of new unions where jurisdictions were vacant (Lorwin, 1933: 67-70). Not all of the unions chartered during this period survived, hence the numbers for 1897 and 1904, when considered together with the number of newly chartered unions, do not tally.

[6]   The original eight unions were: United Mine Workers; Amalgamated Clothing Workers of America; International Ladies Garment Workers' Union; United Textile Workers of America; Oil Field, Gas Well and Refinery Workers of America; International Union of Mine, Mill and Smelter Workers; International Typographical Union; and the Cap and Millinery Department of the United Hatters, Cap and Millinery Workers' International Union. These eight unions were later joined by the Federation of the Flat Glass Workers of America; Amalgamated Association of Iron, Steel and Tin Workers; United Automobile Workers of America; and the United Rubber Workers of America, which were also affiliated to the AFL. In addition, two independent unions joined the Committee: United Electrical and Radio Workers and the Industrial Union of Marine and Shipyard Workers.

larger throughout (see Galenson, 1960; Preis, 1964). What is less contentious is that the initial growth of the CIO unions was slowed by the recession of 1938 and that after 1947 expansion was muted, although membership peaked at almost 4 million in 1950 (see Table 11.1). The AFL responded to the CIO challenge by launching its own recruitment campaigns, the success of which owed much to the abandonment of 'genuine' craft unionism and the recruitment of semi-skilled workers. By the time of the merger of the two confederations in 1955, 108 AFL-affiliated unions organised about twice as many members as the remaining thirty CIO affiliates. In addition to the 'softening' of the division between craft and industrial unionism, the merger was also encouraged by shared opposition to the Taft-Hartley Act, assessments of the cost of membership competition and the adoption of more characteristics of business unionism by CIO-affiliated unions (Estey, 1967; Preis, 1964).

Table 11.1: The Distribution of Membership and Unions, 1930-2000

	Total Membership[1] 000s	AFL-CIO Membership[2] 000s	AFL Membership[3] 000s	CIO Membership[3] 000s	Total Number of Unions[4]	Number of AFL-CIO Affiliates	Number of AFL Affiliates	Number of CIO Affiliates	Number of Independents
1930	3,401		2,961		165		104		61
1937	7,001		3,623	1,991	210		102	42	66
1940	8,717		4,247	2,154	222		105	42	75
1945	14,322		6,931	3,928	216		102	40	74
1950	14,267		7,143	3,713	236		107	30	99
1955	16,802	12,622			230	138			92
1960	17,049	12,553			222	139			83
1970	19,381	13,177			266	124			142
1980	19,843	13,602			260	105			155
1990	16,776	13,933			228	91			137
2000	16,258	13,164			201	71			130

[1] Total membership refers to members in the United States and thus excludes Canadian members of US-based trade unions. Membership data for the confederations make no such exclusion.

[2] AFL-CIO membership data excludes associate membership of unions that are affiliated to the confederation.

[3] These data include Canadian members of unions with headquarters in the US.

[4] All the data on the number of unions refer to only national or international unions and thus exclude local unions, state unions and city central unions.

Sources: membership data; Bureau of National Statistics (1930-1980) and Current Population Survey (1990-2000): AFL-CIO membership series; Gifford 2001: AFL membership series; US Bureau of Labor Statistics: CIO membership series; National Bureau of Economic Research: total number of unions; see Footnote 1: number of AFL-CIO affiliates; Gifford various and Fink 1977: number of AFL and number of CIO affiliates; Bureau of Labor Statistics.

The anticipated sharp expansion of membership after the AFL-CIO merger failed to materialise. Instead, membership remained fairly constant throughout the 1960s before rising slowly during the 1970s. Density had peaked during the early 1950s before the confederal merger. Furthermore the share of members organised by AFL-CIO unions did not rise significantly, an issue compounded by a series of expulsions. The number of national unions affiliated to the AFL-CIO also did not increase markedly as a proportion of the total number of unions, reflecting the large number of unions that remain independent of the AFL-CIO (see Table 11.1). The backdrop to the merger process after 1955 is thus one of declining density and, since the late 1970s, declining membership. These declines coincide with the collapse of the New Deal regime and the absence of any political influence through party affiliation.

The Merger Process

Mergers in the United States are not legally regulated, but rely on terms specified in union constitutions. Legal challenges to mergers are usually lodged in terms of failing to meet these constitutional requirements (Chaison, 1996: 29-30). In the absence of legal regulation and the limited authority of the AFL-CIO, mergers are primarily matters for the unions concerned. There is thus no overall direction to the merger process, as unions tend opportunistically to select merger partners, although individual unions may implement specific merger policies intended to consolidate union organisation within particular areas. This section identifies the principal characteristics of the merger process since 1950 and shows how many larger unions have used the merger process to extend their recruitment bases.

The Characteristics of Merger Activity

Figure 1.10 shows that there was no dominant wave of merger intensity in the US after 1950, unlike several of the other countries covered in this volume. Table 11.2 presents the data by reference to amalgamations and acquisitions. In common with other countries, acquisitions tend to outnumber amalgamations, although until 1974 the number of unions disappearing in amalgamations was only slightly lower than the number of unions acquired (46 compared with 59). From 1975, however, acquisitions dominated the merger process: 74 acquisitions and 18 unions disappearing in amalgamations.

**Table 11.2: The Pattern of the Merger Process
in the United States**

	Amalga-mations	Acquisi-tions	Number of unions disappearing in mergers[1]	Number of disappearing unions per year
1950-1954	3	8	16	3.2
1955-1959	5	10	22	4.4
1960-1964	4	9	20	4.0
1965-1969	1	15	19	3.8
1970-1974	4	17	28	5.6
1975-1979	2	12	16	3.2
1980-1984	3	15	23	4.6
1985-1989	/	17	17	3.4
1990-1994	1	19	21	4.2
1995-1999	2	11	15	3.0
TOTAL	25	133	197	

[1] All acquisitions in the US after 1950 involved one union acquiring a second. The number of unions disappearing in an acquisition was thus always one. Amalgamations involved a variable number of unions. The number of unions disappearing in an amalgamation was calculated by reference to the number of pre-merger unions involved. If three unions amalgamated to form a single union, the number of unions disappearing was thus three.

Sources: see footnote 1.

Table 11.3 illustrates the distribution by membership size of unions involved in the merger process. Throughout the period 1950 to 2000 acquired unions tended to be smaller than amalgamating unions. Over 75 per cent of acquired unions organised 20,000 or fewer members, suggesting the presence of a size threshold below which unions were unable to provide sufficient services. Declining employment in the leather, millinery and woodworking industries and in the coopering and siderography trades, for example, resulted in small and contracting unions with jurisdictions of insufficient size to sustain independent organisation. The size distribution of acquisitions did not change markedly before and after 1975. In contrast, amalgamations tended to involve larger unions from 1975. Indeed, several of the smaller unions involved in amalgamations before 1975 were subsequently involved in the merger process again in either an amalgamation or an acquisition, indicating that the initial amalgamation merely delayed more fundamental restructuring.

Table 11.3: The Distribution by Membership
Size of the Merger Process

Membership Size	Acquisitions 1950-1974	Amalgamations 1950-1974	Acquisitions 1975-2000	Amalgamations 1975-2000
2,500 or less	21	5	18	/
2,501-5,000	18	3	14	/
5,001-20,000	11	14	22	3
20,001-50,000	4	9	15	4
50,001-100,000	4	8	3	2
100,001-200,000	1	7	1	4
200,001-500,000	/	/	1	3
500,001 or more	/	/	/	2
Total	59	46	74	18

Sources: see footnote 1.

Continuing a trend evident around the turn of the century (Glocker, 1915), the overwhelming majority of amalgamations involved unions with members in contiguous trades or occupations. The amalgamation to form the United Transportation Union in 1968, for example, involved four pre-merger unions, which each represented a particular occupation within the railway industry.[7] Similar processes were evident among unions in post, printing and publishing, food processing and textiles. Several of these amalgamations comprised a sequence of restructuring, as unions with declining memberships, often in areas of contracting employment, attempted to extend narrow jurisdictions through the merger process. To illustrate: in 1965 the International Photo-engravers Union of North America amalgamated with the Amalgamated Lithographers of America to form the Lithographers and Photo-engravers International Union (LPIU) with a membership of 56,000. Seven years later, with membership of 60,000, the LPIU amalgamated with the International Brotherhood of Bookbinders to form the Graphic Arts International Union (GAIU) with a post-merger membership of 122,500. By 1983 this membership had declined to 82,500 and the GAIU amalgamated with the International Printing and Graphic Communications Union, which had been formed by merger only in 1973, to form the Graphic Communications International Union (GCIU) with a membership of 197,500. By 2000 membership had declined still further to 141,874 members.

---

[7]   The four unions were: the Switchmen's Union of North America; Order of Railway Conductors and Brakemen; Brotherhood of Locomotive Firemen and Enginemen; and the Brotherhood of Railway Trainmen.

Such amalgamations constituted movement towards industrial unions and met the requirement of the AFL-CIO to eliminate the duplication of jurisdictions. Of course, this is neither to argue that such amalgamations necessarily result in industrial unions nor that they eliminate competitive recruitment. While the GCIU certainly has a broader occupational recruitment base than any of its constituent parts, other unions within printing and publishing elected for absorption within even broader unions. The International Typographical Union, for example, was acquired by the Communication Workers of America in 1987, having been earlier rejected by the GCIU 'largely because the cost of providing life-time employment for the Typographers' officers was greater than expected dues from its declining membership' (Strauss, 1993: 41).

Mergers Involving Larger Unions

The diversity of different merger policies can be elaborated by reference to Table 11.4. Ten of the thirteen largest unions in 2000 acquired unions after 1950, whereas only three unions made no acquisitions.[8] These ten unions acquired a total of 51 unions or 38.3 per cent of all national unions acquired since 1950. There is no direct relationship between 'natural growth' and the propensity to acquire unions in the merger process. The National Education Association (NEA), the International Brotherhood of Electrical Workers (IBEW), the American Federation of Teachers (AFT) and the Laborers' International Union of North America (LIUNA) achieved marked natural growth, yet acquired only two unions between them. In contrast, the Service Employees International Union (SEIU), which also achieved substantial membership gains, was very active in the merger process as an acquiring union. Similarly, there is little to link membership decline with acquisitions. The United Food and Commercial Workers International Union (UFCW), for example, completed eleven acquisitions and sustained limited membership losses whereas, both the United Automobile, Aerospace and Agricultural Implement Workers of America (UAW) and the United Steelworkers of America (USWA) made relatively few acquisitions while sustaining huge membership losses. In other words, the specific acquisition policies pursued by different unions are not determined by membership trends. Features of these acquisition policies are examined below with the object of identifying some of the factors that

---

[8]   The National Education Association (NEA) was listed as the largest trade union in the year 2000 (Gifford, 2001). The status of the NEA, however, has not been clear throughout the period since 1950. It has shifted from being a 'genteel association', before 'moving steadily towards more aggressive representation of its members', although remaining 'far from a typical union' (Heckscher, 1988: 186).

influence the outcome of the merger process. Throughout, five themes are apparent;

– acquiring unions have used acquisitions to extend their jurisdiction into areas of employment growth. In consequence, many of the larger unions are becoming more open both industrially and occupationally. This is particularly the case for those unions in manufacturing that traditionally organised as industrial unions. Many large American unions are thus organising increasingly heterogeneous memberships;

– unions selecting a merger partner often have to make a choice between several competing acquiring unions. By offering more favourable terms, an acquiring union may be more successful and thus influence union structural development. The terms of the merger deal often appear as influential as following any principle of union organisation;

– forms of post-merger sectional representation have become commonplace, as unions compete for acquisitions;

– the merger process may have eliminated some areas of competitive recruitment, but it has also generated new areas of competition;

– no consistent evidence emerges to show that mergers arrest the rate of aggregate membership or density decline, although they have resulted in changes among the relative positions of different unions.

The significant natural growth achieved by the NEA after 1950 resulted in the organisation steadily rising through the ranks of unions to assume its current position as the largest union. The extent of this growth insulated the NEA from financial difficulties and resulted in a limited interest in mergers. Furthermore, the occupational definition of the NEA restricted the range of potential merger partners. During the 1970s, however, when bargaining arrangements for teachers were reformed, the NEA was involved in merger discussions with the AFT. Interest in a merger was driven from the state level, where structures of the two unions were merged at the behest of local unionists wishing to facilitate bargaining with state-based education employers. At national level, merger negotiations broke down over a range of issues including AFL-CIO affiliation and internal democracy, with the consequence that several of the mergers between state-level structures were subsequently dissolved (Janus, 1978: 21-22). During the 1990s attempts were made to revive the merger initiative involving the NEA and AFT, initially in the form of a no-raiding agreement. At the time of writing, informal merger discussions are underway, but no early merger agreement is anticipated.

Table 11.4: Acquisitions Completed
by the Largest Unions in 2000

Acquiring Union	Member-ship[1]	Date[1]	No. of Unions Acqui-red	Mem-bers Acqui-red	Member-ship 2000	'Natural' Growth[2]
National Education Association	453,797	1950	/	/	2,530,000	+2,076,203
Int. Bro. Teamsters, Chauffeurs, Warehousemen and Helpers	1,417,400	1957	5	147,498	1,402,000	-162,898
United Food and Commercial Workers International Union	1,235,000	1979	11	223,500	1,380,722	-77,778
Service Employees International Union	553,500	1980	8[3]	292,000	1,374,300	+528,800
American Federation of State, County and Municipal Employees	125,200	1956	1[4]	27,000	1,300,000	+1,147,800
Labourers' International Union of North America	457,700	1968	2	33,700	818,412	+327,012
Int. Assoc. of Machinists and Aerospace Workers	771,400	1956	6	48,400	730,673	-89,127
International Brotherhood of Electrical Workers	478,100	1950	/	/	727,836	+249,736
American Federation of Teachers	41,400	1950	/	/	706,973	+665,573
United Automobile, Aerospace and Agricultural Implement Workers of America	1,389,500	1979	4	47,400	671,853	-765,743
United Steelworkers of America	957,200	1967	6	395,100	612,157	-850,143
United Brotherhood of Carpenters and Joiners of America	637,700	1979	2	25,000	434,023	-228,677
Communication Workers of America	269,100	1960	6[5]	71,300	499,557	+159,157

[1] The membership data refer to the date on which the first acquisition was made after 1950 or, as in the case of the United Food and Commercial Workers, the year during which the union was formed. If no acquisitions were completed, 1950 is used as the start date.

[2] For our purposes 'natural' growth is calculated by subtracting the number of members acquired from the difference between the membership at column 1 and the membership in the year 2000. This assumes that the membership trend of the acquired union follows that of the acquiring union after the merger. While it is acknowledged that this is unlikely, the 'natural' growth figures illustrate a broad relationship between member-ship achieved through mergers and recruitment.

[3] The Service Employees International Union also acquired no fewer than seven unions that organised within particular states: Illinois State Employees Association acquired in 1974, Oregon State Employees Association (1980), California State Employees Association (1984), New Hampshire State Employees Association (1984), Connecticut State Employees Association (1985), Georgia State Employees Association (1985) and the Maine State Employees Association (1988). The acquisition of the Illinois State

Employees Association lasted only a year (Janus 1978). In total, these state unions organised about 105,000 members. As in the case of the two unions below, the membership acquired in these acquisitions are excluded from consideration in the 'natural' growth calculation.

[4] The American Federation of State, County and Municipal Employees also acquired a further six unions that organised within particular states: State of Iowa Employees Association acquired in 1975, Civil Service Employee Associations of New York State (1978), Arizona Public Employees (1982), Ohio Civil Service Employees (1983), Ohio Association of Public School Employees (1984), and Michigan State Employees Association (1986). When they were acquired these organisations represented about 80,000 members.

[5] The Communication Workers of America also acquired the West Virginia Public Employees Association in 1984.

Sources: see footnote 1.

For the thirty years after its expulsion from the AFL-CIO in 1957 for improper activities and financial irregularities, the International Brotherhood of Teamsters, Chauffeurs, Warehousemen and Helpers (IBT) remained unaffiliated. During this period the IBT acquired five other independent unions. The political separation of the IBT from the AFL-CIO was thus a sufficient barrier to preclude acquisitions by the IBT from among AFL-CIO affiliates. Furthermore, three of the five unions acquired by the IBT had also been expelled from either the CIO or the AFL-CIO (Chaison, 1986: 26-27). Expulsion from the confederation removed protection against raiding and, in several cases, led to the confederation establishing a new union to compete directly with the expelled union. Acquisition by the IBT thus provided some security in terms of being part of a larger union and, in particular, offered employment security to the employees of the expelled union.

Following its formation by amalgamation in 1979, the UFCW was one of the more active acquiring unions. Integral to this process of acquisition was the allowance of some degree of post-merger autonomy. The Barbers, Beauticians and Allied Industries International Union (1980), the Insurance Workers International Union (1983) and the United Garment Workers of America (1994) were acquired as separate sections of the UFCW with the authority to implement independent bargaining policies for specific sections of the membership. Subsequently, the International Union of Life Insurance Agents (1993) was acquired as an extension of the Professional Insurance and Finance Division of the UFCW. Similarly, the United Retail Workers Union, the membership of which was concentrated solely in Illinois and Indiana, became Local 881 of the UFCW, thus retaining elements of its pre-merger autonomy (Adams, 1984). The allowance of some degree of post-merger autonomy enabled the UFCW to expand industrially and occupationally from its initial recruitment base in retail, wholesale and meat products. Unions acquired with membership from within this initial jurisdiction were absorbed as part of the core UFCW structure, rather than as separate sections.

Both the SEIU and American Federation of State, County and Municipal Employees (AFSCME) acquired unions, while concurrently recording marked increases in membership through natural growth. Both unions organised in services and implemented expansionary policies. The SEIU's 'Reach Out' programme, for example, was intended to accelerate the rate of membership increase through recruitment and mergers. The two unions pursued different acquisition policies, although they were often in direct competition. The SEIU acquired unions from within the public and private sector services, albeit with particular concentrations among state, health and federal government employees, whereas AFSCME's acquisition policy rested exclusively on the public sector. Competition between the two unions was intense in the public sector, with unions often presented with a choice between the SEIU and AFSCME. Factors associated with the structure and practice of bargaining together with forms of post-merger union government facilitated these acquisitions. In particular, the terms and conditions of state employees are settled through a number of bargaining units at state level. If a state employees' association was acquired by either SEIU or AFSCME and allowed to operate as a post-merger section or local, state-wide bargaining structures meant that the acquisition had relatively little effect on the day-to-day practices of union members. Acquisition in this context merely placed more resources at the disposal of the acquired unions, while also enabling the expansion of the acquiring union.

The Communication Workers of America (CWA) is a third union with an active policy of acquisition and an expanding membership base located in an area of growing employment. Similarly to AFSCME, the acquisitions completed were concentrated within the core area of the membership of the CWA. Furthermore, the CWA acquired several of these unions when faced with competition from other unions, indicating that the terms offered by the CWA were more attractive than other offers. Certainly, different degrees of post-merger autonomy were allowed to acquired unions and the constitutions of acquired unions were maintained post-merger. From an initial membership base among telegraph and telephone workers, the CWA has thus used the merger process to meet the intention of becoming a sectoral communications union.

Employment among the core membership of the UAW, USWA and the International Association of Machinists and Aerospace Workers (IAM) contracted markedly after the mid-1970s. Furthermore, the system of pattern bargaining, which was central to the practice of these unions, was dismantled by employers throughout steel and engineering, thus requiring new forms of union organisation to adjust to decentralisation. These unions used the merger process to serve two ends. First, it was used to consolidate union organisation within core areas. The USWA, for example, acquired the International Union of Mine, Mill and Smelter Workers (1967), while the IAM acquired the International Die Sinkers Conference (1987) and the Pattern Makers League of North America (1991). The membership of each of these acquired unions had declined sharply, thus jeopardising the support provided to members. Second, the merger process was used to secure jurisdictions in areas of employment growth. The acquisition by the USWA of the heterogeneous International Union of District 50 (1972), for example, secured members from throughout manufacturing, public services and private sector services (Chitayat, 1979: 64-65).[9] Similarly, the UAW acquired the Distributive Workers of America (1979) with members among retail, wholesale and university clerical staff. Since this acquisition, the UAW has actively campaigned at universities, initially to deepen recruitment among clerical staff and latterly to extend organisation to teaching assistants. Associated with involvement in the merger process was some decentralisation of union decision-making. In the case of the USWA, Industry Committees were established to allow members to devise bargaining, recruitment and other strategies appropriate for their specific industries. The extent of the autonomy allowed by these arrangements has, however, been questioned (Chaison, 1986: 97).

The wealth of the UAW and USWA has enabled them to exploit some of the recruitment opportunities that arose from these acquisitions. In contrast, the LIUNA, which had earlier pursued a similar strategy in acquiring unions in the stone industry and in the postal service, was restricted in its attempts to develop the membership base established through these acquisitions by limited finances (Chitayat, 1979: 80-89). Irrespective of the resources available to the IAM, UAW and USWA, they were unable to recruit members from new areas of organisation in sufficient numbers to replace those lost from steel and engineering. In consequence, the three unions proposed an amalgamation in 1995 to unify organisation within engineering. Although the proposal was not realised, due to a failure to agree a post-merger system of government, it

---

[9]   The International Union of District 50 claimed members in chemicals; paper and allied products; public utilities including gas, electricity and water; transportation; construction; marine operations; ferrous and non-ferrous mining; stone, clay and glass products; petroleum and coal products; food and dairy machinery; rubber; textiles; leather; and wood products (Chitayat, 1979: 64-65).

illustrates that industrial unionism has not been rejected, even within unions that have diversified their memberships (Clark and Gray, 2000).

The United Brotherhood of Carpenters and Joiners of America (UBC) sustained marked membership losses, yet acquired only two relatively small unions: the Wood, Wire and Metal Lathers International Union (WWML) in 1979 and the Association of Western Pulp and Paper Workers (AWPPW) in 1994. Density rates in the construction industry remain low, however, with the consequence that recruitment opportunities for the UBC remain wide-ranging.[10] Both acquired unions had sustained long-term pre-merger membership decline and organised within declining jurisdictions. The crafts around which the WWML organised were declining and being replaced by construction methods, which the UBC claimed were within its jurisdiction. The acquisition of the WWML was thus influenced by technological change, eliminated jurisdictional disputes between the two unions and consolidated union organisation within construction. The AWPPW was formed as a break-away union in 1964, comprising members from the International Brotherhood of Pulp, Sulphite and Paper Mill Workers (IBPSPMW) and the United Papermakers and Paperworkers (UPP) employed on the West Coast. The IBPSPMW and the UPP amalgamated in 1972 to form the United Paperworkers International Union (UPIU), which continued to claim jurisdiction over areas organised by the AWPPW. For the AWPPW, merger with the UIPU was thus not a viable option, as the issues underpinning the breakaway remained. The AWPPW sought an alternative merger within the terms of which it would retain some autonomy. Such terms were offered by the UBC.

What Promotes Mergers?

Three broad factors are reviewed here as promoting mergers; membership decline and financial weakness, changing bargaining structure, and confederal policy. In reviewing these factors two points should be noted. First, these factors promote mergers, but are not sufficient to ensure that a merger is ratified. A range of issues, described as 'barriers to merger' (Chaison, 1986: 67-90) must be overcome during pre-merger negotiations. Such barriers include differences in union government and representation, in dues and benefit structures, and in terms and conditions of union employment. Attempts to conclude agreements that reconcile these differences are likely to be contested and may provoke internal opposition to the merger. In other words, the three factors may

---

[10] Union density in construction in 2000 was 18 per cent, having declined from about 25 per cent during the mid-1980s (Gifford, various).

promote mergers in general, but are insufficient to explain the terms of each individual merger. Secondly, the three factors that promote mergers are inter-related. It is often their combined effect, rather than any single factor acting in isolation, that is the stimulus to merger.

Membership Decline and Financial Considerations

Long-term membership decline has had a significant effect on the merger process. Employer downsizing and labour intensification, the shift of employment to Southern states and the overt anti-unionism of many employers contributed to membership decline and encouraged involvement in the merger process (Goldfield, 1987). For many former AFL craft unions, technological change undermined or weakened the basis on which the craft had been established. Contractions in craft employment often resulted in membership decline, financial weakness and a search for a merger partner. Industrial unions were similarly affected when technological change led to the contraction of the industry, as, for example, in the case of the woodworking industry. In both of these cases, the impact of membership decline cannot be separated from the impact of policies directed towards exclusive jurisdiction. Once the labour market was divided into jurisdictions, the opportunities for unions to extend organisation were limited. Effectively, some unions were trapped within a contracting jurisdiction. In such circumstances, larger unions sought to acquire unions as a means to expand their jurisdiction, while smaller unions accepted offers of acquisition provided some form of post-merger autonomy was allowed and support services to members were improved.

Many individual cases illustrate the impact of membership decline in promoting mergers (Chitayat, 1979; Brooks and Gamm, 1979). Furthermore, the impact of the business cycle in promoting membership change is also associated with merger activity (Freeman and Brittain, 1977). Analysis of all US mergers between 1900 and 1978, however, revealed that 60.6 per cent of acquired unions and 64.4 per cent of amalgamating unions experienced declining or unchanged membership during the five years prior to merger (Chaison, 1981). In contrast, only 28.0 per cent of acquiring unions underwent similar pre-merger membership trends. With aggregate membership decline after 1979, these proportions rose to the extent that during the 1990s more than 90 per cent of acquired unions and all amalgamating unions sustained declining or unchanged membership during the five years prior to merger.

Although the American trade union movement is one of the wealthiest covered in this volume, like its European counterparts it relies on membership dues for the majority of its annual income (Troy, 1975;

Sheflin and Troy, 1983; Masters, 1997). Membership decline may thus promote financial weakness, which, in turn, encourages merger involvement. Research traces a long-term deterioration in union finances. Union finances were substantially weaker during the 1970s compared to the situation in the 1960s (Sheflin and Troy, 1983) and, following a brief revival during the early 1980s, deteriorated from the mid-1980s and throughout the 1990s (Masters, 1997). Furthermore, union finances have become more concentrated in this period, suggesting that larger, better-resourced unions are in relatively stronger positions than their smaller counterparts. Case study evidence indicates that financial problems, arising from long-term membership decline, certainly promoted the acquisition of several unions (Chitayat, 1979; Chaison, 1986). Short-term financial concerns also promoted mergers, albeit less frequently than long-term membership decline. The United Rubber, Cork, Linoleum and Plastic Workers (URCLPW), for example, merged with the USWA in 1995 during a protracted and costly strike at Bridgestone, the tyre manufacturing company. Before the merger the URCLPW had borrowed heavily and levied significant increases in dues to sustain the strike. Acquisition by the USWA thus provided greater financial security.

Membership decline and financial weakness are not necessarily directly related. For example, declining unions have implemented a range of measures to cut operating costs, such as the closure of offices and departments, reducing the number of locals and redundancies among staff. The point remains, however, that a union embarking on such cuts may opt for a merger as a means whereby services can be restored or improved and the jobs of union employees protected. In addition, the choice of merger partner may be influenced by the remuneration package offered to full-time officers by unions competing to complete an acquisition (Conant, 1993).

Influence of Bargaining Structure

The establishment of national bargaining for particular trades during the twenty years around the turn of the twentieth century promoted some mergers in the pottery, stove and glass industries (Ulman, 1955: 519-535). Wide-ranging national industrial bargaining in the European sense was not established, however, so pressure for the wholesale reform of craft organisation through mergers was limited. The combined influence of employers, concerned to resist rank and file pressure, and the activities of the War Labor Board acted to promote pattern bargaining,[11]

---

[11]   In pattern bargaining the wage settlement concluded by management and a union at a major bargaining unit serves as a guide for settlements in other units. The pattern

which was influential in, amongst others, the automobile, steel, road transport and meat packing industries until the late 1970s (Kochan, 1980: 113-121). Such bargaining arrangements promoted mergers as unions sought to join those unions that 'set' the pattern. The International Union of Mine, Mill and Smelter Workers (IUMMSW), for example, elected to merge with the USWA in 1967 because its financially precarious position resulted in employers attempting to set the pattern with it, rather than with stronger unions in the industry (Chitayat, 1979: 46-48). Within the USWA the acquisition of the IUMMSW presented the opportunity to prevent employers using the weakened position of the IUMMSW to undermine the bargaining position of members of the USWA. Pattern bargaining thus encouraged mergers among unions in the same or similar industries.

The decentralisation of bargaining to company and plant level contributed to the establishment of a different merger dynamic. In the context of decentralised bargaining, the sheer size of the country made it more difficult for smaller unions to support geographically dispersed memberships. Furthermore, the system of exclusive jurisdiction operated by the AFL-CIO made it difficult for unions with jurisdictions in areas of employment contraction to embark on expansionary recruitment initiatives. Both of these pressures promoted the sharp rise in the merger process comprising acquisitions after 1974 (see Table 11.2), as small unions sought access to the support facilities of their larger counterparts and larger unions in areas of employment contraction sought to expand their jurisdictions. The absence of any national industrial bargaining institutions resulted in few limits to the extent of diversifying merger activity. In practice, smaller unions seeking support chose the merger partner that offered the best package of support, irrespective of the industrial origins of the acquiring union. In contrast to other countries covered by this volume, there is also evidence to suggest that employers try to influence trade unionists involved in mergers. 'Merger initiatives are more likely to be successful in situations where the employer is less likely to conduct an intensive "vote no" campaign' (McClendon *et al.*, 1995: 19).

The merger process was also influenced by changes in bargaining structure brought about by legislation. The cases of post and state employees illustrate the impact of legislative change on bargaining structure and the merger process.

---

may be followed in the industry within which the major bargaining unit operates and, in some circumstances, in related industries.

The Postal Reorganisation Act 1970 introduced a system of central-ised bargaining for the Postal Service and brought the Service within the framework of the NLRB. The legislation replaced a system whereby improvements in terms and conditions for postal workers were secured by reference to federal legislation. Before 1970 the seven unions that were recognised within the Postal Service co-ordinated their activities through a federation, the Council of American Postal Employees (CAPE). Within several of the affiliates of CAPE, the enactment of the Postal Reorganisation Act promoted consideration of a structural ad-justment, to participate in the new centralised bargaining arrangements. In practice, the unions sought to centralise their structure to 'match' that of the bargaining structure. Two issues pervaded attempts to reform union structure. First, the largest union in the Postal Service, the Na-tional Association of Letter Carriers (NALC), was concerned to main-tain a dominant position. Second, several postal unions represented craft or occupational interests and, in consequence, were relatively small, but wished to retain their identity within any post-merger structure.

During 1970 and 1971 five craft and occupational unions, which or-ganised a combined membership of 280,000 members, concluded a merger to form the American Postal Workers' Union (APWU). The post-merger structure of the APWU comprised four Craft Divisions, each of which represented one of the pre-merger unions. Only the National Postal Union (NPU) was not accorded such a status (Dewey 1971). The NPU was an independent union that had broken away from the United Federation of Postal Clerks (UFPC) in 1958 and continued to organise similar grades. Hence, the memberships of the NPU and the UFPC were largely assigned to the same post-merger Craft Division. The divisional structure of the APWU thus ensured the retention of craft identities. This was particularly important for the National Association of Post Office and General Service Maintenance Employees, the Na-tional Federation of Post Office Motor Vehicle Employees and the National Association of Special Delivery Messengers, the combined membership of which was no more than 25,000 at the time of the merger.

Almost immediately after the announcement to reform the Postal Service in 1967, the National Association of Post Office Mail Handlers, Watchmen, Messengers and Group Leaders (NAPOMH), with a mem-bership of 32,000, signalled an intention to form a section of LIUNA. The NAPOMH competed for members with several of the unions that went on to form the APWU. A merger with LIUNA thus represented the opportunity to retain some independence for the NAPOMH while also securing access to the support facilities offered by LIUNA. The acquisi-tion of the NAPOMH was ratified by a narrow majority at a special convention of the union and became effective in April 1968 (Chitayat, 1979: 81-82). Some NAPOMH representatives subsequently challenged this acquisition in the courts. These representatives sought involvement in the then ongoing APWU merger discussions, where the divisional structure under discussion offered opportunities for NAPOMH members to retain some autonomy. Although the courts upheld the acquisition, thus supporting the position of LIUNA, the NAPOMH remained a financially independent Division of LIUNA with a separate constitution.

The NALC remained apart from the merger to form the APWU, as it had been able to exert influence on the terms of the legislative reform of the Postal Service (Fink, 1977: 182-183). In other words, the NALC retained sufficient influence to justify maintaining its independence. Legislation to reform the bargaining arrangements within the Postal Service thus prompted substantial reforms of union structure. The federal structure adopted by the APWU facilitated the merging of different craft and occupational interests. Furthermore, it allowed the formation of a union that could challenge the position of the NALC.

Throughout the post-war period workers employed by state governments were represented by either trade unions or state employee associations. State employee associations tend to rely on lobbying rather than collective bargaining or strikes and are inclusive insofar as they incorporate supervisory and managerial staff, who were often reluctant to join trade unions (Nelson, 1973; Steiber, 1973). This division in worker representation was initially underpinned by the weak legal position of public sector employees regarding the settlement of their terms and conditions of employment. The growth of public sector employment between 1960 and 1975, however, was accompanied by legislation that provided unionisation and bargaining rights, and President Kennedy's Executive Order, issued in 1962, that authorised unionism and collective bargaining for federal employees (Lewin, 1986). Public sector unionisation rates rose sharply and competition between trade unions and state employee associations heightened. In order to secure broader influence, several employee associations formed a federation, the Assembly of Governmental Employees (AGE), through which it was anticipated some economies of scale might be realised. By the mid-1970s over 650,000 members were attached to the AGE through more than twenty state associations (Troy and Sheflin, 1985: A-3). The extension of collective bargaining and the growth of strike activity during the 1970s, among state employees and in the public sector generally (Lewin, 1986: 247), weakened the initial policy stance of AGE and the state employee associations. The relatively small size of the state employee associations precluded the economies of scale achieved by the major AFL-CIO affiliates with which they were in competition. Furthermore, the absence of bargaining and campaigning expertise limited the capacity of the associations to secure improvements for members. Although managers were less likely to support acquisition by a trade union, defections from AGE accelerated after the mid-1970s to the extent that AGE dissolved in 1985 (Cornfield, 1991). Changes in bargaining structure and practice, therefore, promoted mergers among public sector organisations as members of state employee associations sought improved forms of representation.

Confederal Policy and the Merger Process

The absence of any direct confederal constitutional authority over affiliated unions has limited the capacity of the AFL and the AFL-CIO to influence structural development. Confederal influence over the merger process in the US is thus similar to that of most other countries covered by this volume. In two regards, however, the pattern of confederal influence in the US is noteworthy. First, the merger of the AFL and the CIO was expected to generate a wave in merger activity as union structure was 'rationalised'. Second, the policy of expulsion implemented by the AFL, CIO and AFL-CIO indirectly stimulated merger activity.

Prior to the merger with the CIO in 1955, the AFL implemented two key policies regarding union structural development. First, the confederation relied on exclusive jurisdiction. Second, the AFL was precluded from interfering in the internal affairs of affiliated union. These two policies were contradictory when affiliated unions disputed jurisdiction over groups of workers. In situations where it proved impossible to resolve such disputes or where jurisdictions were too narrowly defined to sustain a separate union, the AFL encouraged mergers between affiliated unions. Furthermore, when affiliated unions refused to complete mergers recommended by the AFL, the confederation threatened expulsion, and, in several cases, expelled affiliated unions (Chaison, 1986: 20-21). Thus, prior to the emergence of the CIO, the AFL had a direct influence on the merger process. However, the merger process during this period was not extensive. Between 1900 and 1931, for example, only 29 mergers were completed within the AFL, the majority of which comprised the acquisition of a small, declining union (Lorwin, 1933: 343).

The terms of the merger between the AFL and the CIO necessitated a marked policy shift. In particular, the merger agreement between the two confederations stipulated that the jurisdiction of affiliated unions would remain unchanged and that each union would retain its autonomy. As both confederations had chartered unions to compete with each other since the mid-1930s, the confederal merger meant that overlapping jurisdictions were inevitable. To reduce these overlaps, the constitution of the AFL-CIO encouraged 'the elimination of conflicting and duplicating organisations and jurisdictions through the process of voluntary merger'. As is evident from Figure 1.10, however, the merger between the AFL and the CIO was not followed by a wave of merger activity involving affiliated unions. To the contrary, only 6 of the 36 mergers completed between 1956 and 1971 involved both a former AFL and a former CIO affiliated union (Janus, 1978). While these mergers certainly consolidated organisation in the paper, insurance, printing and food industries, the scale of merger activity did not meet expectations. Indeed, during this period AFL-CIO affiliated unions were more likely to acquire independent unions, rather than consolidate organisation by completing mergers of former AFL and former CIO affiliated unions.

Throughout the 1960 and 1970s the AFL-CIO maintained a position of supporting mergers between affiliated unions and provided support to unions involved in merger negotiations. No attempt was made to interfere in the internal government of affiliated unions. Recognising the paucity of progress, the AFL-CIO published a series of 'merger guidelines' in 1985, central to which was an understanding that mergers were more likely to be effective if the unions involved shared 'a community of interests based on their employment sector' (AFL-CIO, 1985: 33). A satisfactory community of interests was defined in terms of unions that organise members in industries that are vertically integrated or members that work for the same conglomerate company. In other words, the AFL-CIO offered guidance, which was intended to limit the extension of jurisdictions through merger involvement. As is apparent from the acquisitions completed by the larger unions, however, there is little evidence to suggest that several of these unions are restricting the breadth of their merger activity.

A second confederal impact on the merger process arises from the policy of expulsions. As mentioned above, the AFL expelled several unions before 1955 for failure to comply with confederal merger policy. In addition, eleven unions were expelled from the CIO during 1949 and 1950 and a further five from the AFL-CIO between 1957 and 1959 (Chaison, 1972). Underpinning these later expulsions were issues concerning corruption, financial irregularities, communist influence and dual unionism (*ibid.*). Once expelled these unions were no longer protected by the confederation from recruitment initiatives taken by affiliated unions. While several of the larger union were relatively unaffected by their confederal expulsion, smaller unions and unions that organised in areas of acute membership competition were adversely affected. In consequence, the overwhelming majority of the expelled unions either dissolved or merged, in most cases within five years of their expulsion (Chaison, 1972). Confederal expulsion thus indirectly contributed to an increase in merger intensity. The politics of these expulsions also influenced the choice of merger partner. In particular, the expelled unions that chose to merge tended to select another expelled union as a merger partner. The IBT, for example, implemented an extensive merger policy based on the acquisition of unions expelled from either the CIO or the AFL-CIO.

Conclusion: Has the Merger Process Made a Difference?

This chapter has shown that most mergers in the US are a reaction to some form of adverse environmental change. The hostility of employers towards unions, coupled to the weak industrial relations regulatory regime, resulted in long-term membership and density decline, which, in turn, promoted mergers. The politics of bargaining were compounded by a split in the confederations according to principle of union organisation and the operation of the doctrine of exclusive jurisdiction.

No overarching strategy has held sway over the US merger process, the character of which remains within the control of individual unions. Larger unions are characterised by rising membership heterogeneity and increases in the number of sections intended to accommodate such diversity. Furthermore, membership, finance and other resources are becoming more concentrated in these large, diverse unions. There is little evidence to suggest that these trends, and the contribution of the merger process to them, are likely to slacken in the immediate future. Indeed, the debate is couched in terms of how few AFL-CIO unions will remain, with estimates varying from two dozen (Chatak, 1991) to eleven (Masters, 1997).

The merger process has thus transformed US trade union structure, but has it enabled unionists to confront broader challenges? With reference to reversing the decline in membership and density, the answer is an unequivocal 'no'. The long-term decline in membership and density has accelerated as the merger process has intensified. As was demonstrated above, some unions have used mergers as a substitute for organising and have thus enhanced their position without influencing aggregate trends. More recent efforts to shift from 'servicing' to 'organising' approaches may be facilitated by the concentration of resources that has arisen from the merger process. Analyses of national union organising efforts and results among the larger unions (Fiorito *et al.*, 1995; Fiorito, 2003), however, indicate that merger involvement is not a key variable. Unions with high involvement in merger activity (SEIU and UFCW) were highly committed to organising, as were unions with infrequent merger involvement, such as the Hotel Employees and Restaurant Employees International Union. Mergers may thus contribute to the concentration of resources, but preparedness to adopt an organising approach is independent of merger engagement.

The evidence on the impact of the merger process on membership participation and involvement is not clear-cut. The creation of huge unions with diverse memberships may 'distance' members from union decision-making. The formation of the United Transportation Union, for example, was viewed by members as essential to preserve the bargaining position of railway workers, but undercut the shared identities held by different groups within the workforce and the 'mutual aid logic' through which these groups cohered, with damaging consequences for their union participation (Bacharach *et al.*, 2001: 69-72). Similarly, rank-and-file movements expressed concern for union democracy during the merger discussions involving the IAM, UAW and USWA (*Labor Notes*, 1995; 1996). Greater centralisation of control over the control of collective agreements is also associated with rising membership heterogeneity (Hendricks *et al.*, 1993). As the merger process increases membership heterogeneity, it would thus appear to be linked with the centralisation of union control. Critics of this position argue that post-merger forms of sectional representation protect members' identity and interests and, hence, do not lead to falling participation rates (Chaison, 2001). In a similar vein, the post-merger sectional representation allowed to the National Brotherhood of Packinghouse and Industrial Workers (NBPIW) when acquired by the UFCW in 1989 enabled former NBPIW members to remain as a cohesive unit, which now forms the opposition to the leadership of the UFCW (Strauss, 2000). It thus seems likely that the terms and politics of each merger case differ and post-merger membership participation is, in part, a function of these features.

The absence of formal ties between the union movement and the Democratic Party means that increasing relative membership size through merger involvement does not lead to increases in direct national political influence, as in several Western European countries. Acquisition may enable a small union to gain access to the more extensive lobbying facilities maintained by larger unions. Such an effect is particularly marked at state and local levels (Chaison, 2001). Although unions continue to offer financial and other support to pro-union candidates at all levels within the polity, it has proved insufficient to secure support for legislation that would strengthen the position of unions. The impact of mergers on political activity is thus primarily restricted to the concentration of resources and the deployment of these resources in lobbying.

Similarly to organising and membership participation, union bargaining effectiveness is dependent upon many factors additional to the merger process. Employer hostility and contracting rates of economic growth, for example, clearly impinge on collective bargaining outcomes. Bearing these points in mind, however, it is apparent that mergers may strengthen union bargaining capacities. The acquisition of a small, declining trade union by a large, well-resourced union is one of the clearer cases. In such circumstances access to the greater reservoir of resources held by the acquiring union may enhance the bargaining position of the smaller union. In general, however, unions have been unable to prevent employers from decentralising bargaining arrangements, which has raised the number of bargaining units and, hence, union operating costs.

In brief the merger process in the US has been primarily a defensive measure to retain members of declining unions within the union movement. Although merger policies have contributed to the membership growth achieved by some unions, aggregate decline in density has been a feature since the early 1950s. In other words, more radical measures than structural readjustment through the merger process are required to reverse the decline of the past fifty years.

List of Abbreviations

AFL   American Federation of Labor

AFL-CIO   American Federation of Labor – Congress of Industrial Organizations

AFT   American Federation of Teachers

AFSCME   American Federation of State, County and Municipal Employees

AGE   Assembly of Governmental Employees

APWU   American Postal Workers Union

AWPPL   Association of Western Pulp and Paper Workers

CAPE   Council of American Postal Workers

CIO   Congress of Industrial Organizations

CWA   Communication Workers of America

GAIU   Graphic Arts International Union

GCIU   Graphic Communications International Union

IAM   International Association of Machinists and Aerospace Workers

IBEW   International Brotherhood of Electrical Workers

IBPSPMW   International Brotherhood of Pulp, Sulphite and Paper Mill Workers

IBT   International Brotherhood of Teamsters, Chauffeurs, Warehousemen and Helpers

IUMMSW International Union of Mine, Mill and Smelter Workers

LIUNA   Laborers' International Union of North America

LMG   Labor-Management Group

LPIU   Lithographers and Photo-engravers International Union

NALC   National Association of Letter Carriers

NAPOMH National Association of Post Office Mail Handlers, Watchmen, Messengers and Group Leaders

NBPIW   National Brotherhood of Packinghouse and Industrial Workers

NEA   National Education Association

NLRA   National Labor Relations Act

NLRB   National Labor Relations Board

NPU   National Postal Union

PATCO   Professional Air Traffic Controllers Organization

SEIU   Service Employees International Union

UAW   United Automobile, Aerospace and Agricultural Implement Workers of America

UBC   United Brotherhood of Carpenters and Joiners of America

UFCW   United Food and Commercial Workers' Union

UFPC   United Federation of Postal Clerks

UPIU   United Paperworkers International Union

UPP   United Papermakers and Paperworkers

URCLPW United Rubber, Cork, Linoleum and Plastic Workers

USWA   United Steelworkers of America

WWML   Wood, Wire and Metal Lathers International Union

CHAPTER 12

Closer Working between Unions

The Impact of the Bargaining Framework

Jesper DUE and Berndt KELLER

The point of departure for this chapter is the well-known hypothesis that the structure of collective bargaining influences union structure in a specific way (Clegg, 1976). The degree of centralisation of bargaining forces trade unions to adapt their decision-making processes so that they function effectively at the decisive bargaining levels. If the existing union structure does not hinder effective decision-making in a particular bargaining system, then the bargaining system will legitimate existing union structure. Changes to the bargaining structure may put union structure under pressure, especially if union structure becomes an obstacle to the adoption of new forms of bargaining (Clegg, 1976). Thus, we expect that changing collective bargaining structures will have an impact on different forms of mergers.

The argument of this chapter is presented in the following sequence. In the first section we distinguish different forms and consequences of closer working, including cartels as well as mergers. The second section elaborates the relationship between changing bargaining structures and mergers. The third section deals with the interests of employers and employers' associations in trade unions mergers, whereas the fourth section discusses the changing interests of the state. The fifth and concluding section investigates emerging future consequences of mergers for the supranational, particularly the European, level of interest representation.

Throughout this 'horizontal' chapter we make use of the detailed descriptions within the country chapters using their range of information as 'stylised facts' for the explanation of our specific, comparative issue. The general caveat is that uniform patterns are difficult to detect and general answers are difficult to find. The argument of the chapter is that various formalised forms of closer working including, among others, mergers and cartels, can be regarded as functional equivalents in certain institutional bargaining arrangements, although their organisational consequences differ significantly. Specific advantages and disadvantages of the two forms also depend on institutional and legal circumstances.

Mergers and Cartels as Specific Forms of Closer Working

The general term 'forms of closer working' is indefinite and refers to quite different modes and qualities of inter-union co-operation. We focus our analysis on the specific forms of closer working that require at least some formal protocol or agreement signed and implemented by the participating organisations. These formalised variants of co-operation include mergers, as their closest possible form, and cartels of unions. In obvious contrast to mergers, the main, if not only, purpose of cartels is relatively limited. In Nordic countries cartels serve as bargaining coalitions for a range of specific issues, including wages, salaries and pensions. These issues are dealt with, first of all at national, but sometimes also at the sectoral or the industrial level. The constellation of interests is different in Southern Europe where cartels are primarily agents for political lobbying with the government rather than bargaining agents with employers.

For some countries – common platforms in Portugal and *Verhandlungsgemeinschaften* (bargaining coalitions) in Germany, among others – there is empirical evidence that some forms of less formal co-operation have also been used for other purposes. These include lobbying or consultation for statutory regulation in the public sector.[1] Such informal arrangements may, but do not necessarily, lead to other closer forms of co-operation and in a small number of cases even to mergers. Austria provides another interesting example for this specific constellation of interests (see Chapter 3).

The vertical chapters of this volume clearly demonstrate that cartels of unions do not exist in all countries. They have been part of trade union structure in the Nordic countries; or, to be more precise, in some of them in their private rather than their public sectors. Denmark is an unusual case, in that bargaining cartels are important in the private sector and are predominant in the public sector. Cartels are absent in Austria, Germany, the UK and the US, where mergers have clearly

---

[1]   A systematic analysis of the public sector and the increasing dominance of public sector unions is beyond the scope of this chapter. It is quite remarkable, however, that mergers between private and public sector unions have recently taken place in a range of different countries, including Germany and the UK. From first principles, one would have expected sectoral borderlines to create major barriers to mergers.

dominated. The explanation is fairly simple. The existence of cartels is more likely in countries with more than one confederation, irrespective of whether the confederations are differentiated by education and status or political and ideological cleavages. According to their numerous advocates, different forms of closer working, especially mergers, are supposed to deliver economies of scale. Whether the more efficient use of scarce resources takes place in practice or not is a completely different question. For the countries examined in this volume the empirical evidence favouring this rather optimistic expectation is less clear-cut than usually assumed and predicted before mergers take place. We suggest that economies of scale, at best, are restricted to a small and limited number of functions or tasks.

It is reasonable to argue that, in some regards and in the terminology of systems theory, cartels are, to a degree, functional equivalents of mergers. In other words, to be more cautious, in some countries they fulfil certain, if not many, functions that mergers are supposed to accomplish in others. Thus, in the majority of cases or countries, cartels are not something like mergers in their embryonic, first stages of gradual development towards the complete integration of unions. Quite the contrary, cartels are more or less viable alternatives with strict long-term perspectives and constitute sustained solutions to similar problems. In that regard it is typical that cartels in Denmark and Sweden are almost as old as the collective bargaining system. Co-operation through cartels in Denmark is clearly an alternative to mergers. A centralised bargaining structure dictated by both private and public employers forced the unions to closer working through cartels. The resistance against mergers was strong and forced the unions to use cartels as an alternative procedure to change internal structure. In other words, employers centralised decision-making power within collective bargaining, and unions centralised their structures by forming cartels while simultaneously retaining their independence.

To put this another way, empirical evidence indicates that mergers, which at present seem to be the major instrument of union reform, are more likely to happen and to be more frequent if cartels do not exist. Cartels do not constitute major barriers to mergers in a strict sense, as their lasting existence makes mergers less necessary and less urgent. They constitute realistic alternatives where mergers are either impossible or, at least, unlikely because of political reasons and/or lasting ideological difficulties between participating unions. Last, but not least, cartels are less defensive reactions towards fundamental changes in the environment than mergers in the vast majority of cases, as union 'external shape' is retained.

Certain strategic advantages of the cartel form of joint working are quite apparent. As members of cartels, unions can basically preserve their independence and their separate identity, for example, as professional or white-collar unions. Thus, they are able to avoid the protracted problems of post-merger integration that they would have to overcome if they merged. As members of a cartel, individual unions might not even think of the merger option as a serious alternative because basic and lasting differences of interest or political orientation between participating unions continue to exist, but can be accommodated within the cartel structure. Furthermore, future secessions would be much easier than breakaways from post-merger unions. In other words, the exit option is a less expensive alternative in the case of cartels.

In the majority of countries where different forms of closer working exist, they are more likely to be intra-confederal than cross-confederal. Thus, the well-known barriers between confederations continue to exist in the case of cartels. These patterns can be found in the Nordic model of occupational confederations and the Southern European model of politically fragmented confederations. In Denmark the numerous small unions in the public sector faced serious problems in a highly centralised bargaining system, but initially secured the interests of their members through intra-confederal cartels, each of which was associated with a particular confederation. The employers subsequently wanted co-ordinated negotiations around general demands. The intra-confederal cartels thus had to take a step further and establish cross-confederal bargaining cartels in both the state and the municipal sectors. It was possible to cross confederal borders in a system with only minor ideological differences between the confederations, as is the case of the Nordic industrial relations systems. Such arrangements have not yet been possible in the ideologically divided Southern European models.

Our overall problem of forms of closer working includes horizontal dimensions that refer to changes in the relationships between individual unions and vertical dimensions that relate to changes in the relationships between umbrella or peak organisation(s) and their affiliated unions. From a theoretical point of view, the most far-reaching vertical consequences of various forms of closer working are to be expected in the case of mergers whereas horizontal consequences dominate in other forms. In empirical terms, the involvement of confederations in mergers of their affiliated unions is difficult to detect. With the exception of the ACTU (Australian Council of Trade Unions) in Australia (see Chapter 2), the influence of confederations is limited. In the majority of countries, confederations are neither major barriers to, nor active promoters of, mergers. Furthermore, where confederations have promoted mergers their impact on the merger process has been mitigated by an absence of constitutional authority. Affiliated unions independently choose and decide their future partners and tend to reject blueprints recommended by their confederations when they involve so-called 'logical' mergers, in terms of industry, sector or politics.

In various cases, the exact composition of forthcoming mergers is extremely difficult to predict, as are the precise results or outcomes of a relatively large number of long-lasting talks and negotiations about mergers. Vested and open self-interests of involved, individual and corporate actors tend to differ widely in their perceptions of the situation. In general, mergers across confederal boundaries are rather unlikely. The Danish case is a likely exception, as differences between the confederations are vanishing, making cross-confederal amalgamations a possible outcome of organisational development in the near future. Thus, the theoretically possible range of merger opportunities is fairly restricted. The overall number of mergers is correlated to the number of existing unions and their principles of organisation.

If the number of their affiliates is relatively large, confederations seem more likely to tolerate or even actively support and promote certain mergers for different reasons. These events diminish neither their internal impact on decision-making processes nor their external or political influence on other corporate actors, the government and wider public opinion. To the contrary, mergers could even strengthen the overall power of the confederation. Therefore, it is no coincidence at all that the ACTU in Australia has played an active role in the merger process, while simultaneously offering new services, including strategies of organising, to the remaining affiliates.

When the overall number of unions affiliated to a confederation is relatively small, the internal power of the confederation *vis-à-vis* affiliates is likely to diminish if mergers reduce the number of affiliates even further. As voting rights of affiliates are usually determined by membership size, the larger, post-merger affiliates will have, and will possibly make use of, increased voting power in intra-organisational disputes. In such cases, support of the confederation is less likely, irrespective of its constitutional and/or empirical authority.

Within the vertical relationships between umbrella or peak associations and their affiliates one could, of course, also reverse the perspective and analyse them from the members' point of view. Post-merger unions will increase in terms of their own absolute resources, although not necessarily per member resources, and, in consequence, they may not need as much support from their confederation. Furthermore, their aggregate impact on processes of decision-making within their confederation will increase because their share of the overall membership has grown. Recent prominent examples include UNISON and TUC in the UK as well as ver.di (Unified Services Union) and DGB (German Trade Union Confederation) in Germany (Waddington *et al.*, 2003). Mergers may also concentrate decision-making processes within confederations regarding external relationships and acting as a pressure group *vis-à-vis* the political system, including political parties. These external effects are to be expected not only for divided or multiple confederations, as in Southern Europe or Nordic countries, but also for the equally frequent case of single or unified confederations, as in Austria, Germany, UK or the US.

The Impact of Bargaining Structure on Mergers

At first glance, the relationship between the independent and the dependant variable seems to be evident. Changes in the bargaining structure can be initiated, according to institutional preconditions, either by individual employers or their associations and/or by the state as the major 'driving forces'. They will promote corresponding changes in union structure, which may include mergers. The historical evidence from the UK and Australia provides strong support for the impact of this relationship. Changes in bargaining structure promoted union mergers: initially centralisation towards national or multi-employer bargaining; subsequently, towards decentralisation (Waddington, 1995). Similarly, change to the Australian arbitration system resulted in pressures to reform union structure, which, in the context of the political Accord, allowed the ACTU to implement a policy of reform. In the Danish case, the outcome of the pressure of a centralised collective bargaining system has been the formation of bargaining cartels as an alternative to mergers, thus placing the decision-making power at the required level of collective bargaining without changing external trade union 'shape'.

In general, strongly centralised confederations and bargaining structures may act as a barrier both to cross-confederal mergers and to mergers between unions affiliated to the same confederation. The centralisation of LO-Sweden following the signing of the basic agreement with SAF (Swedish Employers' Confederation) in 1938 was sufficient to coordinate affiliated unions during the long period of centralised bargaining that commenced during the 1950s. Mergers were, therefore, not given high priority by the LO leadership. Instead, they were considered as practical issues to be dealt with by each individual union on the basis of its specific interests (Hadenius, 1976: 159). In Denmark labour legislation introduced in the 1930s had similar centralising effects on collective bargaining (see Chapter 4). The power of the public conciliator to link ballots on draft settlements made the formal centralisation of

LO (Danish Confederation of Trade Unions) more or less superfluous. It also meant that mergers between the affiliated unions became less urgent for many decades.

The incentives for reforming traditional union structures and merging the many small unions were also weakened by the establishment of bargaining cartels which fulfilled important co-ordinating functions, above all, in the public sector. In Norway, Sweden and Denmark public sector wage negotiations were also centralised by the introduction of bargaining cartels, which were demanded by the state as an employer. Forced to co-operate more closely, the Swedish LO unions within the state sector, however, chose to amalgamate in 1970. Within a few years the Cartel of State Servants functioned as a provisional bargaining co-ordinator, but did not meet the demands of the state as a centralised bargaining partner. The reason was that the LO constitution did not permit the forming of real bargaining cartels among its affiliated unions (Hadenius, 1976: 152). A large number of other mergers among public sector unions in the second half of the 1960s and early 1970s can partly be attributed to the policy of the Swedish government to centralise public sector wage negotiations. Similarly, the large wave of acquisitions within the Danish white-collar confederations FTF (Confederation of Salaried Employees and Civil Servants) and AC (Confederation of Professional Associations) was accelerated by the introduction of collective bargaining in the public sector. In contrast to their Swedish equivalents, the AC unions have no bargaining rights in the private sector.

In the Danish metal industry the cartel CO-Metal (Central Organisation of Metal Workers) in the 1990s was widened to include all of manufacturing and unions for blue-collar and white-collar workers, with the exception of unions affiliated to AC. The cartel was renamed CO-Industri (Central Organisation of Employees in Industry). The Swedish manufacturing cartel FI (Unions within Manufacturing) includes primarily unions affiliated to LO, but also includes two white-collar unions affiliated to other confederations. By bringing these unions closer to each other, this cartel might function as an intermediate step towards future mergers. The emergence of FI also encourages unions within private services to merge or to form new alliances to secure their influence. On the other hand, the bargaining cartel founded by the Swedish printing unions in the mid-1920s was a means of forestalling LO demands for a merger (see Chapter 9).

These primarily Nordic examples of forms of closer working through cartels support Clegg's (1976) theory of the influence of collective bargaining on union structure. If we include other countries in the analysis, the overall picture becomes more complicated and trends are less apparent. Mergers can leave the overall organisation, structure and processes of collective bargaining basically untouched. In this case the new, larger union will be required to develop more differentiated organisational sub-structures. Furthermore, it will have to offer a broader, more attractive range of services to its members than its more homogeneous predecessors. These processes of internal restructuring are necessary because post-merger unions have to provide and guarantee ample opportunities for the representation of group-specific or sectional interests within bargaining structures. These protracted processes of further intra-organisational differentiation and higher degrees of bargaining autonomy for specific groups of members reflect the growing diversity and heterogeneity of members' interests. These are an almost necessary consequence of mergers that result in general or multi-industry unions.

In other words, increasing complexity and new challenges for union governance result from the gradually changing patterns of employment and composition of the labour force, *and* from the reform of trade union structure. Indeed, several mergers have been the occasion when reforms have been introduced to systems of trade union government that otherwise might not have occurred. New procedural provisions introduced during the UNISON (Waddington *et al.*, 2003) and ver.di mergers (Keller, 2001), for example, were intended to foster the participation and representation of hitherto under-represented groups of members.

The development of these new, highly differentiated provisions for interest aggregation and intermediation will be the most likely result in all cases of large-scale, vertical mergers with vertical directions, because the heterogeneity of members' interests will increase to a high degree. Predictions about the most likely effects of mergers on organisational structures are even more difficult if 'anything goes'; that is, for mergers with all possible directions including horizontal ones. The most realistic outcome might be the development of a purely additive structure reflecting the sum of the formerly existing old structures.

Historical and more recent evidence demonstrates that mergers can contribute or lead to some rationalisation of bargaining structures, such as the establishment of a smaller number of broader 'bargaining units' and more encompassing collective contracts. Australia provides the most prominent example. Such developments would be the expected result in cases of fragmented and fairly decentralised industrial relations systems, especially 'enterprise bargaining', with a rather high number of comparatively small unions and, therefore, a fairly high number of possible mergers.

One frequent expectation or intended result of mergers is the disappearance, avoidance or 'blurring' of all demarcation and/or jurisdictional disputes and all accompanying inter-union rivalry and conflicts on different issues such as recruitment, services or bargaining. In empirical perspective, however, this assumption refers to the constellation *within* the new organisation only. These borderlines also constitute a major handicap for encompassing bargaining structures. An unintended consequence of mergers, however, could be the emergence of new *external* demarcation disputes; that is, with other extant and competing unions. In other words, mergers that result in general or multi-industry unions instead of other organisational structures, such as craft, occupational or industrial unions, might either solve or, at least, contribute to the solution of internal problems of interest aggregation and representation. Such mergers, however, might create additional problems or, at least, perpetuate other difficulties of external relations. Thus, existing problems of inter-union rivalry and competition will be reduced, or in some cases even eliminated, only internally. They could, however, either persist or even be aggravated externally. Thus, the degree of simplification of previously existing structures remains limited. In any case, it would be highly unrealistic to expect that mergers would be able to provide solutions for all problems of demarcation.

Consequences of Decentralisation

We now turn to the impact of more recent tendencies towards flexibilisation and the decentralisation of collective bargaining structures in general on mergers. Processes of decentralisation have occurred in the majority of countries included in this study. It is important to note from the outset that these processes of decentralisation can take quite different forms and may lead to rather different outcomes (Traxler, 1996). They can follow a co-ordinated path, as in the Nordic countries, Austria and Germany, or an uncoordinated path, as in the UK and US. Decentralisation leads, almost by definition, to a greater number of bargaining units and, thus, to considerably higher costs on the union side if previously established bargaining coverage rates are to be sustained. These gradual developments towards decentralisation in the forms of company agreements and, in some cases, individualisation of bargaining, could indirectly increase the likelihood or necessity of forms of closer working. For example, they might promote mergers for purely economic reasons, because union operating expenses increase, such as the expenditure incurred to support the system of bargaining.

The consequences of these different forms of decentralisation are somewhat counter-intuitive, but are supported by empirical evidence from different countries. The trend towards smaller bargaining units leads to (or maybe even requires) more effort towards concertation, namely cartels or larger, merged unions instead of smaller ones. This is especially the case if processes of decentralisation take place in an uncoordinated form. As already mentioned, post-merger unions have to develop more differentiated internal sub-structures for the representation of sectional interests. This necessity is compounded by the requirement to expand their capacity for coping with consequences of decentralisation. In countries where co-ordinated decentralisation dominates, this relationship seems to be less clear. Major adaptations seem to be less urgent because existing structures prevail, and different forms of opening clauses can be introduced and used as instruments to bridge the widening gap. The exact impact on the direction of mergers, however, is difficult to detect.

Within the highly co-ordinated Danish decentralisation process, pressures on unions to merge have arisen because of the simultaneous process of organisational centralisation on the employers' side. It is, therefore, often labelled 'centralised decentralisation' (Due *et al.*, 1994). A large number of employers' associations are in the process of merging to form a few sector-wide organisations. For example, DI (Confederation of Danish Industries) now covers all of manufacturing. In consequence of the re-organisation introduced by employers to produce DI, trade unions in manufacturing are strengthening and widening their closer working, although the final outcome of the process is still uncertain.

For the majority of countries included in our study, longitudinal data for the decades since the 1950s show that the overall number of unions has considerably decreased (see Figure 1.1). The average size of trade unions, measured in terms of the number of members per union, has significantly increased (see Table 1.1). The 'threshold for viability' thus appears to have increased. These trends can also be detected during the period of decentralisation of bargaining since the 1980s and even more in recent periods of declining overall membership and density, which have led to deteriorating union finance and power, and, therefore, weakened unions.

Employers' Interests in Mergers

Advocates of mergers argue that they increase union bargaining power and, thus, the overall impact of the new, larger union. As the vertical chapters illustrate, the possibility of increases in bargaining power has to be taken into account. Employers' interests, therefore, may be affected by decisions of unions to merge. Employers' specific interests in different forms of closer working are difficult to determine and their reactions are difficult to assess. Furthermore, employers' strategies have significantly changed over time and have differed between countries. It is apparent, however, that employers can exert influence either directly on union decisions to merge or indirectly via the promotion of changes in legislation.

Generally, it seems as if the influence of employers' actions on merger decisions and processes has considerably changed over time from hostility, whether open or latent, in the late-nineteenth and early-twentieth centuries towards toleration, or even acceptance in more recent times. In general terms, the impact of employers on mergers has not been exceptionally strong. The recent case of ver.di in Germany is a prototypical example. Employers' organisations have not shown any major interest or even offered public statements on the very unusual case of a merger of five unions in Germany (Keller, 2001).

Employers may prefer one and only one union per workplace or per plant. Under more centralised legal-institutional preconditions they may prefer one union per sector or industry. In these circumstances employers reject pluralistic and more complicated systems of multi-unionism. Savings in transaction costs, especially bargaining costs, is the major reason underpinning this position. Where multi-unionism already exists, employers may support mergers in the expectation of lower costs arising from labour conflicts, particularly inter-union disputes. In an historical perspective Australia and the UK constitute the major examples that support this line of reasoning leading to a reduction in the number of unions. Employers' organisations, for example, supported the 'easing' of the legislative requirements for mergers in the UK in 1964 in order that union mergers could be promoted (Waddington, 1995).

In contrast, employers may pursue a divide-and-rule strategy and thus impede the merger process. If there are many, relatively small, unions it is likely that none of them will be very strong and thus managerial prerogatives will not be seriously challenged. In this case, different kinds of attempt to prevent mergers could include political pressure on the state to support this strategy by legislative means. This may include employer lobbying on the terms of recognition procedures or, in the case of the UK, lobbying to prevent any easing of the legal requirements for merger, as occurred during the first half of the twentieth century (Elias, 1973). In this regard the sheer size of enterprises may influence the position of employers. Employers operating small and medium-sized enterprises would most likely prefer relatively small partners because large opponents could create a major threat, especially in collective bargaining. Larger enterprises, such as multinational companies, would be more interested in strong unions that might help to reduce transaction costs and to rationalise existing relationships.

In comparative perspective we should, however, distinguish between the interests of individual employers and employers' organisations or, where appropriate, general business associations. The first form exists in 'monistic', fairly decentralised systems of industrial relations, the second in all 'dual' systems where the sectoral and/or industrial level still matters, despite far-reaching trends towards decentralisation. Employers' associations should be particularly interested in strong partners, which they need not only for collective bargaining purposes, but also for various forms of political exchange and co-ordination. From the little evidence available, however, their impact, at least on the result of the merger process, has not been very important.

Employers and employers' associations can exert a strong indirect influence on the merger process via the system of collective bargaining. Danish employers in both the private and public sectors, for example, acted to ensure that a form of centralised collective bargaining was established, thus bringing pressure to bear on trade union structure and its reform by means of the merger process. For the unions it was impossible to avoid structural changes in these circumstances. The form of closer working chosen, however, remained a question for the unions to decide. There have been both amalgamations and acquisitions, but the preference in Denmark has been the establishment of different forms of bargaining cartels.

The Interest of the State in Mergers

The state has to be considered as the 'third', widely neglected corporate actor within industrial relations systems. In the context of mergers, the state can usefully be conceptualised as a legislator or regulator. The overall impact of the state, or to be more precise, the government, on mergers shows an enormous degree of historical and national diversity.

The state can, more or less actively, support or even drive and enforce mergers by applying different strategies of statutory regulation. In historical perspective, the Anglo-Saxon countries, especially Australia and the UK, provide strong and ample empirical evidence for this variant, in their imposition of legal restrictions on the merger process. Other approaches are also in evidence. The legal prescription of a minimum number of members per union is just one example of the actual existence of procedural thresholds. Denmark is here a special example. As a result of the close connection between the trade unions and the unemployment insurance funds, the state practically eliminated all small unions in LO. By legislating during the late 1960s, the Danish parliament stipulated that, in order to obtain state recognition and thus public support for an unemployment insurance fund, a minimum union membership of 1,000 was required. This threshold was subsequently raised to 5,000 by legislation enacted in 1979, albeit operative only from 1985.

As Chapter 4 demonstrates, unions with memberships below these thresholds merged in order to retain their unemployment insurance funds.

Interference in rules of union statutes and/or their constitution is another strategy adopted by the state. For example, the Labor-Management Relations (Taft-Hartley) Act, 1947 and the Labor-Management Reporting and Disclosure (Landrum-Griffin) Act, 1959 in the US restricted opportunities for membership growth and required unions to reform their systems of government. Similarly, in the UK a raft of legislation enacted by the Conservative governments between 1980 and 1993 contributed to membership decline and thus, indirectly, promoted mergers. In both of these instances, governments viewed union movements as inhibiting economic development and considered intervention necessary to change the relative disposition of power in bargaining. On the other hand, the state remains basically neutral within systems where bargaining autonomy and/or complete freedom of association are paramount. This kind of regulatory regime favours self-regulation by private actors, instead of active intervention by the state. This approach can be observed in the majority of countries. In Germany, among others, the state has definitely been a 'non-actor' and considers mergers to be purely an issue of internal union affairs. This is counter-intuitive in that one would have expected exactly the opposite constellation of interests, that is, a strong impact of the state within highly regulated or highly legalised systems, such as in Germany, and next to no impact in the case of traditionally 'voluntary' systems, such as in the UK.

Last, but not least, there is historical evidence from some countries that the state has also *de facto* increased the barriers to mergers. The legally prescribed approval of a qualified majority of the entire membership, or even the necessity of individual ballots before mergers are allowed to take place, constitute such relatively high barriers that are established by external legal provisions. Generally, the empirical evidence concerning the interest of the state is somewhat inconclusive or at least not unilaterally directed. The specific institutional conditions in Australia and the UK demonstrate that legislation can prevent or favour mergers depending on the kind of legislation and its terms, as well as the political opportunities and interests of individual governments and their relationship with the trade union movement.

Furthermore, the state could have some self-interest in a certain, albeit limited, rationalisation of existing union structures. These interests would lead to a smaller overall number of unions, on the assumption that those that remained would be more representative and would constitute more reliable partners for purposes of political exchange and concertation. Such approaches are only likely to be pursued by governments engaged in some form of neo-corporatist interest intermediation or, in more recent terminology, in related forms of social partnership and social dialogue. In this neo-corporatist or tripartite context it should be stressed, however, that most important from the perspective of the state are strong and representative confederations. The structure of trade unionism, in terms of the actual number of trade unions, is of less importance. In practice, the number of unions is important only in so far as it limits the ability of the confederations to act in the tripartite system.

The state could also be interested in more encompassing bargaining units and/or more centralised bargaining structures. This arrangement might lead to more favourable macro-economic results, in terms of employment, growth and price stability, among others. This seems to be the case, among others, in the public sector of various countries. Sweden is just one example of a country where the government demanded centralisation in the public sector. In Australia it was not limited to the public sector. In Denmark the state has also promoted a centralised collective bargaining system in both the private and the public sector, leading, for example, to strong centralised bargaining cartels in both the state and the municipal/county sector.

Outlook: The Impact of National Mergers at the International Level

To this point forms of closer working have been discussed with special reference to the consequences of mergers at national level. During times of growing internationalisation, 'globalisation' and forms of closer regional integration, however, closer working between unions embraces important transnational or supranational dimensions. These have been neglected in the existing literature on mergers.

The needs of institutionalised co-operation are of course different for individual countries and their unions. For Australia such an institutional need hardly exists, maintenance of membership in International Confederation of Free Trade Unions (ICFTU) being apparently the only basic requirement. Of course, this is not to argue that, in particular circumstances, wider forms of co-operation are not required. The recent Australian dock workers' strike, for example, benefited from wider support and co-operation. Such forms of co-operation, however, are beyond our remit, which focuses on more or less permanent forms of co-operation. In the case of the North American Free Trade Agreement, unions from the US and Canada, to date, have not engaged in any permanent forms of closer working. Quite the contrary is the case: US-based international unions have split up into their American and Canadian component parts, have not developed unified strategies for both countries, and a certain degree of hostility has prevailed.

Within the European Union, however, closer co-operation of some kind will be of increasing importance within the continuing processes of European integration. Towards the end of the 1990s, the launching of European Monetary Union created a political pressure that required increasing co-operation at the supranational level. These emerging needs will definitely not be restricted to national confederations and their European peak association, the European Trade Union Confederation (ETUC). They will also have to include different national member unions and their supranational counterparts, the European Industry Federations (EIFs), which are members of the ETUC. The major reason is that, even after an extended period of decentralisation, collective bargaining still takes place at the sectoral/branch level in the majority of European Union member states. The UK is the major exception to this pattern. Various forms of co-operation could be autonomous and sector-specific within national or supranational peak confederations.

The primary problem is that national interests may prevail and that significant transfers of scarce resources, in the form of personnel and mandates, are unlikely in the foreseeable future. Furthermore, union structures at European level do not correspond with the widely differing principles of organisation that prevail at the national level within all member states. Thus, individual national unions have to be members of different EIFs, even if no mergers have occurred.

How is the co-operation between national unions and their 'counter-parts' at supranational level, the EIFs, influenced by mergers? In our terminology, EIFs can be considered as specific forms of closer working at European level. First of all, merged unions will be able to increase their influence within EIFs because of their membership size and voting power. They will be members of a larger number of EIFs than their constituent, pre-merger parts and will have to re-organise their structures for this kind of co-operation. They will have to develop fairly sophisti-cated internal divisions of labour to represent the differing and more heterogeneous interests of their members within different EIFs. Fur-thermore, post-merger unions will need new internal instruments and structures for formal as well as informal co-ordination of these wider ranges of activities at European level. Otherwise, internal frictions and conflicts, as well as losses of external impact, will result.

Table 12.1: European Industry Federations

EUROPEAN INDUSTRY FEDERATION	YEAR OF ESTABLISHMENT	NUMBER OF MEMBER ORGANI- SATIONS	NUMBER OF MEMBERS (IN MILLIONS)	RECENT CONGRESS/ GENERAL ASSEMBLY
Transport Workers' Federation (ETF)[1]	1999	n.a.	3	1999
European Federation of Food Agriculture and Tourism (EFFAT)[2]	2000	120	2.6	2000
European Federation of Building and Wood Workers (EFBWW)	1958	49	2.4	1999
European Federation of Textile, Clothing and Leather (ETUF-TCL)	1964	47	1.5	2000
European Federation of Services and Communi- cation (Uni-Europa)[3]	2000	133	7	2000
European Metalworkers' Federation (EMF)	1971	59	6.4	1999
European Federation of Public Service Unions (EPSU)	1974	180	10	2000
European Trade Union Committee of Education (ETUCE)	1975	81	8	2001
European Federation of Journalists (EFJ)	1988	43	0.16	2001
European Mining, Chemical and Energy Federation (EMCEF)[4]	1996	119	3	2000

[1] Merger of FST (1958) and European affiliates of the ITF.
[2] Merger of EFA (1958) and ECF-IUF (1981).
[3] Merger of CI (1965), EURO-FIET (1972), EGF (1985) and EEA (1993).
[4] Merger of EFCGU (1988) and FEBV (1991).

As far as issues are concerned, this necessity does not refer to collective bargaining in the traditional national sense, which, at least for the time being and for the near future, does not exist at the European level. Union activity will be directed, *inter alia*, toward the development or stabilisation of sectoral social dialogue and to related forms of interest representation, including all forms of sector-specific lobbying activities. All these activities are likely to focus on 'soft' issues and are likely to exclude wages and salaries.

An impact in the opposite direction, from the EIFs towards mergers at national level, does not exist. Mergers of EIFs have occurred, United

Network International – Europe is the most prominent, recent example. Although there are exceptions, these mergers at European level have not generally been in accord with developments at national level. Thus, developments at both levels have been characterised by different patterns. These ongoing processes have created problems for the necessary re-organisation of internal and external forms of co-operation. Ver.di, for example, will be a member of the majority of existing EIFs with consequent difficulties of co-ordinating its internal structures and external organisational affiliations.

To date mergers have happened between unions at national level only. In the long term, however, at international level not only closer forms of co-operation such as EIFs, but also mergers, are likely to take place. They could create an additional, maybe even more viable option for national unions as an appropriate response to ongoing processes of internationalisation or, more specifically europeanisation. It is more likely that they will happen in highly internationalised sectors, such as transport or telecommunications, and not in 'national' sectors, such as major parts of the public sector. In Germany, TRANSNET, the union of railway employees, opted out of the merger process resulting in ver.di, arguing that purely national mergers could not cope with present and future challenges of European integration. One should, however, not underestimate the time needed for the completion of such experiments. In the near future, national unions will hardly be willing to transfer major parts of their scarce resource and, thus, to lose control.

List of Abbreviations

AC	Akademikernes Centralorganisation (Danish Confederation of Professional Associations)
ACTU	Australian Council of Trade Unions
CI	Communications International
CO-industri	Centralorganisationen af industriansatte (Central Organisation of Industrial Employees)
CO-Metal	Centralorganisationen af Metalarbejdere (Central Organisation of Metal Workers)
DGB	Deutsche Gewerkschaftsbund (German Trade Union Confederation)
DI	Dansk Industri (Confederation of Danish Industries)
ECF-IUF	European Committee of Food, Catering and Allied Workers' Unions within the International Union of Foodworkers
EEA	European Alliance of Media and Entertainment
EFA	European Federation of Agricultural Workers' Unions

EFCGU	European Federation of Chemical and General Workers' Unions
EGF	European Graphical Federation
EIF	European Industry Federation
ETUC	European Trade Union Confederation
EURO-FIET	European Regional Organisation of the International Federation of Commercial, Clerical, Professional and Technical Employees
FEBV	European Miners' Federation
FI	Facken inom industrin (Unions within Manufacturing)
FTF	Funktionærernes og Tjenestemændenes Fællesråd (Confederation of Salaried Employees and Civil Servants in Denmark)
FST	Federation of Trnasport Workers' Unions in the European Union
ICFTU	International Confederation of Free Trade Unions
LO	Landsorganisationen i Danmark (Danish Confederation of Trade Unions)
LO	Landsorganisationen (Swedish Confederation of Trade Unions)
SAF	Svenska Arbetsgivareföreningen (Swedish Employers' Confederation)
TRANSNET	Union of Railway Workers
TUC	Trades Union Congress
UNISON	Public Sector Union
ver.di	Vereinte Dienstleistungsgewerkschaft (Unified Services Union)

CHAPTER 13

Confederations and Mergers
Convenience Rather Than True Love

Christos A. IOANNOU and Anders KJELLBERG

The character and power of union confederations vary considerably between countries. How this variation affects mergers between national unions, as well as between confederations, is examined in this chapter. By considering alternative typologies of confederations a number of circumstances that facilitate or obstruct mergers are identified. With respect to the degree of confederal monopoly in a country, three main variants are discerned. First, unitary confederations are contrasted with multiple confederations, with the latter based upon either political/religious or occupational class/status divisions. Despite weakened political/religious links and blurring collar/sectoral borders, these divisions still constitute important obstacles to mergers between and across confederations. Second, strongly centralised and/or state-regulated industrial relations systems may, at least partly, function as substitutes for mergers and, consequently, make mergers appear less urgent. Third, the continued existence of craft and general unions may block confederal efforts to restructure along industrial lines.

The persistence of established union structures and major institutional obstacles to mergers are addressed in the first two sections of this chapter. The third section examines the extent to which confederations promote mergers; in particular, how actively they initiate and implement blueprints. Although we accept that, normally, individual unions decide whether to merge, we classify union confederations according to their activity and success in rationalising union structure.

Union Confederations: Persistence of Established Patterns in Most Countries

To establish a framework for the analysis, this section first classifies confederations. It then reviews the evidence on mergers between confederations and the impact of confederal splits on the trade union merger process. Finally, an assessment of the extent of the trade union merger process before and after confederal mergers is presented.

Types of Union Confederation

Union confederations may be classified by reference to a number of characteristics, including: political orientation; the degree of centralisation or decentralisation; whether they have a direct collective bargaining role or act only as umbrella organisations; the membership composition of affiliated unions and according to principle(s) of organisation, such as industrial, occupational or professional. A single confederation may thus be characterised as politically independent, decentralised, white-collar and professional. A typology based upon socio-economic, political or religious divisions between confederations in a country is presented here. Important dimensions within this typology are the prevalence or absence of such divisions, their strength, and how they are manifested between and/or within confederations. Three main categories of confederation arise from this typology in the late 1990s and early 2000s. As the Greek case illustrates, some countries may not readily be classified in a single category. Instead, they may be regarded as composite cases.

The first category comprises monopoly or almost complete domination of one union confederation, which covers all or almost all categories of worker. Examples of unitary confederations include the British TUC (Trades Union Congress), Austrian ÖGB (Austrian Trade Union Confederation) since 1945, German DGB (German Trade Union Confederation) since 1949, American AFL-CIO (American Federation of Labor-Congress of Industrial Organisations) since 1955, Irish ICTU (Irish Congress of Trade Unions) since 1959, and Australian ACTU (Australian Council of Trade Unions) since 1985. The Greek GSEE (General Confederation of Greek Workers) could also be classified in this group, as it is a monopoly that represents employees working under private law contracts. The existence of a second confederation, ADEDY (Confederation of Greek Civil Servants), which is the monopoly for civil servants, or employees working under public law contracts, however, may also lead Greece to be classified in the second category.

Confederations based on class and/or status, comprise the second category, which is labelled socio-economic unionism. It may be based on education or type of employment relationship (private law or public law) and is often influenced by political orientation. The Nordic countries, with their social democratic blue-collar confederations and politically independent white-collar confederations, are prime examples. In these countries, there is one confederation each for mainly blue-collar workers, university graduates and other white-collar workers (see Table 13.1). This pattern is most pronounced in Sweden and is least developed in Norway, where there are several overlaps between confederations. From a Nordic perspective, relatively large numbers of white-collar unions are affiliated to LO-Norway (Norwegian Confederation of Trade Unions), but in the private sector no attempts have been made to merge blue-collar and white-collar LO unions.

Table 13.1: Union Confederations in the Nordic countries

	BLUE-COLLAR	PROFESSIONAL	OTHER WHITE-COLLAR
Denmark	LO-Denmark	AC	FTF
Norway	LO-Norway	Akademikerne, partly UHO	YS, partly UHO
Sweden	LO-Sweden	SACO	TCO
Finland	SAK	AKAVA	STTK

The Greek confederations only partly correspond to the blue-collar/white-collar divide. They can, therefore, be allocated to the first, but also to the socio-economic category. The latter partly also applies to Switzerland with its white-collar confederation VSA (Confederation of Swiss Trade Union Associations) and socialist SGB (Swiss Trade Union Confederation), mainly organising blue-collar workers. The existence of a catholic confederation, CNG (Christian National Trade Union Confederation), however, places Switzerland more firmly in the third category.

The third category comprises confederations based on political/ideological and/or religious cleavages, or to abbreviate, ideology-based unionism. This does not mean that each of these confederations is homogenous, but rather is dominated by a certain orientation. Included in this group are France, Italy, Portugal, Spain, Switzerland and the Netherlands (Table 13.2). Dutch union structure has become more similar to that of the Nordic countries with the rise of the white-collar confederation MHP (Federation of White-collar Staff Organisations) and the merger between the socialist NVV (Dutch Confederation of Trade Unions) and catholic NKV (Dutch Catholic Trade Union Confederation) to form FNV (Confederation of Dutch Trade Unions). In contrast to the Nordic countries, mergers in the Netherlands partly have integrated blue-collar and white-collar unions (Visser and Waddington, 1996: 45).

Table 13.2: Union Confederations mainly based upon Political/ideological and Religious Cleavages

	CHRISTIAN	COMMUNIST	SOCIALIST AND/OR SOCIAL DEMOCRATIC	OTHERS
France	CFTC	CGT	CFDT	FO, CGC (white-collar) UNSA (white-collar)
Italy	CISL (catholic)	CGIL	UIL	
Netherlands	CNV (protestant)			FNV (socialist+catholic) MHP (white-collar)
Portugal		CGTP	UGT	
Spain		CC.OO	UGT	
Switzerland	CNG (catholic)		SGB	VSA (white-collar)

It is important to isolate any medium-term and long-term trends towards mergers or division and fragmentation at the confederal level. Regarding long-term trends, in most cases the starting point has been a unitary confederation, which, with the development of employment structure and industrial relations systems, has divided along political, religious or status cleavages. A hypothesis related to the present situation of shrinking union density in many countries and other major challenges facing unions is that this may promote a revival of unitary trade unionism. Most of the divisions still persist, with both the Nordic and the Southern European cases providing prominent examples, but new cross-confederal bargaining alliances indicate a trend towards a kind of *de facto* unitary trade union action. Growing economic and political internationalisation is also a driving force for increased union co-operation, not only at the international level, but also between confederations in each country. EU membership has brought Danish, Finnish and Swedish union confederations to intensify their co-operation within the Nordic Trade Union Confederation and the ETUC. To facilitate these activities and to make lobbying more effective, the three Swedish confederations have a shared office in Brussels.

Nordic union movements started in the unitary category, but with the rise of white-collar confederations, the monopoly of the Nordic blue-collar LOs was broken. As late as 1950, LO-Sweden (Swedish Confederation of Trade Unions) organised almost 80 per cent of all union members, despite the appearance of the white-collar confederations in 1944 (TCO, Swedish Confederation of Professional Employees) and in

1947 (SACO, Swedish Confederation of Professional Associations). With rising union density among the expanding number of white-collar workers, LO's share in 2002 had declined to 52 per cent. Similar developments took place in the other Nordic countries.

Sometimes changes have occurred in the course of a few years. Due to a profound political split, the Italian union movement in 1947 left the unitary category and moved to the ideology-based category. Something similar happened in Portugal when Intersindical (1975-78) was divided into the communist CGTP (General Confederation of Portuguese Workers) and the socialist UGT (General Union of Workers). In both cases, the splits occurred just a few years after the fall of fascist dictatorships and the rise of a unitary union movement. In France and Spain unitary confederations were also split after a short period of existence.

Some national systems have moved in the opposite direction. In Germany and Austria the pre-war split was overcome when the union movement was reconstructed after the fall of the Nazi regime. Political divisions were kept, however, as informal factions within the new unitary confederations. The Australian transition to unitary trade unionism took place only gradually, although the traditional, fragmented structures were retained within the increasingly encompassing peak organisation ACTU. Through successive acquisitions of white-collar confederations, by the mid-1980s the ACTU had established a monopoly position, quite contrary to the development in the Nordic countries, where white-collar confederations steadily expanded their share of union members.

Confederal Mergers and Confederal Splits

All confederal mergers in the Nordic countries hitherto have taken place at one or the other side of the collar division. The same applies to breakaways. Thus, the Finnish SAJ (Finnish Union Confederation) left the predominantly blue-collar SAK (Central Organisation of Finnish Trade Unions) in 1960. As few SAK unions escaped this social democratic split, collective bargaining became very complicated when competing unions outbid each other in their negotiation demands and resorted to strikes to obtain better settlements than their rivals. The employers' federation applauded the 1969 reunification, as inter-union rivalry was an obstacle to incomes policy (Lilja, 1992: 206-9). Although bargaining is co-ordinated across the border between the Finnish white-collar confederations STTK (Finnish Confederation of Technical/Salaried Employees) and AKAVA (Central Confederation of Professional Associations), recent attempts to merge them have failed (Kauppinen and Waddington, 2000: 189ff.). On the other hand, a small Swedish confederation of public sector staff associations joined SACO in 1974. Thirty years earlier the private sector white-collar confederation DACO (Central Organisation of Employees) amalgamated with 'old TCO', comprising public sector white-collar unions, into modern TCO. At its 1997 Congress, TCO declared it desirable to merge with SACO, but SACO is cold-hearted. All SACO unions are professional associations, which are profiting from the marked expansion of academic employment, while TCO consists of both horizontal and vertical unions, including many white-collar workers in lower and middle grades. The border between TCO and SACO unions is diluted because of the growing importance of university education in today's working life. A strengthened position in lobbying and public opinion is another motive for closer co-operation between the two white-collar confederations, which signed a co-operation agreement in 1996. In Sweden cross-confederal bargaining cartels were founded within manufacturing (comprising LO, TCO and SACO unions) and among public sector employees (TCO-SACO, see Chapter 9).

Of the Nordic countries, Sweden has the most far-reaching confederal separation of blue-collar unions, professional associations and other white-collar unions. Compared to LO-Sweden, its Danish, Finnish and Norwegian counterparts organise relatively large numbers of white-collar workers and consequently have more fluid borders with their closest white-collar neighbours. In Denmark, some mergers have occurred across LO (Danish Confederation of Trade Unions) and FTF (Central Confederation of Salaried Employees and Civil Servants; see Chapter 4) boundaries, but in contrast to Sweden no bargaining cartels exist across confederations. The recruitment areas of LO-Norway and YS (Confederation of Vocational Unions) markedly overlap. The intense membership competition has resulted in LO manoeuvring to prevent YS from joining the European Trade Union Confederation (ETUC). Both YS and AF (Federation of Norwegian Professional Associations), the predecessor to Akademikerne (Federation of Norwegian Professional Associations) were founded about thirty years after their Swedish equivalents. While YS comprises a smaller white-collar segment than Swedish TCO, AF had a much broader composition than Swedish SACO, which almost exclusively organises university graduates. Akademikerne was founded in 2000 when a number of dissatisfied unions of university graduates left AF, which was dissolved. The remaining unions founded the new confederation UHO (Confederation of Higher Education Unions, Norway) at the end of 2001. With the formation of Akademikerne, Norwegian confederal structure became more similar to the Swedish structure, although it remains more fragmented.

As in Sweden, there are very few cross-confederal union mergers in Norway.

In Australia three white-collar confederations successively (in 1979, 1981 and 1985) joined the increasingly dominant ACTU (see Chapter 2). In several countries, no separate white-collar confederations exist and single unitary confederations have a monopoly position, as with the Austrian ÖGB. The existence of separate blue-collar and white-collar unions within ÖGB has prevented the formation of autonomous white-collar unions outside the confederation (Traxler, 1998: 247). The German white-collar DAG (Union of Salaried Employees), which is more properly described as a trade union, rather than a confederation, joined the DGB in 2001 as a result of the ver.di (Unified Services Union) merger, while DBB (Union of Civil Servants) still stands apart as a separate confederation (see Chapter 5). Other mergers between confederations in the unitary confederal category comprise predominantly blue-collar confederations: the American AFL and CIO; which amalgamated in 1955 into AFL-CIO, and the Irish confederations Irish Trade Union Congress (ITUC) and Conference of Irish Unions (CIU) which reunited in the form of the ICTU in 1959. In Britain the space for separate white-collar unions within TUC has been strongly curtailed due to the rise of conglomerate unionism.

It is common that confederations based on political and/or religious cleavages include white-collar and blue-collar workers in the same unions. Together with the pronounced political character of unionism and the absence of effective mechanisms for joining different political currents in the same peak organisation, it is not surprising that separate white-collar confederations are established in these countries; for example, the Dutch MHP (1964-), French CGC (General Confederation of Managerial Staffs; 1944-) and UNSA (National Federation of Autonomous Unions; 1993-).

Strong political ties also explain why many countries in the ideology-based confederal category are characterised by periods of confederal splits and tense relations between confederations, followed by efforts to bring confederations closer together and to reunite them. Thus, French FO (Workers' Strength) left CGT (General Confederation of Labour) in 1948 in the wake of the Cold War. Almost simultaneously, the Italian CGIL (Italian General Confederation of Labour), created in 1944 as a unitary union movement during the resistance, split into communist CGIL, catholic CISL (Italian Confederation of Workers' Unions) and social democratic UIL (Italian Union of Labour). After its radicalisation in the 1960s the French Christian CFTC split in 1964 into socialist CFDT (French Democratic Confederation of Labour; the majority) and the Christian CFTC (French Confederation of Christian Workers). In

Italy the 'hot autumn' of 1969 was followed by strong pressures from below for bridging cleavages between unions affiliated to different confederations. Together with weakened party-political dominance over the unions, this resulted in the Unitary Federation CGIL-CISL-UIL in 1972-84. Union collaboration was further encouraged by a shared will to avoid a social collapse. It resulted in the 'national solidarity' government of 1976-79. After a new period of inter-union rivalry, the debate on union reunification has revived since the mid-1980s. France has experienced varying union alliances, but, on the whole, intense inter-union rivalry has dominated.

After the fall of the Portuguese and Spanish dictatorships during the 1970s, confederal splits followed short periods of unitary union movements. In Portugal, UGT was founded in 1978 by socialist and social democratic unions leaving Intersindical, while the Spanish socialist and social democratic UGT (Confederation of General Workers) was re-established in 1976 after the transformation of the workers commissions into the communist CC.OO (Workers' Commissions). A growing rapprochement between these two confederations, however, followed the break between UGT and the socialist government and strengthened union autonomy against political parties from 1987.

After the fall of the Greek dictatorship (1967-74), GSEE remained united. The informal *ad hoc* co-ordination of opposition unions, that expressed the same centrifugal tendencies as those operating in Portugal and Spain, illustrated by strong political ties with rising left-wing parties, was directed not to the founding of a separate confederation, but towards 'occupying' the existing one, GSEE. After the 1981 rise to power of the PASOK socialist party, socialists and communists jointly took control over GSEE and it was awarded legislated monopoly bargaining rights and was allowed to draw upon state financing for union activities (see Chapter 6). Together with the general weakness of Greek trade unionism, this explains why GSEE remains a unique case that does not follow the Southern European trend towards fragmentation, despite the strong political ties of its trade union factions. In contrast, Spanish and Portuguese unions after the mid-1970s moved faster and further away from state regulation of their internal affairs.

Mergers between and across Confederations

Do cross-confederal union mergers precede confederal mergers or do mergers between national unions occur after confederal mergers, or both? In the Nordic countries there have been very few cross-confederal mergers between trade unions, but also few confederal mergers. When Swedish DACO and 'old TCO' merged into modern TCO in 1944 not very many unions merged, which is explained by DACO being primarily a private sector confederation, while 'old TCO' unions recruited within the public sector.

The North American experience suggests that confederal mergers precede mergers between affiliated unions. The amalgamation of the AFL with the CIO in 1955 and the merger the following year between two Canadian confederations promoted much amalgamation activity in the 1960s and 1970s 'because rival unions in similar industries entered into merger negotiations in the aftermath of the mergers of labor (con)federations' (Chaison, 1996: 57). Similarly, the Finnish SAK-SAJ merger in 1969 preceded the unification of the national unions belonging to the two wings of the labour movement (Lilja, 1992: 207ff.). The Dutch FNV was formed as an umbrella organisation by the social democratic and catholic confederations in 1976, six years before it was constituted as a real confederation. Not until the latter event did the unions affiliated to the two amalgamating confederations start to merge.

Institutional Obstacles to Mergers

Mergers between confederations might be hampered, irrespective of the degree of overlapping recruitment fields. If confederations organise different status groups or segments of the labour market, union identities might deviate sharply, as between the Nordic blue-collar and white-collar confederations. Another major obstacle to mergers is the social democratic orientation of the blue-collar confederations and the political independence of white-collar confederations. In this case, cross-confederal mergers between individual unions will probably precede changes at peak level. Blurring borders between blue-collar and white-collar workers may also open the door for mergers at confederal level, but this presupposes that the Nordic LOs dissociate themselves from the social democratic parties. In others countries mergers between confederations organising the same labour market segments may also be problematic, as these confederations are often keen competitors. Another severe obstacle is usually the distinct political and religious identities of these confederations.

Political/Ideological/Religious and Class/Status Divisions as Obstacles to Mergers

Political/ideological/religious and class/status divisions still constitute major obstacles to mergers. A number of processes, however, are breaking up traditional boundaries between white-collar and blue-collar workers and between private and public sector workers. These boundaries are blurred by new concepts of work organisation and the deregulation or privatisation of public services. Similarly, political and religious cleavages are alleviated by secularisation, depillarisation, the appearance of euro-communism and the end of the cold war. Secularisation paved the way for the 1982 amalgamation between the socialist and catholic confederations in the Netherlands. In many countries, unions and political parties now have less close ties than previously. In Italy the collapse of the traditional party system during the mid-1990s made mergers between unions affiliated to different confederations a real prospect (Regalia and Regini, 1998: 473). In other countries, increased autonomy from political parties may also facilitate mergers. In Finland, decreased political conflicts within the social democratic camp, and between communists and social democrats, made the 1969 reunification of the leading union confederations possible.

During the 1990s in Europe, the social pacts concluded between union confederations and employers' associations and, primarily, social democratic governments, facilitated closer union co-operation (Fajertag and Pochet, 2000). In national systems with more adversarial industrial relations, however, these pacts enhanced tensions between confederations (Portugal) or within confederations (Greece). The move from centre-left to centre-right governments facilitates the closer co-operation of divided union confederations in all the Southern European cases, but they are, in the short run, unlikely to lead to formal mergers.

In Spain, Italy and Portugal the politically divided trade union movements, and in Greece the different factions within confederations, have developed political action cartels for reforming pension systems and labour markets, while not appearing to perceive any need for mergers. The changed political situation with centre-right governments in office, and declining union density, have generated more co-operation in the Italian and Spanish cases, both with respect to political bargaining and sectoral collective bargaining. In Portugal and Greece politically deadlocked positions are still maintained. It remains an open question whether this situation may be altered with the new political development in Portugal and the election of the centre-right in Greece during 2004. Recent Italian experience, however, provides a case in which one of the three major confederations has developed centripetal behaviour, largely influenced by the fluidity of the political system. CISL has embarked on a political project under the term 'competitive unity' with CGIL and UIL, where the emphasis is more on competition between confederations than on unity (Fajertag and Pochet, 2000: 34-35). Despite the collapse of the traditional party system and the development of political cartels by the confederations, the reshaping of the political system does not seem to result in confederal mergers. Under the Olive Tree Coalition

346

of the Left, the political divisions remained untouched, even between CGIL and UIL, which are considered more left-wing than CISL.

The decentralisation of collective bargaining has deprived LO-Sweden of its direct wage bargaining role and has facilitated the appearance of a cross-confederal cartel within manufacturing. Although no merger across the collar cleavage has occurred in Sweden, the door may open in the long-term for such mergers by the blurring of borders between blue-collar and white-collar workers, the development of shared interests in defending the position of manufacturing unions in the 'post-industrial' society, and a growing need for united action against transnational companies. At least two obstacles, however, remain. First, work organisation has not changed at the same pace everywhere. Second, the close links between LO-Sweden and the social democratic party are incompatible with the neutral position of white-collar unions towards political parties. Further contributing to this uncertainty is a fear that union density among white-collar workers would decline if white-collar unions were to lose their own union identity.

LO-Denmark arranged an extraordinary Congress in 2003 to cut economic ties with the social democratic party. The formal ties were abolished in 1995. The aim of ending the financial support to the party was to pave the way for a unitary confederation, in the first instance by a merger between LO and white-collar FTF, which, in the long-run, was also to include AC (Danish Confederation of Professional Associations). Declining membership and a desire to create a more influential union confederation in the national and European arenas are the most conspicuous motives. It should be noted that, similarly to its Norwegian equivalent, but in contrast to LO-Sweden, LO-Denmark has for a long period defined itself as a unitary confederation to which white-collar unions should affiliate.

Centralisation and State-regulation as Substitutes for Mergers

A further barrier to mergers, in addition to collar and/or status divisions and political and/or religious cleavages, is strongly centralised confederations and bargaining structures, which may function as substitutes for union mergers (see Chapter 12). A prominent example is the considerable transfer of power from affiliated unions to LO-Sweden before the introduction of centralised bargaining in the 1950s. As a consequence, mergers between affiliates were not considered very urgent by LO. Danish labour legislation introduced in the 1930s had similar centralising effects by increasing the co-ordination powers given to the public conciliator.

The centralised awards system in Australia also had a freezing effect on traditional union structure. The Australian system perpetuated narrowly based occupational unions that had no resources for enterprise bargaining (see Chapter 2). When the awards system was dissolved, an urgent necessity arose to transform the old union structure and create viable unions. Both in Australia and New Zealand the arbitration system sustained a secure but highly fragmented union movement (Chaison, 1996: 158). In addition, closed-shop clauses in arbitration awards, together with state registration, made organisation efforts, as practised in most other countries, redundant (*ibid.*: 144ff.). Furthermore, by enabling small, weak unions to gain recognition from employers, registration had a strong freezing effect.

French and Greek industrial relations are still characterised by strong state interference. The French state is very important in providing unions with resources and protecting them through the legal doctrine of 'most representative union' (Ebbinghaus and Visser, 2000: 251-253). Membership decline in France has intensified competitive unionism and increased the importance of protection by the state and the dependence of unions on state subsidies (Daley, 1999: 173-189). Since 1980, French unions have been transformed into electoral machines. To participate in the election of works councils and other bodies requires fewer resources than recruiting members (*ibid.*: 199). In addition, the second Auroux Law, enacted by the socialist government in the early 1980s, strengthened the works councils at the expense of unions (*ibid.*: 175).

Like the former arbitration systems in Australia and New Zealand, the frequent use of compulsory arbitration in Greece from 1955 to 1990 had a freezing effect on bargaining and union structures (see Chapter 6). The provision concerning the most representative union prevented bargaining cartels, which is why the lack of mergers in Greece cannot be associated with cartel practices functioning as a substitute for mergers. On the contrary, as in France, inter-union conflict has been intense. Even more than in France, Greek unions are dependent upon economic contributions provided by the state. Until 1989 the government even appointed the GSEE leadership (Ioannou, 2000: 281ff.). Similarly to France, political cleavages have acted as barriers to mergers. This, however, is unlikely to change even if the two Greek union confederations continue to come closer to each other, as a result of joint political bargaining. In addition to organising different segments of the labour force, the reason for their continued separation is the deep political divisions between the two confederations. Only the retreat of political cleavages and the increased financial autonomy from the state will facilitate mergers.

Craft and General Unions Resisting Restructuring Efforts along Industrial Lines

In countries where general unions and craft unions secured a stronghold, confederations have met strong resistance from craft unions unwilling to merge and from general unions unwilling to restructure along industrial lines. The first merger within LO-Denmark, which was formed in 1898, did not take place until 1917! The fragmented nature of the Danish union movement, together with the strongly centralised employers' confederation, explains why bargaining cartels and legislation on balloting rules attained such importance in co-ordinating wage negotiations. It is true that the latter developments helped to conserve union structure, but part of the explanation is in Danish union structure. The large general union SiD (General Workers' Union in Denmark) still blocks the transformation of LO unions into industrial unions, as it refuses to split up (see Chapter 4). Within the engineering industry, Metal (National Union of Metalworkers) has acquired a number of unions of skilled workers, while SiD organises unskilled metal workers, as does the general union of unskilled women, KAD (National Union of Women Workers). Instead of being split up along industrial lines, SiD plans to merge with KAD, thus consolidating its position within LO.

The British union movement has a very fragmented and increasingly complex structure. In the early 1960s, the TUC abandoned industrial unionism as its guiding star. At the same time, the legal restrictions for mergers were eased, followed by a wave of mergers. While craft unions have lost almost all significance, giant general unions, each of which includes more and more industries and occupations, now dominate the scene (Waddington, 1995). Emphasis is placed on size in itself, rather than on a rationally motivated principle of organisation. Ireland is also dominated by a few large, general unions and many small unions, several of which are based in the UK. Most Irish unions affiliate to ICTU, which, like the TUC, has relatively limited authority over its many affiliates, in particular *vis-à-vis* the dominant general unions (Roche, 2000: 344).

Confederal Efforts to Rationalise Union Structure

After examining a number of circumstances that tend to conserve established union structures, our focus now shifts to efforts by confederations to restructure affiliated unions. Considering the degree of ambition and success of implementing union mergers, confederations might be classified in different categories ranging from the highly ambitious and successful Australian ACTU (the 1987-94 merger wave) to confederations with low ambitions, such as the Greek ADEDY and GSEE (see Table 13.3).

In both Austria and Germany unitary movements comprising relatively few unions were established after World War II. Consequently, the need for mergers was limited. In contrast to the centralised and powerful Austrian ÖGB, its German equivalent had, from the outset, little authority over affiliated unions. The intense German merger activity since 1995, which reduced the number of DGB-affiliated unions from sixteen to eight, was not a result of DGB initiatives. Indeed the very role of DGB has been challenged since IG Metall (Engineering Workers' Union) acquired two unions to consolidate its position, and ver.di and IG BCE (Mining, Chemical and Energy Workers' Union) were formed by amalgamations. Together these three unions represent almost 80 per cent of union membership in Germany.

Table 13.3: Degree of Merger Ambition and Success among Union Confederations

	LOW SUCCESS	MODERATE SUCCESS	HIGH SUCCESS
High Ambition	Austrian ÖGB (radical restructuring plan proposed in 1995)	Austrian ÖGB (three small mergers), LO-Denmark	Australian ACTU
Moderate Ambition	British TUC	Nordic confederations except LO-Denmark; Dutch, French and Italian confederations, Portuguese CGTP	
Low Ambition	American AFL-CIO, German DGB, Greek ADEDY and GSEE Portuguese UGT		

Among European trade union confederations, the Austrian ÖGB is marked by exceptionally high ambitions in promoting restructuring among its affiliates. The ÖGB played a major role in developing the radical 1995 proposal to reduce the number of unions from fourteen to three, one each for industry, private services and public sector. If realised, it would have meant breaking up ÖGB's largest union, the white-collar GPA (Union of Salaried Private Sector Employees), and the transfer of its members within manufacturing to blue-collar unions (see Chapter 3). Instead GPA prefers to merge with GMT (Metal and Textile Workers' Union) and three other blue-collar unions, thus making the ÖGB plan obsolete. Since 1945, only three mergers have taken place (in 1978, 1991 and 2000), in each of which ÖGB has played a supportive role. In contrast, ÖGB was taken by surprise by the proposed large-scale merger.

Since the mid-1980s Australia, like Austria, has had a single, relatively powerful, union confederation that proposed several mergers. But here similarities come to an end. In contrast to the Austrian ÖGB, the Australian ACTU actively planned, and *succeeded* in implementing, a 'Top-Down Strategic Restructuring', as the title of Chapter 2 suggests. Several circumstances explain the impressive merger wave in Australia. First, the number of unions was high, 295 as late as 1990, many of them being craft-based. Second, something had to be done because of the paradigmatic shift of Australian industrial relations in terms of the deregulation of the centralised arbitration system. This process included a far-reaching decentralisation of collective bargaining, which challenged unions that were traditionally very weak and fragmented at workplace level. This was compounded by sharply declining union density and associated financial problems. Third, something was able to be achieved because of the powerful position of the ACTU and the active support it received from the state in the political context of the Accord. The desire to avoid more extensive state intervention strengthened ACTU's preparedness to act (see Chapter 2).

Until the 1990s the centralised arbitration system in Australia could be said to have had a freezing effect upon union structure. Conversely, when the system was abolished, the need for union restructuring appeared in full force. The acquisition of all other Australian confederations, together with its strengthened role in the industrial relations system and a political environment supporting mergers, in the 1980s made ACTU powerful enough to undertake the role as 'strategic driver responding to and initiating change' (see Chapter 2). After the merger wave of the early 1990s and the emergence of about twenty key unions, ACTU lost much of its power and retreated to its pre-1980s role, including the maintenance of a limited role with respect to mergers. The success of ACTU's merger programme may be questioned, as it failed to prevent a further decline of union density. Furthermore, despite the recommended restructuring along industrial lines, some very heterogeneous unions covering a significant range of employees have been created, although most industries are now covered by one key union only (see Chapter 2).

Compared to the aggressiveness of Australian ACTU in promoting mergers, union confederations in the UK and the US appear passive. Chaison concludes that the British TUC, like its equivalents in the US and Canada, 'mildly encourages mergers and mediates stalled merger negotiations, but it is careful not to intrude too deeply in internal union affairs by proposing specific mergers or criticising individual unions for not merging' (1996: 157). In short, affiliated unions retain considerable autonomy. The TUC, in particular, has presented restructuring plans and has attempted to influence the merger process in other ways, for example by providing mediators to facilitate merger negotiations (see Chapter 10). The significance of blueprints, however, has been very limited during the wave of mergers that started in the 1960s. The only remaining principle of organisation is membership size, which is also important for gaining influence within TUC. The result is an increasingly complex union structure, containing very heterogeneous general unions. As in Australia, the high frequency of mergers has not prevented a continued decline in union density, maybe partly related to the growing heterogeneity of large unions and, in the British case, also heightened competition for members. In contrast to many other countries, mergers in Britain are regulated by legislation. The TUC played an important lobbying role for making the law more merger-friendly. This TUC initiative was certainly important in promoting the high merger intensity since the mid-1960s (Waddington, 1995).

American unions are also known for their jurisdictional overlapping. Since the 1980s, AFL-CIO has made some efforts to create more clear jurisdictions and promote mergers among unions with similar membership composition (Chaison, 1996: 31ff.). In the absence of a proactive AFL-CIO policy towards mergers and a facilitating legal framework, merger barriers however appear as 'formidable' in the US (*ibid.*: 50).

In contrast, Nordic union confederations have strong constitutional authority *vis-à-vis* affiliated unions. Nonetheless, Nordic blue-collar confederations have usually taken a highly pragmatic attitude to the implementation of blueprints. It should be noted that mergers are just one of many means of advancing industrial unionism. Membership transfers between unions, for example, were more important than mergers in implementing the industrial principle within Swedish engineering (see Chapter 9). To facilitate mergers, the 1926 Congress of LO-Sweden decided that all persons employed by LO unions, which were dissolved or split up due to mergers, should assume a similar position in the unions to which the members were transferred. No immediate results were achieved, which is why the LO in 1936 attained the right to intervene against unions that refused to comply with the terms of the agreed merger blueprint. These rights were never used, however, but functioned as a latent threat (Hadenius, 1976: 142ff., 158ff.). In practice, mergers continued to be completely voluntary, with the final decisions made within affiliated unions. Had a tough policy been followed, LO risked losing obstinate unions, which is what happened in Norway during the 1920s (see Chapter 7). With the new centralising statutes adopted in 1941, LO-Sweden achieved the power to adjudicate inter-union demarcation conflicts, but the increased centralisation of LO partly functioned as a substitute for mergers, which were considered as a matter for each individual union (Hadenius, 1976: 159). The solidaristic wage policy, for which centralised bargaining was a prerequisite, both accelerated and retarded mergers. It accelerated the number of mergers by encouraging shifts of employment, and retarded merger intensity by raising the fear among craft unions, with relatively highly paid members, that they would lose influence if they were absorbed by large industrial unions (see Chapter 9).

LO-Denmark has made several efforts to transform the traditional structure of many small occupational unions and a few large unions into a limited number of huge industrial unions. The 1971 LO Congress adopted a plan to merge about 55 affiliates into nine industrial unions (see Chapter 4). Despite far-reaching mergers of employers' associations within manufacturing industry, the radical LO plan was not realised because of disagreements among unions, especially between Metal and SiD. From the late 1980s, the LO, therefore, tried an alternative course of action aimed at creating five large bargaining cartels. The main result was the extension of the cartel of metalworkers to the whole of manufacturing, which matched the new employers' association covering the same area. Although the grandiose restructuring plans of LO-Denmark have yielded few results, the number of affiliated unions declined from almost 70 in 1960 to 22 in 2000.

At the 1989 Congress LO-Norway failed to obtain support for a large-scale restructuring of affiliated unions (Dølvik, 2000: 436). The modest compromise to build sectoral cartels, although contested, was realised. Disappointment with a similar unsuccessful LO project encouraged five unions within manufacturing and agriculture to form the heterogeneous *Fellesforbundet* (Norwegian United Federation of Trade Unions) in 1988 (see Chapter 7).

Nordic white-collar confederations have also taken several initiatives to 'rationalise' the structure of white-collar unions. For example, the Swedish white-collar DACO merged in 1944 with 'old TCO' into modern TCO. The transformation of an independent occupational association of clerks into a vertical union of private service workers, a requirement for affiliation, was the most prominent DACO effort in this respect. Similarly, in 1952 TCO initiated a merger between the unions of primary school teachers, but it proved to be a lengthy process that was not completed until 1991. The Norwegian *Utdanningsforbundet* (Union of Education) emerged in 2001 after forty years of efforts to bring together teachers' unions into larger units (see Chapter 7). The Norwegian union resulted from a merger between a former AF union and an independent teachers' union, not as in Sweden by a series of mergers between unions affiliated to the same confederation (TCO). The Norwegian union also includes secondary school teachers, which, in Sweden, are organised by a SACO union. Immediately after their formation during the 1970s, the Norwegian white-collar confederations YS and AF encouraged the creation of large unions by mergers. Like the Swedish SACO, YS established a separate union to allow various small unions to join, the difference being that the aim of the SACO union was to absorb the many small public sector staff associations, while the YS union covers the private sector. The founding of SACO's Danish equivalent AC, in 1972, also triggered a wave of mergers.

Although mergers in the Nordic countries are completely voluntary on the part of the individual unions and the role of blueprints has been restricted to recommendations, the long-term influence of blueprints should not be underestimated. First, they have had a normative influence, strengthening forces in favour of mergers. Second, blueprints have functioned as guidelines for restructuring, including transfers of members between unions; for solving demarcation disputes; and allowing or denying affiliation of unions or the expulsion of affiliated unions. Not infrequently, unions wishing to join a confederation had to accept acquisition by an affiliate as a requirement for affiliation. As in other countries confederations do not accept hostile breakaways as affiliates, at least, not until a very long time after the initial breakaway.

The Portuguese UGT belongs within the group of confederations making few, if any, attempts to promote mergers. Founded as late as 1978, UGT adopted a policy of industrial unionism from the outset. The need for further rationalisation is thus limited, compared to its rival the CGTP, which is placed in the group with modest merger ambitions and success, as since 1995 it has promoted restructuring among its affiliates with some success (see Chapter 8). Likewise, the French CFDT has been more successful than other French confederations in its policy of reorganising affiliates on a sectoral basis (Ebbinghaus and Visser, 2000: 251). All three Italian confederations have actively promoted mergers, although UIL has met with somewhat less success than CGIL and CISL (*ibid.*: 392). Nevertheless, we have chosen to locate all these French and Italian confederations in the same group. In both Italy and France, discontent with established confederations, however, has promoted the emergence of new unions and thus increased union fragmentation. The rise of autonomous unions and alternative forms of organisation in Italy after 1980 is explained by the absence of specialised unions or sections for white-collar employees within the major confederations, combined with growing discontent among these groups with the egalitarian bargaining strategy of the traditional confederations (Locke and Baccaro, 1999: 250).

The Greek case illuminates the problems of classifying confederations by merger activity. Neither GSEE nor ADEDY have had any success in influencing the rate of mergers, but plan to amalgamate without consequences for affiliated unions (see Chapter 6). Indeed, the GSEE merger campaigns since the early 1980s have failed, thus perpetuating the fragmentation and weakening of trade union structures. In the Greek case there are some similarities with the Australian experience, where the abolition of centralised bargaining and the arbitration system created a need for union restructuring. In Greece, although more voluntarism was introduced in collective bargaining, the union and bargaining structures remain intact as the threat of quasi-compulsory arbitration still operates.

A similarity between Greece, Australia (before the merger wave) and Portugal is the very large number of occupational, professional and regional unions. While the Australian ACTU succeeded in bringing these unions together, Greek 'multi-level' unionism, comprising regional and occupational primary-level unions, federal (national) unions and confederations, however, obstructed all efforts to rationalise union structure. Similarly, in Portugal, a large number of unions are based on region or occupation, many of which are affiliated to federations which, in practice, function as national unions. Compared to the Greek confederations, the Portuguese CGTP, however, has been relatively successful in promoting mergers.

Conclusions

Overall, it appears that confederal efforts to rationalise union structures remain one source of influence in shaping union mergers but can hardly be described as the main source and/or as an effective one. The exceptional Australian case can be attributed more to the radical change in the bargaining system and less to confederal effectiveness *per se* to implement a blueprint. Normally, as most cases indicate, union mergers are gradual, voluntary processes undertaken by unions, and are generated by changing memberships, declining revenues or an increasing need for economies of scale. Considerable international variations exist regarding the ambitions and success of confederations in restructuring the union landscape, although it is not very easy to rank confederations in these respects. One reason is that confederal influence upon affiliated unions may be indirect and yield results only in the long run. Blueprints thus may have a long-term normative influence, strengthening forces in favour of mergers. Another source of mergers, even less associated with direct pressures or campaigns on the part of confederations, is competition between unions for intra-confederal influence. In Germany both the consolidation of IG Metall by mergers and the giant merger of private and public service unions resulting in ver.di were aimed at strengthening the position of these post-merger unions within DGB (see Chapter 5). Similarly, the proposed large-scale Austrian merger will improve the likelihood of the unions involved preventing ÖGB reforms being implemented against their will (see Chapter 3).

Sometimes blueprints have a more direct influence upon independent unions than on affiliates, as blueprints often require unions contemplating affiliation to be acquired by a union that is already affiliated. Furthermore, several independent American unions have merged with AFL-CIO unions to prevent the 'raiding' of their members by unions affiliated to the confederation (Williamson, 1995). On the other hand, strict entrance rules may result in a preference for remaining independent.

Mergers across confederations are very rare. Generally, they occur only when confederations themselves merge into larger units, such as the Dutch FNV and American AFL-CIO, or when previously split confederations re-unite as in the cases of the Finnish SAK and Irish ICTU. As illuminated by the typology of confederations presented in the beginning of this chapter, severe obstacles limit mergers between confederations and, consequently, mergers between unions affiliated to different confederations. Political and religious divisions still constitute major barriers to mergers in many European countries despite secularisation, depillarisation, the end to the cold war and weakened ties between unions and political parties. Similarly, blurring borders between white-collar and blue-collar workers and between private and public sector workers have not prevented the persistence of union structures based upon class, status or sector in the Nordic countries. In one sense political and religious divisions are external from a labour market perspective, while class/status/sector cleavages are directly related to employment status and employment relations. Rooted in basic socio-economic relations and long-standing cultural traditions, the latter divisions stem, only to a small degree, from voluntary choices by union actors. When confederations with previously different political/religious orientation merge, there is nothing in principle to prevent mergers between their affiliates within the same industry or occupation. Overcoming collar divisions is a much more complicated task, at least in the Nordic countries. Compared to LO-Sweden, its Danish and Norwegian equivalents contain relatively large numbers of white-collar unions, but none of them have joined forces with their blue-collar counterparts. Besides the deep collar division, the absence of mergers is explained by divergent coverage of white-collar and blue-collar unions due to different principles of organisation. The LO-affiliated HK (Union of Commercial and Clerical Employees in Denmark) is an occupational union with members in all sectors (manufacturing, private services and the public sector), which makes a merger with, for example, Metal difficult. Furthermore, the general union SiD (recruiting unskilled workers within all manufacturing industries) has hitherto resisted restructuring along industrial lines.

Diverging principles of organisation may also hamper mergers in unitary confederations like the British TUC or American AFL-CIO. A result of the mergers that are undertaken involving larger unions, however, is the growth of general unions. Some unitary confederations, particularly the German DGB and Austrian ÖGB, were completely reconstructed after World War II, to contain a few affiliates with comparatively clear boundaries. This restructuring weakened the incentives for further mergers. In 1995 the ÖGB proposed a radical restructuring plan, which soon became obsolete due to a merger initiative from some of the largest unions. The Australian ACTU was much more successful in implementing its plans. The paradigmatic shift from a state-regulated, centralised industrial relations system, conserving an extremely fragmented union structure, to a deregulated, decentralised system, forced the ACTU to adopt a radical restructuring plan at the same time as a number of favourable circumstances made it possible to implement it.

Besides the typology of three confederal categories presented in this chapter, we found another set of variables relevant when identifying forces hampering mergers: the degree of centralisation-decentralisation of confederations (and industrial relations systems), and state-regulation versus self-regulation (voluntarism). As we have seen, in several cases centralised and/or state-regulated industrial relations tend to block or, at least, retard mergers. State regulation, in its extreme form, might imply that the government either declares union confederations illegal or grants them more or less monopoly. The position of the Greek GSEE is based on legal provisions concerning bargaining and union rights. French unions also rely to a high degree on financial and other forms of support from the state. The merger process may also be regulated by law. In Britain, merger intensity rose sharply when the requirements for mergers were eased in the mid-1960s (see Figure 1.9).

As for the future, continued decentralisation of collective bargaining and declining union density will probably increase incentives for mergers and cross-confederal alliances, as will blurring collar and sector boundaries and weakened links between unions and political parties. In several countries, a radical restructuring of national unions requires mergers between confederations. At the same time, the significance of confederations tends to decline with the decentralisation of wage negotiations and the emergence of huge general and sectoral unions or cross-confederal and cross-collar bargaining cartels. Depoliticised and secu-larised confederations deprived of bargaining tasks may thus pave the way for future mergers, not by actively promoting restructuring, but by their loss of power. Consequently, the 'institutionalisation thesis' and the 'politics of bargaining' in such cases might be complementary rather than alternative explanations of mergers.

List of Abbreviations

AC	Akademikernes Centralorganisation (Danish Confederation of Professional Associations)
ACTU	Australian Council of Trade Unions
ADEDY	Anotati Diikisis Enoseon Demosion Ypallilon (Confederation of Greek Civil Servants)
AF	Akademikernes Fellesorganisasjon (Federation of Norwegian Professional Associations)
AFL-CIO	American Federation of Labor-Congress of Industrial Organi-zations
AKAVA	Akateeminen Yhteisvaltuuskunta (Central Confederation of Professional Associations)
CC.OO	Comisiones Obreras (Workers' Commissions)
CFDT	Confédération Française Démocratique du Travail (French Democratic Confederation of Labour)
CFTC	Confédération Française des Travailleurs Chrétiens (French Confederation of Christian Workers)
CGC	Confédération Générale des Cadres (General Confederation of Managerial Staffs)
CGIL	Confederazione Generale Italiana del Lavoro (Italian General Confederation of Labour)
CGT	Confédération Générale du Travail (General Confederation of Labour)
CGTP	Confederacão Geral dos Trabalhadores Portugueses (General Confederation of Portuguese Workers)
CISL	Confederazione Italiana Sindicati dei Lavoratori (Italian Confederation of Workers' Unions)
CIU	Conference of Irish Unions
CNG	Christlich Nationaler Gewerkschaftsbund (Christian National Trade Union Confederation)
CNV	Christelijk Nationaal Vakverbond (Confederation of Christian Trade Unions)

CSN	Confédération des Syndicats Nationaux (Confederation of National Trade Unions)
DACO	De Anställdas Centralorganisation (Central Organisation of Employees)
DAG	Deutsche Angestelltengewerkschaft (Union of Salaried Employees)
DBB	Deutscher Beamtenbund (Union of Civil Servants)
DGB	Deutscher Gewerkschaftsbund (German Trade Union Confederation)
FEN	Fédération de l'éducation nationale (Federation of National Education)
FNV	Federatie Nederlandse Vakbeweging (Confederation of Dutch Trade Unions)
FO	Force Ouvrière (Workers' Strength)
FTF	Funktionærernes og Tjenestemændenes Fællesråd (Central Confederation of Salaried Employees and Civil Servants)
GMT	Gewerkschaft Metall-Textil (Metal and Textile Workers' Union)
GPA	Gewerkschaft der Privatangestellten (Union of Salaried Private Sector Employees)
GSEE	Geniki Synomospondia Ergaton Ellados (General Confederation of Greek Workers)
HK	Handels- og Kontorfunktionærernes Forbund i Danmark (Union of Commercial and Clerical Employees in Denmark)
ICTU	Irish Congress of Trade Unions
IG BCE	Industriegewerkschaft Bergbau, Chemie, Energie (Mining, Chemicals and Energy Workers' Union)
IG Metall	Industriegewerkschaft Metall (Engineering Workers' Union)
ITUC	Irish Trade Union Congress
KAD	Kvindeligt Arbejderforbund i Danmark (National Union of Women Workers)
LO-Denmark	Landsorganisationen i Danmark (Danish Confederation of Trade Unions)
LO-Norway	Landsorganisasjonen i Norge (Norwegian Confederation of Trade Unions)
LO-Sweden	Landsorganisationen (Swedish Confederation of Trade Unions)
Metal	Dansk Metalarbejderforbund (National Union of Metalworkers)

MHP	Centrale voor Middelbaar en Hoger Personeel (Federation of White-collar Staff Organisations)
NKV	Nederlands Katholiek Vakverbond (Dutch Catholic Trade Union Confederation)
NVV	Nederlands Verbond van Vakverenigingen (Dutch Confederation of Trade Unions)
ÖGB	Österreichischer Gewerkschaftsbund (Austrian Trade Union Confederation)
SACO	Sveriges Akademikers Centralorganisation (Swedish Confederation of Professional Associations)
SAF	Svenska Arbetsgivareföreningen (Swedish Employers' Confederation)
SAJ	Suomen Ammattijärjestö (Finnish Union Confederation)
SAK	Suomen Ammattiliittojen Keskusjärjestö (Central Organisation of Finnish Trade Unions)
SGB	Schweizerishen Gewerkschaftsbund (Swiss Trade Union Confederation)
SiD	Specialarbejderforbundet i Danmark (General Workers' Union in Denmark)
STTK	Suomen Teknisten Toimihenkilöjärjestöjen Keskuslitto (Finnish Confederation of Technical/Salaried Employees)
TCO	Tjänstemännens Centralorganisation (Swedish Confederation of Professional Employees)
TUC	Trades Union Congress
UGT	Unión General de Trabajadores (Confederation of Workers)
UGT	União Geral dos Trabalhadores (General Union of Workers)
UHO	Utdanningsgruppenes Hovedorganisasjon (Confederation of Higher Education Unions, Norway)
UIL	Unione Italiana del Lavoro (Italian Union of Labour)
UNSA	Union Nationale des Syndicats Autonomes (National Federation of Autonomous Unions)
ver.di	Vereinte Dienstleitungsgewerkschaft (Unified Services Union)
VSA	Vereinigung Schweizerischer Angestelltenverbände (Federation of Swiss Trade Union Associations)
YS	Yrkesorganisasjonenes Sentralforbund (Confederation of Vocational Unions)

CHAPTER 14

Are New Forms of Union Organisation Emerging?

Gerard GRIFFIN

Historically, the basis of trade union structure has been very diverse. The traditional craft basis to union organisation in the United Kingdom and the United States, for example, can be contrasted with the industrial unions found in Austria and Germany. In turn, craft and industrial unions are significantly different to the company unions dominant in Japan. Interspersed with these forms, and often co-existing, are variants such as general and white-collar unions. This diversity is not surprising. Unionism developed in different countries at different times and within a variety of industrial, social and economic environments. Furthermore, trade union structure frequently reflects the impact of factors such as politics, culture, tradition, and in some countries, religion. Accordingly, union structure in any particular society is as diverse as the society in which it is located.

Yet there are also some similarities. Until relatively recent times, for a variety of ideological, political and economic reasons, most union movements in industrialised economies had moved towards, or aspired to move towards, industrial unionism. Certainly some traditional trade union structures were threatened. The craft unions of skilled manual workers were disappearing in most countries, albeit at different rates. White-collar occupational unions, however, have flourished in such areas as education and health. Equally, many general unions were confined to specific sectors of industry. In most countries, however, structural change, as a general rule, was very much evolutionary rather than revolutionary. Events of the 1980s and 1990s accelerated this process of slow change. Unions in many industrialised countries, with the arguable exception of the 'Ghent' countries, faced serious threats and challenges, irrespective of the established union structure. They had to cope with the linked issues of increasingly decentralised bargaining systems and increasingly hostile employers, which were combined with demands for increased labour flexibility. At the same time, unions were losing their influence in the polity, an influence that had sustained many union movements in the post-World War II period. Furthermore, membership was declining as these challenges mounted, thus restricting resources at a time when they were most in demand.

As has been outlined in earlier chapters of this volume, a series of union mergers occurred in several countries as one, major, component of the response to these challenges. The question then arises, what has been the impact of this intense merger activity on trade union structure? Obviously, as detailed in Table 1.1, the number of unions has certainly decreased, and their average membership size has increased. But what has been the impact on different union structures? If the pressures to merge have been similar, are the outcomes also similar? Specifically, have similar pressures on unions in their national context produced an internationally similar structural outcome? The limited number of studies that address this issue point to some common features. Intra-industry union mergers are relatively rare, 'more common are mergers that increase membership heterogeneity' (Waddington, 2001: 453). The outcome of the merger process in countries such as Austria, Denmark, Germany and Norway is an accumulation of industries leading to 'multi-industry unionism' or 'the extension of general unionism' (Waddington, 2001: 453). Comparing and contrasting unions in Germany and the Netherlands, Streeck and Visser argue the case for 'conglomerate unionism', a structural variant driven by the search for organisational viability (1997: 322). Indeed, if we are witnessing the growth of such forms of union organisation within countries where industrial unionism has traditionally prevailed, what is happening elsewhere? Has there been a convergence on a conglomerate structure of trade unionism, regardless of structural tradition, or is there still considerable diversity between union forms despite concurrent change?

This chapter draws on the earlier, country-specific, chapters to provide some answers to these questions. In particular, it analyses how the merger process outlined in these chapters has affected trade union structure. The chapter begins with a brief outline of the main, traditional structural variants of unionism. It then introduces a simple typology of the extant forms of union structure and allocates the dominant form of unionism in each of the ten countries covered in this volume within this typology. The impact of post-merger changes are then assessed and discussed.

Traditional Structures

A wide variety of factors influenced the structure of trade unions in different countries. A range of factors contributing to these differing structures can be subsumed into three general themes: industrialisation, institutionalisation and the politics of bargaining (see Chapter 1). Each of these themes combined to produce five types of union: craft, general, industrial, company, and white-collar. With the proviso that distinctions between each of these types of union are rarely fixed and are subject to almost continuous change, they are defined below and their relative strengths identified in the ten countries.

It is clear that in the earlier industrialising countries, such as the UK and the US, craft unions were usually the initial, dominant form. Unless driven by political developments, skilled workers, the aristocrats of labour with their relatively strong labour market leverage, were much more likely to establish unions successfully in the face of employer and state opposition. While craft unions were often the first and dominant unions in a significant number of countries, their ascendancy was rarely left unchallenged for long. Consequently, this form of unionism evolved to incorporate semi-skilled or what were termed in the UK, 'allied workers'; that is, workers employed in close proximity to craft workers. Thus, by the middle of the twentieth century, few genuine craft unions remained. Most had expanded their boundaries to cover other occupations or had been subsumed within a broader union.

With the passage of time, and usually within a few decades of the success of craft unions, unskilled workers started to establish their own unions. Given their weaker labour market position, these workers sought strategic power and industrial leverage through membership numbers. Initially, these unions were restricted to specific industries or sectors. Relatively rapidly, however, a number of these unions expanded their organisation base by recruiting workers across a number of industries. Gradually, they became known as general unions, although this descriptor was somewhat misleading as the *de facto* coverage of most general unions was restricted, either through custom and practice or through agreement with other unions, to segments of the (predominantly) blue-collar workforce. Despite its prominence for a short period of time in the late nineteenth/early twentieth century, particularly in the English-speaking world, the ultimate outcome of the concept of general union-ism – One Big Union – was never broadly accepted or indeed pursued.

Industrial unionism was a major contributor of the twentieth century to union structural development. The membership parameters of indus-trial unions are usually those of an industry or a specific segment of an industry. Within these parameters, membership is open to all employees, regardless of skill, occupation or work position. In some countries, such as the Nordic countries, divisions between blue-collar and white-collar unions and confederations restrict opportunities for industrial unionism in its 'ideal' form. Industrial unionism became an important structural form in much of Europe, particularly in those countries that industrialised relatively late. Canada and the US were two other countries where industrial unions had a significant impact. In those countries without industrial unions, the model was much admired and a number of union confederations aspired to this form as their organisational goal, but lacked the political or constitutional authority to implement a policy to achieve such an outcome.

Company unionism, where membership is restricted to employees of a particular enterprise, is a rarer form of union structure. Indeed, in many countries, a form of company unionism, 'yellow unionism', is regarded as an employer-dominated form of unionism, which lacks independence and is, thus, not a 'genuine' form of unionism. With the notable exception of Japan, this form of unionism has not been the dominant structure in developed market economies, although in the UK it assumed a position of some importance.

The final, major form of unionism is the white-collar union. During the late nineteenth/early twentieth century, 'new' white-collar workers established occupation-based unions to represent their industrial, and, often, their professional interests. Initially termed associations or federations, this organisational form spread rapidly, usually from an initial base in the public sector, to countries where industrial unionism was firmly established. Throughout much of the twentieth century this was probably the fastest growing form of unionism (for details, see Bain, 1970).

The structural basis of union movements in all democratic, industrialised societies was usually a mix of these five organisational forms. While one or two structural forms might dominate, it was not unusual to find three or more forms co-existing within the same country. As a general rule, societies with industrial unions tended to have fewer different structural forms of unionism than those countries with horizontal or occupational-based unionism. But, even in countries where union movements were structured around industries, complexities existed. For example, in the former West Germany, usually advanced as the epitome of industrial unionism, until very recent times the white-collar DAG (Union of Salaried Employees) co-existed with industrial unions, but was excluded from the confederation. Furthermore, Chapter 5 notes that some of these 'industrial' unions were based on occupation or employer. In the Nordic countries white-collar unions, with their divided confederations, also co-existed with industrial unions for manual workers.

Indeed, in the particular circumstances of the high-density Nordic countries, the notion of the industrial, white-collar union was developed, usually with reference to industries such as banking, insurance and finance, where the overwhelming majority of the workforce was employed in white-collar occupations. With the further 'tertiarisation' of the labour force, this category of union is likely to assume a greater importance, thus suggesting that the number and relevance of the various union structures will continue to change over time.

Nevertheless, despite the multiplicity of forms and changes over time, in a general sense it is possible to categorise the main structural forms, and their relative strengths, found within most countries. Tables 14.1 and 14.2 attempt to do so for the ten countries covered in this volume for the decades before about 1990. An initial attempt to encapsulate these data in one table foundered on the differences between blue-collar and white-collar workers, particularly in the Nordic countries. Indeed, despite utilising two tables to accommodate this particular dichotomy, the tables still cannot possibly capture the richness of union structure. The impact of district and region in Portugal and of university education in the Nordic countries, for example, are not incorporated into the tables. A further complication is the increased blurring of the borderline between categories of workers. To illustrate, in Germany, the emergence of the *Entgeltverträge* payment agreements – joint collective contracts covering wages for both white-collar and blue-collar workers – is eroding the traditional rigid differences between *Angestellte* (white-collar) and *Arbeiter* (blue-collar) workers. In addition, an increasing number of unions, such as the public sector unions in Austria, organise both white-collar and blue-collar workers. Nevertheless, utilising this white-collar/blue-collar dichotomy is a useful, if somewhat crude, tool to help assess the macro-level question of the impact of the merger process on union structural form. Specifically, Tables 14.1 and 14.2 outline the relative importance of various union structures for blue-collar and for white-collar unions.

As detailed in Table 14.1, among the four main structural forms, industrial and craft/occupational unions battled for dominance of blue-collar unionism during the period before 1990. Craft/occupational unions were found in all countries, but industrial unions were particularly strong in central Europe. General unionism was of some importance in Austria, Denmark, the US and the UK, while company unionism was restricted mainly to Greece. For white-collar workers the craft-equivalent professional/occupational union was similarly found in all countries and, with some exceptions, such as Sweden, was generally a more important structural form than industrial unionism. General unionism held some attraction to white-collar workers in Austria and Portugal, while company unions were of some importance in the UK. Overall, the contrasting occupational and industrial forms of union organisation were dominant, while general unions were confined to a few countries and company unionism was non-existent in some countries. Within these categories it was possible to identify 'blocks' of countries with broadly similar structures. However, such blocks invariably contained divisions. Even within the most obvious block, the geographical group of countries running north from Austria through central Europe to Norway, the dominance of the industrial union was mitigated by the key role of occupational unionism in Denmark and among white-collar workers in Norway, and the presence of DAG in Germany.

Table 14.1: Traditional Structure
for Blue-collar Unions, 1950-90

Country	Craft/Occupational	Company	General	Industrial
Australia	XXX		X	
Austria	X		XX	XX
Denmark	XXX		XX	X
Germany	X	X		XXX
Greece	XX	XX		XX
Norway	X		X	XXX
Portugal	XX			XX
Sweden	X			XXX
United Kingdom	XX		XX	X
United States	XX			XX

X: Minor form
XX: Important form
XXX: Dominant form

Table 14.2: Traditional Structure
for White-collar Unions, 1950-90

Country	Professional/ Occupational	Company	General	Industrial
Australia	XXX	X		
Austria	X		XX	XX
Denmark	XXX	X		X
Germany	X			XX
Greece	XX			XX
Norway	XXX		X	X
Portugal	XX		XX	XX
Sweden	XX			XXX
United Kingdom	XX	X	XX	
United States	XX			XX

X: Minor form
XX: Important form
XXX: Dominant form.

New Structures

Tables 14.1 and 14.2 classify earlier union structural developments. This section identifies the current dominant forms of union organisation. Drawing on the earlier chapters, three distinct forms of organisation can be identified. This is not to argue that there is no overlap between these forms, nor that other organisational forms do not exist. Rather it is to assert that these three forms have different distinct characteristics and that they are clearly the dominant forms of organisation. Other possible forms, such as the company form contained in the earlier tables, are omitted because of their relative lack of, or declining, importance.

- the first form is occupational unionism. This category subsumes both craft and professional forms of organisation and retains at its core the horizontal organising principle;
- the second form is industrial unionism, the traditional organisational form to which many union movements aspired, and a form that is defined by its vertical organising principle. Recall however that in some countries, particularly the Nordic countries, industrial unionism remains structurally divided along occupational grounds;
- the third form comprises general and sectoral unions. This form comprises the traditional general unions with their organising principle of 'open to all-comers' and the more recent development pursued with a defined sectoral recruitment base in mind, such as UNISON (public sector) in the UK and ver.di (service sector) in Germany. In practice, this multi-industry form of unionism organises both vertically and horizontally. However, in both general and sectoral unions there are frequently limits to recruitment bases, usually arising from industrial or sectoral boundaries or by the division between blue-collar and white-collar organisation. This form of unionism is evolving towards general unionism (UK and USA) or sectoral unionism (Germany).

Tables 14.3 and 14.4 detail the relative presence of the three structural forms in the ten countries. Focusing initially on changes in unions covering blue-collar workers, three inter-related changes can be identified. First, the occupational form of unionism has virtually disappeared for blue-collar unions. Before 1990, craft/occupational unions were found in all ten countries. Due in no small part to the merger process, craft/ occupational unions have virtually disappeared from most countries. Indeed, only in Greece, where the relatively few mergers did not significantly change the traditional structure, do occupational unions remain important. Occupational unions are also found as a minor form in Denmark: a huge change from their earlier dominance. Second, industrial unionism has experienced contradictory fortunes. In some countries, notably Australia, Denmark and Portugal, industrial unions have emerged as the dominant form of unionism for blue-collar workers, and they have retained much of their influence in Sweden. At the same time, in Austria and Germany, the traditional dominance of the industrial union has been ceded to multi-industry or sectoral unions. Third, there is the significant growth of general and sectoral unions. Such unions are now found in virtually all countries, are the dominant form in four countries and an important form in two other countries. Overall, for blue-collar unions, the traditional joust for superiority between industrial and craft/occupational unions has been replaced by a contest between the industrial unions and the general or sectoral unions.

Table 14.3: Post-1990s Forms of Blue-collar Union Structure

Country	Occupational	Industrial	General/Sectoral
Australia		XXX	X
Austria			XXX
Denmark	X	XXX	XX
Germany		X	XXX
Greece	XX	XX	
Norway		X	XX
Portugal		XXX	X
Sweden		XXX	X
United Kingdom	X	X	XXX
United States		X	XXX

X: Minor form
XX: Important form
XXX: Dominant form.

Table 14.4: Post-1990s Forms of White-collar Union Structure

Country	Occupational	Industrial	General/Sectoral
Australia	XX	XX	X
Austria	X	XX	XX
Denmark	XXX	X	
Germany			XXX
Greece	XX	XX	
Norway	XX	XX	XXX
Portugal	XX	XX	XX
Sweden	XX	XX	
United Kingdom	XX	X	XXX
United States	XX	X	XX

X: Minor form
XX: Important form
XXX: Dominant form.

Have similar structural changes been replicated in white-collar organisation? The answer for occupational unionism would appear to be
no. While occupational unions have decreased in overall importance in
three countries, they retain their traditional, pre-1990s status in all other
countries. In Denmark occupational unionism remains by far the dominant structural form. And in those countries where this form of unionism
has declined somewhat – Australia, Germany and Norway – the level of
change has not been marked. Indeed some of this structural change has
seen occupational white-collar unionism replaced by industrial white-
collar unionism. For example, in Australia, six horizontally organised
unions in the banking and insurance industries merged to form the
Finance Sector Union. The experience of the white-collar occupational
structure is thus markedly different to that of the blue-collar form.
Arguably, this could be related to the numerical dominance of white-
collar workers, a development that facilitates an on-going form of
occupational organisation. In short, and regardless of reason, while
occupational unions for white-collar workers have decreased in salience,
they remain important. Similarly, industrial unionism has also lost
adherents in some countries but has actually gained strength in Australia
and Norway. Overall, it remains an important form of organisation. In
contrast, general and sectoral unions have emerged as the dominant
form of white-collar organisation in Germany, Norway and the UK, and
are important in several other countries. In the UK, white-collar unions
that recruited across several industries have tended to become part of
large, general unions comprising both blue-collar and white-collar
workers. Overall, general and sectoral unions have developed rapidly
and are now arguably the leading form of organisation of white-collar
workers. It is far from the dominant form overall, however, since both
occupational and industrial structures remain important across a range of
the countries studied.

Linking together trends in both blue-collar and white-collar union
structural development, a number of general observations should be
stressed. First, while occupational unionism for blue-collar workers has
virtually disappeared, it remains significant for white-collar unions. This
is particularly the case in Denmark and, to a lesser extent, in Norway
and Sweden, where no mergers have linked white-collar to blue-collar
unions. Second, industrial unions, the traditional structure to which
many union movements aspired, seem to have lost much of their attraction. Industrial unionism remains extremely important, however, for
some blue-collar workers and in the Nordic countries, but even in these
countries some mergers have occurred across the public/private divide.
Third, general and sectoral unions have emerged as a major structural
form, particularly in the central European countries, the US and the UK.

Conversely, such structures have had little impact in countries such as Sweden and Portugal.

At the macro level these findings represent something of a mixed picture. Furthermore, it is not difficult to identify additional contradictory trends. For example, while there has been a reduction in the number of structural forms found in some countries, notably Germany, there appears to be expansion in others, notably Sweden, and little change in others, notably Greece. Perhaps this outcome should not have been unexpected. Many of the mergers detailed in the earlier chapters were defensive, a number were opportunistic and, certainly, some strange alliances were politically based. With the possible exception of Australia, where the confederation attempted to drive a programme of restructuring, with the primary objective of attaining industrial unionism, the merger process did not follow any pre-determined blueprint or 'grand plan'. Indeed, in most countries, some apparently 'logical' potential mergers were not consummated and other options were chosen instead.

If few general lessons can be drawn, is it possible that trends in changing structure can be identified across blocks or sub-groups of countries? Based on the structures identified in Tables 14.1 and 14.2, four such sub-groups with relatively similar union structures can be identified:

- the industrial model of central Europe (Austria and Germany);
- the traditionally occupational model of the Anglo-Saxon countries (Australia, the UK and the US);
- the mixed industrial/occupational Nordic model (Denmark, Norway and Sweden);
- the southern European model of large numbers of unions with small memberships (Greece and Portugal).

The possibility that common structures have evolved along similar lines in these sub-groups is now addressed.

Industrial Model of Central Europe

In the post-World War II period, these countries tended towards industrial unionism. Despite the white-collar jurisdiction of the DAG in Germany and the GPA in Austria, the union movements in these two countries implemented what was arguably as pure an industrial model as was possible in industrialised democratic societies. Thus, the scope for intra-industry mergers in both these countries was limited. This is not to argue that some mergers along more industry-linked lines were not possible: indeed, the two country chapters in this book outline such possibilities. Nevertheless, if mergers were to occur, their structures would have to involve multi-industry alliances. This is what happened. The significant reduction in the number of unions in both countries has resulted in multi-industry and, in the unique case of ver.di, sectoral unions. The term conglomerate unionism has been used in this context to characterise developments in Germany and the Netherlands (Streeck and Visser, 1997). This term, however, offers somewhat misleading guidance. Unlike conglomerate businesses, these unions do not have the choice or opportunity to simply move into and operate in any industry. Rather, because of jurisdictional rules, often enforced by confederations, they are restricted to recruiting and operating in a specific number of industries. Thus, the term sectoral or perhaps multi-industry more correctly defines their organisational scope. In countries where industrial unionism was firmly entrenched, there has been a discernible move to such forms of union organisation.

The Occupational Model

In this group of Anglo-Saxon countries, the traditional craft/white-collar occupational structure, with some limited examples of industrial unionism, has evolved away from an occupational focus towards more general forms of union organisation. In the US, because of the decision of the craft unions affiliated to the AFL (American Federation of Labor) not to organise the new mass production industries, the 1930s saw the growth of strong industrial unions in some key sectors of the economy. These two principles of union organisation were reconciled in the form of the AFL-CIO (American Federation of Labor-Congress of Industrial Organisations) in 1955. Subsequent mergers have tended to result in the larger unions organising more heterogeneous memberships and adopting characteristics of general or sectoral unions. Within the complex structure of UK trade unionism, craft unions have virtually disappeared as their larger representatives have been transformed into general unions, largely, but not exclusively, by merger activity, thus complementing the longstanding general unions with their origins in the 'new unionism' of the 1890s. In some ways, because of the traditional structural diversity, the merger process has produced a disordered post-merger outcome, with no obvious 'simplification' of union structure. While general and sectoral structures dominate in the US and the UK, industrial unions and white-collar occupational unions are the key structural forms in Australia. This emergence of the industrial structure is linked to the top-down nature of mergers in Australia, driven by the powerful central confederation. The Australian Council of Trade Unions was established in 1927 with, among other things, a goal of implementing an industrial form of structure. When the opportunity arose in the late 1980s/early 1990s it ruthlessly pursued this objective (see Chapter 2). Yet even the ACTU was not strong enough to enforce such a change on occupational-based white-collar unions with strong identities. Thus, while some, such as finance unions, coalesced into white-collar industrial forms, others such as teachers and nurses retain their occupational basis.

The Nordic Model

Class or differentiation of employees has traditionally characterised this model, leading to a mixture of craft, white-collar and, particularly, industrial unions. Industrial unionism has retained its salience, particularly for white-collar unionism in Sweden and in Denmark, but a number of mergers have resulted in sectoral unions. These sectoral unions cross the public/private sector divide. With the exception of the blurring of some differences between the industrial and services sector in Denmark, the new union structures have not generally crossed the white-collar/blue-collar divide. In effect, different trends are evident within the Nordic countries. Concurrent with the growth of general and sectoral forms of unionism, industrial unionism remains important and occupational white-collar unionism has flourished with factors such as educational qualifications playing a significant role in differentiating groups of unionists.

Southern Europe

Trade union structure in Greece and Portugal has remained relatively constant. This is not to argue that some change is not occurring. For example, in Portugal, the CTGP (General Confederation of Portuguese Workers) adopted a policy of rationalising union structure in 1995, a policy that is now showing some signs of progress (see Chapter 8). And following its formation in 1978, the UGT (General Union of Workers) favoured national 'vertical' unions. In Greece, unions in the privatised utilities are exploring industrial unionism. In general, however, and linked to political developments, particularly the role of the state, both Greece and Portugal retain a union structure that has many similarities to that of earlier industrialisation: large number of unions with very small memberships and few full-time officials at the local level. These union movements have completed relatively few mergers and the short-term possibility of a major reduction in union numbers appears remote. In effect, union organisation remains focused at the local level, and is built around occupational and white-collar identification.

Discussion of developments in the ten countries broken down into these sub-groups helps explain why no overall trend is evident. Rather, it argues that differing trends are occurring both between and within some sub-groups. In some countries, particularly those traditionally based on industrial unions, there is a clear move towards the multi-industry model. In the Nordic countries, there is some movement in this direction but also a strengthening of the occupational-based form. In the Anglo-Saxon countries, the direction of change has been away from occupational towards general unionism (UK and US) and towards industrial unionism (Australia), but still with a significant independent white-collar element in Australia and the US. In Greece and Portugal, there has been little change. Overall, while mergers have significantly reduced the number of unions in most of the countries studied, the resultant trade union structure remains a complex mosaic.

Conclusion

Union structures at the local, regional and national level have been, and remain, the outcome of a complex interaction of factors such as industry structure, law, politics and bargaining levels. These factors vary between nations. Consequently, different union structures are found in different countries. Despite the traditional commitment of a range of union movements to industrial unionism, few succeeded in achieving such a goal. During the 1980s and 1990s there were a significant number of union mergers in most countries. This chapter sought to assess the impact of these recent mergers on union structure. In particular, it sought to ascertain if these mergers have led to a convergence in union structure. A comparison of the post-merger structures in the ten countries covered in this volume shows that no single, dominant form of unionism has emerged to mark the early twenty-first century.

Four significant trends, however, can be identified. First, and perhaps most clear, among blue-collar unions, there has been a major movement away from craft/occupational unions. The 'replacement' form, however, is not so clear: in Australia and in the UK, two countries with traditionally strong craft/occupational unions, the replacement form differed; in the former it was industrial unions, while in the latter it was general unions. Furthermore, for white-collar workers in several countries, the traditional occupational form of unionism remains important. Second, there has been a significant movement towards general and sectoral forms of unionism. In some countries, such as Germany, this form has evolved from industrial unions; in others, such as the UK, from a mixture of union structures. Third, the star of industrial unionism has dimmed somewhat in some countries, such as Norway and Germany, but remains an important, indeed the dominant, form in countries such as Portugal and Sweden. Fourth, while there are tendencies for countries with traditionally similar structures to move in similar directions, divergence is also common. Overall, in the post-1990 period, general and sectoral unions are now the leading forms of organisation among blue-collar unions, but industrial unions remain dominant in some countries. For white-collar unions the general and sectoral form has assumed significance but both the occupational form and the industrial form remain important. In short, while union mergers have significantly influenced union structure, the range and diversity of organisational forms remains broad.

List of Abbreviations

ACTU   Australian Council of Trade Unions

AFL   American Federation of Labor

AFL-CIO   American Federation of Labor – Congress of Industrial Organizations

CGTP   Confederação Geral dos Trabalhadores Portugueses-Intersindical Nacional (General Confederation of Portuguese Workers)

DAG   Deutsche Angestellte-Gewerkschaft (Union of Salaried Employees)

GPA   Gewerkschaft der Privatangestellten (Union of Salaried Private Sector Employees)

UGT   União Geral dos Trabalhadores (General Union of Workers)

UNISON   Public Sector Union

CHAPTER 15. CONCLUSIONS

What Difference Has
the Merger Process Made?

Jeremy WADDINGTON

Since 1950, with the exception of Greece, the merger process has transformed the structure of trade unions in the countries covered by this volume. Features common to this transformation include a decline in the overall number of trade unions, an increase in average trade union membership size and increasing membership heterogeneity among the larger unions. While these indicators of change to the 'external shape' of trade unions suggest that similar national outcomes result from the merger process, there is no consistent evidence to demonstrate a convergence in trade union structure. As decisions on mergers rest within individual unions and a wide range of divergent merger policies are in evidence, the specific combinations of unions arising from merger engagement vary markedly between the different countries. Although the merger process comprises considerable cross-national variation, a feature of the merger process in most countries is the establishment of a small, but rising, number of large unions with increasingly heterogeneous memberships. These memberships require new forms of internal governance and representation to ensure articulation between the different levels of union activity.

To expand on these issues, this chapter follows the structure of Chapter 1 and identifies the contribution of this volume to each of three aspects of the merger process: the reasons for merger, the internal processes of negotiation and the selection of a merger partner, and merger outcomes. It argues that the merger process in recent years has been essentially defensive and was primarily driven by adverse environmental circumstances. Internal processes of merger negotiation and the constitutional outcome of such negotiations tend to be more complex when larger unions are involved and in amalgamations compared to acquisitions. While mergers may be pre-requisite to union renewal or revitalisation, there are very few indicators that suggest post-merger unions have been able to deploy the additional resources at their disposal to reverse pre-merger membership decline, to strengthen union bargaining positions or to restore political influence. To the contrary, many mergers merely constitute a temporary break in the pattern of membership decline, which continues unabated within the post-merger union.

Reasons for Merger

Chapter 1 introduced four broad explanations of the merger process: the industrialisation thesis, the institutionalisation thesis, a political explanation, and an explanation based on the politics of bargaining. In addition, a range of factors was identified, each of which may influence some mergers, but does not impinge on all mergers. This section assesses the viability of the four broad explanations and identifies those factors which have been most prominent in promoting merger activity since 1950.

The peaks and troughs in merger intensity in several countries support the expectation of the industrialisation thesis that trade union structural reform tends to be cyclical. The linear, rather than the cyclical, development of the merger process in Norway and the US, however, is problematic for the industrialisation thesis. A central tenet of the industrialisation thesis, that periods of fundamental unrest promote the merger process, is not confirmed. To the contrary, the most significant peaks in merger intensity occurred in some countries when industrial conflict was marked and in others when industrial conflict was at low ebb. The marked variation in the timing of the peaks in merger intensity between countries also suggests that factors additional to industrialisation influence the merger process. It is clear, for example, that the peak in merger intensity in Australia can be traced to peculiarities in the politics of bargaining rather than industrialisation.

The shift in employment from manufacturing to services illustrates that the recent pattern of industrialisation has had two distinct effects on the merger process. First, in countries where the shift in employment resulted in aggregate membership decline, merger activity intensified as declining unions sought mergers to protect member services and the employment of union staff. For example, the woodworking, leather, clothing, textiles and furniture industries in many countries are now too small to sustain independent unions, irrespective of the level of density that might have been achieved. Second, the decline in manufacturing employment prompted the dominant unions within the sector, which often organised the engineering industry, to seek merger partners in order to sustain their influence within the confederation. Engineering unions in several countries thus became multi-industry or sectoral unions to counter the faster rates of membership growth achieved by unions in services.

Peaks of merger intensity after 1950 in Australia, Denmark, Sweden and the UK allow us to dismiss the variant of the institutionalisation thesis that predicts union structural stability once employers and the state recognised trade unionism (Lester, 1958). Indeed, with the exception of Greece, significant union structural reform has been introduced in all the countries covered by this volume after 1950, the principal difference between countries being in the intensity of merger activity rather than the presence of merger activity *per se*. High levels of merger intensity in Portugal are consistent with the institutionalisation thesis in so far as high rates of structural change are anticipated during the period immediately after totalitarian rule when employers and the state first recognised the legitimacy of independent trade unions. The institutionalisation thesis would expect similarly high rates of structural change in Greece, but this expectation is not met.

Clegg's (1976) variant of the institutionalisation thesis suggests that trade union structural reform will continue after trade unions have been recognised, due to changes in bargaining structure. This variant of the institutionalisation thesis is on firmer ground than the variant proposed by Lester (1958). In many countries the procedures adopted for national bargaining allowed smaller unions to benefit from participating in the same negotiations as larger, more powerful unions, which often set the terms and conditions at which other unions settled. The decentralisation of bargaining raised challenges for unions in terms of supporting a rising number of bargaining units, co-ordinating activities across bargaining units and exposure to bargaining with employers without the protection of other unions. Smaller unions were particularly hard-hit by these developments and, in the absence of sufficient resources or infrastructure, opted to merge to meet these challenges. Mergers among the smaller Danish and Swedish unions clearly illustrate this tendency. Responding to demands from employers for co-ordinated bargaining, white-collar unions in Denmark and Sweden engaged in waves of restructuring during the early and mid-1970s. The settlement of the terms of recognition from employers for bargaining and representation was thus a key influence. Subsequently, had no cartels been formed in these countries to accommodate decentralisation, it is likely that merger intensity would have been higher.

In those countries where the decentralisation of bargaining was not 'organised', specifically the UK and the US, decentralisation was associated with the selection of merger partners from among a large range of unions. In the absence of organised decentralisation, smaller unions tended to opt for the merger partner that offered the best deal, irrespective of any industrial or political 'logic'. In consequence, membership heterogeneity among the larger, acquiring unions increased markedly. The variant of the institutionalisation thesis that allows for structural change generated by shifts in bargaining is thus generally supported by the data. This support assumes that trade union structural change is, at least partially, driven by the desire within unions to maintain bargaining strength and position. In other words, the explanation is similar to that on the politics of bargaining, which is discussed below.

A third strand of argument that has been applied to trade union structural development has the political organisation of labour movements and the impact of social and cultural cleavages at its core. This explanation argues that 'the social cleavage structure at the time of its consolidation is frozen' in trade union structure (Ebbinghaus, 1990). Political differences between confederations in Portugal and the occupational distinctions between Nordic confederations certainly continue to act as social and cultural cleavages that limit the merger process. Within trade union movements dominated by single confederations, the impact of initial cleavages appears less marked. Distinctions between craft, industrial and white-collar unions, for example, have been eroded, as the merger process has regularly involved unions from two or more of these categories. Similarly, the industrially organised Austrian and German union movements have abandoned rigid demarcations between industries and moved towards multi-industry or sectoral forms of union organisation. In other words, some of the social and cultural cleavages, initially frozen in trade union structure are melting. The extent of this process appears to be mediated, in part, by the character of confederal organisation.

A fourth explanation of the merger process emphasises the role of the 'politics of bargaining', and focuses on three elements: bargaining position of unions relative to the state and employers; a union's bargaining position relative to competitor unions; and factional bargaining within unions (Waddington, 1995: 205-213). Within the liberal market economies of the UK and the US, long-term political hostility to trade unionism undoubtedly contributed to membership decline and thus to the promotion of merger activity. In Australia the politics of the Accord afforded the Australian Council of Trade Unions (ACTU) a uniquely powerful position through which it was able to accelerate the merger process and to specify which combinations of unions should merge. In the co-ordinated market economies, the greater distance from trade unionism sought by social democratic parties may have weakened the bargaining position of unions, particularly if a social democratic government was in office. There is no consistent evidence, however, to link this weakened trade union bargaining position with changes in merger intensity. To the contrary, unions continue to merge to retain or to seek influence within confederations, thereby securing influence within social democratic parties, irrespective of the strength of the relationship between trade unionism and social democratic parties.

From the outset, it should be acknowledged that any measurement of either employers' or union bargaining strength is fraught with difficulty (Martin, 1992). It is also accepted that, at any one point in time, there is a huge variation in the bargaining strength of individual unions. With these caveats in mind, there are several indicators of widespread union bargaining weakness during recent years. In particular, trade union movements have been unable to resist employers' initiatives to decentralise bargaining and their introduction of a range of new production techniques at the workplace. Furthermore, several union movements have recently engaged in forms of concession bargaining (Hyman, 1999). In other words, union bargaining weakness would appear to coincide with periods of intense merger activity during recent years. In addition, employer restructuring has eroded demarcations between industries and occupations, and resulted in many industries being too small to support independent unions. There is, however, little evidence to suggest that employers have directly contributed to an acceleration of the merger process. Only in the UK and the US when employers have de-recognised a union or ensured its decertification is there a direct link to mergers. In practice, the de-recognised or decertified union may seek a merger partner in order to restore its position *vis-à-vis* the employer.

The bargaining position of a union relative to that of competitor unions continues to influence the merger process. Union influence within confederations and political parties is usually a function of membership size. The shift in employment from manufacturing to services, membership decline in all but the Nordic countries, and higher rates of membership growth in the public sector have promoted merger involvement. These effects are notable among the larger unions in manufacturing, which sought to extend their recruitment bases in order to retain their position relative to unions in services. Within trade union movements organised by industry where union density is high, the LOs of Denmark, Norway and Sweden for example, mergers are the principal means whereby influential unions in manufacturing can maintain membership sizes and growth rates similar to unions in services. Similarly, in the US, the manner in which the AFL-CIO administers the principle of exclusive jurisdiction promotes merger engagement among the larger unions with jurisdictions lying within declining segments of manufacturing industry.

Factional bargaining within trade unions has certainly not propelled the recent rise in merger intensity. It has, however, influenced the particular combinations of unions on two counts. First, political affinities between factions within prospective merger partners may facilitate a merger, which otherwise may not have succeeded, as the factions jointly campaign for its ratification. If these affinities involve senior officials, the likelihood of a merger agreement is enhanced. Second, similarities between pre-merger union memberships in terms of occupation and industry may also promote factional influence of the merger process. Similarities in occupation, for example, may form the basis of post-merger alliances and thus increase support for the merger.

Apart from Lester's variant of the institutionalisation thesis, there is thus tentative support for each of the broad explanations of the merger process. Neither the industrialisation nor the changing levels of bargaining variant of the institutionalisation thesis, however, incorporate the impact on union structure of changing relations between unions, the state and employers. They also downplay the role of 'agency' in the merger process. As the country chapters illustrate, these features of the politics of bargaining impinge on the merger process in each nation state. Furthermore, they contribute substantially to the cross-national variation of the merger process.

Internal Processes of Negotiation and the Selection of a Merger Partner

Senior officers lead unions into mergers. The latitude of action of senior officers may be constrained by bargaining structure, legislative requirements and/or union rules, and the terms of any merger policy agreed within union decision-making bodies. Furthermore, members may exert a direct influence on merger decisions by reference to issues associated with identity, union governance and bargaining autonomy. In no country, however, was there a member-driven merger movement after 1950.

There is considerable cross-national similarity in the process whereby merger agreements are concluded. Essentially, joint committees are established comprising representatives from the unions involved. The number and scale of these committees depends on the relative size of the unions concerned and the extent to which the post-merger union is intended to be 'new' in terms of its constitution, systems of governance and member participation, and policy objectives. In cases where the intention is to establish a new union, these committees often comprise an equal number of representatives from the unions involved, irrespective of the membership size of the unions. This approach emphasises 'equality' among the merger partners, facilitates the generation of an acceptable post-merger structure and encourages members and employees of the different unions to commit to the new structure. Draft merger agreements drawn up by these committees are usually, but not universally, ratified by special congresses or conferences, comprising elected representatives or delegates of the unions involved. In countries where legislation regulates the merger process, membership ballots are then held to confirm the decisions taken at the special conferences.

The terms of merger agreements specify the formal structures of governance of the post-merger union. In the overwhelming majority of mergers, centralised control is retained over union finances and decisions on industrial action, while allowance is made for different degrees of bargaining autonomy. The support services provided by the post-merger union are usually available to all post-merger sections on demand. Most merger agreements also offer some employment protection for the employees of the unions involved.

Within the framework of these general terms, the central issue in the case of acquisitions is whether the rules of the acquired union apply to the post-merger section that it forms and, if so, is there a time limit on the period of their application to the post-merger section? In addition, there are the issues of the representation of the acquired union at the conference and on the executive of the post-merger union, and whether the acquired union can retain a conference within the post-merger union. The terms on which these issues are settled depend on the relative strengths of the unions that are party to the merger. All other things being equal, the greater the degree of post-merger autonomy offered by an acquiring union, the greater the likelihood that the union will be able to compete successfully in the merger process against other acquiring unions.

While the same basic issues underpin most merger negotiations, they tend to be more complex in the case of an amalgamation. Where the intention is to 'bolt together' two unions rather than create a 'new' union, the additional complexity is limited. Indeed, in many such instances the two pre-merger unions retain their rules, conference and executives as sections of the post-merger union. Merger negotiations in these instances focus on the range and rules of the joint structures, such as executive and conference, which are introduced as 'senior' to those of the pre-merger unions. In these circumstances, much, if not all, of the integration of the pre-merger unions takes place after the merger has been formally ratified and tends to be a 'top-down' process orchestrated by the joint executive.

Where the intention is to amalgamate to create a 'new' union with a constitution, policy objectives and governing structures that are fundamentally different to, and replace, those of the pre-merger unions, the complexity of the merger negotiations is at its most intense. This complexity is deepened if these changes are also linked to the establishment of new means of membership participation. Such new unions, ver.di (Germany), *Fellesforbundet* (Norway) and UNISON (UK) for example, tend to be large and to dominate a sector. The founding mergers of these unions represented an opportunity to introduce a range of constitutional innovations that might not have otherwise been implemented. In particular, the introduction of mechanisms to encourage the participation of women, young and ethnic minority members reflect attempts to incorporate horizontal linkages within these unions, to supplement the vertical sections that are linked to bargaining structure. The scale of these amalgamations and the extent of the constitutional revision associated with them have three key implications. First, such amalgamations tend to be followed by lengthy periods of post-merger adjustment during which people are allocated to roles within the new system and the system is refined to operate in practice rather than as a blueprint developed during the merger negotiations. Second, large numbers of jobs tend to be lost after the merger, through voluntary redundancy, early retirement or not filling vacancies. Third, the initial absence of informal networks which cross the boundaries of the pre-merger unions, tends to slow the development of the post-merger union. These informal processes, which are often reliant on personal networks and linkages, may take many post-merger years to develop. In combination, these three features promote post-merger uncertainty among union staff, which may compound a sense of post-merger introspection, whereby those involved in the union tend to look inward, rather than focus on the development of external policy and relations.

A range of factors also influences the selection of merger partners. In most of the ten countries, representatives of the confederations generated blueprints for mergers that followed some 'logic', usually associated with contiguous industries or trades, and linked to the objective of eliminating smaller unions. In the main these blueprints failed, as control over the selection of a merger partner rested within unions rather than confederations. Failure was most apparent where the blueprint necessitated the break-up of a large and powerful affiliate, such as the GPA (Union of Salaried Private Sector Employees) in Austria and SiD (General Workers' Union) in Denmark. Thus, in practice, confederations tended to promote mergers in general and to facilitate merger negotiations set in train by affiliated unions, rather than impose their blueprints. Three exceptions to this pattern are in evidence. First, in committing affiliated unions to the principle of industrial unionism, the Swedish LO was able to exert some influence over the direction of the merger process, but not the rate at which it took place. This was particularly pronounced when the LO was directly engaged in collective bargaining. Second, the Portuguese confederations tend to have greater influence over the merger process than confederations elsewhere. While this influence is also enhanced by confederal engagement in bargaining and social pacts, the constitutions of the Portuguese confederations afford them greater leverage over both federations and unions.[1] Third, the peculiarities of the politics associated with the Accord in Australia enabled the ACTU to implement a merger blueprint, in several instances, irrespective of the wishes of many affiliated unions.

Numerous mergers follow a 'logic' based on bargaining structure and/or political affinities. Where bargaining was decentralised in an uncoordinated manner, as in the UK and US, many mergers follow no apparent logic and tend to be more influenced by the quality of member support services offered by prospective merger partners, the extent of post-merger autonomy, and the terms of employment of union officers and employees. In other words, uncoordinated, decentralised bargaining is associated with merger processes that fail to simplify union structure significantly. Similarly, in Austria and Germany where structures akin to industrial unionism existed after 1950, many mergers linked unions with different industrial membership concentrations to form multi-industry or sectoral unions. There was no overriding industrial logic to these mergers. To illustrate, in Germany the GGLF (Horticulture, Agriculture and Forestry Workers) merged with IG BSE (Construction Workers' Union), whereas in Austria the GLFG (Agricultural and Forestry Workers' Union) merged with the GLG (Food and Tobacco Workers' Union). In other words, if the merger process starts from a base akin to industrial unionism, the selection of any partner is likely to constitute a step away from industrial unions, but different steps have been taken in different countries.

The presence of competition for membership between unions appears to exert no consistent influence on the choice of merger partners. The involvement of DAG (Union of Salaried Employees) and HBV (Banking and Commerce Union) in the ver.di amalgamation, for example, eliminated competition between the two pre-merger unions in finance and retail. In contrast, the amalgamation between the GMWU (General and Municipal Workers' Union) and the ASBSBSW (Amalgamated Society of Boilermakers, Shipwrights, Blacksmiths and Structural Workers) to form the GMB (General, Municipal and Boilermakers

---

[1]   This situation may be a feature of southern European trade union organisation. Evidence from Italy and Spain, for example, suggests that confederations there also have considerable influence over the merger process (Baccaro *et al.*, 2003; Hamann and Martinez Lucio, 2003).

Union), together with the subsequent acquisitions by the GMB of the GMA (Gas Managers' Association) and the MPO (Managerial and Professional Officers), were mergers that fostered extant membership competition. As post-merger sections of the GMB, the ASBSBSW continued to compete with the AEU (Amalgamated Engineering Union), while the GMA and MPO competed for members with UNISON. Mergers are more likely to shift the location of membership competition, rather than eliminate such competition. Furthermore, membership competition may become more intense if the post-merger unions involved are larger and better resourced. Debate on these topics concerns merger outcomes, to which the analysis now turns.

Merger Outcomes

In terms of the declining number of unions, their increasing average size and rising membership concentration, it is relatively straightforward to document the outcome of the merger process. Similarly, rising membership heterogeneity figures strongly among the larger unions, although occupational concentration remains a feature in some white-collar areas, such as among unions of teachers, doctors and nurses. Furthermore, it is apparent that the influence of craft and industrial unions is waning, whereas that of multi-industry, sectoral and general unions is strengthening. In part, this is due to craft and industrial unions being transformed into these other types through merger involvement. A degree of convergence in union structure can thus be identified at this level of analysis. Given the huge variation in union structure in the different countries and in the specific combinations of unions resulting from merger involvement, it is no surprise that there are marked limits to the extent of any convergence. These limits are reflected in the range of specific outcomes of the merger process. This section reviews the outcome of the merger process in two areas: the restructuring of confederations and the impact of mergers on members. Each section briefly speculates on the likely future impact of the merger process.

The Restructuring of Confederations

Since 1950 the number of unions affiliated to the confederations in the countries covered by this volume has tended to decline. In addition, changes in the composition of union membership have resulted in shifts in membership size and relative strength among affiliated unions. Many affiliated unions have thus sought merger engagement as a means of compensating for their relatively more difficult recruitment terrain, thereby enabling them to retain a similar relative position within confederations. The influence of confederations on the merger process is more marked where they retain some role in collective bargaining or social pacts. At different points in time since 1950 such engagement by the Nordic LOs, the Portuguese CGTP and UGT, and the Australian ACTU enabled confederal influence to be brought to bear on the merger process. Where a confederal bargaining role was lost, the influence of the confederation diminished. Similarly, confederations with no role in bargaining have been unable to exert any significant influence on the merger process. Apart from these general tendencies, two inter-linked issues connected to the merger process have been particularly influential on the restructuring of confederations: the impact of an apparent threshold concerning the number of affiliated unions and revisions to relations between affiliated unions and confederations.

Confederations have traditionally adjudicated on disputes between affiliated unions, acted as a conduit to government and, in certain circumstances, undertaken a role in bargaining. In addition, confederations have provided a range of support services to unions, which smaller affiliates tend to be more dependent upon than their larger counterparts. As smaller unions have been acquired by larger unions or have amalgamated to form a large union, they have tended to withdraw from the support services offered by the confederation and rely on those available within the post-merger union. The merger process has thus diminished reliance on the confederation among smaller unions.

When the number of affiliates falls beneath an apparent threshold, the roles of the confederation in adjudicating disputes between affiliated unions and acting as a conduit to government are brought into question. An obvious example of this tendency is Germany where there are now only eight unions affiliated to the DGB, three of which organise over 80 per cent of affiliated membership. Although a recent agreement on recruitment domains was brokered by the DGB, negotiations between the three largest affiliated unions determined the content of the agreement (Waddington *et al.*, 2003). The DGB was thus marginal in an area in which it traditionally has exerted considerable influence. Similarly, each of the three major unions has the resources and influence to liaise directly with government, rather than through the auspices of the DGB. Negotiations around the *Bundnis für Arbeit* and its collapse, coupled to bargaining on the government's *Agenda 2010* programme, have been characterised by direct relations between affiliated unions and the government. In these circumstances, the position of the DGB is substantially weakened and its future the subject of debate.

The extent of the decline in the number of affiliated unions is more marked in Germany than elsewhere. The merger process, however, has reduced the number of unions affiliated to the Danish and Swedish LOs to fewer than 20, while the number of unions affiliated to the Norwegian

LO has fallen to 25. In Austria the merger process is likely to reduce the number of unions affiliated to the ÖGB to nine by 2005. Furthermore, in these countries similar processes of concentration are underway to that in Germany, marked by the emergence of a small number of very large unions.[2]

The growing share of total membership organised by the competing white-collar and academic confederations accentuates the weaknesses of the Nordic LOs. In each of these Nordic countries the future role of the confederations is the subject of debate. The three Nordic confederations of manual unions have distanced themselves from social democratic parties in an attempt to facilitate the recruitment of white-collar workers. In addition, the prospect of confederal mergers has moved higher up the agenda. In the short term, such mergers would effectively raise the number of affiliated unions and thus reinforce the role of the confederation in adjudicating disputes between affiliates.

In Germany the debate on the future of the confederation starts from the question, should there be a DGB? In Austria the peculiarities arising from the constitution of the ÖGB alter the terms of the debate. In particular, the ÖGB constitution stipulates that unions are not independent, but are sub-units of the confederation, which also exercises some control over union finances. In addition, all full-time officials are formally employees of the ÖGB rather than the member unions. The debate in Austria thus focuses on the development of altered relations between unions and the confederation, rather than the existence of the ÖGB. If extant merger plans are implemented, the largest union will organise about 40 per cent of ÖGB membership and is unlikely to adhere to the terms of the relationship with the confederation outlined above.

The 'Austrian model' is thus under threat in Austria. Elsewhere, however, it is viewed as a desirable strategic objective. While the FNV (Federation of Dutch Trade Unions) encouraged mergers among affiliated unions, measures were also taken to centralise a range of functions, which were carried out by the FNV in support, and on behalf, of affiliated unions, and to 'brand' each union in terms of its FNV affiliation. The Dutch position thus incorporates elements of the Austrian approach. The newly elected Deputy General Secretary of the British TUC (Trades Union Congress) has also indicated her support for a similar approach (*The Times*, Thursday 2 March 2000).[3] Were this proposal to be imple-

---

[2]   In Finland and the Netherlands similar processes are underway. The Finnish SAK has fewer than 25 affiliates, while 15 unions affiliate to the Dutch FNV.

[3]   Matthew Taylor, Director of the influential Institute for Public Policy Research, voiced similar proposals in an interview reported in *Unions Today*, March 2000.

mented, it is envisaged that members would pay a flat-rate membership fee to the TUC for which they would receive a range of support services. The flat-rate fee would be topped-up by additional contributions if the member also wished to join an affiliated union. Underpinning this proposal is the idea that the member would retain TUC membership as s/he moved from job to job, and would thus only have to be recruited once. Loyalty and commitment would primarily be generated between member and the TUC, rather than member and affiliated union. Similarly, representatives from both NJM (Iron and Metalworkers' Union) and NBIF (Norwegian Union of Building Industry Workers), the largest constituent parts of *Fellesforbundet*, wished to transform the Norwegian LO into a union, with affiliated unions re-constituted as industrial or sectoral sub-units. In other words, a move towards the structure adopted by the ÖGB was envisaged. Although this initiative was rejected by other unions affiliated to the LO, the broad sectoral scope of *Fellesforbundet* constitutes a major step in this direction. Moreover, further developments in this direction cannot be ruled out, particularly if *Fellesforbundet* acquires additional affiliates of LO in the merger process.

The merger process has thus made a significant contribution to the opening of debates on the future of confederations. As with the merger process, there is no convergence in the strategic options that are either being debated or implemented. It is clear, however, that the trends evident from the merger process, which drive these debates, particularly declining union numbers and rising membership concentration, will not be reversed in the foreseeable future. The restructuring of confederations is thus likely to assume a more prominent position on the union reform agenda in the short to medium-term.

Mergers and Members

Three aspects of the impact of mergers on members are examined here: the provision of services and support; membership heterogeneity and participation; and levels of membership and density. In each of these areas of impact, the merger process has the potential to contribute to union revitalisation, but very few recent examples have been unearthed where this potential has been realised. In practice, much of the merger process remains defensive and fails to address issues of union renewal.

Services and Support

Advocates of mergers from almost all of the countries considered in this volume argue that mergers will deliver economies of scale and thus constitute opportunities to improve the quality of support services available to members. The country-based studies suggest that such economies of scale are rarely achieved. Instances where unions with overlapping recruitment bases merge represent one of the best opportunities to achieve economies of scale. Recent merger activity, driven by membership decline and financial difficulties, however, tends to be linked to extensive post-merger rationalisation during which staff numbers are reduced. In these circumstances any economies of scale merely allow the maintenance of pre-merger levels of support services, rather than any broadening of their range.

The acquisition of a small union by a large union also offers an opportunity for an improvement in the quality of support services for members of the small union. Small unions are unable to offer wide-ranging services and support to members. In practice, acquisition by a larger union acts as a guarantee of access to such support services for members of the small, acquired union. For members of the acquiring union there is unlikely to be any significant change. Similarly, members of an industrial union in a declining segment of the economy may elect for acquisition in order to protect the level of support services, which may be cut if the union remained independent, due to declining income. In this context, it seems likely that the trend towards mergers for size will continue unabated in the medium term.

Membership Heterogeneity and Participation

Increasing membership heterogeneity, particularly within many of the larger unions, is a feature of the merger process in most countries. To accommodate increasing membership heterogeneity, many unions have supplemented regional and industrial forms of representation with structures for women, white-collar, young and ethnic minority workers. Such structures are often introduced as elements of the merger process and are intended to raise participation levels among such groups, to facilitate co-ordination between different vertically organised groups of members, and to allow the development of union policies that incorporate items of direct concern to these groups. In practice, as membership becomes more heterogeneous, systems of union government become more sophisticated. Arguably, union government also becomes more expensive in such circumstances, thus mitigating the impact of any economies of scale that might arise from merger involvement (Waddington *et al.*, 2003). In particular, it is more expensive to operate with both vertical and horizontal forms of representation. Furthermore, it is far from certain that measures, such as systems of reserved seats, sections for under-represented groups and specialist officers, have achieved their intended results (Garcia *et al.*, n.d.; Colling and Dickens, 1998; Cyba and Papouschek, 1996).

Two developments that arise directly from the merger process have greater potential for change. These can be illustrated by reference to the systems of government adopted by UNISON in the UK and ver.di in Germany, two unions that were founded by mergers. Representatives of the unions involved used the occasion of the founding merger to attempt to establish new unions, which differed fundamentally from their con-stituent pre-merger parts. The introduction of these systems of union government was facilitated by this approach, as, implicit in it, was the rejection of the systems of government employed in the pre-merger unions. Underpinning the approach adopted by UNISON and ver.di is the principle of proportionality, whereby the composition of each com-mittee within the union must reflect the composition of the membership from which its members are drawn. In other words, if 55 per cent of group of members are women, then 55 per cent of the committee that represents the group should also be women. Allied to the adoption of the principle of proportionality in UNISON are novel approaches to fair representation and self-organisation. The initial UNISON rulebook defined fair representation as:

> The broad balance and representation of members of the electorate, taking into account such factors as the balance between part-time and full-time workers, manual and non-manual workers, different occupations, skills, qualifications, responsibilities, race, sexuality and disability (UNISON, 1993: 65).

Self-organisation was also promoted among women members, black members, members with disabilities, gay and lesbian members. In combination, these approaches have reshaped the traditional model of trade union governance (McBride, 2001). Women, black, and gay and lesbian members are engaged in decision-making processes on a wider scale than hitherto and have developed new skills appropriate to this engagement (Humphrey, 2002). Furthermore, alliances between differ-ent self-organised groups are now likely and present opportunities to extend the influence already secured (Colgan and Ledwith, 2000). The situation in ver.di is less developed, primarily because the merger is more recent, but similar processes have been introduced. The point is that these approaches constitute a significant development beyond traditional approaches to equality and present opportunities to main-stream issues of concern to these groups, rather than treat such issues as those of 'special interest' groups. Furthermore, it is likely that vested interests would prohibit the introduction of such systems without the opportunity provided by a founding merger.

While these innovative approaches to union governance generate considerable potential for more wide-ranging membership participation, the overall effect of the merger process on membership participation remains difficult to gauge. The country-based studies provide no unambiguous data. Increasing concentration of membership through merger activity may be associated with centralised systems of governance, particularly regarding financial control and decisions on industrial action. Such centralisation is unlikely to promote greater membership participation. In contrast, the decentralisation of bargaining coupled to the allowance of degrees of post-merger bargaining autonomy enables members to participate in union activities at levels where decisions may have direct implications for workplace practices. The impact of mergers on membership participation is thus not straightforward. Given the current pattern of development of the merger process, it would be particularly beneficial to understand the impact of acquisitions on membership participation. For example, what are the opportunities available to a textile worker, formerly a member of GTB (Textile and Clothing Workers' Union), and are they taken up, to participate within IG Metall (Engineering Workers' Union), almost 90 per cent of the members of which are in the engineering industry?

Levels of Membership and Density

Throughout, supporters of union structural change claim that the merger process is important as a means to enable unions to reverse membership decline and to extend unionisation into the expanding areas of private sector services. The evidence to support these contentions is thin on the ground. In those countries where membership decline has been marked, the UK and the US since the late 1970s, Austria and Australia since the mid-1980s and Germany after unification, the merger process does not appear to have arrested the rate of aggregate membership decline. The acquisition of small, declining unions, which are restricted to contracting segments of the economy, has prevented the membership of such unions from being lost to unionism, but little more.

Specific unions, however, have used the merger process as a low-cost, low-risk alternative to organising the unorganised sectors of the economy. Such approaches enable unions to maintain relative membership size and have been particularly effective when used by unions that organise in manufacturing. More positively, there are also instances of unions making an acquisition and using the membership secured by such means as a basis from which to expand organisation. In the UK, the acquisition of the National Health and Human Service Employees by the Service Employees International Union (SEIU) in 1998, for example, almost doubled the acquiring union's membership in health. The subsequent allocation of additional resources to organising in the health industry enabled the SEIU to establish a dominant position within the industry. The initial acquisition thus presented an opportunity for expansion. In the case of the SEIU, the subsequent allocation of resources enabled the union to realise the potential of the opportunity. Such a development is the exception rather than the rule. In the majority of instances where a merger creates such an opportunity, either the absence of resources or an unwillingness to deploy them, results in the dissipation of the potential that arose from the merger. In short, the merger process is insufficient as a measure to reverse membership decline, but, in certain circumstances, it may create opportunities for membership growth. The post-merger union must implement other measures if the opportunity created by the merger is to be exploited.

The defensive character of much of the merger process is thus perpetuated in post-merger developments. More radical measures are required if union movements are to extend membership throughout private sector services. There is no consistent evidence from the ten countries examined here, for example, to indicate that post-merger unions have deployed additional resources to improve working relationships with other social movements or to transform unionism into an element of a more influential social movement.

List of Abbreviations

ACTU	Australian Council of Trade Unions
CGTP	Confederação Geral dos Trabalhadores Portugueses-Intersindical Nacional (General Confederation of Portuguese Workers)
DGB	Deutscher Gewerkschaftsbund (German Trade Union Confederation)
FNV	Federatie Nederlandse Vakbeweging (Federation of Dutch Trade Unions)
GGLF	Gewerkschaft Gartenbau, Land und Forstwirtschaft (Horticulture, Agriculture and Forestry Workers' Union)
GLFG	Gewerkschaft Land-Forst-Garten (Agriculture and Forestry Workers' Union)
GLG	Gewerkschaft der Lebens- und Genußmittelarbeiter (Food and Tobacco Workers' Union)
GPA	Gewerkschaft der Privatangestellten (Union of Salaried Private Sector Employees)
GTB	Gewerkschaft Textil-Bekleidung (Textile and Clothing Workers' Union)
IG BSE	Industriegewerkschaft Bau-Steine-Erden (Construction Workers' Union)
IG Metall	Industriegewerkschaft Metall (Engineering Workers' Union)

NBIF   Norsk Bygningsindustriarbeiderforbund (Norwegian Union of Building Industry Workers)

NJM   Norsk Jern- og Metallarbeiderforbund (Iron and Metalworkers' Union)

ÖGB   Österreichischer Gewerkschaftsbund (Austrian Trade Union Confederation)

SAK   Suomen Ammattiliittojen Keskusjärjestö (Central Organisation of Finnish Trade Unions)

SEIU   Service Employees International Union

SiD   Specialarbejderforbundet i Danmark (General Workers' Union)

TUC   Trades Union Congress

UGT   União Geral dos Trabalhadores (General Union of Workers)

UNISON   Public Sector Union

ver.di   Vereinte Dienstleistungsgewerkschaft (Unified Services Union)

References

Abrahamsson, B. (1993), "Union Structural Change", *Economic and Industrial Democracy*, Vol. 14, No. 3, pp. 399-421.

AC, FTF, LO and DA annual reports, various years.

ACTU (1987), *Future Strategies for the Trade Union Movement*, Document No. D229/87, Melbourne, Australian Council of Trade Unions.

Adams, L. (1984), "Labor Organization Mergers 1979-84: Adapting to Change", *Monthly Labor Review*, September, pp. 21-27.

AF (various), *Beretning for Akademikernes Fellesorganisasjon*. Annual reports, 1975 – 1999, Oslo, Akademikernes Fellesorganisasjon

AFL (1923), *Kongressen 1923. Dagsorden og protokol*, Oslo, Arbeidernes Faglige Landsorganisasjon.

AFL (1957), *Forbundenes organisasjonsområde. Innstilling fra Organisasjonskomitéen av 1953*, Oslo, Arbeidernes Faglige Landsorganisasjon.

AFL-CIO (1985), *The Changing Situation of Workers and Their Unions*, A Report by the AFL-CIO Committee on the Evolution of Work, Washington, D.C., American Federation of Labor-Congress of Industrial Organizations.

Åmark, K. (1998), *Solidaritetens gränser. LO och industriförbundsfrågan under 1900-talet*, Stockholm, Atlas.

Andersen, R. (1999), *De første: glimt fra Norsk grafisk forbunds historie*, Oslo, NGF.

AscW and ASSET (1967), "The Case for Amalgamation to Form the Association of Scientific, Technical and Managerial Staffs", reproduced in Hughes, J. and Pollins, H. (1973), *Trade Unions in Great Britain*, London, David and Charles.

Auer, M. and Welte, H. (1994), "Öffnungsklauseln in der tariflichen Lohnpolitik Österreichs – Umsetzung in Betriebsvereinbarungen und politische Einschätzung", *Industrielle Beziehungen*, Vol. 1, No. 3, pp. 297-314.

Baccaro, L., Carrieri, M. and Damiano, C. (2003), "The Resurgence of the Italian Confederal Unions: Will It Last?", *European Journal of Industrial Relations*, Vol. 9, No. 1, pp. 43-59.

Bacharach, S., Bamberger, P. and Sonnenstuhl, W. (2001), *Mutual Aid and Union Renewal*, Ithaca, ILR Press.

Bain, G. (1970), *The Growth of White-Collar Unionism*, Oxford, Oxford University Press.

Bain, G. and Price, R. (1980), *Profiles of Union Growth*, London, Blackwell.

Bakka, D. Jr. (1995), *I hårdt vær. Skipsfartskrise og samlingsprosess*, Oslo, Norsk Sjøoffisersforbund.

Barling, J., Fullagar, C. and Kelloway, E. (1992), *The Union and Its Members: A Psychological Approach*, New York, Oxford University Press.

Barreto, J. (1992), *A Formação das Centrais Sindicais e do Sindicalismo Contemporâneo em Portugal (1968-1990)*, Lisboa, ICS.

Barreto, J. (1994), "Comunistas, católicos e os sindicatos sob Salazar", *Análise Social*, No. 125-126, pp. 287-317.

Barreto, J. and Naumann, R. (1998), "Portugal: Industrial Relations under Democracy", in Ferner, A. and Hyman, R. (eds.), *Changing Industrial Relations in Europe*, Oxford, Blackwell, pp. 395-425.

Benson, J. (1991), *Unions at the Workplace*, Melbourne, Oxford University Press.

Bergh, T. (1985), *Lønnskamp og etatspolitikk. Den norske Postorganisasjon 1884 – 1984*, Oslo, Den Norske Postorganisasjon.

Bergh, T. (1989), *Postvesenets underklasser i Norge. Hovedlinjer i Norsk Postforbunds historie*, Oslo, Norsk Postforbund.

Bernstein, I. (1960), "Union Growth and Structural Cycles", in Galenson, W. and Lipset, S. (eds.), *Labor and Trade Unionism: An Interdisciplinary Reader*, New York, Wiley, pp. 73-101.

Berntsen, H. (1993), *Hvem bygde landet – for hvem? Norsk bygningsindustriarbeiderforbund fra gjenreisning til krise 1945-1988*, Oslo, Fellesforbundet, seksjon Bygning.

Berry, P. and Kitchener, G. (1989), *Can Unions Survive?* Dickson (ACT), Building Workers Industrial Union (ACT Branch).

Björklund, B. (1965), *Svenska Typografförbundet*, Stockholm, Tidens förlag.

Blackburn, R. (1967), *Union Character and Social Class*, London, B.T. Batsford.

Blaschke, S. (1999), "Gewerkschaftlicher Organisationsgrad in Österreich", *Zeitschrift für Soziologie*, Vol. 28, No. 1, pp. 60-71.

Bodham, P. (1998), "Trade Union Amalgamations, Openness and the Decline in Australian Trade Union Membership", *Australian Bulletin of Labour*, Vol. 21, No. 1, pp. 18-45.

Brenner, R. (1998), "The Economics of Global Turbulence", *New Left Review*, No. 229, special issue.

Brody, D. (1993), "Workplace Contractualism in Comparative Perspective", in Lichtenstein, N. and Harris, H. (eds.), *Industrial Democracy in America: The Ambiguous Promise*, Cambridge, Cambridge University Press.

Bronfenbrenner, K. (1997), "The Effects of Plant Closing or Threat of Plant Closing on the Right of Workers to Organize", supplement to *Plant Closings and Workers Rights: A Report to the Council of Ministers by the Secretariat of the Commission for Labor Cooperation*, Dallas, TX, Bernan Press.

Brooks, G. and Gamm, S. (1976), *The Causes and Effects of Union Mergers, with Special Reference to Selected Cases in the 1960s and 1970s*, Washington, D.C., US Department of Labor.

Buchanan, R. (1974), "Merger Waves in British Unionism", *Industrial Relations Journal*, Vol. 5, No. 2, pp. 37-44.

Buchanan, R. (1981), "Mergers in British Trade Unions: 1949-1979", *Industrial Relations Journal*, Vol. 12, No. 3, pp. 40-49.

Buiting, H. (1990), "The Netherlands", in van der Linden, M. and Rojahn, J. (eds.), *The Formation of Labour Movements, 1870-1914*, Leyden, E. J. Brill, pp. 57-84.

Buksti, J. (ed.) (1980), *Organisationer under forandring. Studier i organisationssystemet i Danmark*, Århus, Politica.

Callesen, G., Christensen, S. and Grelle, H. (eds.) (1996), *Udfordring og omstilling. Bidrag til Socialdemokratiets historie 1971-1996*, Copenhagen, Fremad.

Callus, R., Morehead, A., Cully, M. and Buchanan, J. (1991), *Industrial Relations at Work: The Australian Workplace Industrial Relations Survey*, Canberra, AGPS.

Campling, J. and Michelson, G. (1997), "Trade Union Mergers in British and Australian Television Broadcasting", *British Journal of Industrial Relations*, Vol. 35, No. 2, pp. 215-242.

Carle, T., Kinnander, S., and Salin, S. (2000), *Lärarnas Riksförbund 1884-2000*, Stockholm, Informationsförlaget.

Carney, S. (1988), *Australia in Accord: Politics and Industrial Relations under the Hawke Government*, Melbourne, Sun Books/Macmillan.

Carter, B. (1991), "Politics and Process in the Making of Manufacturing, Science and Finance", *Capital and Class*, No. 45, pp. 35-71.

Cerdeira, M. (1997), "A Evolução da Sindicalização Portuguesa de 1974 a 1995", Colecção Estudos Serie C: Trabalho, Lisboa, Ministério para a Qualificação e o Emprego.

Cerdeira, M. (1997), "A Sindicalização Portuguesa de 1974 a 1995", *Sociedade e Trabalho*, No. 1, Outubro, pp. 46-53.

Cerdeira, M. and Padilha, E. (1988), *As Estruturas Sindicais Portuguesas (1933-1987)*, 3 Vols., Lisboa, MSST (Série C-Trabalho).

Certification Officer (various), Annual Reports, London, Certification Office for Trade Unions and Employers' Associations.

Chaison, G. (1972), "Federation Expulsions and Union Mergers in the United States", *Relations Industrielles*, Vol. 28, No. 2, pp. 343-361.

Chaison, G. (1981), "Union Growth and Union Mergers", *Industrial Relations*, Vol. 20, No. 1, pp. 98-108.

Chaison, G. (1982), "A Note on the Critical Dimensions of the Union Merger Process", *Relations Industrielles*, Vol. 37, No. 1, pp. 198-206.

Chaison, G. (1986), *When Unions Merge*, Lexington Mass., Lexington Books.

Chaison, G. (1996), *Union Mergers in Hard Times: The View from Five Countries*, Ithaca, Cornell University Press.

Chaison, G. (1997), "Reforming and Rationalizing Union Structure: New Directions and Unanswered Questions", in Sverke, M. (ed.), *The Future of Trade Unionism*, Aldershot, Ashgate, pp. 19-36.

Chaison, G. (2001), "Union Mergers and Union Revival: Are We Asking Too Much?", in Turner, L., Katz, H. and Hurd, R. (eds.), *Rekindling the Movement: Labor's Quest for Relevance in the Twenty-First Century*, Ithaca, ILR Press, pp. 238-255.

Chaison, G., Sverke, M. and Sjöberg, A. (2001), "How Union Mergers Affect Membership Participation", *Journal of Labor Research*, Vol. XXII, No. 2, pp. 355-372.

Chatak, E. (1991), "A Unionist's Perspective on the Future of American Unions", *Journal of Labor Research*, Vol. 12, No. 4, pp. 327-332.

Chitayat, G. (1979), *Trade Union Mergers and Labor Conglomerates*, New York, Praeger.

Clark, G. (1989), *Unions and Communities under Siege: American Communities and the Crisis of Organized Labor*, Cambridge, Cambridge University Press.

Clark, P. and Gray, L. (2000), "Assessing the Proposed IAM, UAW and USW Merger: Critical Issues and Potential Outcomes", *Journal of Labor Research*, Vol. 21, No. 1, pp. 65-82.

Clegg, H. (1976), *Trade Unionism under Collective Bargaining: A Theory Based on Comparisons of Six Countries*, Oxford, Blackwell.

Colgan, F. and Ledwith, S. (2000), "Diversity, Identities and Strategies of Women Trade Union Activists", *Gender, Work and Organization*, Vol. 7, No. 4, pp. 242-257.

Colling, T. and Dickens, L. (1998), "Selling the Case for Gender Equality: Deregulation and Equality Bargaining", *British Journal of Industrial Relations*, Vol. 36, No. 3, pp. 389-412.

Conant, J. (1993), "The Role of Managerial Discretion in Union Mergers", *Journal of Economic Behaviour and Organisation*, Vol. 20, No. 1, pp. 49-62.

Cornfield, D. (1991), "The Attitude of Employee Association Members Toward Union Mergers: The Effect of Socio-economic Status", *Industrial and Labor Relations Review*, Vol. 44, No. 2, pp. 334-348.

Costa, M. (1995), "Super Unions: Dinosaurs of the Information Age", *Southland Magazine*, Vol. 7, Autumn, pp. 13-14.

Costa, M. and Duffy, M. (1991), *Labor, Prosperity and the Nineties: Beyond the Bonsai Economy*, Sydney, Federation Press.

Crosby, M. and Easson, M. (1992), *What Should Unions Do?* Leichhardt, Pluto.

Crouch, C. (1993), *Industrial Relations and European State Traditions*, Oxford, Clarendon Press.

Cyba, E. and Papouschek, U. (1996), "Women's Interests in the Workplace: Between Delegation and Self-representation", *Transfer*, Vol. 2, No. 1, pp. 61-81.

Dabscheck, B. (1989), *Australian Industrial Relations in the 1980s*, Melbourne, Oxford University Press.

Daley, A. (1999), "The Hollowing Out of French Unions: Politics and Industrial Relations After 1981", in Martin, A. and Ross, G. (eds.), *The New Brave World of European Labor. European Trade Unions at the Millennium*, New York, Berghahn Books, pp. 167-216.

Davis, E. (1990), "The 1989 ACTU Congress: Seeking Change Within", *Journal of Industrial Relations*, Vol. 32, No. 1, pp. 100-110.

Davis, E. (1992), "The 1991 ACTU Congress: Together for Tomorrow", *Journal of Industrial Relations*, Vol. 34, No. 1, pp. 87-101.

Davis, M. (1980), "The Barren Marriage of American Labour and the Democratic Party", *New Left Review*, No. 124, pp. 43-84.

Davis, M. (1999), "Is Bigger Better? Union Size and Expenditure on Members", *Journal of Industrial Relations*, Vol. 41, No. 1, pp. 3-34.

de Lucena, M. (1976a), *O Salazarismo*, Lisboa, Perspectivas e Realidades.

de Lucena, M. (1976b), *O Marcelismo*, Lisboa, Perspectivas e Realidades.

Department of Employment and Productivity (1971), *British Labour Statistics: Historical Abstract 1886-1968*. London: HMSO.

Dewey, L. (1971), "Union Merger Pace Quickens", *Monthly Labor Review*, June, pp. 63-70.

Dølvik, J. E. (2000), "Norwegian Trade Unionism between Traditionalism and Modernisation", in Waddington, J. and Hoffman, R. (eds.), *Trade Unions in Europe*, Brussels, European Trade Union Institute, pp. 417-449.

Dølvik, J E. and Waddington, J. (2004), "Organising Marketised Services: Are Trade Unions up to the Job?", *Economic and Industrial Democracy*, Vol. 25, No. 1.

Drucker, J. (1988), "Unions in the 1990s: Fewer but Fitter?", *Personnel Management*, August, pp. 24-29.

Due, J. and Madsen, J. S. (1996a), *Forligsmagerne. De kollektive forhandlingers sociologi*, Copenhagen, DJØF Publishing.

Due, J. and Madsen, J. S. (1996b), "Socialdemokratiet og fagbevægelsen i en opbrudsperiode", in Callesen *et al.* (eds.), *Udfordring og omstilling. Bidrag til Socialdemokratiets historie 1971-1996*, Copenhagen, Fremad, pp. 485-534.

Due, J. and Madsen, J. S. (2000b), "Fagbevægelsens struktur i det 20. Århundrede", *LO-Dokumentation*, No. 1, Copenhagen, LO.

Due, J., Madsen, J. S. and Strøby Jensen, C. (1993), *Den danske Model. En historisk sociologisk analyse af det kollektive aftalesystem*, Copenhagen, DJØF Publishing.

Due, J., Madsen, J. S. and Strøby Jensen, C. (2000), "The September Compromise: A Strategic Choice by Danish Employers in 1899", *Historical Studies in Industrial Relations*, No. 10, Autumn, pp. 39-66.

Due, J., Madsen, J. S., Strøby Jensen, C. and Petersen, L. (1994), *The Survival of the Danish Model. A Historical Sociological Analysis of the Danish System of Collective Bargaining*, Copenhagen, DJØF Publishing.

Dunlop, J. (1948), "The Development of Labour Organisation", in Lester, R. and Shister, J. (eds.), *Insights into Labor Issues*, New York, Wiley, pp. 163-193.

Dworkin, J. and Extejt, M. (1979), "Why Workers Decertify their Unions", *Proceedings of the 39th Annual Meeting of the Academy of Management*, Georgia, August, pp. 241-245.

Ebbinghaus, B. (1990), "Where Does Trade Union Diversity Come From? Studying the Formation and Transformation of Western European Trade Union Systems", paper presented at European University Institute, Florence, June, 81 pp.

Ebbinghaus, B. and Visser, J. (1990), "Where Does Trade Union Diversity Come From?", paper presented at XII World Congress of Sociology, Madrid, July, 32 pp.

Ebbinghaus, B. and Visser, J. (eds.) (2000), *Trade Union in Western Europe since 1945*, London, Macmillan Reference.

Ebbinghaus, B., in co-operation with Scheuer, S. (2000), "Denmark", in Ebbinghaus and Visser (eds.), *Trade Union in Western Europe since 1945*, London, Macmillan Reference, pp. 157-99.

Edwards, R. and Podgursky, M. (1986), "The Unraveling Accord: American Unions in Crisis", in Edwards, R., Garonna, P. and Todtling, F. (eds.), *Unions in Crisis and Beyond: Perspectives from Six Countries*, Dover, Mass., Auburn House, pp. 14-60.

Elias, P. (1973), "Trade Union Amalgamations: Patterns and Procedures", *Industrial Law Journal*, Vol. 2, No. 3, pp. 125-136.

Estey, M. (1966), "Trends in Concentration of Union Membership, 1897-1962", *Quarterly Journal of Economics*, Vol. 80, pp. 343-360.

Estey, M. (1967), *The Unions: Structure, Development and Management*, New York, Harcourt, Brace & World Inc.

Fajertag, G. and Pochet, P. (eds.) (2000), *Social Pacts in Europe – New Dynamics*, Brussels, European Trade Union Institute.

Fakiolas P. (1978), *Trade Unionism in Greece*, Athens, Papazisis (in Greek).

Farner, K. (1991), *Norges Juristforbund gjennom 25 år*, Oslo, Norges Juristforbund.

Ferner, A. and Hyman, R. (eds.) (1992), *Industrial Relations in the New Europe*, Oxford, Blackwell.

Ferner, A. and Hyman, R. (eds.) 1998, *Changing Industrial Relations in Europe*, Oxford, Blackwell.

Fichter, M. (1990), *Einheit und Organisation. Der Deutsche Gewerkschaftsbund im Aufbau 1945 bis 1949*, Köln, Bund-Verlag.

Fink, G. (1977), *Labor Unions*, Westport, Greenwood Press.

Fiorito, J. (2003), "Union Organizing in the United States", in Gall, G. (ed.), *Union Organizing: Campaigning for Trade Union Recognition*, London, Routledge, pp. 191-210.

Fiorito, J., Jarley, P. and Delaney, J. (1995), "National Union Effectiveness in Organizing: Measures and Influences", *Industrial and Labor Relations Review*, Vol. 48, No. 4, pp. 613-635.

Flecker, J. and Schulten, T. (1999), "The End of Institutional Stability: What Future for the German Model?", *Economic and Industrial Democracy*, Vol. 20, No. 1, pp. 81-115.

Florin, C. (1987), *Kampen om katedern. Feminiserings- och professionaliseringsprocessen inom den svenska folkskolans lärarkår 1860-1906*, Stockholm, Almqvist & Wiksell International.

Floryan, J. and Lindholm, S. (1980), "Akademikernes organisering – udvikling, struktur og problemer", in Buksti, J. (ed.), *Organisationer under forandring. Studier i organisationssystemet i Danmark*, Århus, Politica, pp. 170-214.

Freeman, J. and Brittain, J. (1977), "Union Merger Process and Industrial Environment", *Industrial Relations*, Vol. 16, No. 2, pp. 173-185.

Fulcher, J. (1991), *Labour Movements, Employers and the State. Conflict and Co-operation in Britain and Sweden*, Oxford, Clarendon Press.

Gahan, P. (1996), "Did Arbitration Make for Dependent Unionism? Evidence from Historical Case Studies", *Journal of Industrial Relations*, Vol. 38, No. 4, pp. 648-698.

Galenson, W. (1952), *The Danish System of Labor Relations: A Study in Industrial Peace*, Cambridge, Mass., Harvard University Press.

Galenson, W. (1960), *The CIO Challenge to the AFL*, Cambridge, Mass., Harvard University Press.

Garcia, A., Hacourt, B. and Lega, H. (1999), *The Second Sex of European Trade Unionism*, Brussels, European Trade Union Confederation.

Geroski, P. and Knight, K. (1984), "Corporate Merger and Collective Bargaining in the UK", *Industrial Relations Journal*, Vol. 15, No. 2, pp. 51-60.

Gifford, C. (various), *Directory of U.S. Labor Organizations*, Washington, D.C., The Bureau of National Affairs.

Gill, H. and Griffin, V. (1981), "The Fetish of Order: Reform in Australian Union Structure", *Journal of Industrial Relations*, Vol. 23, No. 3, pp. 362-382.

Gilson, C. and Wagar, T. (1992) "Accounting for Union Success in Representation Elections: Some Canadian Evidence", International Industrial Relations Association, World Congress, Sydney, September.

Gitelman, H. (1965), "Adolph Strasser and the Origins of Pure and Simple Unionism", *Labor History*, Vol. 6, pp. 71-83.

Glocker, T. (1915), "Amalgamation of Related Trades in American Unions", *American Economic Review*, Vol. 5, No. 3, pp. 554-575.

Goldfield, M. (1987), *The Decline of Organised Labor in the United States*, Chicago, University of Chicago Press.

Greve, A. (1995), *Førskolelærernes historie: på vei mot en yrkesidentitet*, Oslo, Universitetsforlaget.

Griffin, G. (1994), "The Authority of the ACTU", *The Economic and Labour Relations Review*, Vol. 5, No. 1. pp. 81-103.

Griffin, G. and Giuca, V. (1986), "One Union Peak Council: The Merger of ACSPA and CAGEO with the ACTU", *Journal of Industrial Relations*, Vol. 28, No. 4, pp. 483-503.

Griffin, G. and Scarcebrook, V. (1989), "Trends in Mergers of Federally Registered Unions, 1904-1986", *Journal of Industrial Relations*, Vol. 31, No. 2, pp. 257-262.

Griffin, G. and Svensen, S. (1996), "The Decline of Australian Union Density – A Survey of the Literature", *Journal of Industrial Relations*, Vol. 38, No. 4, pp. 507-547.

Griffin, G., Svensen, S. and Teicher, J. (1997), "Trade Union Non-Industrial Services: Membership Attitudes", *Labour and Industry*, Vol. 7, No. 3, pp. 31-42.

GSEE (1995), *Organisational Restructures of Federations, Labour Centres and Primary Level Unions*, mimeo, 12 pages. (in Greek).

Hadenius, A. (1976), *Facklig organisationsutveckling*, Uppsala, Statsvetenskapliga föreningen.

Hadenius, A. (1976), *Facklig organisationsutveckling. En studie av Landsorganisationen i Sverige*, Stockholm, Rabén & Sjögren.

Hagemann, G. (1992), *Skolefolk: lærernes historie i Norge*, Oslo, Ad notam Gyldendal.

Hallenstvedt, A. *et al.* (1983), *Norske organisasjoner*, 4. rev. og ajourførte utg., Oslo, Tanum-Norli.

Halvorsen, T. (1990), *Jern og metall 100 år. 1941-1991*, Oslo, Fellesforbundet Seksjon Jern og Metall/Tiden Norsk Forlag.

Hamann, K. and Martinez Lucio, M. (2003), "Strategies of Union Revitalization in Spain: Negotiating Change and Fragmentation", *European Journal of Industrial Relations*, Vol. 9, No. 1, pp. 61-78.

Hanley, G. (1999), "Member-Union Satisfaction in Australia", *Australian Bulletin of Labour*, Vol. 25, No. 4, pp. 306-333.

Hansen, A. (1949), *Norsk høvleriarbeiderforbund: Sagbruks- og høvleriarbeidernes organisasjonshistorie 1889 – 1949*, Oslo, Forbundet.

Hansson, S. (1925), *Svenska Träarbetareförbundets historia 1889-1923*, Stockholm, Svenska Träarbetareförbundet.

Hassel, A. (1999), "The Erosion of the German System of Industrial Relations", *British Journal of Industrial Relations*, Vol. 37, No. 3, pp. 483-506.

Heckscher, C. (1988), *The New Unionism*, New York, Basic Books.

Heidenheimer, A. (1976), "Professional Unions, Public Sector Growth and the Swedish Equality Policy", *Comparative Politics*, Vol. 9, No. 1, pp. 49-73.

Hendricks, W., Gramm, C. and Fiorito, J. (1993), "Centralization of Bargaining Decisions in American Unions", *Industrial Relations*, Vol. 32, No. 3, pp. 367-390.

Hoffmann, J. (2001), "Industrial Relations and Trade Unions in Germany: The Pressure of Modernisation and Globalisation", in Waddington, J. and Hoffmann, R. (eds.), *Trade Unions in Europe: Facing Challenges and Searching for Solutions*, Brussels, ETUI.

Hoffmann, J., Hoffmann, R., Lange, D. and Mückenberger, U. (eds.) (1990), *Jenseits der Beschlußlage: Gewerkschaft als Zukunftswerkstatt*, Köln, Bund-Verlag.

Hoffmann, R. and Waddington, J. (1998), "Tendenzen gewerkschaftlicher Organisationspolitik in Europa", *Gewerkschaftliche Monatshefte*, Vol. 49, No. 5, pp. 297-309.

Howard, W. (1987), "Australian Trade Unions in the Context of Union Theory", *Journal of Industrial Relations*, Vol. 19, No. 3, pp. 255-73.

Howells, J. and Cathro, S. (1981), "Union Growth and Concentration Revisited", *Journal of Industrial Relations*, Vol. 23, No. 1, pp. 23-32.

Hughes, J. (1967), *Trade Union Structure and Government: Structure and Government*, Research Paper 5, Part 1, Royal Commission on Trade Unions and Employers' Associations, London, HMSO.

Humphrey, J. (2002), *Towards a Politics of the Rainbow: Self-organization in the Trade Union Movement*, Aldershot, Ashgate.

Huzzard, T. (2000), *Labouring to Learn: Union Renewal in Swedish Manufacturing*, Umeå, Boréa.

Hyman, R. (1999), "Imagined Solidarities: Can Trade Unions Resist Globalization?", in Leisink, P. (ed.), *Globalization and Labour Relations*, Cheltenham, Edward Elgar, pp. 94-115.

ILO (1997), *World Labour Report 1997-98: Industrial Relations, Democracy and Social Stability*, Geneva, International Labour Office.

Ioannou, C. (1989), *Salaried Employment and Trade Unionism in Greece*, Athens, Mediterranean Studies Foundation (in Greek)

Ioannou, C. (1994), "The National System of Industrial Relations in Post-war Greece, 1955-67", in Sakis Karagiorgas Foundation, *The Post-war Greek Society 1945-67*, Athens, Sakis Karagiorgas Foundation, pp. 73-105 (in Greek).

Ioannou, C. (1995), "Free Collective Bargaining and Elements of Continuity in Laws 3239/1955 and 1876/1990", *Labour Law Review*, Vol. 54, No. 20, pp. 908-911. (in Greek).

Ioannou, C. (1996), "Trade Unions in Greece: Change and Continuity", *Transfer*, Vol. 2, No. 3, pp. 500-518.

Ioannou, C. (1997), "The Unequal Development of Greek Trade Unionism: A Microeconomic Analysis", *Industrial Relations Journal*, Vol. 2, No. 5, pp. 21-37. (in Greek)

Ioannou, C. (1999), *Trade Unions in Greece: Development Structures and Prospects*, Athens, Friedrich Ebert Foundation.

Ioannou, C. (2000), "Change and Continuity in Greek Industrial Relations: The Role and Impact on Trade Unions", in Waddington, J. and Hoffmann, R. (eds.), *Trade Unions in Europe*, Brussels, European Trade Union Institute, pp. 277-304.

Ioannou, C. (2000), "Social Pacts in Hellenic Industrial Relations: Odysseys or Sisyphus?", in Fajertag, G. and Pochet, P. (eds.), *Social Pacts in Europe*, Brussels, European Trade Union Institute and Observatoire Social Européen, pp. 219-236.

IRS (1992), "Germany – Debate on Union Reform", *European Industrial Relations Review*, April, No. 219, pp. 12-14.

IRS (1996), "Metal and Wood Workers' Unions to Merge", *European Industrial Relations Review*, December, No. 275, p. 6.

Janus, C. (1978), "Union Mergers in the 1970s: A Look at the Reasons and Results", *Monthly Labor Review*, October, pp. 13-23.

Jecchinis, C. (1967), *Trade Unionism in Greece: A Study in Political Paternalism*, Chicago, Roosevelt University.

Johnsson, L. (1998), *Förbund på sju hav*, Vol. 3, Stockholm, Seko sjöfolk.

Jørgensen, C. (1999), "Danish Union of Graphical Workers Dissolves", eironline, www.eiro.eurofound.ie, 4 pp.

Kamsvåg, J. (1990), *Med nål og tråd gjennom 100 år: Bekledningsarbeiderforbundet 1890-1990*, Oslo, Fellesforbundet, Seksjon bekledning/Tiden Norsk Forlag.

Karlhofer, F. (1999), "Verbände: Organisation, Mitgliederintegration, Regierbarkeit", in Karlhofer, F. and Tálos, E. (eds.), *Zukunft der Sozialpartnerschaft. Veränderungsdynamik und Reformbedarf*, Vienna: Signum, pp. 15-46.

Katsanevas, T. (1984), *Trade Unions in Greece*, Athens, National Centre for Social Research (EKKE).

Kauppinen, T. and Waddington, J. (2000), "Finland: Adapting to Decentralisation", in Waddington, J. and Hoffmann, R. (eds.), *Trade Unions in Europe*, Brussels, European Trade Union Institute, pp. 183-214.

Keller, B. (2001), *Ver.di: Triumphmarsch oder Gefangenenchor? Neustrukturierung der Interessenvertretung im Dienstleistungssektor*, Hamburg, VSA.

Kelley, M. (2000), "The Participatory Bureaucracy", in Ichniowski, C., Levine, D., Olson, C. and Strauss, G. (eds.), *The American Workplace: Skills, Compensation and Employee Involvement*, Cambridge, Cambridge University Press, pp. 81-110.

Kelly, D. (1994), "Trade Unionism in 1993", *Journal of Industrial Relations*, Vol. 36, No. 1, pp. 135-146.

Kerr, C. (1983), *The Future of Industrial Societies: Convergence or Continuing Diversity?*, Cambridge, Mass., Harvard University Press.

Kircher, W. (1968), *Testimony before the Special Subcommittee on Labor of the Committee on Education and Labor of the US House of Representatives*, H.R. 11725, Washington D.C., Government Printing Office.

Kittel, B. and Tálos, E. (1999), "Interessenvermittlung und politischer Entscheidungsprozeß: Sozialpartnerschaft in den 1990er Jahren", in Karlhofer, F. and Tálos, E. (eds.), *Zukunft der Sozialpartnerschaft. Veränderungsdynamik und Reformbedarf*, Vienna, Signum, pp. 95-136.

Kjellberg, A. (1983), *Facklig organisering i tolv länder*, Lund, Arkiv förlag.

Kjellberg, A. (1998), "Sweden: Restoring the Model?" in Ferner, A. and Hyman, R. (eds.), *Changing Industrial Relations in Europe*, Oxford, Blackwell.

Kjellberg, A. (2000a), "Sweden", in Ebbinghaus, B. and Visser, J., *Trade Unions in Western Europe since 1945*, London, Macmillan Reference.

Kjellberg, A. (2000b), "The Multitude of Challenges Facing Swedish Trade Unions", in Waddington, J. and Hoffmann, R. (eds.), *Trade Unions in Europe. Facing Challenges and Searching for Solutions*, Brussels, ETUI.

Kjellberg, A. (2001), *Fackliga organisationer och medlemmar i dagens Sverige*, Lund, Arkiv förlag.

Klenner, F. and Pellar, B. (1999), *Die österreichische Gewerkschaftsbewegung. Von den Anfängen bis 1999*, Vienna, Verlag des österreichischen Gewerkschaftbundes.

Kochan, T. (1980), *Collective Bargaining and Industrial Relations: From Theory to Policy and Practice*, Homewood, Irwin.

Kochan, T. and Wever, K. (1991), "American Unions and the Future of Worker Representation", in Strauss, G., Gallagher, D. and Fiorito, J. (eds.), *The State of the Unions*, Madison, Industrial Relations Research Association, pp. 363-386.

Kochan, T., Katz, H. and McKersie, R. (1986), *The Transformation of American Industrial Relations*, New York, Basic Books.

Kohaut, S. and Bellmann, L. (1997), "Betriebliche Determinanten der Tarifbindung: Eine empirische Analyse auf der Basis des IAB-Betriebspanels 1995", *Industrielle Beziehungen*, Vol. 4, No. 4, pp. 317-334.

Koopmann, P. (2000), *Gewerkschaftsfusion und Tarifautonomie*, Berlin, Duncker und Humblot.

Koukiadis, I. (1981), *Labour Law, Collective Industrial Relations*, Thessaloniki, Paratiritis (in Greek).

Koukoules G. (1984), *Greek Trade Unions: Financial Independence and Dependency*, Athens, Odysseas (in Greek)

Kuhn, R. (1993), "The Limits of Social Democratic Economic Policy in Australia", *Capital and Class*, Vol. 51, Autumn, pp. 17-43.

Labor Notes. (1995), "Union Merger: Is Bigger Better?", September, pp. 1 and 14.

Labor Notes (1996), "Activists to Press for Democracy in UAW-IAM-USWA Merger", March, pp. 4 and 13-14.

Latta, G. (1972), "Trade Union Finance", *British Journal of Industrial Relations*, Vol. 10, No. 3, pp. 392-411.

Lester, R. (1958), *As Unions Mature: an analysis of the evolution of American unionism*, Princeton, Princeton University Press.

Lewin, D. (1986), "Public Employee Unionism and Labor Relations in the 1980s: An Analysis of Transformation", in Lipset, S. (ed.), *Unions in Transition: entering the second century*, San Francisco, ICS Press, pp. 241-264.

Lichtenstein, N. (1989), "From Corporatism to Collective Bargaining: Organized Labor and the Eclipse of Social Democracy in the Postwar Era", in Fraser, S. and Gerstle, G. (eds.), *The Rise and Fall of the New Deal Order 1930-1980*, Princeton, Princeton University Press, pp. 122-152.

Lilja, K. (1992), "Finland: No Longer the Nordic Exception", in Ferner, A. and Hyman, R. (eds.), *Industrial Relations in the New Europe*, Oxford, Blackwell, pp. 198-217.

Lindgren, J. (1938), *Svenska Metallindustriarbetareförbundets historia 1888-1905*, Vol. I, Stockholm, Tiden.

Lindgren, J., Tingsten, H. and Westerståhl, J. (1948), *Svenska Metallindustriarbetareförbundets historia 1906-1925*, Vol. II, Stockholm, Tiden.

Lipset, S. and Rokkan, S. (1967), "Cleavage Structures, Party Systems and voter alignments: An Introduction", in Lipset, S. and Rokkan, S. (eds.), *Party systems and Voter Alignments: Cross National Perspectives*, New York, Free Press, pp. 1-64.

LO (various), *Beretning*. Annual reports, 1946 – 1999, Oslo, Landsorganisasjonen i Norge.

Locke, R.M. and Baccaro, L. (1999), "The Resurgence of Italian Unions?", in Martin, A. and Ross, G. (eds.), *The New Brave World of European Labor. European Trade Unions at the Millennium*, New York, Berghahn Books, pp. 217-268.

Lorwin, L. (1933), *The American Federation of Labor: History, Policies and Prospects*, Washington, D.C., The Brookings Institution.

Madsen, M. (2000), "Fagbevægelsens rekrutteringsgrundlag", in *LO-Dokumentation*, No. 1, Copenhagen, LO, pp. 33-55.

Maranto, C. and Fiorito, J. (1987), "The Effects of Union Characteristics on the Outcome of NLRB Elections", *Industrial and Labor Relations Review*, Vol. 40, No. 2, pp. 225-240.

Markovits, A. (1986), *The Politics of the West German Trade Unions: Strategies of Class and Interest Representation in Growth and Crisis*, Cambridge, Cambridge University Press.

Martin, A. and Ross, G. (1999), *The New Brave World of European Labor. European Trade Unions at the Millennium*, New York, Berghahn Books.

Martin, R. (1980), *TUC: The Growth of a Pressure Group 1868-1976*, Oxford, Clarendon Press.

Martin, R. (1992), *Bargaining Power*, Oxford, Clarendon Press.

Masters, M. (1997), *Unions at the Crossroads: Strategic Membership, Financial, and Political Perspectives*, Westport, Connecticut, Quorum Books.

Masters, M. and Atkin, R. (1997), "The Finances of Major U.S. Unions", *Industrial Relations*, Vol. 36, No. 4, pp. 489-506.

McBride, A. (2001), *Gender Democracy in Trade Unions*, Aldershot, Ashgate.

McClendon, J., Kriesky, J. and Eaton, A. (1995), "Member Support for Union Mergers: An Analysis of an Affiliation Referendum", *Journal of Labor Research*, Vol. 16, No. 1, pp. 9-23.

Mielke, S., Rütters, P. and Tudyka, K. (1994), "Trade Union Organisation and Employee Representation", in Lecher, W. (ed.), *Trade Unions in the European Union. A Handbook*, London, Lawrence and Wishart, pp. 129-234.

Mitsou, T. (1992), *La Représentativité des Partenaires Sociaux en Grèce*, Etude pour la Commission des Communautés Européennes, Athènes, Mimeo.

Mitsou, T. (1993), *Les Organisations Ouvrières les plus représentatives en Grèce*, Etude pour la Commission des Communautés Européennes, Athènes, mimeo.

Moody, K. (1988), *An Injury to All*, London, Verso.

Moren, J. (1966), *Oppslagsboken norske organisasjoner*, Oslo, Tanum.

Moren, J., *et al.* (1972), *Norske organisasjoner. Ny, rev. og ajourført utg*, Oslo, Tanum.

Morris, T. (1986), "Trade Union Mergers and Competition in British Banking", *Industrial Relations Journal*, Vol. 17, No. 2, pp. 129-140.

Morris, T., Storey, J., Wilkinson, A. and Cressey, P. (2001), "Industry Change and Union Mergers in British Retail Finance", *British Journal of Industrial Relations*, Vol. 39, No. 2, pp. 237-256.

Mortimer, J.E. (1982), *History of the Boilermakers' Society (1906-1935)*, Vol. 2, London, George Allen and Unwin.

Müller-Jentsch, W. and Ittermann. P. (2000), *Industrielle Beziehungen: Daten, Zeitreihen, Trends, 1950-1999*, Frankfurt, Campus.

Müller-Jentsch, W. And Weitbrecht, H. (eds.) (2003), *The Changing Contours of German Industrial Relations*, München and Mehring, Rainer Hampp Verlag.

NaFo (1995), "Norsk Naturforvalterforbund 25 år", *NaFo-nytt*, No. 16, Oslo, Norsk Naturforvalterforbund, p. 5.

Naumann, R. and Stoleroff, A. (1996), "Portugal", in *Handbook of Trade Unions in Europe*, Brussels, European Trade Union Institute, pp. 1-44.

Nelson, R. (1973), "Assembly of Governmental Employees Stresses Professionalism", *Monthly Labor Review*, Vol. 96, No. 11, pp. 56-57.

Niedenhoff, H-U. and Wilke, M. (1991), *Der neue DGB – Vom Industrieverband zur Multibranchen-gewerkschaft*, Köln, Deutscher Instituts-Verlag.

Nilsson, B. (1996), *Kvinnor i statens tjänst – från biträden till tjänstemän*, Stockholm, Almqvist & Wiksell International.

NNN (1998), *Næringsmiddelarbeideren. 1923-1998 NNN 75 år*, 71. årgang, No. 8-9, Oslo, Norsk Nærings- og Nytelsesmiddelarbeiderforbund.

Norges Juristforbund (2000), *Nye løsninger for en ny virkelighet!*, Sluttrapport fra utvalget som har vurdert organisasjonsoppbygging og ressursbruk i Norges Juristforbund, Levert forbundsstyret 28. august 2000, Oslo, Norges Juristforbund.

NWC (National Wage Case) (1986), Canberra, AGPS.

Offe, C. and Wiesenthal, S. (1985), "Two Logics of Collective Action", in Offe, C. (ed.), *Disorganized Capitalism*, Cambridge Mass., The MIT Press.

Optenhogel, U. and Stoleroff, A. (1985), "The Logics of Politically Competing Trade Union Confederations in Portugal: 1974-1984", in Ferreira, E-S. and Opello, W. (eds.), *Conflict and Change in Portugal 1974-1984*, Lisboa, Teorema, pp. 179-190.

Östberg, K. (1997), *Efter rösträtten. Kvinnors utrymme efter det demokratiska genombrottet*, Stockholm/Stehag, Brutus Östlings Bokförlag Symposion.

Palaiologos, N. (2002), "From Tradition to the Need for Reform: Critical Comments on the Structure and Operation of the Greek Trade Unions Movement", in *Labour 2002*, Athens, Panteion University, pp. 283-295 (in Greek).

Parker, M. and Slaughter, J. (1988), *Choosing Sides: Unions and the Team Concept*, Boston, South End Press.

Patriarca, F. (1994), "A regulamentação de trabalho nos primeiros anos do regime corporativo", *Análise Social*, Vol. XXIX, No. 128, pp. 801-839.

Patriarca, F. (1995), *A questão social no Salazarismo 1930-1947*, Lisboa, Imprensa Nacional, Casa da Moeda.

Pedersen, C. (1980), "FTF's dannelsen og udvikling", in Buksti, J. (ed.), *Organisationer under forandring. Studier i organisationssystemet i Danmark*, Århus, Politica, pp. 133-169.

Peetz, D. (1998), *Unions in a Contrary World: The Future of the Australian Trade Union Movement*, Melbourne, Cambridge University Press.

Peissl, W. (1994), *Das "bessere" Proletariat*, Vienna, Verlag für Gesellschaftskritik.

Perlman, S. (1928), *A Theory of the Labor Movement*, New York, MacMillan.

Preis, A. (1964), *Labor's Giant Step: Twenty Years of the CIO*, New York, Pioneer Publishers.

Quinlan, M. (1987), "Early Trade Union Organization in Australia: Three Australian Colonies, 1829-1850", *Labour and Industry*, Vol. 1, No. 3, pp. 61-95.

Rappe, H. (1992), "Gespräch mit Hermann Rappe über die Fusionspläne von IG Papier-Chemie-Keramik und IG Bergbau und Energie und das Verhältnis zwischen Gewerkschaften und DGB", *Gewerkschaftliche Monatshefte*, No. 1, pp. 8-13.

Rawson, D. (1992), "Has Unionism a Future?", in Crosby. M. and Easson, M. (eds.), *What Should Unions Do?*, Leichhardt, Pluto.

Regalia, I. and Regini, M. (1998), "Italy: The Dual Character of Industrial Relations", in Ferner, A. and Hyman, R. (eds.), *Changing Industrial Relations in Europe*, Oxford, Blackwell, pp. 459-503.

Rimmer, M. (1981), "Long Run Structural Change in Australian Trade Unionism", *Journal of Industrial Relations*, Vol. 23 No. 3, pp. 323-343.

Roche, W. (2000), "Ireland", in Ebbinghaus, B. and Visser, J. (eds.), *Trade Unions in Western Europe since 1945*, London, Macmillan, pp. 339-369.

Seip, Å. (1990), *Lektorene. Profesjon, organisasjon og politikk 1890 – 1980*, Fafo Report 108, Oslo, Fafo.

Sheflin, N. and Troy, L. (1983), "Finances of American Unions in the 1970s", *Journal of Labor Research*, Vol. 4, No. 2, pp. 149-157.

Sheridan, T. (1975), *Mindful Militants: The Amalgamated Engineering Union in Australia 1920-72*, Melbourne, Cambridge University Press.

Sneade, A. (2001), "Trade Union Membership 1999-2000: An Analysis of Data from the Certification Officer and the Labour Force Survey", *Labour Market Trends*, September, pp. 433-444.

Statistics Norway (various), *Statistisk Årbok (Statistical Yearbook)*, Annual volumes 1956 – 2000, Oslo, Statistics Norway.

Stieber, J. (1973), *Public Employee Unionism: Structure, Growth, Policy*, Washington, D.C., Brookings Institution.

Stinchcombe, A. (1965), "Social Structure and Organisations", in March, J. (ed.), *Handbook of Organisations*, Chicago, Rand McNally, pp. 142-193.

Stokke, T-A. (1998), *Lønnsforhandlinger og konfliktløsning. Norge i et skandinavisk perspektiv*, Dissertation, Fafo-Report No. 246, Oslo, Fafo.

Stokke, T-A. (2000), *Organisasjonsgrader i norsk arbeidsliv 1945-1998*, Fafo-notat 10, Oslo, Fafo.

Stokke, T-A., Evju, S. and Frøland, H-O. (2003), *Det kollektive arbeidslivet. Organisasjoner, tariffavtaler, lønnsoppgjør og inntektspolitikk*, Oslo, Universitetsforlaget.

Stoleroff, A. (1988), "Relações Industriais e Sindicalismo em Portugal", *Sociologia: Problemas e Práticas*, No. 4, Maio, pp. 147-164.

Stoleroff, A. (2000), "The Professional Urge in the Formation of Unions and Union Practice in Democratic Portugal", paper presented to Interim Conference of ISA Research Committee Sociology of Professional Groups, RC52, Lisbon, Portugal, 13-15 September.

Stoleroff, A. (2001), "Unemployment and Trade Union Strength in Portugal", in Bermeo, N. (ed.), *Unemployment in the New Europe*, Cambridge, Cambridge University Press, pp. 173-202.

Stoleroff, A. and Naumann, R. (1994), "A Sindicalização em Portugal: A Sua Medida e a Sua Distribuição", *Sociologia: Problemas e Práticas*, No. 14, Setembro, pp. 19-47.

Stratton-Devine, K. (1992), "Union Merger Benefits: An Empirical Analysis", *Journal of Labor Research*, Vol. 13, No. 1, pp. 133-143.

Strauss, G. (1993), "Issues in Union Structure", *Research in the Sociology of Organizations*, Vol. 12, pp. 1-49.

Strauss, G. (2000), "What's Happening inside US Unions: Democracy and Union Politics", *Journal of Labor Research*, Vol. 21, No. 2, pp. 211-225.

Streeck, W. and Visser, J. (1997), "An Evolutionary Dynamic of Trade Union Systems", MPIfG Discussion Paper No. 4, Cologne, Max Planck Institute for the Study of Societies.

Streeck, W. and Visser, J. (1997), "The Rise of the Conglomerate Union", *European Journal of Industrial Relations*, Vol. 3, No. 3, pp. 305-332.

Streeck, W. and Visser, J. (1998), "An Evolutionary Dynamic of Trade Union Systems", MPIfG Discussion Paper, No. 4, Cologne, Max Planck Institute for the Study of Societies.

Strøby Jensen, C. (ed.) (2001), *Arbejdsgivere i Norden. En sociologisk analyse af arbejdsgiverorganiseringen i Norge, Sverige, Finland og Danmark*, Copenhagen, Nordisk Ministerråd.

Strøby Jensen, C., Madsen, J. S. and Due, J. (2001), "Arbejdsgiverorganisering i Danmark – et institutionssociologisk perspektiv på arbejdsgiverorganiseringens betydning for den danske arbejdsmarkedsmodel", in Strøby Jensen, C. (ed.), *Arbejdsgivere i Norden. En sociologisk analyse af arbejdsgiverorganiseringen i Norge, Sverige, Finland og Danmark*, Copenhagen, Nordisk Ministerråd, pp. 83-154.

Sverke, M. and Sjöberg, A. (1997), "Short-term Merger Effects on Member Attitudes and Behaviour", in Sverke, M. (ed.), *The Future of Trade Unionism: International Perspectives on Emerging Union Structures*, Aldershot, Ashgate, pp. 347-360.

Swabe, A. and Price, P. (1984), "Building a Permanent Association? The Development of Staff Associations in the Building Societies", *British Journal of Industrial Relations*, Vol. 22, No. 2, pp. 195-204.

Taft, P. (1963), "On the Origins of Business Unionism", *Industrial and Labor Relations Review*, Vol. 17, No. 1, pp. 20-38.

TCO (1944, 1946), *Tjänstemännens Centralorganisation. Styrelsens och revisorernas berättelser*, Stockholm, TCO.

Tenfelde, K., Schönhoven, K., Schneider, M., Peukert, D. (1987), *Geschichte der Deutschen Gewerkschaften, von den Anfängen bis 1945*, Köln, Bund-Verlag.

Thue, L. (1986), *Fra bestillingsmannsforening til moderne fagforbund. Kommunalansattes Fellesorganisasjon 1936-1986*, Oslo, Kommunalansattes Fellesorganisasjon.

Tomasek, H. (1999), "Organisationsreformprozesse im ÖGB", in Kaiser, E., Berndt, A., Füreder, H. and Greif, W. (eds.), *Auf zu neuen Ufern. Gewerkschaftliche Organisierungsmodelle in Österreich und Europa*, Vienna, Verlag des österreichischen Gewerkschaftbundes, pp. 139-160.

Tomkins, M. (1999), "Trade Union Amalgamations: Explaining the Recent Spate of Mergers in Australia", *Labour and Industry*, Vol. 9, No. 3, pp. 61-77.

Traxler, F. (1996), "Collective Bargaining and Industrial Change, A Case of Disorganisation: A Comparative Analysis of Eighteen OECD Countries", *European Sociological Review*, Vol. 12, No. 3, pp. 271-287.

Traxler, F. (1998), "Austria: Still the Country of Corporatism", in Ferner, A. and Hyman, R. (eds.), *Changing Industrial Relations in Europe*, Oxford, Blackwell, pp. 239-261.

Traxler, F. (2000), *European Employment and Industrial Relations Glossary: Austria*, London, Sweet and Maxwell.

Troy, L. (1975), "American Unions and Their Wealth", *Industrial Relations*, Vol. 14, No. 2, pp. 134-144.

Troy, L. and Sheflin, N. (1985), *Union Sourcebook: Membership, Finances, Structure, Directory*, West Orange, New Jersey, Industrial Relations Data and Information Services.

TUC (1947), *Trade Union Structure and Closer Unity*, London, Trades Union Congress.

TUC (1966), *Report of the 98th Annual Congress*, London, Trade Union Congress.

TUC (1999), *Meeting the Millennial Challenge*, London, Trades Union Congress.

TUC (various), *Annual Report*, London, Trades Union Congress.

Ulman, L. (1955), *The Rise of the National Trade Union: The Development and Significance of Its Structure, Governing Institutions, And Economic Policy*, Cambridge Mass., Harvard University Press.

Undy, R. (1999), "Negotiating Amalgamations: Territorial and Political Consolidation and Administrative Reform in Public-Sector Unions in the UK", *British Journal of Industrial Relations*, Vol. 37, No. 3, pp. 445-463.

Undy, R., Ellis, V., McCarthy, W. and Halmos, A. (1981), *Change in Trade Unions: The Development of UK Unions since the 1960s*, London, Hutchinson.

Undy, R., Fosh, P., Morris, H., Smith, P. and Martin, R. (1996), *Managing the Unions: The Impact of Legislation on Trade Unions' Behaviour*, New York, Oxford University Press.

UNISON. (1993), *Rules as at Vesting Day*, London, UNISON.

Vester, M., Oertzen, P., Gelling, H., Hermann, T. and Müller, D. (1993), *Soziale Milieus im gesellschaftlichen Strukturwandel*, Köln, Bund Verlag.

Restructuring Representation

Visser, J. and Waddington, J. (1996), "Industrialisation and Politics: A Century of Union Structural Development in Three European Countries", *European Journal of Industrial Relations*, Vol. 2, No. 1, pp. 21-53.

Vlastos, S. (1996), *Civil Associations, Trade Unions and Employers' Organisations*, Athens, P.N. Sakkoulas (in Greek).

Voos, P. (1983), "Union Organising: Costs and Benefits", *Industrial and Labor Relations Review*, Vol. 36, No. 4, pp. 576-591.

Voos, P. (1984), "Trends in Union Organizing Expenditures, 1953-1977", *Industrial and Labor Relations Review*, Vol. 38, No. 1, pp. 52-63.

Voss, K. and Sherman, R. (2000), "Breaking the Iron Law of Oligarchy: Union Revitalization in the American Labor Movement", *American Journal of Sociology*, Vol. 103, No. 2, pp. 303-349.

Waddington, J. (1988), "Business Unionism and Fragmentation within the TUC", *Capital and Class*, No. 36, pp. 7-15.

Waddington, J. (1988), "Trade Union Mergers: A Study of Trade Union Structural Dynamics", *British Journal of Industrial Relations*, Vol. 26, No. 3, pp. 409-430.

Waddington, J. (1992), "Trade Union Membership in Britain, 1980-1987: Unemployment and Restructuring", *British Journal of Industrial Relations*, Vol. 30, No. 2, pp. 287-324.

Waddington, J. (1992), "Trade Union Mergers, in Cox, D. (ed.), *Facing the Future*, Nottingham, University of Nottingham.

Waddington, J. (1993), "Trade Union Membership Concentration, 1892-1987: Development and Causation", *British journal of Industrial Relations*, Vol. 31, No. 3, pp. 433-457.

Waddington, J. (1995), *The Politics of Bargaining: The Merger Process and British Trade Union Structural Development, 1892-1987*, London, Mansell.

Waddington, J. (2000), "Towards a Reform Agenda? European Trade Unions in Transition", *Industrial Relations Journal*, Vol. 31, No. 4, pp. 317-330.

Waddington, J. (2001), "Articulating Trade Union Organisation for the New Europe", *Industrial Relations Journal*, Vol. 32, No. 5, pp. 449-463

Waddington, J. and Hoffmann, J. (2000), "The German Union Movement in Structural Transition: Defensive Adjustment or Setting a New Agenda?", in Hoffmann, R., Jacobi, O., Keller, B. and Weiss, M. (eds.), *Transnational Industrial Relations in Europe*, Düsseldorf, Hans-Böckler Stiftung, pp. 113-138.

Waddington, J. and Hoffmann, R. (2000) (eds.), *Trade Unions in Europe*, Brussels, European Trade Union Institute.

Waddington, J. and Kerr, A. (1999), "Trying to Stem the Flow: Union Membership Turnover in the Public Sector", *Industrial Relations Journal*, Vol. 30, No. 3, pp. 184-196.

Waddington, J., Kahmann, M. and Hoffmann, J. (2003), *United We Stand? A Comparison of the Trade Union Merger Process in Britain and Germany*, London, Anglo-German Foundation, www.agf.org.uk.

Wallén, T. (1989), *Suveränitet och Samverkan*, Stockholm, TCO/TAM.

Western, B. (1997), *Between Class and Market: Postwar Unionization in the Capitalist Democracies*, Princeton, Princeton University Press.

Westerståhl, J. (1945), *Svensk fackföreningsrörelse*, Stockholm, Tidens förlag.

Williamson, L. (1995), "Union Mergers: 1985-94 Update", *Monthly Labor Review*, No. 2, February, pp. 18-25.

Willman, P. (1989), "The Logic of Market-Share Trade Unionism: Is Membership Decline Inevitable?", *Industrial Relations Journal*, Vol. 20, No. 4, pp. 260-271.

Willman, P. and Cave, A. (1994), "The Union of the Future: Super-unions or Joint Ventures?", *British Journal of Industrial Relations*, Vol. 32, No. 3, pp. 395-412.

Willman, P. and Morris, T. (1988), *The Finances of British Trade Unions 1975-1985*, Research Paper No. 62, London, Department of Employment.

Willman, P., Morris, T. and Aston, B. (1993), *Union Business: trade union organisation and financial reform in the Thatcher years*, Cambridge, Cambridge University Press.

Windmuller, J. (1981), "Concentration Trends in Union Structure: An International Comparison", *Industrial and Labor Relations Review*, Vol. 35, No. 1, pp. 43-57.

Wolman, L. (1936), *Ebb and Flow in Trade Unionism*, New York, National Bureau of Economic Research.

Wooden, M. (1999), "Union Amalgamations and the Decline in Union Density", *Journal of Industrial Relations*, Vol. 41, No. 1, pp. 35-52.

Wyller, T. (1970), *Landsforbund og lønnskamp: En studie av Embetsmennenes landsforbund: 1918-68*, Oslo, Cappelen.

YS. (various), *Beretning* (Annual reports), 1977 – 1999, Oslo, Yrkesorganisasjonenes Sentralforbund.

Notes on Contributors

Sabine Blaschke

Lecturer, Institute of Sociology, University of Vienna.

Jesper Due

Director, FAOS-Employment Relations Research Centre, University of Copenhagen, Denmark.

Gerard Griffin

Professor, Faculty of Business and Enterprise, and Pro Vice Chancellor, University of South Australia, Australia.

Jürgen Hoffmann

Professor, Hochschule für Wirtschaft und Politik, Hamburg, Germany.

Christos A. Ioannou

Director, Hellenic Institute for Occupational Health and Safety (ELINYAE), Member of the Body of Mediators and Arbitrators, Organisation for Mediation and Arbitration (OMED), Athens, Greece.

Berndt Keller

Professor of Labour and Social Policy, Universität Konstanz, Germany.

Anders Kjellberg

Associate Professor of Sociology, Lund University, and Researcher, National Institute for Working Life, Norrköping, Sweden.

Jørgen Steen Madsen

Head of Research, FAOS-Employment Relations Research Centre, University of Copenhagen, Denmark.

Kristine Nergaard

Senior Researcher, FAFO Institute for Applied Social Science, Oslo, Norway.

Alan Stoleroff

Researcher, Instituto Superior de Ciencias do Trabalho e da Empressa, Lisbon, Portugal.

Jeremy Waddington

Professor of Industrial Relations, University of Manchester, Britain; and Project Co-ordinator, European Trade Union Institute, Brussels, Belgium.

"Work & Society"

The series "Work & Society" analyses the development of employment and social policies, as well as the strategies of the different social actors, both at national and European levels. It puts forward a multi-disciplinary approach – political, sociological, economic, legal and historical – in a bid for dialogue and complementarity.
The series is not confined to the social field *stricto sensu*, but also aims to illustrate the indirect social impacts of economic and monetary policies. It endeavours to clarify social developments, from a comparative and a historical perspective, thus portraying the process of convergence and divergence in the diverse national societal contexts. The manner in which European integration impacts on employment and social policies constitutes the backbone of the analyses.

Series Editor: Philippe POCHET, Director of the Observatoire Social Européen (Brussels) and Digest Editor of the Journal of European Social Policy.

Recent Titles

No.47– *A European Social Citizenship? Preconditions for Future Policies from a Historical Perspective*, Lars MAGNUSSON & Bo STRÅTH (eds.) (2004), 361 p., ISBN 90-5201-269-5.

No.46– *Restructuring Representation. The Merger Process and Trade Union Structural Development in Ten Countries*, Jeremy WADDINGTON (ed.) (2004), 414 p., ISBN 90-5201-253-9

No.45– *Labour and Employment Regulation in Europe*, Jens LIND, Herman KNUDSEN & Henning JØRGENSEN (eds.) (2004), 408 p., ISBN 90-5201-246-6

N° 44– *L'État social actif. Vers un changement de paradigme ?* (provisional title), Pascale VIELLE, Isabelle CASSIERS & Philippe POCHET (dir.) (forthcoming), ISBN 90-5201-227-X

No.43– *Wage and Welfare. New Perspectives on Employment and Social Rights in Europe*, Bernadette CLASQUIN, Nathalie MONCEL, Mark HARVEY & Bernard FRIOT (eds.) (2004), 206 p., ISBN 90-5201-214-8

No.42– *Job Insecurity and Union Membership. European Unions in the Wake of Flexible Production*, M. SVERKE, J. HELLGREN, K. NÄSWELL, A. CHIRUMBOLO, H. DE WITTE & S. GOSLINGA (eds.) (2004), 202 p., ISBN 90-5201-202-4

N° 41– *L'aide au conditionnel. La contrepartie dans les mesures envers les personnes sans emploi en Europe et en Amérique du Nord*, Pascale DUFOUR, Gérard BOISMENU & Alain NOËL (2003) en coéd. avec les PUM, 248 p., ISBN 90-5201-198-2

N° 40– *Protection sociale et fédéralisme*, Bruno THÉRET (2002) en coéd. avec les PUM, 2002, 495 p., ISBN 90-5201-107-9.

No.39– *The Impact of EU Law on Health Care Systems*, Martin MCKEE, Elias MOSSIALOS & Rita BAETEN (eds.) (2002, 2nd printing 2003), 314 p., ISBN 90-5201-106-0.

No.38– *EU Law and the Social Character of Health Care*, Elias MOSSIALOS & Martin MCKEE (2002, 2nd printing 2004), 259 p., ISBN 90-5201-110-9.

P.I.E.-Peter Lang – The website

Discover the general website of the Peter Lang publishing group:

www.peterlang.net